WESTERN MANUSCRIPTS FROM CLASSICAL ANTIQUITY TO THE RENAISSANCE

GARLAND REFERENCE LIBRARY
OF THE HUMANITIES
(VOL. 139)

WESTERN MANUSCRIPTS FROM CLASSICAL ANTIQUITY TO THE RENAISSANCE
A Handbook

Laurel Nichols Braswell

GARLAND PUBLISHING, INC. • NEW YORK & LONDON
1981

Library of Congress Cataloging in Publication Data

Braswell, Laurel Nichols, 1931–
  Western manuscripts from classical antiquity to the
Renaissance.

  (Garland reference library of the humanities ; v. 139)
  Includes bibliographical references and index.
  1. Manuscripts—Handbooks, manuals, etc. 2. Paleog-
raphy—Handbooks, manuals, etc. I. Title. II. Series.
Z105. B73   091   79-7908
ISBN 0-8240-9541-3   AACR2

Printed on acid-free, 250-year-life paper
Manufactured in the United States of America

To the Memory of My Sister
Judith Lea Nichols Huffman
(1934–1977)

CONTENTS

PREFACE

All those who have ever suffered the long and painstaking demands of bibliographical studies will know that, as a reward for their efforts, bibliographies can never be definitive, that they are out of date the moment they go to press, and that they must furthermore undergo continuous additions and corrections if they are to remain viable. To this end I should be grateful for further suggestions and corrections, especially since this *Handbook* is a pioneer effort of sorts with no earlier model for its conception as a general guide to the study of early manuscripts and its choice of categories for investigation.

It is inevitable that some *lacunae* among these categories and among the items listed will occur. Some will no doubt be due to my own omission, but others will be the result of a lack of scholarship in certain areas. Perhaps the most obvious and immediate need is for more manuscript catalogues of the quality and accuracy of M.B. Parkes' for Keble College, Oxford, and the comprehensiveness of N.R. Ker's survey of medieval manuscripts in British libraries. All of this leads one to suspect that even with the present *Handbook* we are merely "in the vestibule of knowledge," to adapt Ulisse Chevalier's paleographical motto: *Qui scit ubi sit scientia, habenti est proximus*.

Outweighing the difficulties of bibliographical work are the pleasures in acknowledging the inevitably extensive help received in many ways from many individuals and institutions. I should like, first of all, to thank the librarians: those of the Mills Memorial Library at McMaster University, especially Mr. N. Passi of the reference section; those of the Pontifical Institute of Mediaeval Studies, Toronto, especially the Head Librarian, Mrs. L. Egsgard; and those of the Bodleian Library, Oxford, especially Dr. de la Mare and Mr. Robin Harris. All have been both skilled and tireless in directing me toward the more relevant resources. The libraries of St. John's College, Cambridge; Trinity College, Cambridge; the British Library; and the University Library of the Free University of Berlin, have generously provided access to their collections and pleasant working conditions. I am also grateful to Mr. Michael Reeve of Exeter College, Oxford, to Dr. Virginia Brown, Editor of *Mediaeval Studies*, to Father Leonard Boyle of the Pontifical Institute, and to Dr. A.S.G. Edwards of the University of Victoria: all provided astute comments on the scope, contents, and arrangement of this *Handbook*. Dr. Bruce Braswell of the University of Fribourg offered many useful suggestions about Classical references, while Dr. Wolfgang Milde of the Herzog August Bibliothek in Wolfenbüttel kindly answered inquiries about his forthcoming work. To my McMaster colleagues, Professors Chauncey Wood, Maqbool Aziz, Ronald Vince, Brian John, Graham Roebuck, Sharon Adams, and Bryan Mangrum I am indebted for specific references in their respective fields and for general encouragement, most of all for the opportunity to discuss problems in scholarship and methodology relevant to what must by now seem a group project. My thanks are due to Miss Mary Monaco, who, as my summer assistant under the McMaster Studentship Award Programme, skillfully and cheerfully fulfilled many of the tedious research and clerical tasks required by a complex manuscript in its final stages. To my editors, Mr. Lawrence Davidow and Mr. Richard Newman of Garland Publishing, I am grateful for patience, practical suggestions, and sensitivity toward the major academic exigencies of this work.

Finally, to my former teachers of paleography, Professors N.R. Ker and M.B. Parkes of Oxford and P. Lefèvre of Louvain, I owe perhaps the greatest but most intangible debt of gratitude. Although they can in no way be held responsible for the inadequacies and errors of this *Handbook*, they should still be credited with imparting to its compiler the fascination and challenge of manuscript study.

L.N.B.

INTRODUCTION

The present *Handbook* is innovative for three reasons. First, it brings together for the first time a number of disciplines, usually considered bibliographic topics in themselves, in order to facilitate the study of Western manuscripts. Of this more will be said later, but suffice it for the moment to suggest that paleography is not only an interdisciplinary study but is most often used as a tool for the advancement of scholarship in other areas, and that, hence, an interdisciplinary bibliography is an obvious approach to the subject. Secondly, this *Handbook* defines an area of primary sources for paleography, illumination, and codicology and brings together for the first time a selection of medieval documents which illustrate the practices of the *scriptorium*, the scribe, and the making of the medieval book. Thirdly, and perhaps most importantly, this *Handbook* is arranged in such a way as to serve as a guide from the first steps in identifying a manuscript to its transcription and ultimately its edition. Each section is conceived as one possible stage in the study of a manuscript, and each is intended to further through its bibliographical references knowledge of the manuscript's physical features, whether script, date, decoration, or provenance, and knowledge of the manuscript's relevance both to other manuscripts within a given textual tradition and to a larger cultural context. The methodological procedure which the fifteen sections of this *Handbook* suggest will be discussed more fully below.

Paleography as a Discipline

Paleography was first conceived as a discipline in its own right by Bernard de Montfaucon and so described in his *Palaeographia Graeca Sive de Ortu et Progressu Literarum* of 1708. While in de Montfaucon's mind and in eighteenth-century practice paleography meant only the decipherment of letters hand-written on papyrus or parchment, it has in our own time come to represent a recognized discipline dependent upon a wide range of acquired knowledge and practiced skills. Today the paleographer not only "deciphers" but must also use what have been distinguished as "archaeological skills," that is, those which involve the materials, the making, and the transmission of the manuscript book. To read and assess a script a paleographer must combine a knowledge of much factual data covering several historical periods with all the technical skills of a scientist and the intuitive judgment of a detective.

Although the initial task of the student of manuscripts is indeed to decipher and identify the script of the document before him, his efforts probably will not cease once this task is complete. There may next be required the subsequential tasks of cataloguing, indexing, or editing. The present *Handbook* has assumed that one or all of such activities may be required by the researcher at some stage. He may, for example, need to be able to recognize the distinguishing features of a particular bastarda script and at the same time require a basic knowledge of English fourteenth-century ecclesiastical history. Moreover, the tasks of cataloguing, indexing, or editing are seminal in that they may initiate further study by placing a manuscript within a larger context, and thus it must be the responsibility of the paleographer to identify those features of greatest relevance and significance for future scholarship.

Paleography and Bibliography

The interdisciplinary nature of paleography ideally requires a correspondingly comprehensive bibliography, one which can provide a handy reference source to related methodologies and subjects, one which the student can keep literally "at hand" beside his manuscript or microfilm-reader and take if necessary to the card catalogues and other areas of the library. He may need to know which facsimiles in a printed collection might help to date the script of his own manuscript; it might be crucial in establishing the provenance of his manuscript to recognize that the clasp marks on the binding are characteristic of a particular monastery; he may be confronted with illuminated initials which are crucial factors in identifying the manuscript with a certain *scriptorium*; he may suspect that the scribe and the decorator were one and the same and that therefore the scribe might be identifiable through other features of script and format; he may discover liturgical fragments with musical notation in an historical chronicle and have to decide whether these are later interpolations; he may be forced to leave the manuscript and its library for reasons of time and to investigate microfilm facilities in order to continue his work elsewhere; if he intends to edit the manuscript, he may need to consult works on textual criticism in order to determine the most appropriate methods, to distinguish dialectal from scribal variants, and eventually to consult historical, literary, or other works in order to assess what potential value such an edition might have in these fields. For such reasons the present *Handbook* has assumed an interdisciplinary form, and one designed to refer the student to the major and most helpful works in those areas he is most likely to encounter.

Bibliographical Classifications and Divisions

In order to facilitate reference to so many areas of scholarship, I have divided these areas into fifteen major groups. Within groups, citation usually begins with a section on bibliographical materials, then proceeds to individual areas of study. Many of these subsections are divided according to period, country, or specific topic. In subsections involving an historical period, as in the case of VI.D, "Writing and Scripts," order is more or less chronological. In sections involving geographical location, sections are arranged in alphabetical order by country.

Within each section and subsection, order of citation is alphabetical. The names of authors beginning with "De" or "Van" are cited under the main form, e.g., Ancona for D'Ancona, except for Anglicized names such as de la Mare. Series with a succession of editors are generally cited under the series title, as for the Oxford History of Art.

It may nevertheless occasionally appear to the user of this *Handbook* that some divisions are arbitrary and that some items are ill-placed. He may well query whether Briquet's *Les Filigranes* should be classified as a miscellaneous reference work or as a history of watermarks. He might wonder whether Eis's *Altdeutsche Handschriften* really belongs among the titles of facsimile collections rather than among studies of individual scripts. My own decisions about such classifications have stemmed from what I have considered the essential nature of a work and how it might most often be used. Thus, because Briquet's work on watermarks would probably serve more often as a reference manual for locating and dating paper manuscripts than for establishing the history of paper manufacture, I have accordingly cited it among reference manuals. I have, however, also made a cross-reference to it under "Materials" in Section XI.D. Because Eis's work on medieval German manuscripts provides not so much a facsimile collection of representative German hands as a critical analysis of German hands based upon facsimile examples, I have cited it among general studies rather than among national facsimile collections. My reasons for decisions in classification and grouping have generally been summarized in introductory rubrics to each section. The principal criteria upon which they are based will be manifest in the general nature of the works listed. I hope that cross-referencing and indexing may solve some of the problems caused by the choice of one classification rather than another.

Also included among the divisions of this *Handbook* are sections on Diplomatics and Archives, Decoration and Illumination, and Music; many references to Papyrology occur in sections relating to Classical studies and journals. Although some critics might consider these areas of study beyond the present scope of this *Handbook*, I have felt that their inclusion could be justified for reasons already suggested above with reference to the interdisciplinary nature of paleography. Papyrology can hardly be separated from the study of Classical and Byzantine manuscripts, as such scholars as Kenyon and Omont have demonstrated. That Diplomatics and Archivicology—the study of official public documents—may be required for assessing the script and provenance of nonarchival manuscripts is illustrated by the work of Bischoff and Ker; it can be used as well for the advancement of scholarship in other disciplines, a possibility more recently proven through the activities of the Records for Early

English Drama project in Toronto. And finally, that illumination and music can scarcely be ignored in certain aspects of paleographical research has been illustrated in the work of such scholars as Wormald and Reaney. The practical considerations of this *Handbook*, however, have restricted bibliographical references in these areas to select, representative works. They are intended only to provide initial references, to indicate possible directions a researcher might take in pursuit of more precise and detailed information. They are intended to suggest, once again, that the divisions of this *Handbook* represent a complete and interrelated system of references.

Principles of Selection within Divisions

Although a handbook must include several disciplines in order to provide a research tool with multiple uses, it must nevertheless exert some principles of selection within each in order to be practicable. I have therefore avoided those titles which would contribute little toward this end, whether by reason of faulty information, popular level of scholarship, or unavailability.

The most significant contributing factor in the selection of titles has been my conception of the most important problems of manuscript studies today. These appear to be the identity of documents and their relationship to others. All paleographers have been at one time or another confronted by a manuscript which betrayed not the slightest indication of authorship, not the least hint of date, or provenance, or subsequent ownership. Even supposing that some of these questions have already been answered by earlier cataloguers or editors, there is still the strong likelihood that these answers need reexamining on the basis of more recent evidence. This leads inevitably to the second problem, which is one of relating documents to one another, whether in terms of historical, literary, or linguistic features, or, in more codicological terms, in regard to script, parchment, collation, or binding. For these reasons my selection of titles has been for the most part determined by what would appear to be those works most conducive to the solution of such problems.

For these and other reasons I have not provided full lists of all available manuscript catalogues in Section II. It is an unfortunate fact that many manuscript catalogues are of little help in establishing identity and therefore not to be trusted for guidance in determining possible relationships between manuscripts. Such lists would be not only impossibly long, but also unnecessary, since further bibliographic lists are provided in reference works such as Downs's *British Library Resources*. For similar reasons, too, I have not devoted many references to the classification and preservation of manuscripts; these would lie more properly within the area of library science, rather than the proper study of paleographical features.

Scope

The scope of the *Handbook* covers Classical Antiquity through the Middle Ages to the early Renaissance. It does so by reason of historical circumstance. The greatest number of extant manuscripts in the West date from the ninth to the fifteenth century, that is, from the time when the *scriptoria* of Monte Cassino, Bobbio, and other monasteries began to preserve earlier Classical writing to that time in the mid-fifteenth century when handwritten manuscripts gave way to printed books. Within this period I have concentrated upon the bibliographical resources for British manuscripts, mainly because I assume that this *Handbook* will receive a wider circulation among English speakers working with manuscript collections in Great Britain and North America. Among these resources I have focused more specifically upon English literary and scientific manuscripts, chiefly because in these lie my own interest and experience.

While the scope of historical coverage is largely determined by chronological fact, the linguistic scope represented by the titles of this *Handbook* may seem to be unlimited. Many titles in languages other than English have had to be included, for these provide the many works on paleography never written in English but essential to paleographical studies; they also provide a richness of referential material not to be overlooked by the serious scholar. Paleography has always been an international subject. Most students of Western manuscripts will be working with resources located in more than one country, whether by nature of the provenance of the manuscripts or because of the location of the libraries in which they are found. But since it would obviously be impossible to list all the major resources for North America, Great Britain, Ireland, and all Western European countries—including the Slavic countries where Western manuscripts are to be found in some collections—I have once again tried to select those key works which would lead through their bibliographical references to others and so eventually to those specialized works most relevant to the researcher's topic.

Use

This *Handbook* is arranged in such a way that the ordering of the sections should guide the researcher through the various stages of his investigation, and thus in itself provide the basic methodology for whatever aspect of paleographical or codicological study concerns him. Some sections, of course, will be by-passed, and the final section on textual criticism will never be considered by some scholars as their final destination. Yet, generally speaking, the order of whatever sections may be relevant should lead from the general, introductory stage of investigation to the most precise.

On the basic assumption that identification or initial knowledge about the general nature of a manuscript must be the starting point for further study, the first section of this *Handbook* is devoted to *Bibliographical Materials*. If the manuscript has already been identified specifically and definitively, either in the library's catalogue or in an edition, the question of identity will not normally be relevant. The researcher has only to proceed through "interpretation," "study and scholarship," and finally to "edition," if editing the manuscript is the ultimate goal (see diagram). But if the identity of the manuscript has been challenged, or improperly or insufficiently made, or not made at all, then initial research will be necessary through Sections I–VI (*bibliography, libraries, microforms, incipits, indexes*, and *paleography*) before "interpretation" can begin.

"Interpretation," of course, depends initially upon *paleography* and *codicology* (Sections VI and XI), with reference to "special problems" if the manuscript contains *archival* material

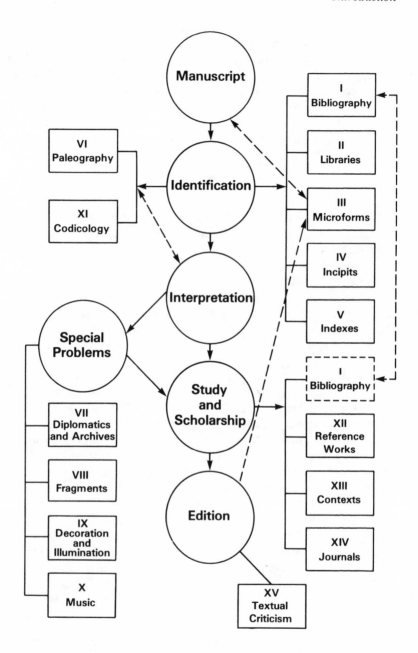

(Section VII), is a *fragment* (Section VIII), involves significant *decoration* or *illumination* (Section IX), or contains *music* (Section X). It will also depend upon "study and scholarship" and thus refer to Sections XII–XIV (*reference works, contexts,* and *journals*), with consultation necessary back to Section I on *bibliography.*

"Identity" and "study" established, the manuscript can then be edited on the basis of material gathered from Sections I–XIV, possibly with reference to Section III (*microforms*) if microfilm is used for checking transcriptions or as a substitute for the original manuscript when that is inaccessible or subsequently lost. Editing may proceed according to any number of textual principles established in Section XV, whether these follow traditional recensionist methods initiated by Lachmann or are adapted to the open-text methods of later editors such as Kane and Görlach. The edition might also utilize more recently developed mechanized aids, such as computerized collation, or depend entirely upon the computer programming described by Froger and Kochendörfer.

Although the main stages of manuscript research outlined in this *Handbook* are indicated by the circles of the diagram, and these circles are arranged in a certain order from "identification" to "edition," such an order should be considered only as a general guide. It will be necessary, as every student of manuscripts knows, to proceed tediously as often backwards as forwards. The order might very well be, for example, from *bibliography* to *libraries* to *codicology* to *illumination* to *topics* to *paleography* and back again to *libraries* as various questions arise and as needs for specific answers demand. It may also happen that only one problem is involved, that the researcher need deal only with the exegetical implication of a particular historiated initial, for example, and so consult only Section IX. For such purposes this work will constitute more a reference work than a handbook and provide an initial starting point to a highly specialized line of inquiry.

I. BIBLIOGRAPHICAL MATERIALS

The following titles include those of general
medieval interest, then those pertinent to various
specialized subjects, e.g., history, literature,
science, and others for which paleographic resources
may be required. Periodical bibliographies issued
in journals are noted in Section XIV, while bibliographies for art and music are included in Sections
IX and X. Some works listed in Section XI as *indexes*
or *repertoria* also provide bibliographical lists.

CONTENTS

A. GENERAL MEDIEVAL

1. PERIODIC

1 *British Humanities Index*. London: Library Association, 1962-.

   A general index on individual subjects within the humanities
   which continues the *Subject Index to Periodicals*, 1919-61.

2 *Essay and General Literature Index*, ed. M.E. Sears, M. Shaw,
   et al. New York: H.W. Wilson, 1934-.

   An index to over 2,144 volumes of collections of essays and
   miscellaneous works from 1900; arrangement is alphabetical by
   topic and author; see especially "manuscripts," "paleography."
   Reviews are cited for many items, and cumulations published about
   every five years, the last in 1978.

3 *International Guide to Medieval Studies, An*. Darien, Conn.:
   American Bibliographic Service, 1961-.

   A quarterly index to periodical literature on all medieval subjects; indexes; see also next item.

4 *International Medieval Bibliography*. Leeds: University Press,
   1967-.

   Published approximately semi-annually under the joint auspices
   of the universities of Leeds and Minnesota, this bibliography
   lists articles, notes, reviews, and *Festschriften* published each
   year in periodicals and other publications. There are subject
   and author indexes. Sections devoted to "Palaeography and Diplomatic" (1969-) and "Manuscripts" (1972-) list articles on all
   aspects of these subjects.

5 *Library and Information Science Abstracts*, ed. Tom Edwards.
   London: Library Association, 1969- .

   Published six times per year, this periodical lists with
   critical résumés current publications on library science. Author/
   subject indexes conclude each fascicle, with a cumulative index
   published for 1969-73. Many items on manuscript cataloguing,
   preservation, and individual library collections are cited.

6 Modern Language Association of America. *MLA International
   Bibliography of Books and Articles on the Modern Languages and
   Literatures*. New York, N.Y.: The Association, 1921-, 1925-.

A critical bibliography usually appearing as the June issue of
PMLA, with international coverage since 1957. There are some
references to paleographical matters, especially in the area of
textual criticism. Indexes are included.

7   *Quarterly Check-List of Medievalia: An International Index of
    Current Books, Monographs, Brochures, and Separates.* Darien,
    Conn.: American Bibliographic Service, 1958-.

    This is a companion bibliography to item 3, which offers critical
    notes on non-periodical studies in all medieval subjects. Arrange-
    ment is alphabetical by author with a subject index.

8   *Social Sciences and Humanities Index.* New York, N.Y.: H.W. Wilson,
    1921-.

    An index to articles and reviews in periodical literature,
    especially *Studies in Philology*, *Modern Philology*, *Modern Language
    Quarterly*, and *PMLA*.

                                2. CLOSED

9   Besterman, Theodore. *A World Bibliography of Bibliographies.*
    Lausanne: Societas Bibliographica/Totowa, N.J.: Rowman and
    Littlefield, 1965-.

    A series of inclusive bibliographies on separate subjects such
    as history, medicine, music and drama. Indexed by author.

10 Bohatta, Hanns, and Hodes, Franz, eds. *Internationale Bibliographie
    der Bibliographien.* Frankfurt-am-Main: Klostermann, 1950.

    This work provides an excellent guide to international resources
    for paleographical studies; see especially *"Bibliographien"* and
    "Buch und Bibliothekswesen." Arrangement is by country, then by
    topic and author, with full indexes.

11 Hain, Ludwig Friedrich Theodor. *Repertorium Bibliographicum.*
    4 vols. Stuttgart: 1826-38/Milan: Görlich, 1948. *Supplement* by
    Walter Arthur Copinger. 2 vols. in 3. Milan: Görlich, 1950.

    The standard and earliest comprehensive catalogue for incunabula.
    Vol. 2.2 includes an index of cities and types; Copinger's *Supple-
    ment*, vol. 1, makes nearly 7,000 corrections and adds ten colla-
    tions of works described or mentioned by Hain; vol. 2 gives critical
    lists of nearly 6,000 volumes printed in the fifteenth century.
    Such bibliographies of early printed books (see also items 15, 30,
    31, and 32) provide important indications of the survival of cer-
    tain manuscript traditions and, in some cases, copies of manu-
    scripts since lost. For further catalogues, consult individual
    library catalogues or union lists.

12 *Index Bibliographicus.* 4th ed. The Hague: Federation Internationale
    de Documentation, 1956-64.

An international directory to current abstracting and bibliographic activites; sections include science and technology, social sciences, humanities, and general bibliographies. Entries are arranged by the universal decimal classification system. Subject/title indexes are provided.

13   Labande, Edmond René, and Leplant, Bernadette, eds. *Répertoire internationale des médiévistes*. Centre d'Etudes Supérieures de Civilisation Médiévale. Poitiers: CECM, 1971.

A dictionary of medievalists with addresses, areas of scholarship, major works, and works in progress; first issued in 1960; to be continued by a *Directory of Medievalists in North America* under the auspices of the Medieval Institute (Kalamazoo, Mich.: Western Michigan University Press, forthcoming).

14   Leistner, O. *Internationale Bibliographie der Festschriften*. Osnabrück: Biblio-Verlag, 1976.

A list, with resumés, of most *Festschriften* up to 1974; includes subject indexes.

15   Pollard, Alfred W., and Redgrave, G.R., comp. *A Short-Title Catalogue of Books Printed in England, Scotland and Ireland and of English Books Printed Abroad 1475-1640*. London: The Bibliographical Society, 1946; 2nd ed. rev. and enlarged by W.A. Jackson and F.S. Ferguson, completed by K. Pantzer. London: The Society, 1976. *Index of Printers, Publishers, and Booksellers*, by Paul G. Morrison. Charlottesville, Va.; Bibliographical Society of the University of Virginia, 1950.

This work is the standard catalogue for early English editions and contains some useful critical and bibliographical matter; its use is greatly facilitated by Morrison's *Index*; on the use of incunabula see under item 11 above.

16   Rouse, Richard H. *A Guide to Serial Bibliographies for Medieval Studies*. Publications of the Center for Medieval and Renaissance Studies, 3. Berkeley, Calif.: University of California Press, 1969.

A comprehensive list of 283 bibliographies with brief annotations of serial bibliographies. Arrangement is by subject with title/author indexes.

17   Willard, James F., ed. *Progress of Medieval and Renaissance Studies in the United States and Canada*. Boulder, Colo.: University of Colorado Press, 1923-60.

Published under the patronage of the University of Colorado and ACLS, this work developed from the annual publication edited by S. Harrison Thompson and issued biannually. It includes articles on special areas of medieval scholarship, including paleography, lists papers read and books in press, features individual scholars with bibliographies of their writings, and provides name/subject/field-of-interest indexes.

18   Zamarriego, Tomás. *Enciclopedia de orientación bibliográfica.*
      Barcelona: J. Flores, 1964-65.

      Although the focus of this bibliography is upon Hispanic resources,
      it is nevertheless useful for all areas of paleographical studies.
      Arrangement is by subject, with some annotation.

                              B. SPECIALIZED

      1. CLASSICAL, PATRISTIC, BYZANTINE, AND MEDIEVAL LATIN STUDIES

19   Adamson, N.L.; Bartlett, K.R.; Eisenbichler, K.; and Svilpis,
      J.E., eds. *Humanist Editions of the Classics at the C.R.R.S.*
      Centre for Reformation and Renaissance Studies, Occasional
      Publications, 1. Toronto: CRRS, 1979.

      A catalogue, arranged alphabetically by author, of the collec-
      tion of Humanist Classical editions in the E.J. Pratt Library at
      Victoria College, University of Toronto; it numbers some 500
      volumes, the earliest of which dates from 1492. The catalogue
      constitutes a representative bibliography of Humanist editions.

20   Altaner, Berthold, and Stuiber, Alfred. *Patrologie: Leben,*
      Schriften und Lehre der Kirchenvater. 7th ed. (from 1938).
      Freiburg: Herder, 1966.

      This comprehensive survey of Patristic writers contains ex-
      cellent bibliographies on individual Fathers, with a brief biog-
      raphy, list of writings, and bibliography of critical works.
      The English translation is based upon the 5th ed., trans. Hilda
      C. Graef, 2nd ed. (New York, N.Y.: Herder, 1961).

21   *L'Année philologique: Bibliographie critique et analytique de*
      l'antiquité greco-latine, gen. eds. Jules Marouzeau, Juliette
      Ernst, *et al.* Paris: Société d'Edition 'Les Belles Lettres,'
      1927-.

      The standard and most comprehensive annual critical bibliography
      on all aspects of Classical studies, including textual criticism.
      Sections include literary history, language, texts, paleography,
      papyrology, archaeology, history, and humanism. Indexes are pro-
      vided for ancient authors and locations as well as for modern
      authors. See item 29 for earlier bibliography. This bibliography
      tends to run about three years behind publication dates of works
      cited; for more up-to-date bibliographies, see items 37, 46, 48,
      52, 54.

22   Berkowitz, Luci. *Thesaurus Linguae Graecae; Canon of Greek Authors*
      and Works from Homer to A.D. 200. Costa Mesa, Calif.: TLG
      Publications, 1977.

      A list of authors, works, and editions with some critical
      commentary. Treatment and coverage are somewhat uneven, with
      reported inaccuracies.

23 *Bibliography: Graeco-Roman Egypt. Papyri (1930-31).* London: Egypt
    Exploration Society, 1936. Repr. from *The Journal of Egyptian
    Archaeology*, 18-22 (1932-36).

    A descriptive bibliography divided into topics, e.g., literary
    texts, religion, with an account of the year's work.

24 *Bibliotheca Philologica Classica: Bursians Jahresbericht über
    die Fortschritte der klassischen Altertumswissenschaft, begründet
    von Conrad Bursian. Supplements.* Leipzig: O.R. Reisland, 1873-
    1943.

    A bibliography issued annually to 1943 in four parts: I. Greek
    Authors; II. Latin Authors; III. *Altertumswissenschaft* (i.e.,
    philosophy, history, etc.); and IV. *Bibliotheca Philologica Classica*
    (i.e., an international, classified list of books, articles, and
    reviews for the preceding year). Nos. 172, 193, and 209 (1914-
    29) contain bibliographies for Greek and Latin paleography.

25 *Blackwell's Byzantine Hand-List: A Catalogue of Byzantine Authors
    and Books on Byzantine Literature, History, Religion, Art,
    Archaeology, etc.* Oxford: Basil Blackwell, 1938.

    This work is now greatly outdated, but the sectional and alpha-
    betical arrangement facilitates reference to earlier titles.

26 Cairo, National Library. *A Bibliography of Works about Papyrology.*
    Cairo: National Library Press, 1960.

    A brief (63pp.) introductory bibliography with limited annota-
    tion.

27 *Classical World Bibliographies*, introd. Walter Donlan. 5 vols.
    New York, N.Y.: Garland Publishing, Inc., 1978.

    A collection and re-publication of critical bibliographies of
    Classical scholarship from ca. 1950. They include: *Greek Drama
    and Poetry*; *Greek and Roman History*; *Philosophy, Religion, and
    Rhetoric*; *Vergil*; and *Roman Drama and Poetry and Ancient Fiction*;
    arrangement is by genre and author/work, with a summary analysis
    of major books and articles published 1950-76.

28 Dekkers, E., and Gaar, E. *Clavis Patrum Latinorum.* 2nd ed. (from
    1951). Sacris Erudiri: Jaarboek voor Godsdienstwetenschappen,
    3. The Hague: M. Nijhoff, 1961.

    A bibliography of patristic writings in collections and period-
    icals; contains three indexes: *index nominum et operum*, *index
    sytematicus*, and *initia*; the last, as a list of *incipits*, is
    especially valuable for the paleographer. A *Clavis Patrum Graecorum*
    is in preparation.

29 Engelmann, Wilhelm. *Bibliotheca Scriptorum Classicorum.* 8th ed.
    E. Preuss, ed. Leipzig: 1880; Hildesheim: Georg Olms, 1959.
    2 vols.

    A detailed but non-critical bibliography of editions of
    Classical works from 1700; vol. 1 is devoted to *Scriptores Graeci*,
    vol. 2 to *Scriptores Latini*; continued to 1896 by Rudolf Klussmann,

Bibliotheca Scriptorum Classicorum et Graecorum et Latinorum.
2 vols. Leipzig: 1908; Hildesheim: Georg Olms, 1961; continued
by Scarlat Lambrino, *Bibliographie de l'antiquité classique, 1896-
1914.* Paris: Société d'Edition 'Les Belles Lettres,' 1951; continued by J. Marouzeau, *Dix années de bibliographie classique
(années 1914 à 1924).* 2nd ed. (from 1928), 1969; and finally by
item 20.

30   Flodr, Miroslav. *Incunabula Classicorum: Wiegendrucke der griechis-
     chen und römischen Literatur.* Amsterdam: Hakkert, 1973.

     A critical bibliography of incunabula, which offers useful in-
     formation on the later traditions and survival of Classical manu-
     scripts; see also next item.

31   *Gesamtkatalog der Wiegendrucke.* 2nd ed. (from 1925-). Stuttgart:
     A. Hiersemann for the Kommission für den Gesamtkatalog, 1968-.

     This continuing catalogue provides good bibliographical refer-
     ences to library collections of incunabula and individual Classical
     texts.

32   *Index Aureliensis, Catalogus Librorum Sedecimo Impressorum. Prima
     Pars,* vols. 1-17, A-Bucke. Baden-Baden: Biblioteca Biblio-
     graphica Aureliana, 1965-73; *Tertia Pars,* vols. 1-2, *Indexes,*
     1967-73.

     An alphabetical main-entry listing of sixteenth-century printed
     books, with locations, in over 500 libraries; the indexes are for
     printer, personal names, and places. See also items 11 and 15.

33   *Index Scriptorum Novus Mediae Latinitatis ab anno DCCC usque ad
     annum MCC.* 2nd ed. (from 1957). Copenhagen: E. Munksgaard, 1973.

     A list of works with editions used for the *Novum Glossarium*
     (item 1595), arranged by title or author alphabetically ("De
     abbatibus abbendoniae" to "Zacharias chrysopolitanus episcopus")
     with dates.

34   International Congress of Papyrology. *Proceedings.* London:
     Published for the British Academy by the Egypt Exploration
     Society, 1901-.

     A periodical publication containing notices and bibliography.

35   Koenen, L. "Papyrology in the Federal Republic of Germany, and
     Field Work of the International Photographic Archive in Cairo."
     Studies in Papyrology, 15 (1976), 39-79.

     This bibliographical article is representative of periodical
     publications in the journal, which feature individual countries.

36   Leeman, Anton. *Bibliographia Latina Selecta.* Chicago, Ill.:
     Argonaut, 1967.

     A critical bibliography for Latin language and literature.

37   *Lustrum: Internationale Forschungsberichte aus dem Bereich des
     klassischen Altertums,* ed. Hans Joachim Mette and Andreas Thier-
     felder. Göttingen: Vandenhoeck and Ruprecht, 1957-.

An annual, international bibliography issued in fascicles; different Classical authors are featured in each issue, with full critical commentary for items listed. An author/editor index concludes each fascicle. One of the most comprehensive and accurate Classical bibliographies.

38   McGuire, Martin R.P. *Introduction to Classical Scholarship: A Syllabus and Bibliographical Guide*. 2nd rev. ed. Washington, D.C.: Catholic University of America Press, 1961.

39   ———, and Dressler, Hermigild, O.F.M. *Introduction to Mediaeval Latin Studies: A Syllabus and Bibliographical Guide*. 2nd ed. (from 1964). Washington, D.C.: Catholic University of America Press, 1971.

Both works define the principal areas for study and investigation, e.g., historical periods and topics. Bibliographical references are usually not annotated. Indexes refer to historical authors and texts, and to modern scholars and reference works. As a Patristic scholar, McGuire devotes fair coverage to that subject in item 38, while item 39 offers an "elementary orientation" to Latin paleography, pp. 239-41.

40   Musurillo, Herbert. "Some Recent Books on Greek Patristics." *Traditio*, 10 (1954), 567-78, and offprint.

An especially valuable bibliography among those in the series on Patristic studies appearing periodically in *Traditio*; the critical surveys of recent scholarship usually focus upon single topics, e.g., Patristic theology (1958) or Ecumenism (1964).

41   Nairn, John A. *A Classical Handlist*. 3rd ed. (from 1931). Oxford: Basil Blackwell, 1953.

An handlist which offers succinct guides to all areas of Classical studies, including general studies, authors, history, language, paleography, and textual criticism.

42   Ooteghem, J. van, S.J. *Bibliotheca Graeca et Latina à l'usage des professeurs des humanités greco-latines*. 3rd ed. (from 1936). Brussels: Les Etudes Classiques, 1969.

A comprehensive, non-critical bibliography of Classical studies from a pedagogical point of view. Arranged by topic, e.g., ancient geography, authors. No indexes are provided.

43   Pack, Roger A. *The Greek and Latin Literary Texts from Greco-Roman Egypt*. 2nd ed. (from 1952). Ann Arbor, Mich.: University of Michigan Press, 1965.

The author, listing Classical texts preserved in papyri, cites editions and studies for each. Arrangement is alphabetical by author. Indexes are provided.

44   *Penguin Companion to Literature*, 4: *Classical and Byzantine*, ed. D.R. Dudley. Harmondsworth: Penguin Books, 1969.

A useful, compact bibliography is provided after individual entries, with additional bibliography concluding each section of this encyclopedic dictionary. Similar in format to item 1633, which provides only limited bibliography.

45 Pöschl, Viktor, gen. ed. *Bibliographie zur antiken Bildersprache.* Heidelberger Akademie der Wissenschaften. Heidelberg: Carl Winter, 1964.

An indispensable bibliography devoted to Latin and Greek figures of speech, in two parts: an alphabetical list of subjects and authors, with editions; and an iconographical index, arranged alphabetically by subject, e.g., "*Aal*," "*Berg*."

46 *Quarterly Check-List of Classical Studies: An International Index of Current Books, Monographs, Brochures, and Separates.* Darien, Conn.: American Bibliographic Service, 1958-.

A non-critical quarterly bibliography, arranged alphabetically by author; an author/editor/translator index concludes each issue.

47 Roey, A. van, and Dreesen, G. *Bibliographia Patristica: Patres Latini 1900-1914.* Louvain: University Press, 1974.

A critical bibliography of Patristic studies devoted to this period.

48 Schneemelcher, W. von, ed. *Bibliographia Patristica.* Berlin: De Gruyter, 1956-, 1959.

An international, comprehensive, and periodic bibliography, arranged mainly by author or subject under eight headings, with extensive cross-referencing; contains lists of editions and critical works. Some entries are annotated.

49 Schweiger, F.L.A. *Handbuch der classischen Bibliographie.* 2 vols. Leipzig: Fleischer, 1930-32/Amsterdam: Hakkert, 1962.

This work provides an excellent bibliography of early printed Classical texts; arrangement is alphabetical by author or work.

50 Stewardson, Jerry L. *A Bibliography of Bibliographies on Patristics.* Evanston, Ill.: Garrett Theological Seminary Library Typescript, 1967.

A useful critical bibliography of bibliographies on Patristics and early Christian literature; a few copies are in circulation, e.g., at the Pontifical Institute of Mediaeval Studies, Toronto.

51 Tobey, Jeremy L. *The History of Ideas: A Bibliographical Intro-duction.* I. *Classical Antiquity.* Santa Barbara, Calif.: Clio Books, 1975.

A bibliography of mainly Classical philosophical writings, little more than a handlist.

52 Toumanoff, Cyril. "Caucasi and Byzantine Studies." *Traditio*, 12 (1956), 409-25.

An important article in the bibliographical series devoted to these subjects, which appear periodically in the journal.

53   Verdenius, W.J. *Beknopte Bibliographie voor de Studie der Griekse
     Taal- en Letterkunde.* 4th ed. (from 1956). Amsterdam: Adolf M.
     Hakkert, 1967.

     A condensed, non-critical bibliography, arranged alphabetically
     by author. Emphasis is upon Greek studies by Dutch scholars.

54   *Year's Work in Classical Studies, The.* The English Classical
     Association. London: The Association, 1906-47.

     An annual bibliography, which focuses upon Greek and Roman
     history and which includes some items on paleography and textual
     criticism. Arrangement is alphabetical by author and topic; in-
     dexes.

See also items 1756, 1777, 1785, 1791-3, 1796-1800, 1812-4, 1824-6,
1856, 1865-6, 1882-3, and 1892.

2. HUMANIST STUDIES

55   *Bibliographie internationale de l'humanisme et de la renaissance.*
     Fédération Internationale des Sociétés et Instituts pour l'Etude
     de la Renaissance. Geneva: E. Droz, 1965-.

     The coverage for this bibliography, appearing annually, is
     mainly fifteenth and sixteenth centuries, but some items relate
     to earlier Humanist studies. Arrangement is alphabetical by author,
     with a name/place/subject index. Non-critical, but comprehensive
     on an international scale.

56   Ladner, Gerhard B. "Some Recent Publications on the Classical
     Tradition in the Middle Ages and Renaissance and on Byzantium."
     Traditio, 10 (1954), 578-94. Offprint.

     A critical resumé of mainly 1953 scholarship on Humanist and
     Byzantine literature. Similar bibliographies occur periodically
     in this journal.

57   Warburg Institute. *A Bibliography on the Survival of the Classics*,
     trans. from German with an English Introduction. 2 vols. London:
     Cassell, 1934-38.

     An invaluable bibliography and one conveniently divided into
     such topics as folklore, religion, or philosophy. Summaries of
     books and articles appear under each heading. Indexes, with ample
     cross-references, are provided.

See also items 647, 1780, 1831, 1839, 1869, 1878, 1884, 1892, and 1894.

3. HISTORY

(a) General

58   *Bibliographie internationale de l'histoire des universités*, ed.
      R. Gibert, J. Paquet, S. Ellehoj, F. Kavka, and J. Havranek.
      Commission internationale pour l'histoire des universités,
      Etudes et Travaux, 2. Vol. I. Geneva: E. Droz, 1973-.

      The first volume in a series of proposed bibliographies on the
      history of European universities; it includes Spain, Louvain,
      Copenhagen, and Prague; the references are arranged according to
      subject, faculty, biography, library, and manuscript collection.
      See also items 75, 88, 419.

59   *Bibliographie internationale des travaux historiques publiés dans
      les volumes de 'Mélanges,' 1880-1939*. Paris: Librairie Armand
      Colin, 1955.

      A bibliography of Festschriften, arranged first by country of
      origin then chronologically by date of publication; a subject/
      author index is provided.

60   Caron, P., and Jaryc, M. *World List of Historical Periodicals and
      Bibliographies*. Oxford: The International Committee of Historical
      Sciences, 1939.

      A non-critical but comprehensive listing of all publications
      relating to the historical sciences; continued by the *International
      Bibliography*, item 66.

61   Commission Internationale d'Histoire Ecclésiastique Comparée.
      Bibliographie de cartographie ecclésiastique. I. *Germany-Austria*.
      Leiden: E.J. Brill, 1968; II. *Poland*, 1971.

      A good critical bibliography of ecclesiastical cartography, with
      entries arranged by district in chronological order by date of
      publication. The volumes are divided into two historical periods:
      pre- and post-Reformation. An author index is provided.

62   Constable, Giles. *Medieval Monasticism: A Select Bibliography*.
      Toronto Medieval Bibliographies, 6. Toronto: University Press,
      1976.

      A useful and comprehensive bibliography on all aspects of
      medieval monasteries, although entries are generally not annotated.
      Entries are arranged according to: Reference Works, Monastic
      History, and Monastic Life and Institutions. An author/editor
      index concludes. One should also consult this work for the numer-
      ous bibliographies published for individual religious orders.

63   Dutcher, G.M.; Shipman, H.R.; Fay, S.B.; Shearer, A.H.; and
      Allison, W.H., eds. *Guide to Historical Literature*. New York:
      P. Smith, 1949.

      This bibliography provides full critical comments for the major
      books, articles, and periodicals within all historical periods.

Indispensable for the paleographer for the pre-1948 period.
Brought up to 1961 by item 65.

64 Halphen, Louis. *Initiation aux études d'histoire du moyen âge.*
3rd rev. ed. (from 1940), by Y. Renouard. Paris: Presses Universitaires de France, 1951.

A valuable bibliographical tool for historical resources and
reference works, especially for France and Belgium. Provides full
critical commentary, although the loose, essay-type presentation
is somewhat incommodious. Part 3 summarizes library resources
and manuscript collections, with a short bibliography of catalogues; the majority of items are more relevant to the libraries
of Paris.

65 Howe, G.F.,; Boyce, G.C.; Broughton, R.S.; Cline, H.F.; Fay, S.B.;
Kraus, M.; Pritchard, E.H.; and Shafer, B.C., eds. *A Guide to
Historical Literature.* American Historical Association. New
York: Macmillan, 1961.

An updating of item 63 with a more convenient arrangement but
less critical commentary. The section on current bibliographies
and dissertations is especially useful.

66 International Committee of Historical Sciences. *International
Bibliography of Historical Sciences.* Paris: Librairie Armand
Colin, 1930-.

An international critical bibliography appearing approximately
every three years. Now a continuation of item 60.

67 Paetow, L.J. *Guide to the Study of Medieval History.* 2nd ed.
(from 1917). New York, N.Y.: F.S. Crofts, for the Mediaeval
Academy of America, 1931/1960.

This work represents probably the best critical bibliography on
medieval history and documentary sources for pre-1930 items. Much
of the section on library resources and catalogues is still valid.

68 Potthast, August. *Bibliotheca Historica Medii Aevi: Wegweiser
durch die Geschichtswerke des europäischen Mittelalters bis
1500.* Berlin: W. Weber, 1862; 2nd ed. 2 vols. 1896; repr. Graz:
Akademische Druck- und Verlagsanstalt, 1957.

A critical bibliography of mainly historical documents, e.g.,
chronicles, biographies, and saints' legends, with lists of editions to 1896. Some *caveat* is necessary in the use of this other-
wise valuable work, however, for many inaccuracies in dates,
pagination, etc., occur. For a revised version, see Wattenback,
item 90.

69 Thompson, James Westfall. *Reference Studies in Medieval History.*
Chicago, Ill.: University Press, 1907; rev. ed. (from 1916).
3 vols. 1925-30.

This bibliography is limited to works in English; arrangement
is alphabetical under general and specialized headings. Highly
accurate and clearly presented, with a useful introduction on
historical methodology.

See also items 97, 646, and 943.

(b) British and Irish

70   Asplin, P.W.A. *Medieval Ireland c. 1170-1495*. Dublin: Royal Irish
     Academy, 1971.

     A specialized, descriptive bibliography, which brings Kenny's
     work, item 79, up to date. There is a good section of repositories
     and manuscripts, pp. 7-9, which includes a list of catalogues of
     Irish manuscripts abroad.

71   *Bibliography of Historical Writings Published in Great Britain
     and the Empire (1940-45)*. British National Committee of the
     International Committee of Historical Sciences. Oxford: Basil
     Blackwell, 1947.

     A general bibliography of books and articles published on all
     periods of British history for this five-year period and brought
     up to date by item 78. A subject/author index is provided.

72   Bonser, Wilfrid. *A Romano-British Bibliography (55 B.C. - A.D.
     449)*. 2 vols. Oxford: Basil Blackwell, 1964.

     The section on historical documents and repositories is of
     special interest for the paleographer; vol. 2 contains indexes.
     See also items 104-5.

73   *Checklist of Research in British Legal Manuscripts*, ed. Sue
     Sheridan Walker. Chicago, Ill.: Northeastern Illinois University,
     1974-.

     A checklist of work in progress, listed alphabetically by
     scholar's name, and a list of papers read at the Plea Roll Con-
     ference, 1971. Thus far two vols. have appeared: 1 (1974) and 2
     (1977).

74   Cordeaux, E.H., and Merry, D.H. *A Bibliography of Printed Works
     Relating to the University of Oxford*. Oxford: Clarendon Press,
     1968.

     This work provides a useful bibliography of manuscript materials
     relevant to the history of the university, which are classified
     according to types of documents and location by college, hall, or
     other type of institution.

75   Gabriel, Astrik L. *Summary Bibliography of the History of the
     Universities of Great Britain and Ireland up to 1800, Covering
     Publications between 1900 and 1968*. Texts and Studies in the
     History of Mediaeval Education, 14. Notre Dame, Ind.: The Medi-
     aeval Institute, 1974.

     The format is similar to items 58 and 88; see item 419. Of
     special interest for the paleographer are lists of manuscript
     catalogues for each college and university in Great Britain and
     Ireland. For a general study with bibliography, see 1653.

76   Gross, Charles. *A Bibliography of English History to 1485*, ed.
     Edgar B. Graves. Oxford: Clarendon Press, 1975.

A complete and updated bibliography usually annotated; arrangement is by type of work, e.g., bibliography, journal, or auxiliary subject, then alphabetical within each section; one section, IV, is devoted to archival and library resources.

77 Historical Association. *English Local History Handlist: A Select Bibliography and List of Sources for the Study of Local History and Antiquities*, ed. F.W. Kuhlicke and F.G. Emmison. 4th ed. (from 1947). London: The Association, 1969.

Although the entries are abbreviated and non-critical, the work provides a useful bibliographical survey of parish records, genealogy, and local book production.

78 Institute of Historical Research. *Writings on British History*. London: The Institute, 1946, 1956-66, 1970-.

A comprehensive non-critical series of bibliographies covering every aspect of British history. Arrangement is by topic, e.g., paleography, chronology, iconography, archives and collections, genealogy, etc., then by chronological period within each topic. See also item 81.

79 Kenny, James F. *The Sources for the Early History of Ireland*. I. *Ecclesiastical. An Introduction and Guide*. Records of Civilization Sources and Studies, Columbia University Department of History, 11. New York, N.Y.: Octagon, 1966-.

The most comprehensive and accurate bibliography of early Irish history and literature to appear thus far. The entries are fully annotated and rich in cross-references; the work also provides lists of manuscript collections and catalogues.

80 Martin, G.H., and McIntyre, Sylvia, eds. *A Bibliography of British and Irish Municipal History*. Leicester: University Press, 1972.

The section on bibliographies, guides to records, and resource materials is especially helpful in this well-organized and annotated bibliography. A subject/name/place index is provided.

81 Mullins, E.L.C., comp. *A Guide to the Historical and Archaeological Publications of Societies in England and Wales, 1901-1933*. Institute for Historical Research. London: Athlone Press, 1968.

Lists societies alphabetically and provides a summary of serial and other publications. A general index is included.

82 ————. *Texts and Calendars. An Analytical Guide to Serial Publications*. Royal Historical Society, Guides and Handbooks, 7. London: The Society, 1958.

A guide to published texts and calendars relating to English and Welsh history, which have been issued in series by (mainly) societies. Arrangement is by society, then chronological by item.

83 Royal Historical Society. *Annual Bibliography of British and Irish History*, gen. ed. G.R. Elton. London: Jonathan Cape for the Society, 1976-.

Published annually (vol. 1976 for publications from 1975), this
bibliography lists publications under periods and then by topic,
e.g., politics, intellectual history, and religion.

See also items 513, 640-1, 646, 935, 971-1013, 1751, 1764, 1770, 1782,
1787, 1809-10, 1821, 1823, 1827, 1830, 1854, 1873, and 1878.

(c) French

84   *Bibliographie annuelle de l'histoire de France*. Paris: Centre
     National de la Recherche Scientifique, 1953-.

     This annual bibliography replaces the *Répertoire bibliographique
     de l'histoire de France*, ed. Pierre Caron, which ceased publica-
     tion in 1931. It includes sections on bibliographies, methodology,
     libraries, and museums. Arrangement is chronological by period.
     No annotation is provided, but there are indexes.

85   Chevalier, Ulysse. *Répertoire des sources historiques du moyen
     âge: bio-bibliographie*. Paris: 1877-88; 2nd ed. 2 vols. Paris:
     1905-07/New York, N.Y.: Kraus, 1960.

86   ————. *Répertoire des sources historiques du moyen âge: topo-
     bibliographie*. 2 vols. Paris: 1894-1903/New York: Kraus, 1960.

     These two excellent works list documentary sources pertaining
     to persons and places, respectively. Although they are out of
     date and non-discriminatory, they do provide valuable surveys of
     historical personages and institutions and cite some lesser-known
     French sources. Now updated by the next item.

87   Cottineau, Dom Laurent H. *Répertoire topo-bibliographique des
     abbayes et prieures*. 3 vols. Mâcon: Prôtat Frères, 1939-70.

     An updating of the preceding item; especially useful are the
     indexes, ed. Gregoire Poras as vol. 3. Arrangement is by location,
     with a brief history of each house and a list of bibliographical
     references.

     Répertoire bibliographique de l'histoire de France. See item 84.

See also items 130, 136, 1752, 1765-6, 1770, 1794, 1836, 1847, 1852,
1863-4, 1869-75, 1877-8, and 1892.

(d) German

88   *Bibliographie zur Universitätsgeschichte: Verzeichnis der im
     Gebiet der Bundesrepublik Deutschland 1945-1971 veröffent-
     lichen Literatur*, ed. Edwin Stark and E. Hassinger. Freiburg/
     Munich: Karl Alber, 1974.

     A bibliography of published items on German university history
     for this period. Division is by university, then individual topics
     such as subject, faculty, biography, see items 58 and 75. The
     emphasis is upon more recent history.

89   Dahlmann, F.C., and Waitz, G. *Quellen Kunde der deutschen Geschichte*. 9th ed. (from 1838), ed. Hermann Haering, *et al*. Leipzig: K.F. Koehler, 1931.

A survey of the historical sources for German history. Although outdated, the sections devoted to medieval sources, e.g., geographical names (1.2), language (1.3), and paleography (1.4), offer many still valid references. The *Registerband*, serving as a general index, was published in 1932.

90   Wattenbach, W. *Deutschlands Geschichtsquellen im Mittelalter bis zur Mitte des dreizehnten Jahrhunderts*. 2 vols. Berlin: Wilhelm Hertz, 1893; continued by Wilhelm Levison, *et al*., in 5 fascicles. Weimar: Böhlaus, 1952-63.

An account, dependent largely upon Potthast, item 68, of mainly Carolingian German works and writers; the notes provide bibliographical information on texts and studies. The *Beiheft*, ed. Rudolf Buckner (1953), is devoted to legal sources, although one should also consult the list of supplementary references in Luitpold Wallach's review, *Speculum*, 30 (1955), 92-96.

See also items 967-70, 1758, 1761-3, 1770, 1806, 1816-7, 1827, 1876-8, 1892, and 1897.

(e) Hispanic

91   Foulché-Delbosc, Raymond, and Barrau-Dihigo, Louis. *Manual de l'Hispanisant*. 2 vols. New York, N.Y.: G.P. Putnam's Sons, 1920/ Kraus, 1960.

A select guide to Hispanic historical studies. While it offers more comprehensive lists for the Renaissance period and later history, it does include the medieval period. Some general items are relevant to literature, language, and art.

92   Sáez, Emilio, and Rossell, Mercé, eds. *Repertorio de medievalisimo hispanico (1955-1975)*. I. *A-F*. Barcelona: Ediciones 'El Albir,' 1976-.

The first volume in a proposed comprehensive bibliography for mainly Spanish publications on medieval Spain. Although the topics include history, language, literature, and art, they are arranged alphabetically under author's name. Also cited are works in progress. There is no subject index.

See also items 143-7, 1014-21, and 1815.

(f) Italian

See items 148-50, 1022-33, 1768-9, 1776, 1778, 1789, 1834, 1851, 1859, 1879, 1884, and 1888-9.

(g) Netherlandic

See items 151, 1766, 1863, and 1893-4.

(h) Scandinavian

93   Erichsen, B., and Krarup, A. *Dansk Historisk Bibliografi*. 3 vols.
      Copenhagen: I Kommission Hos G.E.C. Gad, 1929.

      This non-critical bibliography lists items only to 1912, but
      Vol. 1, pp. 4-7, contains references to significant early works
      on archives, diplomatics, and paleography relating to medieval
      Scandinavian history.

94   *Excerpta Historica Nordica*, ed. Poul Bagge, *et al*. The Inter-
      national Committee of Historical Sciences. Copenhagen: Rosen-
      kilde and Bagger, 1955-.

      An invaluable biannual bibliography for early Scandinavian
      history. It provides summaries of recent publications, with full
      indexes.

See also items 152-3, 1036-8, 1625, and 1818.

4. LANGUAGE AND LITERATURE

(a) General

95   Ashworth, E.J. *The Tradition of Medieval Logic and Speculative
      Grammar*. Subsidia Mediaevalia, 9. Toronto: Pontifical Institute
      of Mediaeval Studies, 1978.

      A bibliography of secondary works and modern editions of all
      books and articles on formal logic and semantics from Anselm to
      the late seventeenth century. It includes such individual topics
      as consequences, syllogistic, supposition, theory, and speculative
      grammar, but excludes the categories, the struggle between nominal-
      ism and realism, and pure grammar. Arrangement is by author and
      work, with indexes to both.

96   Baldensperger, F., and Friederich, Werner P. *Bibliography of
      Comparative Literature*. New York: Russell and Russell, 1960.

      Lists works on literary themes and types, e.g., fables and
      fabliaux, sagas, myths, etc., with cross-referencing and indexes;
      brought up to date by item 103.

97   Caenegem, R.C. van, and Ganshof, F.L. *Kurze Quellenkunde des
      westeuropäischen Mittelalters: Eine typologische, historische
      und bibliographische Einführung*. Göttingen: Vandenhoeck and
      Ruprecht, 1964.

A bibliography of sources for European literature, adapted from an earlier edition designed for Dutch and Flemish scholars as a general guide to types. There are five sections: types of narrative sources and collections of diplomatic material and historical documents; a survey of the major libraries and archives; general reference works; and encyclopedias, dictionaries, and other reference materials. Indexes cite authors and works.

98   Fisher, John H., ed. *The Medieval Literature of Western Europe: A Review of Research Mainly 1930-1960*. New York, N.Y.: New York University Press for the Modern Language Association, 1966.

A general, critical survey of scholarship and a guide to definitive editions of major medieval literary works; divided into sections on English, Latin, Celtic, French, German, and Spanish literature.

99   International Arthurian Society. *Bulletin bibliographique de la société internationale Arthurienne*. Paris: The Society, 1949-.

An annual critical bibliography of Arthurian literature in all medieval vernacular languages, with cumulative indexes. A continuation of the "Bibliography of Critical Arthurian Literature," *Modern Language Quarterly*, 1940-63.

100   Murphy, James J. *Medieval Rhetoric: A Select Bibliography*. Toronto Medieval Bibliographies, 3. Toronto: University Press, 1971.

A selective guide to rhetorical texts, their relationship, and current publications in the field; somewhat brought up to date by the notes of item 1701. A second edition is in progress.

101   Stratman, Carl J., C.S.V. *Bibliography of Medieval Drama*. 2nd ed. (from 1954) 2 vols. New York, N.Y.: Frederick Ungar, 1972.

A valuable bibliography for the various forms of medieval drama in Latin and individual vernaculars. Arrangement is chronological under topic. A comprehensive index greatly facilitates use.

102   Tucker, Lena L., and Benham, Allen R. *A Bibliography of Fifteenth-Century Literature with Special Reference to the History of English Culture*. University of Washington Publications in Language and Literature, 2.3. Seattle, Wash.: University of Washington Press, 1928.

Out of date but nevertheless useful as a starting point for paleographers of late medieval literature. The sections include bibliography, political background, social and economic background, cultural background, and literature; under the last are listed texts, drama, authors, and anonymous works.

103   *Yearbook of Comparative and General Literature*. Chapel Hill, N.C.: University of North Carolina Press, 1952-.

An annual bibliography which also provides lists of translations into English from other languages. It includes cumulative indexes and cross-references.

(b) Celtic

104   Bonser, Wilfrid. *An Anglo-Saxon and Celtic Bibliography (450-*
       1087). 2 vols. Berkeley and Los Angeles, Calif.: University
       of California Press, 1957.

       Vol. 1 provides bibliographies on all aspects of Celtic history,
       religion, archaeology, numismatics and seals, epigraphy, and art.
       Entries are arranged alphabetically by topic. Vol. 2 indexes
       authors, subjects, and places. For some significant omissions,
       many of which have been rectified in the next item, see R.J.
       Schoeck's review, *Speculum*, 33 (1958), 267-8.

105   Bromwich, Rachael. *Medieval Celtic Literature: A Select Bibliog-*
       raphy. Toronto Medieval Bibliographies, 5. Toronto: University
       Press, 1974.

       Like all bibliographies in this series, with the exception of
       Hughes' on music (item 1262), this bibliography represents a
       highly select list designed primarily for undergraduates. It is,
       however, the most comprehensive bibliography of Celtic medieval
       literature to date and provides an indispensable starting point
       for all paleographers working in the field. In addition to
       specialized titles, the author includes introductory aids to the
       language. General sections cover introductory matter (i.e.,
       bibliographies and catalogues of manuscripts); language studies;
       literary history and criticism; texts and translations; and
       background material, including Irish and Welsh civilization.
       Indexes are provided for authors and editors, but not for titles
       and topics.

(c) English

106   *Abstracts of English Studies*. Boulder, Colo.: University of
       Colorado Press, 1958-.

       A cumulative bibliography of over 1,100 journals. Published
       ten times per year, it includes abstracts of articles and essays
       on English, American, and Canadian literature.

107   Ackerman, Robert W., and Ackerman, Gretchen P. *Sir Frederic*
       Madden: A Biographical Sketch and Bibliography. Garland Refer-
       ence Library of the Humanities. New York, N.Y.: Garland Pub-
       lishing, Inc., 1979.

       A critical bibliography which reflects Madden's extensive in-
       volvement with manuscripts and paleographical concerns as Keeper
       of Manuscripts in the British Library, 1827-66.

108   Beale, Walter H. *Old and Middle English Poetry to 1500: A Guide*
       to Information Sources. Gale Information Guide Library. Detroit,
       Mich.: Gale Research Co., 1976.

       A critical bibliography, arranged by general topic, then al-
       phabetically by author. Some sections are of interest for the
       areas of scholarship in textual studies and literary background,
       especially Parts 1.1 and 2.1.

109   Booker, J.M. *A Middle English Bibliography: Dates, Dialects, and Sources of the XII, XIII, and XIV Century Monuments and Manuscripts Exclusive of the Works of Wyclif, Gower, and Chaucer and the Documents of the London Dialect.* Heidelberg: Carl Winter, 1912.

       Although this critical bibliography is out of date, it does provide some listing of Middle English manuscripts with comments on dates, dialects, and provenances.

110   *Fourteenth-Century English Mystics Newsletter*, ed. Ritamary Bradley and Valerie M. Lagorio, English Department, University of Iowa, Iowa City, Ia. 52240.

       Since 1975 this newsletter has been published four times per year. It contains international work in progress, recent publications, and general information on current university courses in the subject.

111   Kennedy, Arthur G. *A Bibliography of Writings on the English Language from the Beginning of Printing to the End of 1922.* Cambridge, Mass.: Harvard University Press/New Haven, Conn.: Yale University Press, 1927.

       A bibliography of works, mainly from the sixteenth century. The lists of glosses, dictionaries, and other works are a good source of information on the language of some late Middle English manuscripts.

112   Matthews, William, ed. *Later Medieval English Prose.* Goldentree Books. New York, N.Y.: Appleton-Century-Crofts, 1963.

       While this represents merely a general introduction to the subject and one designed for undergraduates, it does contain some useful bibliographical references for the paleographer working in late Middle English didactic literature.

113   ————, ed. *Old and Middle English Literature.* Goldentree Bibliographies. New York, N.Y.: Appleton-Century-Crofts, 1968.

       A non-critical listing of basic works in Old and Middle English. It includes standard editions and some secondary material.

114   *Medieval Sermon Studies Newsletter*, ed. Gloria Cigman, English Department, University of Warwick, Coventry, England, CV4 7AL.

       Issued approximately twice per year since 1977, this newsletter includes international lists of scholars, work in progress, some critical bibliography, and desiderata.

115   Modern Humanities Research Association. *Annual Bibliography of English Language and Literature.* Cambridge: Bowes and Bowes, 1920-.

       A periodical listing of books, articles, dissertations, and reviews on all aspects of English studies, which also gives critical summaries of the preceding year's work. Author/subject indexes are provided.

116   Morrell, Minnie Cate. *A Manual of Old English Biblical Materials*.
      Knoxville, Tenn.: University of Tennessee Press, 1965.

      A bibliographical guide and index to Old English materials
      containing translations or paraphrases of the Bible. Manuscripts
      are described in terms of origin, dialect, editions, etc. The
      indexes and bibliography are invaluable, while appendixes give
      information on chronology, Latin origins, and notes to the texts.

117   *New Cambridge Bibliography of English Literature*, gen. ed. George
      Watson. 4 vols. Cambridge: University Press, 1969.

      This work is the standard, critical bibliography of British
      authors. It also includes references to background and reference
      matter. Arrangement is by author or genre within a chronological
      framework. It represents a revised edition of the *CBEL*, ed.
      F. Bateson (1954), and *Supplement* (1957).

118   New Chaucer Society. *The Chaucer Newsletter*, ed. Donald M. Rose,
      J. Lane Goodall, Nancy Zorn, and Lynne H. Levy, The University
      of Oklahoma, 760 Van Vleet Oval, Norman, Okla. 73019.

      Somewhat more than a newsletter, this publication contains
      short articles, notes, and announcements of conferences, research
      in progress, and publications. Published twice annually in
      January and June since 1979. See also item 1888.

      Newsletter, see items 110, 114, 119, 121, 122, and 123.

119   New Wyclif Society. *Newsletter*, ed. L.M. Eldredge, Dept. of
      English, University of Ottawa, Ottawa, Ont., Canada, K1N 6N5.

      An account of recent publications and work in progress, pub-
      lished since December, 1979, approximately twice yearly. These
      concern mainly the developments in university thought in England
      from ca. 1350 to ca. 1420.

120   Oizumi, Akio. *A Classified Bibliography of Writings on English
      Philology and Medieval English Literature*. 2nd ed. Tokyo:
      Nan'un-Do, 1966.

      A rather eclectic bibliography which lists, e.g., the *Supple-
      ment* but not the *Index of Middle English Verse*. It contains some
      lists of editions of medieval English texts, but its entries are
      of more interest for reflecting bibliographical items available
      in Japanese libraries and private collections. In view of the
      increasing number of Middle English manuscripts now available
      to scholars in Japan, this work may prove a useful aid to their
      study.

121   *Old and Middle English Medical Manuscripts*, ed. Laurel Braswell,
      Dept. of English, McMaster University, Hamilton, Ont., Canada,
      L8S 4L9.

      Notes, announcements, and work in progress on an international
      basis in the form of an appendix to the *Society for Ancient
      Medicine Newsletter*, ed. John Scarborough, University of Kentucky,
      Lexington, Ky. See item 176.

122   *Old English Newsletter*, ed. Paul Szarmach for the Old English
       Group of the Modern Language Association of America, Center
       for Medieval and Renaissance Studies, Ohio State University,
       Columbus, Ohio, 1967-, 1972-.

       An annual bibliography and review of year's work in Old English
       language and literature, published in two issues per year. In-
       cluded are short articles and notes.

123   *Records of Early English Drama*, ed. JoAnna Dutka, English Section,
       Erindale College, University of Toronto, Mississauga, Ont.,
       Canada, L5L 1C6.

       Published approximately twice per year since 1976, this news-
       letter is devoted to short articles and news of research and
       publications pertaining to the production of early drama in
       England, 1300-1600.

124   Robinson, Fred C. *Old English Literature: A Select Bibliography*.
       Toronto Medieval Bibliographies, 2. Toronto: University Press,
       1970.

       A select bibliography of 304 items, with some critical comment
       on most; items 294-6 relate to paleography. The index lists
       modern authors only.

125   Severs, J. Burke, ed. *Recent Middle English Scholarship and
       Criticism: Survey and Desiderata*. Pittsburgh, Pa.: Duquesne
       University Press, 1971.

       A critical survey of recent work on the major Middle English
       literary works, with bibliographical lists.

126   Simms, Norman T., comp. *Ritual and Rhetoric: Intellectual and
       Ceremonial Backgrounds to Middle English Literature; a Critical
       Survey of Relevant Scholarship*. Norwood, Pa.: Norwood Editions,
       1973.

       A select list of critical studies on such subjects as rhetoric
       and iconography. An index of editions is provided.

127   Wells, J.E. *A Manual of the Writings in Middle English 1050-1400,
       with Supplements*. New Haven, Conn.: Yale University Press,
       1916-57.

       An invaluable critical and descriptive bibliography, with
       bibliographical references continually brought up to date in
       subsequent supplements. The lists of manuscripts for each work
       are also revised and expanded in the supplements. Since 1967
       the work has been continued by members of the Middle English
       Group of the Modern Language Association under the direction of
       J. Burke Severs and Albert Hartung (New Haven, Conn.: Connecticut
       Academy of Arts and Sciences, 1967-), with individual vols.
       devoted to major works or genres; the chronological coverage has
       been extended to 1500.

128   *Year's Work in English Studies, The*. The English Association.
       Oxford: Murray, 1921-.

An annual, critical review of published books and articles on the whole range of English studies; arrangement is chronological and indexes are provided.

See also items 1729, 1738, 1747, 1750-1, 1753-4, 1754-5, 1757, 1788, 1797, 1804-5, 1808, 1810, 1832-3, 1836-7, 1839-40, 1843-6, 1849, 1857, 1862, 1878, 1881, 1886-7, 1890, 1892.

(d) French

129   Bossuat, Robert. *Manual bibliographique de la littérature française du moyen âge*. Melun: Librairie d'Argences, 1951; *Second Supplement*, 1961.

This appears to be the most comprehensive bibliography of Old French literature to date, although not so well annotated as Cabeen's (next item). Its numbered items are arranged by genre. An author/title/editor index is provided.

130   Cabeen, D.C., gen. ed. *A Critical Bibliography of French Literature*. I. *The Mediaeval Period*, ed. Urban T. Holmes, Jr. Syracuse, N.Y.: Syracuse University Press, 1952/1964.

A bibliography enlarged from the 1st ed. of 1947. It contains items on general studies and genres, and the full critical comments also list reviews. A name/title index is provided.

131   Klapp, Otto, ed. *Bibliographie der französichen Literaturwissenschaft*. Frankfurt-am-Main: Vittorio Klostermann, 1961-.

A periodical bibliography, non-critical, and arranged in chronological sections; of special interest to paleographers is Section II, "Moyen Rom. Age, Manuscrits et Bibliographies." There is a name/subject index in each vol.

132   *Romanische Bibliographie. Bibliographie romane. Romance Bibliography*. Tübingen: M. Niemeyer, 1961/1962-.

A biannual continuation of the bibliography issued originally as a supplement to the *Zeitschrift für romanische Philologie*.

133   Spanke, Hans. *G. Raynauds Bibliographie des altfranzöschen Liedes*. Leiden: E.J. Brill, 1955.

A critical bibliography of Old French songs from the thirteenth to the fourteenth centuries, with lists of manuscripts.

134   Taylor, Robert A. *La Littérature occitane du moyen âge: bibliographie selective et critique*. Toronto Medieval Bibliographies, 7. Toronto: University of Toronto Press, 1977.

A highly selective, critical bibliography of Provençal literature, arranged by genre and author with indexes provided for both.

135   Woledge, Brian. *Bibliographie des romans et nouvelles en prose française antérieurs à 1500*. Publications Romanes et Françaises, 42. Geneva: E. Droz, 1954.

An alphabetical index of prose romances and tales, arranged by title. Listed are manuscripts, editions, sources (when known), and relations to other literature. The indexes include manuscripts, printers, and author/work/theme.

136 ————, and Clive, H.P. *Répertoire des plus anciens textes en prose française depuis 842 jusqu'aux premières années du XIIIe siècle*. Publications Romanes et Françaises, 79.

Somewhat more than a bibliography, this useful work provides a general introduction to the origins of French prose, then gives an alphabetical index by item or author, with lists of manuscripts and printed editions, Whenever possible, notes are included on sources and relationships to other literature. There is a list of *incipits*, pp. 146-50.

See also items 84-7, 1794, 1843-7, 1863, 1869, 1877-8, 1886, 1890, 1892, and 1898.

(e) German

137 Bostock, J. Knight. *A Handbook on Old High German Literature*. Oxford: Clarendon Press, 1955; 2nd ed. K.C. King and D.R. McLintock. Oxford: Clarendon Press/New York, N.Y.: Oxford University Press, 1976.

This work constitutes a comprehensive bibliography on German background, early translations from Latin, and individual Old High German documents with editions and studies.

138 Faulhaber, Uwe K., and Goff, Penrith B. *German Literature: An Annotated Reference Guide*. New York, N.Y.: Garland Publishing, Inc., 1979.

A comprehensive critical bibliography on all aspects of German language and literature, arranged by author and genre in chronological sequence. An index is provided.

139 *Jahresbericht für deutsche Sprache und Literatur*, gen. ed. Gerhard Marx. Deutsche Akademie der Wissenschaften zu Berlin, Institut für deutsche Sprache und Literatur. Berlin: The Academy, 1886-.

A periodic non-critical bibliography for German language and literature, arranged by genre and period. Indexes are provided for editors/authors/subjects.

140 Körner, Josef. *Bibliographisches Handbuch des deutschen Schrifttums*. 3rd ed. (from 1933). Bern: A. Francke, 1949.

A general bibliography of German literature; for medieval and paleographical items, see especially *Allegemeiner Teil* and Part A: *Deutsche Schrifttum vor Goethe*.

141 Morvay, Karin, and Grube, Dagmar, comp. *Bibliographie der deutschen Predigt des Mittelalters*. Münchener Texte und Untersuchungen zur deutschen Literatur des Mittelalters, 47. Munich: C.H. Beck, 1974.

A critical bibliography exclusively devoted to medieval German sermons and homiletic materials. Indexed.

142   Schlütter, Hans Jurgen, ed. *Bibliographien zur deutschen Litera-tur*. Hildesheim: G. Olms, 1974-.

A continuing periodic bibliography, issued approximately annually. Each vol. covers one genre or author. Indexed.

See also items 88-90, 1757, 1760, 1762, 1772, 1803, 1806, 1808, 1836, 1843-6, 1849-50, 1877-8, 1881, 1892, 1895-6, 1899.

(f) Hispanic

143   Cardenas, Anthony; Gilkison, Jean; Nitti, John; and Anderson, Ellen. *A Bibliography of Old Spanish Texts*. I. *Literary Texts*. Hispanic Seminary of Medieval Studies. 2nd ed. (from 1975). Madison, Wis.: University of Wisconsin Press, 1977.

A bibliography representing the initial stage of the computer-ized Old Spanish Dictionary project currently in progress at the University of Wisconsin; items represent the source texts for dictionary entries. Arrangement is alphabetical by author, with lists of manuscripts and editions provided. The indexes include title, manuscript location, date of composition and production, printer or scribe, author, and subject. See item 901.

144   Foster, David W., and Foster, Virginia Ramos. *Manual of Hispanic Bibliography*. Seattle, Wash.: University of Washington Press, 1970. 2nd ed. New York, N.Y.: Garland Publishing, Inc., 1977.

A four-part bibliography divided into bibliographical materials, Spanish literature, Spanish-American literature, and Spanish-American National bibliographies; the emphasis is upon post-1500 writings, but references to bibliographical and resource mate-rials in the first two sections are also of value to the paleog-rapher.

145   Peers, Edgar Allison. *Spain: A Companion to Spanish Studies*. 5th ed. (from 1929). London: Methuen, 1956.

An invaluable handbook to Spanish language, literature, and history. There are nine individual bibliographies on separate areas of study, with author/title indexes.

146   Simón Díaz, José. *Bibliografía de la literaturia hispánica*. Consejo Superior de Investigaciones Científicas. Madrid: The Institute, 1950-.

Vol. 1 includes sections on the history of literature, collec-tions of texts, and studies; vol. 2 gives comprehensive, critical bibliographies; subsequent vols. focus on specific areas. The bibliographical matter is condensed in a *Manual* (Barcelona: Gustavo Gili, 1963).

147   Voltes, María José Buxo-Dulce de. *Catálogo de publicaciones de
       la diputación provincial de Barcelona*. Barcelona: Province of
       Barcelona, 1966.

       A critical bibliography of official publications for Barcelona;
       included are library catalogues for the Biblioteca Cataluña and
       other provincial collections.

See also items 91-2, 1014-21, and 1815.

                              (g) Italian

148   Harvard University Library. *Italian History and Literature*.
       2 vols. Cambridge, Mass.: Harvard University Press, 1974.

       A non-critical bibliography of publications on Italian history
       and literature based upon the holdings of the Widener library,
       constituting in effect a library catalogue. Vol 1 gives classi-
       fied listings arranged by subject chronologically; vol. 2 lists
       works by author or title.

149   Prezzolini, Giuseppe. *Repertorio bibliografico della storia e
       della critica della litteratura italiana*. 4 vols. Rome: Edi-
       zioni Roma, 1937-48.

       This work provides a bibliographical list of Italian writers
       and writings on literature and history; arrangement is alpha-
       betical by author; updated by Umberto Bosco, ed., 2 vols.,
       Florence: Sansoni, 1959.

150   Puppo, Mario. *Manuale critico-bibliografico per lo studio della
       letteratura italiana*. 5th rev. ed. (from 1954). Torino:
       Società Editrice Internazionale, 1964.

       A work somewhat erratically selective in spite of its many
       revisions, but one which is still useful as the only critical
       bibliography to include medieval Italian language and literature
       and many items of paleographical interest.

See also items 1768-9, 1776, 1778, 1789, 1834, 1851, 1859, 1879, 1884,
       and 1888-9.

                            (h) Netherlandic

151   Bath, B.H. Slicher van. "Guide to the Work of Dutch Medievalists,
       1919-1947." *Speculum*, 23 (1948), 236-66. Offprint.

       An excellent guide to bibliographic surveys, philology,
       chronology, diplomatics, and paleography; see subsequent issues
       for further bibliographic information.

See also items 1766, 1863, 1893-4.

(i) Scandinavian

152   Bekker-Nielsen, Hans. *Old-Norse-Icelandic Studies: A Select
       Bibliography*. Toronto Medieval Bibliographies, 1. Toronto:
       University Press, 1967.

       A bibliography limited in selection and annotation, but one
       of special interest for paleographers, since Section II.d, pp.
       23-25, lists items on manuscript study and catalogues for the
       major Scandinavian collections.

153   ————, and Olsen, Thorkil Damsgaard, eds. *Bibliography of Old
       Norse Icelandic Studies*. Copenhagen: Munksgaard, 1964-.

       An annual, annotated list of editions, books, articles, and
       reviews on all aspects of medieval Scandinavian studies; the
       emphasis is upon literary subjects; indexes are included in each
       issue.

See also items 93-4, 1625, 1818.

5. PHILOSOPHY AND THEOLOGY

154   *Bibliographie critique*. Paris: G. Beauchesne, 1924-.

       Biannual since 1930, this critical bibliography consists of
       reviews of principal books and articles on philosophy for the
       preceding two years. Cumulative indexes on philosophy are
       provided.

155   Institut International de Philosophie. *Bibliographie de la
       philosophie*. Paris: J. Vrin, 1937-.

       This fully critical bibliography is issued quarterly. Arrange-
       ment is by type of philosophy, e.g., general theory, logic, or
       by name of philosopher, then alphabetical by author. Indexes
       are provided.

156   Principe, Walter H. *Bibliographies and Bulletins in Theology*.
       Toronto: The Author, 1967.

       A useful, critical bibliography of the major bibliographies
       and bibliographical materials in the subject, with some emphasis
       upon the medieval period.

157   *Répertoire bibliographique de la philosophie*. Louvain: 1976-.

       A quarterly, classified bibliography, non-critical, published
       by the Institut International de Philosophie. The categories
       are arranged according to general studies, and chronologically
       from Classical to the modern periods.

158   Totok, Wilhelm, ed. *Handbuch der Geschichte der Philosophie*.
       3 vols. Frankfurt-am-Main, Vittorio Klostermann, 1964-77.

       A comprehensive, accurate, but non-critical and often highly
       abbreviated bibliography. Vol. 1 lists general works and items

on ancient philosophies, with arrangement by author, then division into type of work; vol. 2 is devoted to medieval philosophy, and vol. 3 to the modern period. Under the section entitled "*Hilfs-mittel*" are to be found items on manuscript and textual studies. Extensive name/subject indexes are provided.

See also items 1759, 1762, 1773, 1784, 1794, 1801, 1815, 1823, 1829, 1836, 1855, 1860-1, 1864, 1867-8, 1871, 1875-6, 1878, 1880, 1883, 1891-4, and 1897.

6. RELIGION AND THE BIBLE

159   Ackroyd, Peter R., ed. *Bible Bibliography 1967-1973: Old Testa-ment. The Book Lists of the Society for Old Testament Study*. Oxford: Basil Blackwell, 1974.

An excellent, critical bibliography for Old Testament studies, which lists them according to topics such as general, archae-ology, epigraphy, history, and literary criticism, then under year of publication. Indexes are provided. For New Testament bibliography, see items 160, 163.

160   Barrow, John G. *A Bibliography of Bibliographies in Religion*. Ann Arbor, Mich.: Edwards, 1955.

This work provides a non-critical list of further bibliographies on many subjects within the general area of religion. For the paleographer the most useful sections are on the Bible, Church History (arranged by country), Patristics, and individuals such as Albertus Magnus.

161   *Catholic Periodical and Literature Index*. Haverford, Pa.: Catholic Library Association, 1967-.

A continuation and amalgamation of *The Guide to Catholic Literature* (1888-1967) and *The Catholic Periodical Index* (1930-66). It provides an annotated author/title/subject bibliography on all subjects pertaining to the Roman Catholic Church, although many are on the popular level.

162   Grundmann, Herbert. *Bibliographie zur Ketzergeschichte des Mittelalters (1903-1966)*. Rome: Edizioni di Storia e Lettera-tura, 1967.

A critical bibliography, with indexes, of medieval sects, heresies, and heretics.

163   Hurd, John Cooledge, Jr., comp. *A Bibliography of New Testament Bibliographies*. New York, N.Y.: Seabury Press, 1966.

A good, critical bibliography of bibliographies for the whole New Testament, then individual books. It also lists reference works, works by individual scholars, and periodical bibliographies.

164   *Internationale Zeitschriftenschau für Bibelwissenschaft und
       Grenzegebiete.* Düsseldorf: 1951/52-.

       A biannual bibliography for the major international articles
       on Biblical studies. Abstracts are provided in German.

165   Scholar, David. *A Basic Bibliographical Guide for New Testament
       Exegesis.* 2nd ed. (from 1971). Grand Rapids, Mich.: William
       B. Eerdmans, 1973.

       This bibliography is a pleasure to use in its clean, concise
       arrangement by type of study (reference works, critical studies,
       etc.) and helpful annotations. It also lists bibliographic sur-
       veys for Bible studies and theological research, pp. 11-12.

166   *Répertoire générale de sciences religieuses: bibliographie 1950-
       59.* Rome: L'Airone/Paris: Colmar Alsatia, 1953-1968.

       A critical bibliography of all books, articles, and separates
       published during this period; indexed.

See also items 1749, 1755, 1774-5, 1784, 1811, 1815, 1823, 1836, 1855,
    1860-1, 1864, 1867-9, 1871-2, 1875-8, 1883, 1888, 1892-4, and 1897.

7. SCIENCE AND MEDICINE

167   Carmody, Francis J. *Arabic Astronomical and Astrological Sciences
       in Latin Translation: A Critical Bibliography.* Berkeley and
       Los Angeles, Calif.: University of California Press, 1956.

       This bibliography lists works in chronological order for the
       ninth and tenth centuries, then anonymous and Western compila-
       tions such as the *Theorica Planetorum* by Guido Bonatti. Its use
       is greatly facilitated by lists of incipits and indexes of names
       and topics.

168   Cassedy, James H., comp. *Research in Progress.* American Associa-
       tion for the History of Medicine. Bethesda, Md.: The Associa-
       tion, 1976-.

       A bibliographic bulletin, issued annually, which lists re-
       searcher, address, name and brief description of project, and
       probable date of completion. Arrangement is alphabetical by name
       of researcher. Topics include all aspects of medicine from
       Classical antiquity to the present, but unfortunately no subject
       index is provided.

169   Darmstaedter, Ludwig. *Handbuch zur Geschichte der Naturwissen-
       schaften und der Technik.* 2nd ed. (from 1895). Berlin: J.A.
       Stargardt, 1908/New York, N.Y.: Kraus, 1960.

       A bibliographical guide to the resources and methodology of
       the history of the natural sciences, which offers comprehensive
       coverage of late nineteenth-century German items. Arrangement
       is by topic and chronology.

170   Garrison, Fielding, and Morton, Leslie. *Garrison and Morton's Medical Bibliography: An Annotated Checklist of Texts Illustrating the History of Medicine.* 3rd ed. (from 1943). London: Grafton, 1970.

This invaluable work provides extensive, critical summaries or bibliographical references to the major published texts. It was originally published in the *Bulletin of the Institute of the History of Medicine,* 1 (Baltimore, Md.: 1933), 333-434.

171   *Isis Cumulative Bibliography,* ed. Magda Whitrow. 2 vols. Baltimore, Md.: History of Science Society, 1971.

A critical bibliography compiled from the journal *Isis,* vols. 1-90 (1913-65); for current items see *Isis,* item 1822.

172   Leitner, Helmut. *Bibliography to the Ancient Medical Authors.* Bern: H. Huber, 1973.

A brief (61pp.) compilation of ancient medical sources; arrangement is alphabetical under writer's name, e.g., "Galenus," with lists of works and texts.

173   National Library of Medicine. *Bibliography of the History of Medicine.* Bethesda, Md.: U.S. Department of Health, Education, and Welfare, Public Health Service, 1965-.

Although this annual bibliography focuses upon research in more recent medicine, its organization by subject and historical period and full indexes make it make it a handy, initial bibliographical tool for the paleographer in checking the most recent publications on the subject of ancient and medieval medicine.

174   Osler, W. *Incunabula Medica. A Study of the Earliest Printed Medical Books, 1467-1480.* Bibliographical Society, Illustrated Monographs, 19. London: The Society, 1923.

This critical and bibliographical study of medical incunabula is a valuable guide to late manuscript traditions and survivals. See Hain, item 11, for more comprehensive lists of incunabula in the subject.

175   Read, J. *Prelude to Chemistry: An Outline of Alchemy, Its Literature and Relationships.* London: G. Bell and Sons, 1936.

An essay-type bibliography, now out of date but still useful as a starting point for further research. For more recent bibliography on alchemy, see items 177, 688.

176   Scarborough, John, comp. *Society for Ancient Medicine Newsletter.* Lexington, Ky.: The Author, 1975-.

Published approximately annually, this xeroxed bibliography offers an excellent critical review of recently published books and articles on the subject of ancient and medieval medicine. It also lists forthcoming volumes and work in progress; see also item 121.

177   Schuler, Robert M., comp. *English Magical and Scientific Poems to 1700: An Annotated Bibliography*. New York, N.Y.: Garland Publishing, Inc., 1979.

      A census of all English poetry concerning science or magic to 1700 (over 500 published and unpublished texts). Included are descriptive comments and name/subject indexes.

178   Thornton, John L. *Medical Books, Libraries, and Collections: A Study of Bibliography and the Book Trade in Relation to Medical Sciences*, introd. Geoffrey L. Keynes. London: Grafton, 1949.

      The first two chapters of this work, "Medical Literature before the Invention of Printing," and "Medical Incunabula" offer a general résumé with notes of the more important, late medieval texts.

179   Wellcome Institute for the History of Medicine. *Current Work in the History of Medicine*. London: The Institute, 1960-.

      An invaluable, current bibliography on the subject; organization is by subject for articles and by author for books, with full indexes; included is British, Continental, and North American scholarship, as well as Asian, East European, and Russian.

See also items 687-708, 1754, 1767, 1783, 1786, 1802, 1822, 1828, 1836, 1838, and 1842.

8. TRANSLATIONS

180   *Cumulative Index to English Translations, 1948-68*. 2 vols. London: G.K. Hall, 1973.

      A list of English translations from other languages, produced in conjunction with the UNESCO *Index*, item 188. Arrangement is alphabetical by original author.

181   Farrar, C.P., and Evans, A.P. *A Bibliography of English Translations from Medieval Sources*. Records of Civilization, Sources and Studies, 39. New York, N.Y.: Columbia University Press, 1946.

      A critical bibliography, arranged alphabetically by author's name; cited are editions and other references; an author index is provided. Continued by next item.

182   Ferguson, Mary Anne, comp. *A Bibliography of English Translations from Medieval Sources 1944-68*. New York, N.Y.: Columbia University Press, 1973.

      A continuation and updating of the preceding item, with similar arrangement and citation.

183   Kristeller, Paul O., *et al. Catalogus Translationum et Commentariorum: Medieval and Renaissance Latin Translations and Commentaries*. Washington, D.C.: Catholic University of America, 1960-.

A bibliography in progress of all Latin translations to 1600 of pre-A.D. 600 Greek works and Latin commentaries on Ancient Greek and Latin authors; in two parts for Greek and Latin authors respectively, and arranged alphabetically by author or work.

184 *Literatures of the World in English Translation, The: A Bibliography*. I. *The Greek and Latin Literatures*, ed. George B. Parks and Ruth Z. Temple. New York, N.Y.: Frederick Ungar, 1968; III. *The Romance Literatures*, ed. Parks and Temple, 1970.

This bibliography first lists collections of translations, then individual translations alphabetically by author. The proposed vol. IV, *Celtic, Germanic and Other Literatures of Europe*, has not yet appeared.

185 Lucas, Robert. "Medieval French Translations of Latin Classics to 1500." *Speculum*, 45 (1976), 225-53.

An inventory of translations, exclusive of Patristic writers and Roman legal texts. Arrangement is alphabetical by author: Boethius-Vergil. Appended is a list of library catalogues of French manuscript collections outside France, arranged by country.

186 Muckle, J.T. "Greek Works Translated Directly into Latin Before 1350." *Mediaeval Studies*, 4 (1942), 33-42; 5 (1943), 102-14.

Greek authors are listed alphabetically within two historical periods, before A.D. 1000 and from that date to 1350. Cited are editions of Greek texts, mainly in *Patrologia Graeca*, and medieval Latin translations. Detailed coverage is given for Aristotelian and pseudo-Aristotelian works.

187 *Speculum*. "Periodic Bibliography of Editions and Translations in Progress" (1973-).

An annual bibliography of translations, usually carried in the January issue (see item 1878). Arrangement is alphabetical by title, author, or subject, with cross-references. Offprints are available through the Medieval Text Association, Baruch College of the City University of New York, 17 Lexington Ave., New York, N.Y. 10010.

188 UNESCO. *Index Translationum, Répertoire internationale des traductions*. Paris: UNESCO, 1948-.

An international and periodic list of translations of literary, scientific, and other works. There are extensive indexes provided for authors, translators, and publishers.

See also items 38-9.

II. LIBRARIES

CONTENTS

A. MODERN LIBRARIES

The following titles represent a selection of the
more important bibliographical guides to library resources. For individual countries only the more significant or representative catalogues of manuscripts have
been listed, since to list all such works would be beyond the scope of the present *Handbook*. I have, instead,
focused upon general guides or bibliographical works
which would provide a key to additional and in some
cases more specialized catalogues. Further references
may be found in the catalogues of printed books issued
by most major libraries; probably the most convenient
and up to date are the *Subject* volumes issued by the
Library of Congress for their *Union Catalogues*, which
list under "Manuscripts" most library catalogues or other
documents on manuscript collections within a year of
publication. Catalogues or lists of manuscripts devoted
to one topic from more than one library are cited in
Section V.

More specific references to Diplomatic and Archival
collections are found in Section VII. Most of these are
cross-referenced below.

1. GENERAL

189   Altick, Richard D., and Wright, Andrew, eds. "Guides to Libraries
      American, British, Continental," in *Selective Bibliography
      for the Study of English and American Literature*. 2nd ed.
      New York, N.Y.: Macmillan, 1963; pp. 35-43.

190   Collison, Robert. *Published Library Catalogues: An Introduction
      to their Contents and Use*. London: Mansell Information and
      Publishing, 1973.

      Part 1 of this work includes descriptive lists of library cata-
      logues arranged by subject, e.g., "Auction Sale Catalogues" and
      Part 2 provides a key to abbreviations and brief bibliography.
      The latter also includes a subject index.

191   Fischer, Irmgard. *Die Handbibliothek in Handschriftenlesesälen:
      Überlegungen zu ihrer Entstehung, Aufgabe und Benutzung. Mit
      einem Modellvorschlag für die systematische Aufstellung*.
      Arbeiten aus dem Bibliothekar- Lehrinstitut des Landes Nord-
      rhein-Westfallen, 44. Cologne: Greven, 1974.

      While this represents a handbook for consulting manuscripts
      in mainly German libraries, its more general applications may
      be seen from its classifications of manuscript descriptions and
      select bibliography of international reference works.

192   Haenel, Gustav, ed. *Catalogi Librorum Manuscriptorum, qui in
        Bibliothecis Galiae, Helvetiae, Belgii, Britanniae, Hispaniae,
        Lusitaniae Esservantur*. Leipzig: C. Hinrichs, 1830.

        Summary, but intended as comprehensive, this early catalogue
        lists all European manuscripts by country and library collection.

193   *Internationales Bibliotheks-Handbuch. World Guide to Libraries*.
        4th ed. (from 1966). 2 vols. Pullach-bei-Munich: Verlag Doku-
        mentation, 1974.

        A summary guide to all major libraries of the world. Vol. 1
        includes Europe and America, while vol. 2 lists the libraries
        of Africa, Asia, and Oceania. Arrangement is alphabetical by
        continent and country. The information given includes address,
        holdings, number and letter-codes for subject fields, and
        specialized areas.

194   Köttelwesch, C., ed. *Zur Katalogisierung mittelalterlicher und
        neuerer Handschriften*. Zeitschrift für Bibliothekswesen und
        Bibliographie, Sonderheft, 1. Frankfurt: Klostermann, 1963.

        A series of articles on cataloguing problems, including the
        special difficulties of fragments (see section VII below).

195   Kristeller, Paul O. *Latin Manuscript Books before 1600: A List
        of the Printed Catalogues and Unpublished Inventories of
        Extant Collections*. 2nd ed. from earlier publication in
        Traditio, 6 (1948), 227–317; 9 (1953), 393–418. New York, N.Y.:
        Fordham University Press, 1960; 3rd ed. 1965.

        This important work presents a list of printed catalogues and
        unpublished inventories of manuscript collections in America and
        Europe. Although limited to those manuscripts in Latin, it makes
        some reference to manuscript contents in vernacular languages.
        A new edition is currently in preparation by Dr. Wolfgang Milde,
        Herzog-August-Bibliothek, Wolfenbüttel.

196   Lewanski, Richard C., comp. *Special Collections in European
        Libraries: A Directory and Bibliographical Guide*. New York,
        N.Y.: Bowker, 1965.

        An expansion of Lee Ash's *Subject Collections*, 2nd ed. (New
        York, N.Y.: Bowker, 1961), this highly useful directory groups
        libraries under topics based upon the Dewey Decimal system, then
        under country. The information includes address, director, hold-
        ings, and a bibliography of catalogues, although the last is
        not always complete. A final, general bibliography cites library
        guides to individual countries. There is a subject index.

197   Löffler, Karl. *Einführung in die Katalogkunde*. Leipzig: Hierse-
        mann, 1935.

        This account of methodology in cataloguing and classification
        is intended as a companion to the author's introduction to
        paleography, item 744.

198   Munby, A.N.L., and Towner, Lawrence W., eds. *The Flow of Books
        and Manuscripts: Papers Read at a Clark Library Seminar, March*

30, 1968. Los Angeles, Calif.: University of California Press, 1969.

A collection of papers on topics such as the protection of cultural property, collecting manuscripts, and the establishment of library collections.

199   Philippart, G. "Catalogues récents de manuscrits. 10 Ser. Manu-
      scrits en écriture latin," *Analecta Bollandiana*, 94 (1976),
      160-82.

This critical bibliography of catalogues for Latin manuscripts represents an especially useful issue of a bibliography of manuscript catalogues issued periodically in this journal; each issue is devoted to one particular classification of manuscripts.

200   Powitz, Herhardt. "Zur Textaufnahme in Handschriftenkatalogen,"
      in item 716, 4, pp. 59-66.

Powitz discusses methods of manuscript description and compares them with the methods of medieval manuscript cataloguing.

201   Richardson, Ernest Cushing, ed. *A Union World Catalog of Manu-
      script Books, Preliminary Studies in Method*, in *A History of
      Catalogs of Manuscript Books*. 6 vols. New York, N.Y.; H.W.
      Wilson, 1933-35/Burt Franklin: 1972.

Although this work is reportedly plagued with errors, it represents nevertheless a useful starting point for catalogue bibliography; it lists manuscript catalogues alphabetically by country. The key to abbreviations is included in "Preliminary Studies," 2, and in the *Union List of Periodicals*.

202   Steele, Colin. *Major Libraries of the World: A Selective Guide*.
      London/New York: Bowker, 1976.

An alphabetical guide to major libraries and research centers, from Albania to Zagreb; it gives address, director, and history, and indicates major and special collections. The existence of printed catalogues is noted, although they are not cited individually.

203   Thorpe, James Ernest. *The Use of Manuscripts in Literary Research:
      Problems of Access and Literary Property Rights*. New York,
      N.Y.: MLA, 1974.

A brief (40pp.) guide on the location and use of manuscript collections and individual manuscripts in North America and Great Britain. It describes procedures for initial inquiries, microform requests, copyrights, etc.

204   Weinberger, Wilhelm. *Catalogus Catalogorum. Verzeichnis des
      Bibliotheken, die ältere Handschriften lateinischer Kirchen-
      schriftsteller enthalten*. Kaiserlichen Akademie der Wissen-
      schaften. Vienna: F. Tempsky, 1902.

This brief (56pp.) catalogue lists pre-1900 manuscript printed catalogues under individual European countries.

205   Wilson, William Jerome. "Manuscript Cataloguing." *Traditio*, 12
      (1956), 457-556.

Wilson describes the techniques and terminology of manuscript cataloguing and provides a guide to the methodology of more recent catalogues.

See also items 941, 943-4, 949, 956.

2. INDIVIDUAL COUNTRIES

(a) Austria

206   Förstner, K. *Die karolingischen Handschriften und Fragmente in den Salzburger Bibliotheken.* Salzburg: Gesellschaft für Salzburger Landeskunde, 1962.

A descriptive catalogue of Carolingian manuscripts in this collection; it incidentally serves as a guide to the classification and description of fragments used in later bindings, see section VIII.

207   *Handschriftenverzeichnisse in österreichischer Bibliotheken.* Vienna: Akademie der Wissenschaften, 1942-.

These volumes now in progress are devoted to one library or a group of smaller libraries, e.g., vol. 3 (1967) lists the manuscripts and relevant catalogues for the Universitätsbibliothek, Graz.

208   Kraft, Walter C. *Codices Vindobonenses Hispanici: A Catalogue of Spanish, Portuguese, and Catalan Manuscripts in the Austrian National Library in Vienna.* Corvallis: Oregon State College Press, 1957.

A brief (64pp.) descriptive catalogue of all manuscripts within this linguistic group. Some illustrating facsimiles are provided.

209   Mazal, O., and Unterkircher, Franz, eds. *Katalog der abendländischen Handschriften der österreichischen Nationalbibliothek.* Series Nova. Vienna: Georg Prachner, 1963-.

These catalogues, now in progress, of Western manuscripts in the National Library are fully descriptive and contain further bibliographical notes; manuscripts are cited by collection number and indexes are provided. On Mazal's methodology, see his "Handschriftenbeschreibung in Österreich," published among the papers from conferences at Kremsmünster (1973) and Zwettl (1974).

210   Unterkircher, Franz. *Katalog der datierten Handschriften in lateinischen Schrift in Österreich*: I. *Nationalbibliothek.* 3 vols. Vienna: Akademie der Wissenschaften, 1969-74.

The first in Austria's series of inventories of all datable Western manuscripts. The project was first proposed at the First International Colloquium on Palaeography in Paris, 1953, when it was established that individual countries would issue fully descriptive catalogues by region and that the information given

would include accounts of scribes and scripts, a facsimile ex-
tract, paleographical notes, and further bibliographical references. By "lateinischen schrift"/"écriture latine" is meant not
only Latin manuscripts but also those in Western vernaculars,
see items 218, 233, 346. On the relative scope and merits of
this catalogue series, see M.L. Colker, "Some Recent Works for
Paleographers," *Medievalia et Humanistica*, 8 (1971), 235-42.

For microfilms of Austrian library catalogues, see items 541, 549.
See also items 958, 1091, 1093, 1098.

(b) Belgium

211   *Bibliotheca Belgica Manuscripta*, ed. A. Sanderus. Lille: T.
      Leclercq, 1641; repr. 2 vols. Farnborough: Gregg International,
      1969.

      A catalogue of manuscripts found in Belgian collections during
      the first quarter of the seventeenth century.

212   Bollandist Institute. *Catalogus Codicum Hagiographicorum
      Bibliothecae Regiae Bruxellensis*. 2 vols. Brussels: The Insti-
      tute, 1886-89.

      A descriptive catalogue of hagiographical manuscripts in the
      Royal Library; they are also cited under individual saints' names
      in *BHG* and *BHL*, see items 634-5.

213   Calcoen, R. *Inventaire des manuscrits scientifiques de la
      Bibliothèque Royale de Belgique*. Brussels: Bibliothèque Royale,
      1965-.

      This series of inventories now in progress offers a descriptive
      catalogue of all manuscripts containing scientific matter
      (treatises, poems, etc.). Indexes are provided.

214   Faider, Paul. *Bibliographie des catalogues des manuscrits des
      bibliothèques de Belgique*. Bruges: Imprimérie Sainte-Catherine,
      1933.

      An early inventory of manuscript catalogues, sponsored by the
      Academie Royale de Belgique. For some indication of certain limi-
      tations, see *The Library Quarterly*, 8 (1938), 156-7.

215   ————, ed. *Catalogue général des manuscrits des bibliothèques
      de Belgique*. Gembloux: J. Duclot, 1934-.

      A proposed comprehensive survey of manuscript collections,
      arranged geographically by volume and published under the names
      of individual contributors, e.g., vol. 2: A. De Poorter, *Catalogue
      des manuscrits de la bibliothèque publique de la ville de Bruges*,
      1934.

216   Ghent, University of. *Census van de Handschriften*. Ghent: Uni-
      versity Press, 1955-.

A series of descriptive inventories, now in progress, of all manuscripts in university collections; indexes are provided.

217   Gheyn, J. van den, S.J. *Catalogue des manuscrits de la Biblio-thèque Royale de Belgique*. 12 vols. Brussels: Bibliothèque Royale, 1901–36.

This fully descriptive series of volumes represent the most complete catalogue to date for the Royal Library; included are bibliographical references and indexes.

218   Masai, François, and Wittek, Martin, gen. eds. *Manuscrits datés conservés en Belgique. I. 819–1400*. Brussels/Ghent: Editions Scientifiques, 1968; II. *1401–1500, Manuscrits conservés à la Bibliothèque Royale Albert Ier*. Brussels: 1972.

This represents the first in the dated-manuscript series proposed for Belgium, see item 210 above.

See also items 461, 1093, 1348.

(c) France

i. General

219   Direction des Bibliothèques et de la Lecture Publique. *Réper-toire des bibliothèques et organismes de documentation*. Paris: Bibliothèque Nationale, 1971; *Supplement*, 1973.

An indispensable, general guide to most libraries in France; arrangement is, first, by Paris region, then by individual provinces. Given for each library are address, major holdings, and printed catalogues.

220   UNESCO. *Répertoire des bibliothèques de France*: I. *Paris*; II. *Departements*; III. *Centres et services de documentation*. Paris: UNESCO, 1950–51.

A description of research facilities and major library collec-tions in France, arranged by Paris region and province. This work is now replaced by the preceding item.

ii. Individual Libraries

221   Avril, François. *Manuscrits Normands XIe-XIIeme siècles de la Rouen Bibliothèque Municipale*. Paris: Musée des Beaux-Arts, 1975.

A brief, descriptive catalogue with bibliography and some facsimiles. Arrangement is by collection, then chronological.

222   Bibliothèque Nationale, Département des Manuscrits. *Catalogue alphabétique des livres imprimés mis à la disposition des lecteurs dans la salle de travail, suivi de la liste des catalogues usuels au Département des Manuscrits*. Paris: Im-primérie Nationale, 1933.

A descriptive catalogue of printed books and manuscripts, which also contains a bibliography of pre-1932 printed catalogues for manuscripts and archives. A *Bibliographie Annuelle* brings the work periodically up to date; see especially Sect. 6, "Archives et Bibliothèques"; for microfilms see items 529, 532.

223 ————. *Catalogue général des manuscrits latins*, ed. Marie-Thérèse D'Alverny, *et al.*, 1939-.

A series of new catalogues for the 21,000 Latin manuscripts in the Bibliothèque Nationale. Arrangement is by collection number, with frequent cross-references. Full bibliographical references are included.

224 Cadell, Helène. *Papyrus of the Sorbonne.* Publications de la Faculté des Lettres et Sciences Humaines de Paris, Textes et Documents, 10. Travaux de l'Institut de Papyrologie de Paris, 4. Paris: Presses Universitaires de France, 1966-.

A catalogue of papyri arranged by genre, e.g., literary, documentary. A name/subject index is provided, along with a word index. Plates (29) serve as illustrations.

225 Carrière, V., ed. *L'Introduction aux études d'histoire ecclésiastique locale. I. Les Sources manuscrits.* Paris: Letouzay et Ané, 1934-.

A survey, which includes bilbiography, of ecclesiastical manuscripts by region and collection.

226 Delisle, Léopold. *Le Cabinet des manuscrits de la Bibliothèque Nationale.* 3 vols. and atlas. Paris: Imprimérie Nationale, 1868-81.

Delisle's historical account of the formation of the BN collection of manuscripts and a summary of respective "fonds" such as the Latin, Greek, Oriental, and French. There is a useful list of copies made during the seventeenth and eighteenth centuries.

227 ————. *Instructions pour la rédaction d'un catalogue de manuscrits et pour la rédaction d'un catalogue des incunables conservés dans les bibliothèques publiques de France.* Paris: Champion, 1910.

This serves as a methodological introduction to the preceding item and to later catalogues of both manuscripts and incunabula in French collections.

228 Hauréau, J., ed. *Notices et extraits de quelques manuscrits latins de la Bibliothèque Nationale.* 6 vols. Paris: Klincksieck, 1890-93.

A series of "journals" covering all aspects of the Latin manuscripts in the BN. These include paleographical notes as well as articles on textual criticism. Indexed.

229   Leroquais, Victor. *Les Livres d'heures manuscrits de la Biblio-
       thèque Nationale*. 3 vols. Paris: Prôtat Frères, 1927; *Supplé-
       ment*, 1943.

       A descriptive catalogue which includes a portfolio of plates
       of Books of Hours. See also items 606-8.

230   Morel-Fatio, Alfred. *Catalogues des manuscrits portugais de la
       Bibliothèque Nationale*. Paris: Imprimérie Nationale, 1881.

       A descriptive catalogue of Portuguese manuscripts arranged by
       BN number. Later additions are also listed and an author index
       is provided.

231   Omont, Henri. *Catalogue des manuscrits de la Bibliothèque de
       Sir Thomas Phillipps récemment acquis pour la Bibliothèque
       Nationale*. Paris: Bibliothèque de l'Ecole des Chartes, 1903.

       On the manuscripts of Sir Thomas Phillipps and their dispersal,
       see items 246, 284, 498-500.

232   Rand, E.K. *A Survey of the Manuscripts of Tours*. 2 vols. Boston,
       Mass.: Mediaeval Academy of America, 1929.

       This exemplary piece of scholarship provides a fully descrip-
       tive account of most of the early Latin manuscripts attributed
       to Tours with many bibliographical references. Vol. 1 provides
       extracts, and vol. 2 illustrating facsimiles.

233   Samaran, Charles, and Marichal, Robert, eds. *Catalogue des
       manuscrits en écriture latine pourtant des indications de date,
       de lieu ou de copiste*. I. *Musée Condée et Bibliothèques Parisi-
       enne*, Paris: CNRS, 1959; II. *Bibliothèque Nationale, fonds
       latin (nos. 1-8,000)*, 1962; III. *Bibliothèque Nationale, fonds
       latin (nos. 8,001-18,613)*, 1974; V. *Est de la France*, 1965;
       VI. *Bourgogne, Centre, Sud-Est et Sud-Ouest de la France*,
       1968.

       These represent the volumes for France which have thus far
       appeared in the proposed dated-manuscript series of catalogues.
       For a description of format and content, see item 210.

See also items 643, 962-6, 1079, 1087.

(d) Germany

i. General

233.1 Härtel, Helmar. *Adressbuch der Sammlungen mittelälterlicher
       Handschriften in Niedersachsen*. Wolfenbüttel: Herzog August
       Bibliothek, 1976.

       A brief description of libraries in lower Saxony containing
       medieval manuscripts including the Herzog August Bibliothek in
       Wolfenbüttel. Details include address, number of manuscripts with
       sigla, and printed catalogues.

234   Meyen, Fritz, ed. *Verzeichnis der Spezialbibliotheken im der*
      Bundesrepublik Deutschland einschliesslich West Berlin. 2nd
      ed. Braunschweig: F. Vieweg and Sons, 1970.

      A directory of special libraries, including those in West
      Berlin, arranged by subject. The information gives address,
      director, type of library, and research facilities. Indexes are
      provided for subject, place, and name.

235   Reichert, Franz Rudolf. *Handbuch der kirchlichen katholisch-*
      theologischen Bibliotheken in der Bundesrepublik Deutschland
      und in West-Berlin. Trier: Arbeitsgemeinschaft, 1972.

      An invaluable handbook and guide to the use and contents of
      ecclesiastical libraries in the Federal Republic of West Germany
      and West Berlin. Libraries are described in alphabetical order,
      with address, general nature, and major collections. Concluding
      the handbook is a list of directors and indexes for names, places,
      and subjects.

236   Schmidt, Wieland. "Zur Katalogisierung abenländischen Hand-
      schriften in Deutschland." *Zeitschrift für Bibliotheken- und*
      Bibliographie, 16 (1969), 201-16.

      The author describes the project begun in 1961 and sponsored
      by the Deutsche Forschungsgemeinschaft to compile a catalogue
      of codices, manuscripts, and other unpublished material for all
      of Germany. Participating in this union catalogue of manuscripts
      were 26 individual libraries. For a more recent account of the
      project, see A. Derolez, "Les Nouvelles Instructions pour le
      catalogue des manuscrits en République Fédérale Allemande,"
      Scriptorium, 28 (1974), 299-320. On similar projects for Great
      Britain and North America, see Hepworth, items 978-9.

See also items 189-204, 967, 970, 1086, 1088, and 1095.

ii. Individual Libraries

237   *Die Handschriften der Universitätsbibliothek Würzburg. I. Die*
      Handschriften der zisterzienserabtei Ebrach, ed. Hans Thurn.
      Wiesbaden: Harrassowitz, 1970-.

      This represents the first volume in a proposed series of manu-
      script catalogues for the University of Wurzburg Library and
      smaller institutional libraries of the area which now form part
      of it. Vol. 1 describes the 146 manuscripts from the Cistercian
      Abbey of Ebrach and includes bibliography, indexes for author,
      person, place, subject, scribe, editor, and incipit; the manu-
      scripts are illustrated by 32 facsimile plates.

238   Fischer, Hans. *Die lateinischen Pergamenthandschriften der*
      Universitätsbibliothek Erlangen. 2 vols. Erlangen: Universi-
      tätsbibliothek, 1928.

      A descriptive catalogue with many bibliographical references
      and a person/title/subject index. Since 1928 further catalogues
      for the Erlangen University Library include: III. *Papyrushand-*
      schriften, ed. Wilhelm Schubart (Leipzig: Harrassowitz, 1942);

and VI. *Illuminiertenhandschriften*, ed. Eberhard Lutze (Erlangen:
Universitätsbibliothek, 1936). See also item 791.

239   *Katalog der Handschriften der königlichen Bibliothek zu Bamburg*,
      ed. Friedrich Leitschuh. 1 vol. in 2 pts. Bamburg: Buchner,
      1895; reissued in 4 pts. Wiesbaden: Harrassowitz, 1966.

      The 1966 version of this descriptive catalogue arranges manu-
      scripts according to genre: biblical, liturgical, Classical, and
      historical.

240   *Kataloge der Handschriften der Stadt- und Universitätsbibliothek
      Hamburg*. Hamburg: Ernst Hauswedell, 1967-.

      A series similar to those for Würzburg and Frankfurt which
      also includes the manuscript holdings of regional churches; the
      full descriptions are provided with bibliographies; indexes and
      incipits conclude each volume.

241   *Kataloge der Stadt- und Universitätsbibliothek Frankfurt-am-
      Main*, ed. C. Köttelwesch. Frankfurt-am-Main: Klostermann,
      1968-.

      An excellent series of descriptive catalogues, each devoted to
      one civic or insitutional library; vol. 2, e.g., is Gerhardt
      Powitz's *Die Handschriften des Dominikanerklosters und des
      Leonhardstifts im Frankfurt-am-Main* (1968). The catalogues in-
      clude first-line indexes.

242   *Kataloge der Universitätsbibliothek Freiburg-im-Breisgau*, ed.
      Wolfgang Kehr. I. *Die lateinischen mittelalterlichen Hand-
      schriften der Universitätsbibliothek Freiburg-im-Breisgau*,
      ed. Winfried Hagenmaier. Wiesbaden: Harrassowitz, 1974.

      The first in a series of descriptive catalogues for Freiburg-
      im-Breisgau, similar in scope and format to those for Erlangen.

243   Kraft, Benedikt, with Eduard Gebele. *Die Handschriften der
      Bischöfl. Ordinariatsbibliothek in Augsburg*. Augsburg: Liter-
      arisches Institut von Haas und Grabherr, 1954.

      A descriptive catalogue arranged according to collection, e.g.,
      the Füssener; the separate chapters on scripts provide detailed,
      paleographical analyses. See item 1274.

244   Lehmann, P., and Glauning, O. *Mittelalterliche Handschriften-
      bruckstücke der Universitätsbibliothek und des Gregorianum
      zu München*. Beiheft zum Zentralblatt für Bibliothekswesen,
      78. Leipzig: O. Harrassowitz, 1940.

      A descriptive catalogue of fragments; see Section VIII.

245   Marks, Richard B. *The Medieval Manuscript Library of the Charter-
      house of St. Barbara in Cologne*. Institut für Englischen
      Sprache und Literatur, Salzburg. 2 vols. Salzburg: James Hogg,
      1974.

      A descriptive catalogue of manuscripts in the Carthusian
      Library of St. Barbara. The introduction gives a general history,

and the extensive bibliography, pp. 454-73, serves to relate
the manuscripts to other documents and their historical context.

246   Rose, Valentin. *Verzeichniss der lateinischen Handschriften der
       königlichen Bibliothek zu Berlin.* 73 vols. Berlin: A. Asher,
       1889-1905.

       Although many of these manuscripts have since been destroyed
       or dislocated, this catalogue is worth consulting for its full
       descriptions, which include incipits and explicits of all items,
       and rich bibliography of nineteenth-century German texts and
       studies. The volumes have been published on individual collec-
       tions such as the *Codices Phillippii.*

See also items 658, 663, 667, 670.

(e) Great Britain and Ireland

i. General

247   *ASLIB Directory*, ed. Brian J. Wilson. 2nd ed. 2 vols. London:
       The Library Association, 1968.

       A guide prepared for the Association of Special Libraries and
       Information Bureaux, which gives general and practical informa-
       tion on special collections of manuscripts and publications.

248   Central Council for the Care of Churches. *The Parochial Libraries
       of the Church of England.* London: Faith Press, 1959.

       A descriptive list of parochial libraries in England, arranged
       alphabetically by parish. Some medieval manuscripts are indicated
       and general indexes are provided.

249   Corbett, Edmund V., ed. *The Libraries, Museums, and Art Galleries
       Year Book.* London: J. Clarke and Co., 1968-.

       A guide to the libraries, museums, and art galleries of Great
       Britain and Ireland. The information cites location, summary
       holdings, and special collections; an appendix includes late
       entries.

250   Downs, Robert B. *British Library Resources: A Bibliographical
       Guide.* Chicago, Ill.: University Press, 1973.

       This guide lists over 5,000 catalogues, checklists, union
       lists, calendars, and other published material relevant to
       library holdings in Great Britain. It also provides author and
       subject indexes.

251   Ker, N.R. *Medieval Manuscripts in British Libraries.* Oxford:
       Clarendon Press, 1969-. I. *London*, 1969; II. *Abbotsford-
       Keele*, 1977.

       These two excellent descriptive catalogues provide detailed
       accounts of all pre-1500 manuscripts in British libraries accord-
       ing to geographical location and individual collection. Incipits,

explicits, and indexes are provided, along with bibliographical
references. When complete, this series will be the most comprehensive and accurate catalogue of medieval British manuscripts.

252   Maggs, M. June, ed. *Library Resources in Wales*. London: The
      Library Association, 1977.

      A comprehensive, specialized list of all libraries in Wales,
      arranged alphabetically by location; the information given in-
      cludes address, staff, hours, nature of holdings, classification,
      types of services offered, and whether catalogues are available;
      a subject/name index concludes. This guide represents the first
      in a series: proposed are similar guides for London, York, East
      Midlands, North West, South West, and the West Midlands; see
      also Tait, item 258.

253   Percival, Alicia C. *The English Association Handbook of Societies
      and Collections*. London: The Library Association for the
      English Association, 1977.

      An invaluable, current guide to societies and their publica-
      tions and to special collections in British libraries, e.g.,
      the Warburg Institute, London. Arrangement is alphabetical and
      details are provided on location, hours, catalogues, etc.

254   Pfaff, Richard W. "M.R. James: 'On the Cataloguing of Manuscripts':
      A Draft Essay of 1906." *Scriptorium*, 31 (1977), 103-18.

      Pfaff has edited here the text of James' statements about
      those methods and principles he was to employ in his many cata-
      logues from a draft found in one of his notebooks, Fitzwilliam
      Museum, *James Notebook* 7, vi, pp. 1-81. The text provides a
      detailed and illustrated account of James' methods of classi-
      fication and use of symbols.

255   Philip, A.J. *Index to the Special Collections in Libraries,
      Museums and Art Galleries* ... *in Great Britain and Ireland*.
      London: F.G. Brown, 1949.

      Facile to use in its practical arrangment, this general guide
      is still useful in terms of basic information and historical
      notes. More current information may be found in the *Yearbook*,
      item 249.

256   Read, E. Anne. *A Checklist of Books, Catalogues and Periodical
      Articles Relating to the Cathedral Libraries of England*.
      Oxford Bibliographical Society Occasional Publications, 6.
      Oxford: The Society, 1970.

      This work provides an indispensable starting point for manu-
      script study in English cathedral collections. Arrangement is
      alphabetical by cathedral, with a general description of hold-
      ings and a bibliography of printed catalogues.

257 *Research Libraries and Collections in the United Kingdom. A
    Selective Inventory and Guide*, comp. Stephen Roberts, Alan
    Cooper, and Lesley Gilder. London: Clive Bingley/Hamden,
    Conn.: Linnet, 1978.

The best and most recent source of information on libraries
containing manuscript and archival material in Great Britain.
Libraries are listed alphabetically by location, with address,
brief description of holdings, and printed catalogues.

Royal Commission on Historical Manuscripts. See item 987

258 Tait, James A., and Tait, Heather F.C. *Library Resources in
    Scotland*. Glasgow: Scottish Library Association, 1976.

This comprehensive directory to all Scottish libraries is
arranged in format and scope as Maggs' guide to the Welsh libraries, see item 252.

See also items 971-2, 976-8, 980-3, and 986-7.

ii. *Individual Libraries*

Cambridge

For Cambridge and other specific areas of Great
Britain and Ireland only bibliographies of manuscript
catalogues or individual catalogues of special interest
are cited. Munby, item 259, lists catalogues for the
Cambridge colleges published by M.R. James and others,
while Morgan, item 287, lists those for Oxford. Although
James' many catalogues for Cambridge, Oxford, and other
British libraries do provide valuable summaries of manuscript repositories with descriptions of individual
manuscripts, they are nevertheless known to be often
inaccurate and capable of *lacunae*. They should therefore be used only in conjunction with more recent catalogues when possible, or with caution when no other
catalogue for a particular collection is available.

259 Munby, A.N.L. *Cambridge College Libraries: Aids for Research
    Students*. 2nd ed. Cambridge: W. Heffer, 1962.

A general guide to the 80 institutional libraries in Cambridge,
with a bibliography of their manuscript catalogues.

260 Vaughan, R., and Fines, J. *A Handlist of Manuscripts in the
    Library of Corpus Christi College, Cambridge, Not Described
    by M.R. James*. Cambridge: The Society, 1961. Reprinted from
    Transactions of the Cambridge Bibliographical Society, 3.2
    (1960), 113-23.

A descriptive list, with bibliographical references, of manuscripts not included in James' catalogue, 1912.

261 Wormald, F., and Giles, Phillis M. *A Handlist of the Additional
    Manuscripts in the Fitzwilliam Museum Received Since the
    Publication of the Catalogue by Dr. M.R. James in 1895, Ex-
    cluding the McClean Bequest*. Cambridge: The Society, 1954.
    Reprinted from *Transactions of the Cambridge Bibliographical
    Society*, 1.3 (1951); 1.4 (1952); 1.5 (1953), and 2 (1954).

A descriptive list of additional manuscripts acquired by the Fitzwilliam Museum 1895-1950; some bibliographical references are included.

See also item 1000.

London

262   Bill, E.G.W. *A Catalogue of Manuscripts in Lambeth Public Library*. 2 vols. Oxford: Clarendon Press, 1972-76.

A résumé of previous Lambeth catalogues, including James' of 1932, but with corrections and the addition of later items from the sixteenth to the twentieth centuries. A person/place index is provided. Bill describes the library generally in *The Library*, 5th ser., 21 (1966), 192-206.

263   British Library. *The British Library: Guide to the Catalogues and Indexes of the Department of Manuscripts*, comp. M.A.E. Nickson. London: Trustees of the British Library, 1978.

The most complete and up-to-date guide to the British Library, formerly the British Museum, and its manuscript collections. For an earlier guide, see item 266.

264   ———. *Catalogue of Additions to the Manuscripts in the British Museum in the Years 1783-1935*. 20 vols. London: Trustees of the British Library, 1850-.

A series of descriptive catalogues of manuscripts added to the British Library Department of Manuscripts from 1783. It comments on collections and individual manuscripts, with summary descriptions of contents. There are name indexes for each volume and cumulative indexes 1880/1968; 1970.

265   ———. *Catalogue of the Literary Papyri in the British Museum*, ed. H.J.M. Milne. London: Trustees of the British Library, 1927/Milan: Cisalpino-Goliardica, 1977.

A detailed catalogue of papyri from Egypt in the Department of Manuscripts and other Departments of the British Library. Arrangement is by genre according to the major divisions: poetry, prose, Christian literature, and devotional and liturgical. Inventory and Catalogue numbers are given, with an index and accompanying plates.

266   ———. *Catalogues of the Manuscript Collection*, rev. ed. Theodore C. Skeat. London: Trustees of the British Library, 1962.

A descriptive list of the pre-1960 catalogues for such collections as the Egerton, Stowe, Harleian, Arundel, Cottonian, Royal, and others. A simpler but for that reason less useful guide was published by J.P. Gilson, *A Student's Guide to the Manuscripts in the British Museum* (1920).

267   ———. *Catalogue of Romances in the Department of Manuscripts*, ed. H.L.D. Ward, continued (vol. 3) by J.A. Herbert. 3 vols. London: Trustees of the British Library, 1883-1910/1961-63.

This is a fully descriptive catalogue of manuscripts containing romances; listed are contents, incipits, and bibliography.
Arrangement is by types of romance, e.g., Classical or British
and English.

268 ————. *Greek Papyri in the British Museum: Catalogue with
Texts*, ed. F.G. Kenyon, *et al*. 5 vols. London: Trustees of
the British Library, 1893-1917/Milan: Cisalpino-Goliardica,
1973.

A descriptive catalogue with bibliography and edited texts.

Gilson, J.P. See item 266.

Herbert, J.A. See item 267.

269 Irwin, Raymond, and Staveley, Ronald. *The Libraries of London*.
London: The Library Association, 1961.

Chapters 1 and 2 of this guide describe the holdings of the
British Library; chapter 3 describes the science libraries
throughout the city. See also items 270, 272.

Kenyon, F.G. See item 268.

270 Library Resources Coordinating Committee. *Guide to Admission to
Libraries of London*. London: The Committee, 1976.

This guide contains detailed and practical information about
the use of all London libraries--their hours, requirements for
admission, general holdings, and location.

271 Moorat, S.A.J. *Wellcome Historical Medical Library Catalogue
of Western Manuscripts on Medicine and Science. I. Manuscripts
Written before 1650*. London: University of London, Athlone
Press, 1962.

A descriptive catalogue of mainly late medieval medical and
scientific manuscripts, with bibliographical references (often
to early printed editions); indexed.

Nickson, M.A.E. See item 263.

272 Rye, Reginald Arthur. *The Student's Guide to the Libraries of
London: with an Account of the Most Important Archives and
Other Aids to Study*. 3rd ed. (from 1908). London: University
of London, 1927.

Although this practical guide has been superseded by item
269, its historical notes are still of interest in their account
of the development and scope of certain collections.

Ward, H.L.D. See item 267.

273 Watson, Rowan. *A Descriptive List of Fragments of Medieval
Manuscripts in the University of London Library*. London:
University of London, Typescript, 1976.

A brief list (xvii, 40pp.) of 56 fragments, grouped by subject; it includes books in London libraries which contain fragments of medieval manuscripts in their bindings.

274   Wright, C.E. *Fontes Harleiani*. London: Trustees of the British Library, 1972.

An alphabetical dictionary of former owners of the Harleian manuscripts, both individuals and institutions; given are details of ownership, dates, lists of other manuscripts at one time in their possession. A concluding table of manuscripts refers to key words in the dictionary.

See also items 967-8, 1001.

Oxford

275   Black, W.H. *A Descriptive, Analytical, and Critical Catalogue of the Manuscripts Bequeathed unto the University of Oxford by Elias Ashmole, Esq*. Oxford: University Press, 1845.

A descriptive "quarto" catalogue, arranged by collection number; manuscript contents are usually summarized, but incipits and other details are often lacking. W.D. Macray provided a subject/name index, 1866.

276   Coxe, Henry O. *Catalogi Codicum Manuscriptorum Bibliothecae Bodleianae*. Oxford: University Press, 1853-60. I. *Graeca*, 1853/1969; III. *Canonici*, 1854; IV. *Tanner*, 1860/1966.

A descriptive catalogue of Bodleian Library manuscripts, issued by collection.

277   ————. *Catalogi Codicum Manuscriptorum qui in Collegiis Aulisque Oxoniensibus Hodie ad Servantur*. 2 vols. Oxford: University Press, 1852/1972.

A descriptive catalogue of manuscripts found in Oxford College libraries; for St. John's College, see the *Supplement*, comp. M. Colvin, Oxford: Bodleian Library, Typescript, 1956. See also item 287.

278   ————. *Catalogue of the Printed Books and Manuscripts Bequeathed by Francis Douce, Esq., to the Bodleian Library*. Oxford: University Press, 1840.

This catalogue contains more descriptive information than the two preceding items, and is illustrated with many plates.

279   ————. *Laudian Manuscripts*. Oxford: University Press, 1858-85; rev. ed. by R.W. Hunt, 1973.

A descriptive "quarto" catalogue of the Laud manuscripts, similar in format and scope to items 275, 286, 288.

280   Craster, Sir Edmund. *History of the Bodleian Library, 1845-1945*. Oxford: Clarendon Press, 1952.

An account of later manuscript and other collections with descriptions of their contents and organization.

281 ────. *The Western Manuscripts of the Bodleian Library.* Helps
for Students of History, 43. London: Society for Promoting
Christian Knowledge, 1921.

A general, essay-type introduction to the history and collections of the library and their bibliography.

282 de la Mare, Albinia, comp. *Catalogue of the Collection of Medieval Manuscripts Bequeathed to the Bodleian Library, Oxford,
by James P.R. Lyell.* Oxford: Clarendon Press, 1971.

An excellent, fully descriptive catalogue with 96 illustrations and a general index.

283 Dyk, S.J.P. van. *Handlist of the Latin Liturgical Manuscripts
in the Bodleian Library.* 6 vols. Oxford: Bodleian Library,
Typescript, 1960.

A descriptive list, arranged by collection.

284 Hunt, R.W. "A List of Phillipps Manuscripts in the Bodleian
Library." *Bodleian Library Record*, 6 (1957), 348-69.

On the composition and dispersal of the Phillipps collection,
see items 231, 246, 498-500.

285 ────. "The Manuscript Collections of University College,
Oxford: Origins and Growth." *Bodleian Library Record*, 3
(1950), 13-34.

A history and descriptive survey of the manuscript collection.

286 Macray, W.D. *Catalogi Codicum Manuscriptorum Bibliothecae
Bodleianae, Partes Quintae.* Oxford: University Press, 1862-
83.

A descriptive "quarto" catalogue of the Rawlinson and Digby
manuscripts with indexes.

287 Morgan, Paul. *Oxford Libraries Outside the Bodleian: A Guide.*
Oxford: Clarendon Press, 1972/1974.

A descriptive guide to all college and hall library collections, and one which also includes various faculty, departmental,
institutional, and other libraries; Appendix 1 lists additional
manuscript collections, and Appendix 2 offers a select index
of manuscript collections in Oxford college and other libraries
not described by Coxe, item 277.

288 Mortava, Alessandro, comp. *Catalogo dei manoscritti ... codici
canoniciani Italici.* Oxford: Clarendon Press, 1864.

A descriptive "quarto" catalogue.

289 Mynors, R.A.B. *Catalogue of the Manuscripts of Balliol College
Oxford.* Oxford: Clarendon Press, 1963.

A model manuscript catalogue in scope, accuracy, and bibliographical detail; each manuscript is carefully presented and
related, whenever possible, to other manuscripts outside the
college collection; indexed.

290   Parkes, M.B. *The Medieval Manuscripts of Keble College, Oxford:*
      A Descriptive Catalogue, with Summary Descriptions of the
      Greek and Oriental Manuscripts. London: Oxford University
      Press, 1978.

      This excellent catalogue describes the 71 Western manuscripts
      fully, the Greek and Oriental collection less so. Included are
      several ninth-century and later fragments. Parkes' is a signifi-
      cant catalogue insofar as it offers the first full account of
      Keble manuscripts and is also invaluable for its accurate de-
      tail and bibliographical references. Many facsimiles are in-
      cluded.

291   *Summary Catalogue of Western Manuscripts in the Bodleian*
      Library, A, ed. Falconer Madan, H.E. Craster, Noel Denholm-
      Young, *et al.* 7 vols. Oxford: Clarendon Press, 1953.

      Vol. 1 of this important catalogue contains an historical
      introduction and list of shelf-marks, ed. R.W. Hunt; vol. 7
      includes the *Index* by P.D. Record; the volumes between list
      manuscripts according to series number in collection and *S.C.*
      number. Often there is little or no description, although the
      Bodleian Library copy contains many hand-written additions and
      corrections. Later *Accessions 1916-23* are available in the
      Library in three typescript volumes.

See also items 421, 493, 539, 546, 998-9, 1002, 1078, 1092.

      Other Areas

292   Brighton Public Libraries. *A Catalogue of Manuscripts and*
      Printed Books before 1500. Brighton: The Libraries, 1962.

      A descriptive catalogue of this small, varied collection.

293   Charles, B.G., and Emanuel, H.D. "Notes on Old Libraries and
      Books." *National Library of Wales Journal,* 6 (1950), 353-7.

      Annotations on manuscripts and early books in Hereford
      Cathedral Library. See also item 256.

294   Eward, S.M., comp. *A Catalogue of Gloucester Cathedral Library.*
      Gloucester: Dean and Chapter of Gloucester Cathedral, 1972.

      A comprehensive, descriptive catalogue. It also contains a
      section by N.R. Ker on "Medieval Literary Manuscripts," pp. 1-6.

295   Fawtier, Robert. "Handlist of Additions to the Collection of
      Latin Manuscripts in the John Rylands Library, 1908-1920."
      Bulletin of the John Rylands Library, 6 (1921), 120-56.

      A handlist with critical annotation and some bibliographical
      references, including several to earlier notices of Latin
      manuscripts in this collection. See also next item, 298, and
      308.1.

296   Kraft, Robert A., and Tripolitis, A. "Some Uncatalogued Papyri
      of Theological and Other Interest in the John Rylands Library."
      Bulletin of the John Rylands Library, 51 (1968-69), 137-63.

A full description of three theological pieces and five miscellaneous, non-literary samples, from the third to the seventh
centuries. Of some interest to paleographers is item 8, a double
alphabet from the seventh century, with examples of Byzantine
cursive and Coptic uncial letters; see pp. 162-3.

297   Liverpool University Library. *A Guide to the Manuscript Collec-
       tions in the Liverpool University Library*. Library Publica-
       tions, 1. Liverpool: University Press, 1962.

       A brief but well-organized guide to the arrangement and con-
       tents of the manuscript collections. References include printed
       catalogues.

298   Manchester, John Rylands Library. *Catalogue of Greek and Latin
       Papyri in the John Rylands Library, Manchester*, ed. A.S. Hunt,
       C.H. Roberts, E.G. Turner, *et al.* 4 vols. Manchester: Uni-
       versity Press, 1911-52.

       A descriptive catalogue of the collection of literary, the-
       ological, and documentary papyri of Ptolemaic, Roman, and
       Byzantine origin. See also items 295-6, 302.

299   Mathews, N. *Early Printed Books and Manuscripts in the City
       Reference Library, Bristol*. Bristol: City Library, 1879.

       A descriptive catalogue, with entries for early manuscripts
       annotated and corrected by N.R. Ker in the City Library copy,
       June 25, 1946. See also item 251.

300   Mynors, R.A.B. *Durham Cathedral Manuscripts to the End of the
       Twelfth Century*. Oxford: Clarendon Press, 1939.

       This excellent catalogue is fully descriptive, with good
       bibliographical references. It is limited, however, to only
       the earliest manuscripts; for later manuscripts in this collec-
       tion, see items 251 and 256.

301   Nottingham University. *The Library*. Nottingham: University Press,
       1950.

       A brief (21pp.) guide to the manuscript holdings and special
       collections of this library, with bibliographical references
       to catalogue material.

302   Roberts, Colin H. "The Rylands Collection of Greek and Latin
       Papyri." *Bulletin of the John Rylands Library*, 36 (1953-54),
       97-110.

       See also items 296 and 298.

303   Roscoe, W.; Madan, F.; and Ricci, S. de. *A Handlist of Manu-
       scripts in the Library of the Earl of Leicester at Holkham
       Hall*. Supplement to the Bibliographical Society Transactions,
       7. Oxford: The Society, 1932.

       A descriptive handlist to this collection, which includes some
       medieval manuscripts. Included are bibliographical references
       to editions and other catalogues.

304   Symington, J.A. *The Brotherton Library. A Catalogue of Ancient
       Manuscripts and Early Printed Books Collected by Edward Allen,
       Baron Brotherton of Wakefield*. Leeds: Printed for Private
       Circulation, 1931.

       A descriptive catalogue, with 186 illustrations from the
       library's manuscript and early printed book collection.

305   Taylor, Frank. "A Hand-List of the Additions to the Collection
       of English Manuscripts in the John Rylands Library, 1937-51."
       Bulletin of the John Rylands Library, 34 (1951-52), 191-240.

       This article provides a list of local documents, mainly post-
       sixteenth century and relating to Cheshire and Lancashire. Items
       951-6 are medieval and include the *Siege of Jerusalem*, *Life of
       St. Christopher*, *Marvels of the East*, and Laʒamon's *Brut*. See
       next three items.

306   ———. *A Supplementary Hand-list of Western Manuscripts in
       the John Rylands Library, 1937*. Manchester: University Press,
       1937.

       A descriptive handlist; see also items 295-6, 298, 302, 305,
       and 307-308.1.

307   ———, and Matheson, Glenice A. *A Handlist of Additions to the
       Collections of English Manuscripts in the John Rylands Uni-
       versity Library of Manchester, 1952-70*. Manchester: John
       Rylands Library, 1977.

       A descriptive handlist of additions to the list provided in
       item 305. Reprinted from *Bulletin of the John Rylands Library*,
       60 (1977), 213-67. While no medieval manuscripts are listed,
       the bibliographical references to earlier handlists are useful.

308   Tyson, M. "Hand-List of the Collection of English Manuscripts
       in the John Rylands Library." *Bulletin of the John Rylands
       Library*, 13 (1929), 152-212.

       While most of the manuscripts listed are post-sixteenth
       century, the medieval English manuscripts include works by
       Lydgate, Wyclif, Richard Rolle, and Chaucer. Many are from the
       Phillipps and Ashburnham collections. For later additions, see
       two preceding items.

308.1 ———. *A Handlist of Additions to the Collection of Latin
       Manuscripts in the John Rylands Library, 1908-28*. Manchester:
       The Library, 1928.

       A descriptive handlist of additions to the list provided in
       item 295. Reprinted from the *Bulletin of the John Rylands Li-
       brary*, 12 (1928), 581-609.

See items 977-8, 980-7, and 1077.

Ireland and Northern Ireland

309   Abbot, T.K. *Catalogue of Irish Manuscripts in the Library of Trinity College Dublin.* Dublin: Hodges and Figgis/London: Longman, Green, 1900; continued by E.J. Gwynn. Dublin: Hodges and Figgis, 1921.

      A summary catalogue, based partly on E. Bernard's *Catalogi Librorum Manuscriptorum Angliae et Hiberniae* (Oxford: 1697).

310   Hayes, R.J., ed. *The Manuscript Sources for the History of Irish Civilization.* 11 vols. Boston, Mass.: G.K. Hall, 1965.

      This comprehensive and impressive work provides a descriptive catalogue of manuscripts arranged by topic, e.g., persons, subjects, and places. Section xi lists manuscript catalogues for all public and private collections and concludes with a descriptive index of manuscripts in 678 libraries, 1,278 collections, and 30 countries in Latin, English, Irish, and other languages. For those manuscripts omitted from the Trinity College Library, see item 309.

311   Hogan, James. *The Irish Manuscripts Commission: Work in Progress.* Cork: University Press, 1954.

      An account of research and cataloguing, with bibliography. Updated to 1966 by next item.

312   Irish Manuscripts Commission. *Catalogue of Publications Issued and in Preparation, 1928-66.* Dublin: Stationery Office, 1966.

      A descriptive list, which provides full accounts of the contents of the periodical *Analecta Hibernica*, a journal publishing and reporting on work in Irish manuscript and other studies.

313   Murray, Robert Henry. *A Short Guide to Some Manuscripts in the Library of Trinity College Dublin.* Society for the Promotion of Christian Knowledge: Helps for the Student of History, 32. New York, N.Y.: Macmillan, 1920.

      An introductory guide, similar in scope and format to item 281. It describes the nature of individual collections and gives a select bibliography of catalogues and other reference works.

314   O'Rahilly, T.F.; Mulchrone, K.; Byrne, M.E.; Murphy, Gerald, *et al. Catalogue of Irish Manuscripts in the Royal Irish Academy.* Dublin: The Academy, 1926-58.

      A descriptive catalogue of the Academy collection of manuscripts, in 30 fascicles, with an additional fascicle by Tómas Uconcheanainn, 1971. A first-line and general index are included.

315   Shéaghdha, Nessa Ní. *Catalogue of Irish Manuscripts in the National Library of Ireland.* Dublin Institute for Advanced Studies. Dublin: The Institute, 1961-67.

      This work offers a descriptive catalogue in two fascicles. A comprehensive bibliography and an index are provided.

See also items 70-2, 79-83, and 104-5.

Scotland

316   Borland, C.R. *A Descriptive Catalogue of the Western Mediaeval
      Manuscripts in the Edinburgh University Library*. Edinburgh:
      T. and A. Constable at the University Press, 1916.

      A descriptive catalogue arranged by library number, with a
      name/place/subject index. This work should not be used without
      first consulting C.P. Finlayson's "Notes on C.R. Borland's 'A
      Descriptive Catalogue in the Edinburgh University Library',"
      The Bibliothek, 32 (1960), 44–52.

317   Edinburgh, University Library. *Index to Manuscripts*. 2 vols.
      Boston, Mass.: Harvard University Press, 1964.

      This index to the manuscript collections is arranged by series
      and genre, with many cross-references.

318   James, M.R. *A Catalogue of Medieval Manuscripts in the University
      Library, Aberdeen*. Cambridge: University Press, 1932.

      A descriptive catalogue which provides some bibliographical
      references.

319   Young, J., and Aitken, P.H. *A Catalogue of the Manuscripts in
      the Library of the Hunterian Museum in the University of
      Glasgow*. Glasgow: University Press, 1908.

      This descriptive catalogue serves as a useful starting point
      for research on the Hunterian manuscripts, but its bibliographical
      matter is now largely out of date.

See also items 80, 83, 665, and 1009–13.

Wales

320   Davies, J.H. *Catalogue of Additional Manuscripts in the National
      Library of Wales*. Aberystwyth: National Library, 1921.

      A descriptive catalogue of manuscripts in the collection of
      Sir John Williams, Bart. It should be used in conjunction with
      item 323.

321   Gwynne Jones, E., and Johnston, J.R., comp. *Catalogue of the
      Bangor Cathedral Library*. Bangor: University College of North
      Wales, 1961.

      A descriptive catalogue of the Cathedral manuscripts, with
      bibliographical references and an index.

322   Jack, R. Ian. *Medieval Wales. The Sources of History: Studies
      in the Uses of Historical Evidence*. Ithaca, N.Y.: Cornell
      University Press, 1972.

      Although primarily on the uses of historical evidence, this
      useful work provides a general guide to the libraries of Wales
      and their manuscript collections. See especially chapters 2–6.

323   National Library of Wales. *Handlist of Manuscripts in the
      National Library of Wales*. 3 vols. Aberystwyth: National Library
      of Wales, 1950; *Supplements*, 1950–.

A descriptive list, with index. Parts 1-3 were reissued in one vol., 1959. See also item 320.

See also items 80, 83, and 662.

(f) Hispanic Countries

i. General

324 Grubbs, H.A. *The Manuscript Book Collections of Spain and Portugal: Supplement*. New York, N.Y.: H.W. Wilson, 1933-35.

This general inventory forms part of the *Union World Catalog of Manuscript Books*, item 201.

325 Rodriquez Marin, F. *Guía historica e descriptiva de las archivos, bibliotecas y museos arquelógicos de España*. Madrid: Dirección General, 1916-25.

A general survey of archives, libraries, and museums, with an account of their location, manuscript collections, and research facilities. Some bibliographical references are included.

326 Valentinelli, G. *Delle biblioteche della Spagna*. Sitzungsberichte der Phil.-histor. Klasse der kaiserliche Akademie der Wissenschaften, 33. Vienna: The Academy, 1860.

A descriptive survey of Spanish libraries and their manuscript collections. Although this work is now largely superseded by item 324 and the international directories cited in section VII.A.1 of this *Handbook*, it contains some useful bibliographical references to earlier catalogues.

See also items 587, 639, and 1014-21.

ii. Individual Libraries

327 Anselmo, Antonio. *Los codices alcobacenses da Biblioteca Nacional*. Lisbon: Biblioteca Nacional, 1926.

This is an excellent, descriptive catalogue of the manuscripts from the Cistercian abbey of Alcobaca, which are now included in the Biblioteca Nacional collection. See also item 329.

328 Antolin, G. *Catálogo de los codices latinos de la Real Biblioteca del Escorial*. 5 vols. Madrid: Helénica, 1910-23.

Describes Latin manuscripts by collection order. Extensive indexes provide reference to authors, copyists, possessors, miniatures, arms, and other topics.

329 Ataide e Melo, A.F. de. *Inventario dos codices alcobacenses*. Lisbon: Biblioteca Nacional, 1962.

More complete than item 327. A bibliography is included.

330   Beaujouan, Guy. *Manuscrits scientifiques médiévaux de l'univer-*
       sité de Salamanique et de ses 'colegios mayores.' Bibliothèque
       de l'Ecole des Hautes Etudes Hispaniques, 32. Bordeaux: Feret,
       1962.

       An account of the history of the library with lists of present
       holdings. It contains some incipits not in Thorndike and Kibre.

331   Beer, Rudolf. *Handschriftenschätze Spaniens*. Vienna: Akademie
       der Wissenschaften/Amsterdam: Gerard Th. van Heusden, 1970.

       From 616 libraries and archival collections, the author lists
       medieval "*biblioteca*" and "*archivo*" entries, with critical notes.
       Arranged by city; author/library index.

332   Dirección General de Archivos y Bibliotecas. *Instrucciones para*
       la catalogación de manuscritos. Madrid: Dirección General,
       1969.

       On the methodology of cataloguing manuscripts. A reference
       guide to and bibliography of the major catalogues for Spanish
       libraries.

333   Freyre, E. Ponce de Leon. *Guía del lector en la Biblioteca Nacional*.
       Madrid: Biblioteca Nacional, 1942.

       A brief guide to the use and holdings of the National Library;
       bibliography of catalogues.

334   Garcia y Garcia, Antonio. *Catálogo de los manuscritos jurídicos*
       medievales de la catedral de Toledo. Madrid: Instituto Jurídico
       Español, 1970.

       A descriptive catalogue of legal manuscripts, most of them
       post-thirteenth century, in the Toledo Cathedral Library.

335   Miller, E. *Catalogue des manuscrits grecs de la Bibliothèque de*
       l'Escurial. Amsterdam: Hakkert, 1966.

       This work describes the Greek manuscripts of the library, but
       with a minumum of bibliographical annotation. An author/subject
       index is provided.

336   Olivar, Alexandre. *Els manuscrits liturgics de la Biblioteca de*
       Montserrat. Scripta et Documenta, 18. Montserrat: The Abbey,
       1969.

       An excellent, descriptive catalogue, which also includes an
       appendix of edited extracts. The bibliography is valuable for the
       study of Spanish liturgical manuscripts in general.

337   Paz Remola, Ramon, and Toro, José Lopez de. *Inventorio general*
       de manuscritos de la Biblioteca National, 1101-1598. 7 vols.
       Madrid: Ministerio de Educación Nacional, 1953-63.

       An important catalogue, representing the only complete descrip-
       tion of this collection. Arrangement is by numbered entries.
       Bibliographical references, and a name/subject index are provided,
       the latter in vol. 7.

338   Rosell, Francisco Miguel. *Inventario general de manuscritos de
       la Biblioteca Universitaria de Barcelona.* 3 vols. Madrid:
       The University, 1958.

       A descriptive catalogue, arranged by library numbers; it in-
       cludes a bibliography and index.

339   Zarco Chevas, Eusebio Julian. *Catálogo de los manuscritos
       castellanos de la Real Biblioteca de El Escorial.* 2 vols.
       Madrid: Dirección General, 1921-26.

       The general introduction of this descriptive catalogue of
       Catalonian manuscripts in the Escorial also provides useful
       information on their nature, provenance, and bibliography.

For microfilm resources, see item 519.
See also items 144, 146-7, 483, 660, 666, 669.

(g) Italy

i. General

340   *Annuario delle biblioteche italiane.* Rev. ed. 4 vols. Rome:
       Fratelli Palombi Editori, 1969-76.

       This work serves as a general guide to Italian libraries and
       gives information on location, collections, research facilities,
       and catalogues. Arrangement is alphabetical by location of
       library. A fifth volume is expected to appear 1979-80.

341   Ministero della Pubblica Instruzione. *Indicie e cataloghi.*
       11 vols. Rome: Presso i Principali Librai, 1884-1950.

       A descriptive bibliography of catalogues of manuscripts and
       archives in Italian libraries, with lists of Italian manuscripts
       found in other libraries. Arrangement is by the geographical
       location of the library, e.g., the Bibliotheca Medicea Laurenti-
       ana of Florence.

ii. Individual Libraries

342   Abate, Giuseppe, and Luisetto, Giovanni. *Codici e manoscritti
       della Biblioteca Antoniana col catalogo delle miniature a cura
       di Francois Avril, Francesco d'Arcais et Guidana Mariani Canova.*
       2 vols. Venice: Neri Pozza Editore, 1975.

       This work provides a good paleographical description of the
       manuscripts in the Biblioteca Antoniana of Padua, with facsimile
       illustrations for the miniatures.

343   Fare, Paolo A., ed. *I manoscritti T. inf. della Biblioteca
       Ambrosiana di Milano.* Milan: Societa Editrica Vita e Pensiero,
       1968.

       A descriptive catalogue of the Biblioteca Ambrosiana. For an
       account of the scope of this library and its microfilm collection,
       see item 527.

344   Gregoire, Reginald. "Repertorium liturgicum italicum." *Studi medievali*, 3rd ser., 9 (1968), 510-14; "Addenda, I," 11 (1970), 537-56.

      A descriptive list of liturgical manuscripts in the Chapter Library of Ivrea. Information includes collection number, date, provenance, nature of the liturgical work, and select bibliography. See also item 349.

345   *Inventario dei codici superstiti greci et latini antichi della Biblioteca Nazionale di Torino*. Estratto dalla Rivista di Filologia Edistruzione Classica Diretta da Ettore Stampini, 32. Turin: E. Loescher, 1904.

      A summary catalogue of early Latin and Greek manuscripts contained in the manuscript collections.

346   Jemolo, Viviana, gen. ed. *Catalogo dei manoscritti in scrittura datati o databili per indicazione di anno, di luogo o di copista. I. Biblioteca Nationale Centrale di Roma*. Turin: Bottega d'Erasmo, 1971.

      This work is of special importance as the first Italian volume in the dated-manuscript project; see item 210. The scope and format are similar to the other international catalogues.

347   Mazzatinti, G., and Sorbelli, A. *Inventari dei manoscritti delle biblioteche d'Italia*. 76 vols. Forli: Bordandini, 1891-1948; Florence: Leo S. Olschki, 1969-.

      A continuing inventory of individual Italian manuscript and archival collections, issued by library or by several libraries arranged alphabetically within one volume. Each volume is indexed.

348   Pellégrin, Elisabeth, *et al. Les manuscrits classiques latins de la Bibliothèque Vaticane*. 2 vols. Paris: CNRS, 1975-78.

      An excellent, descriptive catalogue of Latin manuscripts in the Vatican Library containing whole or fragmentary Classical texts. It includes bibliographical references and indexes. See also the *Index des auteurs et textes classiques des manuscrits classiques latins de la Bibliothèque Vaticane*, n.p.: n.d., which lists authors and their works with reference to Vatican manuscripts.

349   Professione, Alfonso. *Inventario dei manoscritti della Biblioteca Capitolare di Ivrea*. Ivrea: Domenicaine-Alpa, 1967.

      A fully descriptive catalogue of the library, with editions and bibliographical references. Arranged by catalogue number. Tables collate manuscript numbers with other references. See also item 344.

350   Salmon, P. *Les Manuscrits liturgiques latins de la Bibliothèque Vaticane*. 3 vols. Studi e Testi, 251, 253, 260. Rome: Vatican, 1968-70.

      This is a descriptive catalogue as well as a general study of liturgical manuscripts in the Vatican collection. Arrangement is by genre and collection, with bibliographical references in each volume to other liturgical catalogues and related matter.

351   Silverstein, Theodore. *Medieval Latin Scientific Writings in the
      Barberini Collection. A Provisional Catalogue.* Chicago, Ill.:
      University of Chicago Press, 1957.

      A descriptive list of all medieval Latin writings on the
      natural sciences in this collection. It provides incipits, in-
      dexes, and a useful bibliography.

352   Turrini, Giuseppe. *Index Alphabeticum Bibliothecae Capitularis
      Veronensis A.D. 1940 Exaratus.* Verona: Typescript, n.d.

      An unpublished catalogue of manuscripts listed alphabetically
      in the Biblioteca Capitolare, Verona. Available on microfilm
      in some libraries, e.g., the Pontifical Institute of Mediaeval
      Studies, Toronto, Canada.

353   Turyn, Alexander, ed. *Codices Graeci Vaticani Saeculis XIII et
      XIV Scripti Annorum Notis Instructi.* Codices e Vaticanis
      Selecti, 28. Rome: Vatican, 1964.

      Not so much a catalogue as a collection of facsimiles of Greek
      manuscripts which can be dated, from the Vatican collection of
      thirteenth- and fourteenth-century manuscripts. Each is given a
      paleographical description and some bibliographical references.
      See also Turyn, item 590.

354   Vatasso, M., and Cavalieri, P.F. *Codices Vaticani Latini.* I.
      Codices 1-678; II. *Codices 501-1000*; III. *Codices 1001-1779.*
      Rome/Vatican: Vatican Polyglot Press, 1902-21.

      A summary catalogue of Vatican Latin manuscripts, issued by
      series number. An appendix was added in 1931 to serve as a name
      index. See also Boyle, item 1022, and items 1026, 1029.

See also items 390, 538, 547-8, 590, 600, 949-52, 1023, 1027-8, 1032-3,
1083-4, 1103.

(h) Netherlands

i. General

355   *Catalogus der Bibliotheek.* 7 vols. The Hague: M. Nijhoff, 1920-
      65.

      While this is a catalogue of printed books in The Hague Library,
      it also serves as a source of information for manuscript cata-
      logue bibliography for this and other libraries throughout the
      Netherlands. Each volume is similarly arranged by topic, e.g.,
      libraries or codicology, with accessions added in each successive
      volume.

ii. Individual Libraries

356   *Catalogus Compendiarius Continens Codices Omnes Manuscriptos qui
      in Bibliotheca Academiae Lugduno-Batavae Asservantur.* Leiden:
      E.J. Brill, 1932-.

This series of catalogues lists but does not describe manuscript collections in the Leiden University library. There is a bibliography of manuscript catalogues for the Netherlands, vol. 1, pp. vii-viii.

357   Lieftinck, G.I., ed. *Manuscrits dates conservés dans les Pays-Bas: Catalogue paléographique des manuscrits en écriture latine pourtant des indications de date. I. Les Manuscrits d'origine étrangère (816-ca. 1550).* 2 vols. Amsterdam: North Holland Publishing Co., 1964.

       Issued as the first in the dated-manuscript series, this volume contains a general introduction on the criteria of dating evidence and a catalogue of nearly 300 manuscripts, mainly in Latin, but also in Dutch, Low German, French, and other languages, contained in public and private collections. Arrangement is alphabetical by city and library. See also item 210.

358   Meyier, K.A. de, *et al.*, eds. *Bibliotheca Universitatis Leidensis, Codices Manuscripti.* Leiden: Universitatsbibliotheek, 1912-, 1973-.

       These descriptive catalgues are issued in series for individual collections in the University Library, e.g., *Vossiani Graeci*, 1955, and *Vossiani Latini*, 1973.

See also items 192, 196, 204, 659, 661, 671, 1034-5, 1093.

(i) Scandinavia

i. General

359   Harrison, Kenneth Cecil. *Libraries in Scandinavia.* London: A. Deutsch, 1961.

       An introductory guide to Scandinavian libraries and their resources. It offers a bibliography of library catalogues and provides details of various collections.

ii. Individual Libraries

360   Gödel, Vilhelm. *Katalog öfver Kongelige Bibliotekets fornisländska och fornorska handskrifter.* Stockholm: P.A. Norstedt and Söner, 1897-1900.

       A classified, descriptive catalogue of early Norse and Icelandic manuscripts in the Royal Library, Stockholm. It includes registers of persons, manuscripts, and subjects.

361   ———. *Katalog öfver Upsala Universites Bibliotheks fornisländska och fornorska handscrifter.* Skrifter utgifna af Humanistika Vetenskapssamfundet, 11.1. Uppsala: Almqvist and Wiksell, 1892.

       This a descriptive list of early Icelandic and Norwegian manuscripts in the University Library. It includes name and subject indexes.

362 Hermannsson, Halldór. *Icelandic Manuscripts*. Ithaca, N.Y.:
    Cornell University Press, 1929/Kraus, 1966.

    Hermannsson provides an account and descriptive catalogue of
    the Icelandic manuscripts at Cornell which form the Fiske Collec-
    tion. A bibliography includes further manuscript catalogues for
    Scandinavia.

363 Hornwall, Gert, and Tjäder, Jan-Olof, gen. eds. *Katalog der
    Datierten Handschriften in Lateinischen Schrift vor 1600 in
    Schweden*. Publications in the International Committee on
    Paleography Series for Sweden. I. *Uppsala*, ed. Monica Hedlund.
    2 vols. Stockholm: Almqvist and Wiksell, 1977.

    This represents the first volume to appear in the dated-manu-
    script series for Sweden. It has been issued in two parts, with
    vol. 1 providing a general introduction and descriptive catalogue
    of dated Latin manuscripts in Uppsala, and vol. 2 the illustrat-
    ing facsimiles.

364 Jørgensen, E. *Catalogus Codicum Latinorum Medii Aevi Bibliothecae
    Regiae Hafniensis*. Copenhagen: Gyldendal, 1926.

    A descriptive catalogue which is arranged by genre, e.g.,
    codices theologici, astronomici medici, etc. It includes indexes.

365 Kålund, Kristian. *Katalog over de oldnorsk-islandke handskriften
    i det store kongelige bibliotek og i universitetsbiblioteket*.
    Copenhagen: Gyldendal, 1900.

    A descriptive catalogue of manuscripts in the Royal Library.
    Arrangement is by manuscript number with incipits included. In-
    dexes are provided for name and subject.

366 Kleberg, Tönnes. *Catalogus Graecorum et Latinorum Bibliothecae
    Universitatis Gothoburgensis*. 2nd rev. ed. Göteborg: University
    Press, 1974.

    A good, fully descriptive catalogue with bibliographical refer-
    ences and indexes.

367 Ólason, Páll Eggert. *Skrá um handritasöfn Landsbokasafnsins*.
    Reykjavik: Prentsmið jan Gutenberg, 1918-.

    A series of descriptive catalogues for Icelandic manuscripts,
    with bibliographical references and indexes.

See also items 152-3, 668, 1036-8.

(j) Switzerland

368 Bibliothèque Cantonale et Universitaire. *Das Scriptorium von
    Hauterive: Handschriften des XII, bis XV. Jahrhunderts aus
    Kantons- und Universitätsbibliothek Freiburg*. Fribourg:
    Bibliothèque Cantonale et Universitaire, 1968.

    An account of the *scriptorium* and collection of manuscripts
    in the Cistercian Abbey of Hauterive and one of a series of
    manuscript catalogues for Canton Fribourg.

369   Burckhardt, Max, gen. ed. *Catalogue of Dated Manuscripts Written
       in the Latin Script from the Beginnings of the Middle Ages to
       1550 in the Libraries of Switzerland.* Dietikon-Zurich: Urs
       Graf, 1977-.

       This represents the dated-manuscript series for Switzerland.
       Publication is by location, in alphabetical order, with full
       paleographical and codicological data and many facsimiles; vol.1:
       Aarau, Appenzell, Basel, 1977.

370   Gottwald, B. *Catalogus Codicum Manuscriptorum que Asservantur
       in Bibliotheca Monasterii O.S.B. Engelbergensis in Helvetia.*
       Freiburg-im-Breisgau: Brisgoviae, 1891.

       A descriptive catalogue for the Benedictine monastery of
       Engelberg, with bibliographical references.

371   Hughes, Barnabas B., O.F.M. *Medieval Latin Mathematical Writings
       in the University Library, Basel.* Northridge, Calif.: The
       Author, 1972.

       A descriptive account of 39 codices containing mathematical
       treatises in the Basel University Library collection of Latin
       manuscripts. The author mentions in his introduction that the
       collection is available on microfilm, and he provides a useful
       bibliography for these and related manuscripts.

372   Meier, Gabriel, ed. *Catalogus Codicum Manuscriptorum qui in
       Bibliotheca Monasterii Einsidlensis O.S.B. Servantur.* Einsidler:
       Sumptibus Monasterii, 1899.

       A descriptive catalogue of the manuscript collection in the
       Benedictine monastery of Einsidler. Similar in scope and arrange-
       ment to item 370 above.

373   Meyer, G., and Burckhardt, Max, eds. *Die mittelalterlichen
       Handschriften der Universitätsbibliothek Basel. Beschreibendes
       Verzeichnis. Abteilung B. Theologische Pergamenthandschriften,*
       1. Basel: Universitätsbibliothek, 1960.

       This is an excellent, descriptive catalogue of 321 medieval
       theological manuscripts on parchment in the Basel University
       Library. It includes *sigla,* date, editions, and bibliography,
       but unfortunately no indexes of any kind are provided.

374   Scherrer, G., ed. *Verzeichnis der St. Gallische Handschriften.*
       St. Gall: Von Huber for the Stadtbibliothek Vadiana, 1859/
       1864.

375   ——————, ed. *Verzeichnis der Handschriften der Stiftsbibliothek
       von St. Gallen.* St. Gall: Von Huber, 1875/Hildesheim: G. Olms,
       1975.

       Both works constitute summary catalogues of St. Gall manuscripts,
       with some bibliographical references provided.

See also items 192-3, 196, 202, 204, 1039-40, 1085, 1279.

(k) Others

i. Czechoslovakia

General

376 *Das Bibliothekswesen der Tschechoslowakei. Verfast und zuzammen-
     gestelt von Bibliothekaren der CSSR.* Vienna: Österreichische
     Nationalbibliothek, 1966.

     A general guide to Czechoslovakian libraries, with some details
     given about their collections and research facilities.

Individual Libraries

377 Kotvan, Imrich. *Codices Universitatis Bratislavensis.* Bratislava:
     University Press, 1970.

     A descriptive catalogue of manuscripts in the University
     library. Arrangement is by collection number. A German transla-
     tion of the introduction is included, as well as a good bibliog-
     raphy of Czech catalogues for other manuscript collections, edi-
     tions, and other resources.

378 Truhlar, J. *Catalogus Codicum Manuscriptorum Latinorum qui in
     C.R. Bibliotheca Publica atque Universitatis Pragensis Asser-
     vantur.* 2 vols. Prague: Sumptibus Regiae Societatis Scientiarum
     Bohemicae, 1905-06.

     A descriptive catalogue, arranged by library, of manuscript
     collections in the Charles University and associated institutions.

ii. Greece

379 Weitzmann, Kurt. *Aus den Bibliotheken des Athos.* Hamburg: Fried-
     rich Wittig, 1963.

     A brief, descriptive catalogue of the monastic collections of
     the Lavra Library on Mount Athos and several others. These manu-
     scripts include many Classical and Byzantine texts and a large
     number of Byzantine illuminated manuscripts.

See also items 537, 542, 1181.

iii. Hungary

380 *Codices Manuscripti Latini.* Budapest: Hungarian National Museum,
     1940-. I. *Codices Latini Medii Aevi*, ed. Emma Bartoniek, 1940;
     II. *Codices Latini Medii Aevi Bibliothecae Universitatis Buda-
     pestinensis*, ed. Ladislaus Mezey with Agnes Bolgir, 1961.

     These works are descriptive catalogues of mainly Western Latin
     manuscripts in the National and University libraries. Bibliog-
     raphies and indexes are included in each volume.

See also item 670.

iv. Poland

381   Aland, Kurt. *Die Handschriftenbestände der polnischen Bibliotheken,*
       insbesondere an griechischen und lateinischen Handschriften
       von Autoren und Werken der Klassischer bis zum Ende der patris-
       tischen Zeit. Deutsche Akademie der Wissenschaften zu Berlin,
       Sektion für Altertumswissenschaft, 7. Berlin: Akademie Verlag,
       1956.

       A descriptive handbook on Polish libraries and their collec-
       tions of Greek and Latin manuscripts. The bibliographical refer-
       ences cite individual catalogues.

382   Ziegler, Konrat. *Catalogus Codicum Latinorum Classicorum qui in*
       Bibliotheca Urbi Wratislaviensi Adservantur. Hildesheim/New
       York: G. Olms, 1975.

       Originally published in 1915, this descriptive catalogue of
       Classical Latin manuscripts is arranged by collection number.
       Provided are indexes of authors, persons, libraries, and owners
       and some illustrating facsimiles.

v. Russia

   General

383   Grimsted, P.K. *Archives and Manuscript Repositories in the USSR:*
       Moscow and Leningrad. Princeton, N.J.: Princeton University
       Press, 1972; *Supplement 1: Bibliographical Addenda*, 1976.

       Sponsored by the Russian Institute, Columbia University, New
       York, N.Y., this represents the only comprehensive guide in
       English to Russian libraries. Manuscript catalogues are listed
       in the *Supplement.*

   Individual Libraries

384   Brayer, Edith. "Manuscrits français du moyen âge conservés à
       Leningrad." *Bulletin et Information de l'Institut de Recherche*
       et d'Histoire des Textes, 7 (1958), 23-31.

       This article provides a summary list, with some bibliographical
       references.

385   Staerk, A. *Les Manuscrits latines du Ve au XIIe siècles, con-*
       servés à la Bibliothèque Impériale de Saint-Petersbourg. 2 vols.
       Petersburg/Leningrad: 1910; repr. New York, N.Y./Hildesheim:
       G. Olms, 1976.

       A descriptive catalogue of Latin manuscripts, with bibliograph-
       ical references and 140 facsimile illustrations.

vi. Yugoslavia

   General

386   Jovanović, Slobodan, and Rojnić, Matko, comp. *A Guide to Yugo-*
       slav Libraries and Archives, ed. Paul L. Horecky. The Joint

Committee on Eastern Europe Publication Series, 2. Columbus, Ohio: American Association for the Advancement of Slavic Studies, 1975.

A detailed description of the major libraries, with a bibliography of their publications and catalogues. Arrangement is by province.

Individual Libraries

387   Kaeppeli, T., and Schooner, H.-V. *Les Manuscrits médiévaux de Saint-Dominique de Dubrovnik: Catalogue Sommaire.* Institutum Historicum FF. Praedicaturum, Dissertationes Historicae. Fasc. xvii. Rome: Istituto Storico Domenicano, 1965.

A descriptive catalogue of the library manuscripts, arranged by collection. Some bibliographical references are included.

See also item 527.

(1) North America

i. General

388   *American Library Directory*, ed. Jacques Cattell Press. 31st ed. New York, N.Y.: Bowker, 1978.

A complete directory to all libraries in the United States and Canada. Arrangement is by state, Alabama–Wyoming, or province, Alberta–Québec, with Puerto Rico and the Virgin Islands included. Information gives address, director, size of holdings, special subjects and collections, publications, and other technical details. It lists International Communication Agency Centers and provides an index of names of libraries.

388.1 Ash, Lee, comp. *Subject Collections: A Guide to Special Book Collections and Subject Emphases as Reported by University, College, Public, and Special Libraries and Museums in the United States and Canada.* 5th ed. New York, N.Y.: Bowker, 1978.

Under "Manuscripts" are listed collections by libraries throughout the United States and Canada, arranged by type, e.g., "Collections," "Latin," "Medieval," "Renaissance," and so on. Information includes library address, curator, number and nature of manuscripts, slide and microfilm collections, and catalogues or other bibliographical matter.

389   Downs, Robert B. *American Library Resources: A Bibliographical Guide.* Chicago, Ill.: American Library Association, 1951; *Supplement*, 1950-61, 1962; *Second Supplement*, 1961-70, 1972.

This subject guide lists printed catalogues, union lists, special collections, and library holdings by area of study. All volumes provide author/subject/library indexes.

390   Ermatinger, Charles, J. "A Partial List of Catalogues, Inventories, and Indices, Both Printed and Handwritten on File in the Vatican

Manuscript Depository of the Knights of Columbus Foundation."
Manuscripta, 1-2 (1954), 8-23.

A bibliographical list of manuscript catalogues and other inventories of mainly European manuscripts, especially those in
the Vatican Library. See item 538.

391   Hamer, Philip, M. *A Guide to Archives and Manuscripts in the*
      United States. Compiled for the National Historical Publica-
      tions Commission. New Haven, Conn.: Yale University Press,
      1961.

      Arranged alphabetically by state and then by location, this
      exhaustive guide describes the general character and extent of
      each collection. Extensive subject/author indexes are also pro-
      vided.

392   Library of Congress. *The National Union Catalog of Manuscript*
      Collections. Ann Arbor, Mich.: J.W. Edwards, 1962; Hamden,
      Conn.: 1963; Washington, D.C.: 1964-.

      Published annually since 1964 by the Library of Congress, each
      issue of this catalogue describes a manuscript collection in
      some detail and indicates whether the repository has a descrip-
      tive inventory of contents; volumes are arranged by the number
      sequence of the Library of Congress cards it reproduces. Cumu-
      lative subject/name/repository indexes are published at inter-
      vals.

393   Public Archives of Canada. *Union List of Manuscripts in Canadian*
      Repositories. Rev. ed. Ottawa: Public Archives, 1975.

      A list of manuscripts, arranged by location. Mainly modern
      manuscripts of an historical or literary nature are listed; for
      medieval manuscripts see next item.

394   Ricci, Seymour de, and Wilson, W.J. *Census of Medieval and*
      Renaissance Manuscripts in the United States and Canada.
      3 vols. New York, N.Y.: H.W. Wilson, 1935-40/1961; *Supplement*,
      ed. Christopher Faye and William H. Bond, New York, N.Y.: 1962.

      An extensive union list of medieval and Renaissance manuscripts,
      approximately 12,000, in the United States, Hawaii, and Canada;
      arrangement is alphabetical by state, city, and collection. The
      descriptions include mainly paleographical features of the manu-
      script, its contents, and reference when possible to other
      printed sources of information. Vol. 3 includes indexes for names,
      titles, headings, incipits, and scribes. The *Supplement* adds a
      large number of additional manuscripts and collections. Some
      revisions to this invaluable work have been suggested by Samuel
      A. Ives, "Corrigenda and Addenda to the Description of the
      Plimpton Manuscript as Recorded in the De Ricci *Census*," *Speculum*,
      17 (1942), 33-49, and Offprint.

395   *Subject Directory of Special Libraries and Information Centers*,
      ed. Margaret Labash Young, Harold Chester Young, and Anthony
      T. Kouzas. 5 vols. Detroit, Mich.: Gale, 1977.

The material of this massive directory is taken from the *Directory of Special Libraries and Information Centers*, 4th ed. The five divisions into which American and Canadian libraries are grouped are (1) Business and Law; (2) Education and Information Science; (3) Health Sciences; (4) Social Sciences and Humanities; and (5) Science and Technology. Individual libraries are listed alphabetically under subject, and described by address, director, subjects, special collections, general holdings, catalogues, and services. An alternate name index, for libraries which may be identified in more than one way, concludes.

ii. *Individual Libraries and Collections*

396   Corbett, James Arthur. *Catalogue of the Medieval and Renaissance Manuscripts of the University of Notre Dame*. Notre Dame, Ind.: University of Notre Dame Press, 1978.

A descriptive catalogue of this highly varied collection, with bibliographical references and index.

397   de la Mare, A.C. *The Italian Manuscripts in the Library of Major J.R. Abbey*. New York, N.Y.: Praeger, 1969.

This work provides a fully descriptive catalogue of a Humanist collection containing 63 codices. These range from the twelfth to the sixteenth centuries, and many are illuminated. Each manuscript description is accompanied by a facsimile plate.

398   Fleming, John V. "Medieval Manuscripts in the Taylor Library." *The Princeton University Library Chronicle*, 38 (1977), 107-19.

A brief, descriptive list of medieval manuscripts in the Princeton University Library.

399   Jenkins, John Gilbert. "A Hand-List of the Stowe Collection in the Huntingdon Library, California." *Bucks, Rec. Soc. Lists and Indexes*, 1 (1956): repr. Jordans for the Society, 1956.

A brief (18pp.) descriptive list of manuscripts formerly in the possession of Stowe, with a brief history of earlier provenance when known. Some bibliographical references are given.

400   Pierpont Morgan Library. *Mediaeval and Renaissance Manuscripts*. New York, N.Y.: The Library, 1974.

A descriptive catalogue of early manuscripts to 1500.

401   Pontifical Institute of Mediaeval Studies, Toronto, Canada. *Dictionary Catalogue of the Library of the Pontifical Institute of Mediaeval Studies, Toronto, Canada*. 5 vols. Boston, Mass.: G.K. Hall, 1972.

Vol. 5 of this dictionary catalogue contains a catalogue of the microfilm manuscript collection, see item 547 below. An index of authors is provided.

402   Salinger, Paul. "'The Newberry Library Catalogue of pre-1500 Manuscripts: A Report on Research in Progress'; Abstract of

a Paper Read at the 3rd St. Louis Conference on Manuscript
Studies." *Manuscripta*, 21 (1977), 22–23.

This article is an account, representative of those appearing
regularly in *Manuscripta*, of current research in manuscript
cataloguing in North America.

403   Schulz, Herbert C.; Cuthbert, Norma B.; and Noya, Haydee. *Ten
       Centuries of Manuscripts in the Huntingdon Library*. San Marino,
       Calif.: The Library, 1962.

       A brief, descriptive survey of the manuscript collection, with
       representative facsimiles. A new, revised manuscript catalogue
       for the Huntingdon Library is in progress.

404   United States Army. *Index-Catalogue of the Library of the Surgeon
       General's Office*. 3rd series. 10 vols. Washington, D.C.: United
       States Army, 1918–32.

       A summary catalogue, which includes some early medical manu-
       scripts mainly from the fifteenth century. These are described
       more fully in item 394. See also 544.

See also items 19, 362, 601, 639, 1081, 1089, 1094, 1097, and Section
III.C.

(m) Australia and New Zealand

405   Sinclair, Keith Val, *et al*., eds. *Descriptive Catalogue of
       Medieval and Renaissance Western Manuscripts in Australia*.
       Sidney: Sidney University Press, 1969.

       This is a fully descriptive catalogue of the 264 manuscripts
       currently found in public and private Australian collections.
       Arrangement is by district, beginning with the National Library
       of Australia, Canberra. It provides a list of incipits, a general
       index, and an appendix of manuscripts presumed lost. Illustrated
       with a selection of facsimiles.

406   Taylor, David M. *The Oldest Manuscripts in New Zealand*. Welling-
       ton: New Zealand Council for Educational Research, 1955.

       A descriptive catalogue arranged alphabetically by district
       and library. It provides good bibliographical references, an
       appendix of watermarks, a classified list of manuscripts accord-
       ing to language and subject, and a name/title index. Several
       facsimiles are reproduced in illustrating plates.

B. MEDIEVAL LIBRARIES

The known contents of medieval libraries may offer clues toward establishing the identity and provenance of some manuscripts. Included below, therefore, are references to early catalogues and lists, divided, after an initial section on general references, according to country. Also included here are references to methods of arrangement and identification within various medieval libraries.

1. GENERAL

407   Becker, Gustav H. *Catalogi Bibliothecarum Antiquii*. Bonn: M. Cohen, 1885.

Part 1 of this valuable work lists manuscript catalogues of the thirteenth century, while part 2 lists those from the later medieval period. Included are indexes for anonymous works and libraries.

408   Beddle, J.S. "Libraries in the Twelfth Century: Their Catalogues and Contents," in *Anniversary Essays in Mediaeval History by Students of Charles Homer Haskins*, ed. C.H. Taylor. Freeport, N.Y.: Books for Libraries Press, 1967, pp. 1-35.

A general survey and description of the arrangement of twelfth-century libraries and their holdings, especially in England.

409   *Bibliographie générale de l'Ordre Cistercien*, ed. H. Rochais and E. Manning. Rochefort, Belgium: Abbaye Notre-Dame-de-Saint-Remy, 1977-.

Vols. 21.1 and 21.2 (1977) list Cistercian manuscripts and archives respectively. Arrangement is by house and present library, Abbaye-au-Bois to Zwyveke, with reference to the present location of the documents. Some bibliographical references are included.

410   Christ, Karl. "Bibliotheksgeschichte des Mittelalters, zur Methode und zur neuesten Literatur." *Zentralblatt für Bibliothekswesen*, 61 (1947), 38-56, 149-60, and 233-52.

A methodological essay and bibliography on the history of medieval libraries, with special reference to those in Germany. See also next item.

411   ———. "Mittelalterliche Bibliotheksordnungen für Frauenklöster." *Zentralblatt für Bibliothekswesen*, 59 (1942), 1-29.

The author describes the special provisions made for women's cloister libraries and indicates their general contents.

412   Clark, J.W. *Care of Books: Essay on the Development of Libraries and Their Fittings*. 2nd ed. Cambridge: University Press, 1969.

A general account of the storage and use of books in medieval and Renaissance libraries, especially monastic. See also next item.

413   ————. *Libraries in the Medieval and Renaissance Periods*. Chicago, Ill.: Argonaut, 1894/1968.

A more detailed and focussed version of the preceding item.

414   Gottlieb, Theodor. *Über mitteralterliche Bibliotheken*. Leipzig: 1890; repr. Graz: Akad. Druck- und Verlaganstalt, 1955.

A general account of library holdings, based upon a selection of medieval catalogues from fourteenth and fifteenth-century libraries in Germany, France, Great Britain, Italy, the Netherlands, Scandinavia, Spain, and Portugal. Chapter VII, "Indirekt Quellen," cites earlier sources of information about library contents from such individuals as Theodulf, Bishop of Orleans.

415   Hessel, Alfred. *A History of Libraries*, trans. with *Supplementary Material* by Reuben Preiss. New Brunswick, N.J.: Scarecrow Press, 1955.

A general history of the development and nature of the library during different periods, with some useful references to medieval libraries.

416   Humphreys, K.W. *The Book Provisions of the Mediaeval Friars, 1215-1400*. Amsterdam: Erasmus, 1964.

An account of library regulations for the mendicant orders, with descriptions of library holdings. An excellent bibliography is provided, pp. 137-43, as well as indexes. See also item 62.

417   Lesne, Emile. *Les Livres, 'Scriptoria' et bibliothèques du commencement du VIIIe à la fin du XIe siècle*. Lille: Faculté Catholique de l'Université, 1938.

This work represents vol. 4 of Lesne's *Histoire de la propriété ecclésiastique en France*. 6 vols. (vol. 2 in 3 pts.), Memoires et travaux publiés par des professeurs des facultés Catholiques de Lille, 6, 19, 30, 44, 46, 50, and 53 (Lille/Paris: 1910-43). Lesne discusses the inventories of treasuries and libraries in French churches from the eighth to the eleventh centuries.

418   Manitius, Max. *Handschriften antiker Autoren in mittelalterlichen Bibliothekskatalogen*. Zentraliblatt für Bibliothekswesen, Beiheft 67. Leipzig: Teubner, 1935.

This work surveys generally Classical manuscripts in mainly continental libraries. Especially useful are Manitius' lists of incipits/explicits.

419   Rashdall, H. *Universities of Europe in the Middle Ages*. 2 vols. Oxford: 1895; new ed. by F.M. Powicke and A.B. Emden. Oxford:

Clarendon Press, 1936.

While Rashdall's work is a general history of the medieval university, he gives some account of the library resources for each university. Vol. 1 discusses the universities of Salerno, Bologna, and Paris; vol. 2 other universities of Italy and those of Spain, France, Germany, and Scotland; the third vol., added in 1936, considers English university life. See also items 58, 75, 88.

420   Thompson, James Westfall. *The Medieval Library.* The University of Chicago Studies in Library Science. Chicago, Ill.: University of Chicago Press, 1939; repr. with *Supplement* by Blanche B. Boyer. New York: Hafner, 1957.

An introduction to the subject, followed by essays on individual aspects: the contents of the medieval library, early catalogues, etc. It provides some bibliographical notes, which are updated in the *Supplement*.

2. MEDIEVAL LIBRARIES IN GREAT BRITAIN

421   Allen, Percy S. "Bishop Shirwood (d. 1494) of Durham and His Library." *English Historical Review*, 25 (1910), 445-56.

An account of Shirwood's life and his library of manuscripts and incunabula, acquired by Corpus Christi College, Oxford, in the early sixteenth century. The earliest manuscript is a thirteenth-century copy of Peter Cantor's commentary on the Psalter (now MS. C.C.C. 49). Provenance is given when known for the five manuscripts.

422   Bateson, Mary, ed. *Catalogue of the Library of Syon Monastery, Isleworth.* Cambridge: University Press, 1898.

An early sixteenth-century catalogue of some 1421 manuscripts and early printed books. Given are pressmark, donor's name, and brief description.

423   Craster, Sir Edmund. *The History of All Souls College*, ed. E.F. Jacob. London: Faber and Faber, 1971.

This historical study includes the early history of the All Souls library and its subsequent enlargements. See item 999.

424   Dobson, R.B. *Durham Priory, 1400-1450.* Cambridge: University Press, 1973.

A description of the "New Library," its manuscripts and inventories.

425   Durkan, John, and Ross, Anthony. *Early Scottish Libraries.* Glasgow: J.S. Burns, 1961.

A description of the contents of early Scottish libraries and
the destruction or dispersal of medieval manuscripts from the
sixteenth century. Earlier published in the *Innis Review*, 9.

426   Emden, A.B. *Donors of Books to St. Augustine's Abbey, Canterbury*.
       Oxford Bibliographical Society, *Occasional Papers*, 4. Oxford:
       The Society, 1968.

       A chronological list of donors from the twelfth to the fifteenth
       centuries, with some identification of their manuscript donations
       in terms of present location. It provides a selection of plates
       and a name index.

427   Garrod, Heathcote W. "The Library Regulations of a Medieval
       College." *The Library: Transactions of the Bibliographical
       Society*, 8 (1927), 312-25.

       The regulations of Merton College, Oxford, studied from early
       documents.

428   Gneuss, Helmut. "Englands Bibliotheken im Mittelalter und ihr
       Untergang," in *Festschrift für Walter Hübner*, ed. D. Riesner
       and Helmut Gneuss. Berlin: Erich Schmidt, 1964, pp. 71-121.

       Gneuss makes general observations on medieval, principally
       monastic, English libraries and the later dispersal of their
       manuscripts. The bibliographical references are excellent.

429   Gougaud, Louis. "Inventaires de manuscrits provenant d'anciennes
       bibliothèques monastiques de Grande-Bretagne." *Revue d'Histoire
       Ecclésiastique*, 33 (1937), 789-91.

       A non-critical bibliography of catalogues and other works in-
       dicating library contents; cited by library alphabetically,
       Barking-Worcester.

430   Hunt, R.W. "The Library of the Abbey of St. Albans," item 720,
       pp. 251-77.

       A history of this large Benedictine library beginning with
       the twelfth-century *indiculus*. Included are edited extracts from
       this and other relevant documents.

431   James, M.R. "A List of Manuscripts Formerly in Peterborough
       Abbey Library." *Supplements to the Transactions of the Biblio-
       graphical Society*, 5. London: The Society, 1930; *Supplements*
       1-10, printed in 2 vols., 1926-35.

       One of James' brief surveys of medieval libraries, with some
       bibliographical notes. Many such surveys, e.g., that for Essex
       Monastic libraries (1933), have superseded by Ker's survey,
       items 434-6.

432   ————. *Ancient Libraries of Canterbury and Dover*. Cambridge:
       University Press, 1903.

       A general history of the libraries of Christ Church Priory and
       St. Augustine's Abbey, with an edition of an incomplete twelfth-
       century catalogue from Christ Church. Also edited are Prior

Henry Eastry's book list of Canterbury Cathedral manuscripts (1331), other Christ Church registers, and John Whytefeld's catalogue (1389) of the library of St. Martin at Dover.

433   ———. "Greek Manuscripts in England before the Renaissance."
       The Library, 4th ser., 7 (1927), 337-53.

A brief survey of the nature and present location of Greek manuscripts in English collections.

434   Ker, N.R. "The Chaining, Labelling, and Inventory Numbers of Manuscripts Belonging to the Old University Library." *Bodleian Library Record*, 5 (1955), 176-80.

435   ———. *Medieval Libraries of Great Britain. A List of Surviving Books*. 2nd ed. London: Royal Historical Society, 1964.

An important survey of library holdings based upon extant medieval catalogues and book lists. This work incorporates some of the material in his earlier *English Manuscripts in the Century after the Conquest* (Oxford: Clarendon Press, 1960), and also material later to be expanded in item 251.

436   ———. "More Manuscripts from Essex Monastic Libraries."
       Transactions of the Essex Archaeological Society, n.s., 23 (1945), 56-62.

In this brief article Ker provides additions to James' earlier survey, item 433.

437   Little, A.G. *Grey Friars in Oxford*. Oxford Historical Society, 20. Oxford: The Society, 1892.

An account of Franciscan teaching in medieval Oxford and its library resources from the mid-thirteenth century, with some bibliography.

438   Macray, William Dunn. *Annals of the Bodleian Library Oxford: With a Notice of the Earlier Library of the University*. 2nd ed. Oxford: University Press, 1890.

Macray describes the founding of the Library of Sir Thomas Bodley and provides a list of early donors as well as a brief survey of the collections of manuscripts and early printed books. Brought up to date by Craster, item 280.

439   Ogilvy, J.D.A. *Books Known to Anglo-Latin Writers from Aldhelm to Alcuin*. Cambridge, Mass.: Mediaeval Academy of America, 1936.

440   ———. *Books Known to the English, 597-1066*. Cambridge, Mass.: Mediaeval Academy of America, 1967.

In a similar format, both books list individual authors alphabetically and present a résumé of their works, editions, and other bibliography. The latter item represents an expanded and updated version of the first, with both offering probably the best means of determining the currency of certain texts (chiefly Classical) at particular periods.

441   Oliver, George. *Lives of the Bishops of Exeter and a History of the Cathedral*. Exeter: William Roberts, 1861.

       With its general history of the Cathedral, this work offers editions of inventories of manuscripts, books, vestments, and other items.

442   Piper, A.J. "The Libraries of the Monks of Durham," item 720, pp. 213–49.

       A detailed account of the library from the mid-twelfth century. The illustrations include a diagram of the Cathedral Priory with location of its manuscript books, and several facsimiles.

443   Powicke, F.M. *The Medieval Books of Merton College*. Oxford: Clarendon Press, 1931.

       Besides giving an account of Merton library holdings, the author also describes types of early inventories and their implications for the identification of manuscripts.

444   Rickert, E. "King Richard II's Books." *The Library*, 4th ser., 13 (1932–33), 144–47.

       A list of the king's manuscripts, which appeared on a Memoranda Roll of 1384–5. Rickert makes some possible identifications and suggests some connections between these works and events in Chaucer's life.

445   Rouse, Richard H. "Bostonus Buriensis and the Author of the *Catalogus Scriptorum Ecclesiae*." *Speculum*, 41 (1966), 471–99.

       This article provides a detailed study of John Boston of Bury's "Union Catalogue" of books in England, ca. 1410; the document is extant only in Thomas Tanner's late seventeenth-century transcription. Rouse's documentation is extensive, and he also includes a partial edition with facsimile examples from related manuscripts.

446   Savage, Ernest A. *Old English Libraries: The Making, Collection, and Use of Books During the Middle Ages*. New York, N.Y.: Barnes and Noble, 1911/1970.

       An early but valuable study of medieval book-making and circulation; it describes medieval libraries in England and Ireland, with some focus upon Oxford and Cambridge libraries and notes upon the essential differences between monastic and cathedral collections. An appendix lists book prices for medieval periods, Classical authors found in medieval catalogues, and a survey of records citing medieval library collections.

447   Streeter, Burnett Hillman. *The Chained Library. A Survey of Four Centuries in the Evolution of the English Library*. London: Macmillan, 1931.

       The major chained libraries studied in this work are Oxford and Hereford. Several photographs and diagrams of floor-plans illustrate past and present facilities.

448   Weiss, Roberto. "Henry VI and the Library of All Souls College,
       Oxford." *English Historical Review*, 62 (1942), 102-5.

       See also item 423.

449   Williams, Thomas Webb. *Somerset Medieval Libraries and Miscellane-
       ous Notices of Books in Somerset Prior to the Dissolution of
       the Monasteries*. Bristol: J.W. Arrowsmith, 1897.

       A descriptive account of Somerset medieval libraries with lists
       of manuscripts and present location if known; provides a general
       index.

450   Wilson, R.M. "The Medieval Library of Titchfield Abbey." *Pro-
       ceedings of the Leeds Philosophical and Literary Society*, 5
       (1940), 150-77; 252-76.

       The central and most important part of this article is an
       edition of a manuscript catalogue, ca. 1400, which belonged
       originally to the Duke of Portland.

451   Wormald, Francis, and Wright, C.E., eds. *The English Library
       before 1700: Studies in Its History*. London: University of
       London, Athlone Press, 1958.

       This important collection of essays is the most detailed study
       to date of all aspects of medieval British libraries. Although
       the final "Select Bibliography" is too limited to be of real
       use, the bibliographical notes to individual essays provide
       good documentation and references to further studies. The essays
       consider: II. The Monastic Library; III. The Bibliography of the
       Manuscript Book; IV. The Universities and the Mediaeval Library;
       V. The Contents of the Mediaeval Library; VI. The Private Collec-
       tor and the Revival of Greek Learning; VII. The Preservation of
       the Classics; VIII. The Dispersal of the Libraries in the Six-
       teenth Century; IX. The Elizabethan Society of Antiquaries and
       the Formation of the Cottonian Library; X. The Libraries of
       Cambridge 1570-1700; and XI. Oxford Libraries in the Seventeenth
       and Eighteenth Centuries.

                         3. OTHER MEDIEVAL LIBRARIES

452   Beauvoir, Hiver de. *La Librairie de Jean Duc de Berry au château
       de Mehun-sur-Yevre*. Paris: Auguste Aubry, 1860.

       A descriptive catalogue of the Duke's library in the fifteenth
       and sixteenth centuries, arranged by genre of manuscript, e.g.,
       liturgy or history.

453   Bruckner, A. *Scriptoria Medii Aevi Helvetica*. Denkmäler
       schweizerischer Schreibkunst des Mittelalters. 10 vols.
       Geneva: Roto-Sadag, 1935-64.

       This series of volumes constitutes the most important account
       to date of medieval libraries in Switzerland and the Upper Alsace;
       each is devoted to a particular area, e.g., volume 1 to the

Chur diocese and volume 4 to the Zurich area. Full descriptions
are given of scripts, illumination, decoration, and other features,
and many reproductions are included from selected manuscripts.
Some of the manuscripts are archival documents.

454   Buzas, Ladislaus. *Deutsche Bibliotheksgeschichte des Mittelalters.*
       Wiesbaden: Ludwig Reichert, 1975.

       A study of the religious orders and their libraries, with some
       account of other ecclesiastical and private libraries. An ex-
       cellent bibliography as well as indexes are provided.

455   Champion, P. *La Librairie de Charles d'Orléans.* Paris: Champion,
       1910/1977.

       An account of the poet's manuscript books at the beginning of
       the fifteenth century, accompanied by a portfolio of facsimile
       illustrations. See also items 459, 876.

456   Christ, Karl. *Die Bibliothek des Klosters Fulda im 16. Jahrundert.
       Die Handschriftenverzeichnisse.* Beiheft zum Zentralblatt für
       Bibliothekswesens, 64. Leipzig: O. Harrassowitz, 1933/Nendeln:
       Kraus Reprint, 1968.

       This study provides a catalogue of manuscripts to be found in
       the medieval monastery at Fulda, with historical notes and
       bibliography.

457   Contreni, John J. *The Cathedral School of Laon from 850 to 930:
       Its Manuscripts and Masters.* Münchener Beiträge zur Mediä-
       vistic und Renaissance-Forschung. Munich: Arbeo, 1978.

       An historical study of the Cathedral School and its library.
       Appendix A constitutes a manuscript catalogue. Indexes and
       bibliography are included.

458   Daly, Lloyd W. "Early Alphabetic Indices in the Vatican Archives."
       Traditio, 19 (1963), 483-6.

       A brief note on *rubicelle* and *capitula* used to list the con-
       tents of papal registers from 1227 to ca. 1500.

459   Delisle, Leopold. *Recherches sur la librairie de Charles V.*
       2 vols. Paris: Champion, 1905.

       An inventory with commentary on the libraries of Charles V
       and VI, with some information about the library of Jean, Duc
       de Berry; see items 455, 876.

460   ———. *Recherches sur l'ancienne bibliothèque de Corbia.* Paris:
       Imprimérie Nationale, 1861.

       An early but still useful study of manuscripts in the medieval
       monastic library of Corbie.

461   Derolez, Albert, ed. *Corpus Catalogorum Belgii. De middeleeuwse
       Bibliotheekscatalogi der zuidelijke Nederlanden.* I. *Provincie
       West-Vlaanderen.* Verhandelingen van de Koninklijke Vlaamse
       Academie voor Wetenschappen, Letteren en Schone Kunsten van

Belgie, Klasse der Letteren, 28.61. Brussels: Paleis der
Academien, 1966-.

A proposed series of inventories of medieval manuscript catalogues for mainly Flanders, which thus far contains full descriptions, bibliographies, and indexes; cf. the similar series for
Austria, item 466.

462   Doutrepont, Georges. *Inventaire de la "librairie" de Philippe
le Bon (1420)*. Brussels: 1906/Geneva: Slatkine Reprints, 1977.

This work provides a summary introduction on the library of
Philippe le Bon, based upon inventories 1404-20, followed by an
edition of the 1420 inventory. The text lists manuscripts according to genre, e.g., liturgical works, and gives a brief description. Doutrepont provides a select bibliography for each.

463   Dufour, Jean. *La Bibliothèque et le Scriptorium de Moissac*.
Publications du Centre de Recherches d'Histoire de la IVe
Section de l'Ecole Pratique des Hautes Etudes. Geneva/Paris:
E. Droz, 1972.

A history of the Benedictine Abbey of Moissac, founded 630.
Dufour provides a detailed description of the twelfth-century
scriptorium and its manuscripts.

464   *Elemente des Buch- und Bibliothekswesens*, ed. Fridolin Dressler
and Gerhard Liebers. Wiesbaden: Dr. Ludwig Reichert, 1975-.
I. *Deutsche Bibliotheksgeschichte des Mittelalters*, by Ladislaus Buzas, 1975.

A study of medieval libraries in Germany. After an introduction on the transition from Classical Antiquity to the Middle
Ages, the author devotes individual chapters to types of libraries, e.g., cloister, cathedral, university, private, etc.,
with a final chapter on library administration. An extensive
classified bibliography is provided.

465   Faucon, Maurice. *La Librairie des papes d'Avignon: sa formation,
sa composition, ses catalogues (1316-1420): d'après les registres de comptes et d'inventaires des archives vaticanes*.
Bibliothèque des Ecoles Françaises d'Athènes et de Rome, 43,
50. Paris: Ernest Thorin, 1886-87.

Faucon edits book lists from inventories; these are arranged
according to original collection, e.g., the books purchased by
John XXII in 1317. A name/place/author index is provided.

466   Gottlieb, Theodor, *et al.*, eds. *Mittelalterliche Bibliothekskataloge Österreichs*. I. *Niederösterreich*. Vienna: Adolf
Holzhausen, 1915-1966.

A series of edited medieval catalogues, published by location.
Continued to vol. V. *Salzburg* (1966) with continuation by item
485.

467   Hillgarth, J.N. *Una bibliotheca cistercienne medieval: La Real
(Mallorca)*. Analecta Sacra Tarraconensia, 32. Barcelona: Bal-
mesiana, 1960. Offprint.

This represents the forerunner of a proposed series of editions of medieval Majorcan library catalogues by the author with Juan Pons y Marques. The author here edits four book lists from the Cistercian Abbey of La Real from 1386-1502, which refer to manuscripts no longer identifiable or presumed lost. Classification is by subject. This library is of some interest for its role in the early education of Raymond Llull.

468   Humphreys, K.W., ed. *Studies in the History of Libraries and Librarianship.* II. *The Library of the Carmelites at Florence at the End of the Fourteenth Century.* Amsterdam: Erasmus, 1964. III. *The Library of the Franciscans of the Convent of St. Anthony, Padua, at the Beginning of the Fifteenth Century,* 1966; IV. *The Library of the Franciscans of Siena in the Late Fifteenth Century,* 1978.

These studies provide collections of entries extracted from general inventories of the period. Indexes of authors and incipits are provided.

469   Lebraz, Jacqueline. "La Bibliothèque de Guy de Roye archevêque de Reims 1390-1409." *Bulletin d'Information de l'Institut de Recherche et d'Histoire des Textes,* 6 (1957), 67-100.

A detailed study, based on inventories and other documents, of this early fifteenth-century library.

470   Lehmann, Edgar. *Die Bibliotheksräume der deutschen Klöster im Mittelalter.* Deutsche Akademie der Wissenschaften zu Berlin, Schrifte zur Kunstgeschichte, 2. Berlin: The Academy, 1957.

An archaeological study of the cloister library, with plates and diagrams indicating location of manuscript books, *scriptoria*, and reading areas. See also 472.

471   Lehmann, Paul, and Ruf, Paul. *Mittelalterliche Bibliothekskatalogen Deutschlands und der Schweiz.* Munich: C.H. Beck, 1918-62.

This series of volumes offers descriptive lists of medieval catalogues, arranged by district or canton; incipits/explicits are included; vol. 3.4 provides a *Register* of authors and works.

472   Löffler, Klemens. *Deutsche Klösterbibliotheken.* 2nd ed. (from 1918). Bücherei der Kultur und Geschichte, 27. Bonn/Leipzig: Schröder, 1922.

A general history of individual monastic libraries. Now superseded by item 470.

473   Marks, Richard Bruce. *The Medieval Manuscript Library of the Charterhouse of St. Barbara in Cologne.* 2 vols. Analecta Cartusiana. Salzburg: University Press, 1974.

A study and catalogue of the medieval *scriptorium* and library, with a good bibliography.

474   Mazal, Otto. "Die Salzburger Dom- und Klosterbibliothek in karolingischer Zeit." *Codices Manuscripti,* 3 (1977), 44-64.

A history and survey of manuscripts in the ninth and tenth centuries of the Cathedral and Cloister library.

475   Meinsma, K.O. *Middeleeuwsche Bibliotheken*. Zutphen: The Author, 1903.

A general survey of Dutch medieval libraries with bibliography.

476   Number deleted.

477   Nortier-Marchand, Géneviève. *Les Bibliothèques médiévales des abbayes bénédictines de Normandie*, 2nd ed. (from 1967). Preface by Andre Masson. Bibliothèque d'Histoire et d'Archéologie Chrétienne, 9. Paris: P. Lethielleux, 1971.

This work studies the libraries of Fécamp, Le Bec, Mont-St-Michel, Jumièges, Saint-Wandrille, and Saint-Ouen in terms of *scriptoria* and holdings.

478   Odier, Jeanne B. *La Bibliothèque Vaticane de Sixte IV à Pie XI: Recherches sur l'histoire des collections de manuscrits*. Studi e Testi, 272. Rome/Vatican: Biblioteca Apostolica Vaticana, 1973.

A history of the Vatican Library, from its origins to the time of Pope Pius XI. Described are various individual collections and the influence of successive librarians. The list of administrators 1475-1971 and the full bibliography increase the usefulness of this work for studies in the late medieval library.

479   O'Gorman, James. *The Architecture of the Monastic Library in Italy 1300-1600: Catalogue with Introductory Essay*. New York, N.Y.: New York University Press, 1972.

This essay gives an account of building programs while the accompanying catalogue surveys library holdings in medieval Italy within a geographical arrangement.

480   Oleson, Tryggvi J. "Book Collections of Mediaeval Icelandic Churches." *Speculum*, 32 (1957), 502-10.

A résumé of 76 inventories from the early fourteenth century; described according to genre, e.g., service books or lives of saints.

481   Parsons, Eduard Alexander. *The Alexandrian Library, Glory of the Hellenic World. Its Rise, Antiquities, and Destruction*. Amsterdam: Elsevier, 1952.

An account of the Alexandrian library in the general context of the Hellenistic period. It does not provide many details in the description of manuscripts, although the bibliographic references are of some use as a starting point for further study

482   Pellégrin, Elisabeth. *La Bibliothèque des Visconti et des Sforza ducs de Milan au XVe siècle*. Publications de l'Institut de Recherche et d'Histoire des Textes, 5. Paris: Service des Publications du CNRS, 1955; *Supplément*, Florence: L.S. Olschki, 1969.

An historical account of the library of the Visconti-Sforza
at Pavia, based mainly upon manuscripts subsequently carried off
by Louis XII and presently in the Bibliothèque Nationale, Paris.
Pellégrin gives revised versions of three fifteenth-century inventories. The *Supplément* contains 175 plates in folio.

483   Schiff, Mario. *La Bibliothèque du marquis de Santillane: étude
       historique et bibliographique de la collection des livres manu-
       scrits de Don Iñigo López de Mendoza, 1398-1458, marqués de
       Santillana, conde del Real de Manzanares, humaniste et auteur
       espagnol célèbre.* Bibliothèque de l'Ecole des Hautes Etudes,
       Sciences Historiques et Philologique, 153. Paris: 1905/Amster-
       dam: Gerard Th. van Heusden, 1970.

       A general introduction gives an account of the history and
       nature of the collection. This is followed by a full description
       of each manuscript, arranged by author. A name/subject index is
       provided.

484   Serrurier, Cornelia. *Bibliothèques de France. Description de
       leur fonds et historie de leur formation.* The Hague: M. Nijhof,
       1946.

       A general historical survey of libraries in France by geographi-
       cal area. A bibliography and indexes are included.

485   Uiblein, Paul, *et al.*, eds. *Mittelalterliche Bibliothekskataloge
       Osterreichs. I. Niederösterreich.* Vienna: Böhlaus, 1969-.

       This series of studies of medieval Austrian libraries super-
       cedes the earlier series in item 466. Libraries are arranged
       geographically, e.g., Korneuburg. Indexes are provided.

       4. THE DISPERSAL AND LATER HISTORY OF MEDIEVAL LIBRARIES

486   Barratt, Dorothy M. "The Library of John Selden and Its Later
       History." *Bodleian Library Record*, 3 (1951), 128-42; 208-13;
       256-74.

       A description of Selden's manuscript collection, its provenance
       and later history.

487   *Book-Auction Records: A Priced and Annotated Annual Record of
       London and Other Book Auctions, June, 1902-.* London/New York:
       Henry Stevens, 1903.

       This auction record was published quarterly from 1902-40/41,
       but has appeared annually since 1941-42-. Entries are exact
       reproductions of the auctioneer's catalogue descriptions, and
       include name of buyer, date of sale, and price. Arrangement is
       alphabetical by author of the work sold. Each volume is indexed,
       with general indexes appearing since 1902.

488   Boyer, Blanche B. "Insular Contribution to Medieval Tradition on
       the Continent." *Classical Philology*, 42 (1947), 209-22, and 43
       (1948), 31-39.

This article describes Anglo-Saxon and Irish manuscripts found in continental libraries today. Among the author's interesting conclusions is the inference that these libraries contain twice the number of such manuscripts found in Great Britain.

489   British Library. *A List of Catalogues of English Book Sales, 1676-1900*. London: Trustees of the British Library, 1915.

An additional list of 23 items (1706-1840) has been published by A.I. Doyle, "Sale Catalogues," *Durham Philobiblon*, 1 (1951), 30-39.

Doyle, A.I. See item 489.

490   Hagen, Hermann, ed. *Catalogus Codicum Bernensium (Bibliotheca Bongarsiana)*. Hildesheim: G. Olms, 1974.

A summary catalogue of the library of Jacques Bongars (1554-1612), reprinted from the Bern (1875) edition.

491   James, M.R. *The Sources of Archbishop Parker's Collection of Manuscripts at Corpus Christi College, Cambridge, with a Reprint of the Catalogue of The Thomas Mark Library*. Cambridge: Printed for the Cambridge Antiquarian Society by Deighton, Bell, 1899.

An examination of the provenance of the Parker manuscripts with reference to early catalogues, inscriptions, and other information.

492   ————. *A List of Manuscripts Formerly Owned by Dr. John Dee*. *Supplements* to the Transactions of the Bibliographical Society, 1. London: The Society, 1921.

A reprint of the catalogue of Dee's manuscripts, from the autograph of 1583 and originally ed. J.O. Halliwell-Phillipps for the Camden Society in 1842.

493   ————. "The Manuscripts of St. George's Chapel, Windsor." *The Library*, 4th Ser., 13 (1932-3), 55-76.

A descriptive list of Chapter manuscripts given to the Bodleian Library, Oxford, in 1612, with an additional list of Chapter manuscripts presently in other locations. James also provides a brief history of the library. See also item 294.

494   Ker, N.R. "The Migration of Manuscripts from the English Medieval Libraries." *The Library*, 4th ser., 23 (1942-43), 1-11.

This article represents the best account of the dispersal of English manuscripts at the time of the Reformation. Among Ker's more interesting observations is that based upon a late fifteenth-century library catalogue of St. Augustine's, Canterbury. The catalogue, compared with surviving books, reveals that certain types of manuscripts were more likely to be retained in libraries than others, especially those which were historical, patristic, and biblical, while those containing scholastic, theological, philosophical, and legal matter were sooner dispersed and subsequently lost.

495   ——. *Records of All Souls College Library, 1437-1600*. London:
       Oxford University Press for the Oxford Bibliographical Society,
       1971.

       For Ker the All Souls Library is especially valuable in demon-
       strating how a *libraria* of manuscripts turns into a *bibliotheca*
       of printed books. He prints early lists and inventories, and
       later accessions to 1600. An appendix adds information on bind-
       ing, chaining, and shelf marks. An author/general index is pro-
       vided.

496   *Manuscript Collector's Directory*. New York, N.Y.: Manuscript
       Society, 1953-.

       This directory contains periodic information on sales and on
       the ownership of medieval and modern manuscripts.

497   McKay, George Leslie. *American Book Auction Catalogues, 1713-
       1934. A Union List*, introd. by Clarence S. Brigham. New York,
       N.Y.: New York Public Library, 1937; *Supplement*, 1946-48.

498   Munby, A.N.L. *The Catalogues and Printed Books of Sir Thomas
       Phillipps: Their Composition and Distribution*. Phillipps
       Studies, 1. Cambridge: University Press, 1951.

       A brief, descriptive list with some bibliographical notes.
       A fuller account of Phillipps' collecting habits and manuscripts
       is given in Munby's five volumes of studies, republished by
       Nicolas Barker as *Portrait of an Obsession* (New York, N.Y.:
       Putnam, 1967). See also items 231, 246, 284, 499-500.

499   ——. *Connoisseurs and Medieval Miniatures 1750-1850*. Oxford:
       Clarendon Press, 1972.

       An account of such collectors as Douce, Dibdin, Phillipps,
       and Sneyd, and their taste for medieval illuminated manuscripts;
       an index is provided for manuscripts.

500   Ricci, Seymour de. *English Collectors of Books and Manuscripts
       (1530-1930) and Their Marks of Ownership*. Cambridge: University
       Press, 1930/Bloomington, Ind.: University of Indiana Press,
       1960.

       The Sandars Lectures for 1929-30 on both periods of manuscript
       collecting and individual collectors, e.g., Harley, Beckford,
       Phillipps, and Halliwell. Provided are bibliographical notes and
       an index of names.

501   Rouse, Richard H., and Rouse, Mary A. "The Medieval Circulation
       of Cicero's 'Posterior Academics' and the *De Finibus Bonorum
       et Malorum*," in item 720, pp. 333-67.

       Although primarily concerned with the transmission and pro-
       liferation of Cicero's work, this study also discusses in general
       the circulation of certain manuscripts in the later Middle Ages.

502   Ullman, B.L., and Stadter, Philip A. *The Public Library of
       Renaissance Florence, Niccolò Niccoli, Cosimo de Medici and
       the Library of San Marco*. Padua: Antenore, 1972.

A history and description of several Florentine collections, ca. 1400-1500, with reference to the work of specific Humanists.

503 Watson, Andrew G. *The Manuscripts of Henry Savile of Banke.* London: Bibliographical Society, 1967.

An edition of Savile's manuscript catalogues, with annotations and indications of the present location of manuscripts if known.

504 ———. "Thomas Allen of Oxford and His Manuscripts," in item 720, pp. 279-314.

An account of Allen's collection, acquired from about 1570 to 1632 and now forming part of the Digby, Cotton, and other manuscript collections. Appended is a list of all known Allen manuscripts.

505 Whittaker, John. "Greek Manuscripts from the Library of Giles of Viterbo at the Biblioteca Angelica in Rome." *Scriptorium*, 31 (1977), 212-39.

506 Wright, C.E. "The Dispersal of the Libraries in the Sixteenth Century," in item 451, pp. 148-75.

A summary of the steps taken by Henry VIII to dissolve monastic houses and the resultant effect upon their library holdings.

507 ———. "The Dispersal of the Monastic Libraries and the Beginnings of Anglo-Saxon Studies." *Transactions of the Cambridge Bibliographical Society*, 1 (1949-53), 208-37.

This article focuses upon Archbishop Parker and his collection of manuscripts. The bibliography is a useful guide to further study of early English manuscripts in the sixteenth century.

508 ———. "Humfrey Wanley: Saxonist and Library Keeper." *Proceedings of the British Academy*, 46 (1960), 99-129.

An account of Wanley's interest in Anglo-Saxon manuscript and his catalogue published in 1705, his work on the Cotton manuscripts, and his position as library-keeper to Robert Harley. Some references are made to the provenance and techniques of cataloguing specific manuscripts in the Harleian collection, and the sources of information which Wright uses are largely Wanley's letters and diary; see next item.

509 ———, ed. *The Diary of Humfrey Wanley, 1715-26.* 2 vols. London: The Bibliographical Society, 1966.

An edition of Wanley's diary, outlining the acquisition of his manuscript collection. A general introduction to this edition is provided by the preceding item.

510 Young, P. *Catalogus Librorum Manuscriptorum Bibliothecae Wigorniensis, made in 1622-23*, ed. I. Atkins and N. Ker. Cambridge: University Press, 1944.

An edition of Young's manuscript catalogue for the Worcester Cathedral Library. See Ker's bibliography, item 720, for further studies on Young.

III. MICROFORMS

The references of this section are to materials available in a number of photographic forms. These include microfilm reels in both negative and positive, black and white or color, film strips, slides in black and white or color, microfiche and ultra microfiche cards, and shelf microfiche in case-bound volumes. The matter which these contain may be printed books, such as early printed editions or catalogues, or manuscripts. Individual photographic reproductions may be purchased for some manuscripts, while in other cases an entire manuscript collection may be examined by means of microfilm holdings made available through such institutions as the Knights of Columbus Vatican Film Library in St. Louis, Missouri.

CONTENTS

A. BIBLIOGRAPHICAL MATERIALS

511   Dodson, Suzanne Cates. *Microform Research Collections: A Guide*.
      Westport, Conn.: Microform Review, Inc., 1978.

      A useful bibliography of research collections available on
      microform; of special interest for paleographers are "Early
      English Books: Series 1475-1640" (based on Pollard and Redgrave);
      "The History of Medicine," p. 154; and "Italian Books Before
      1601," p. 178. A general index is included.

512   *Guide to Microforms in Print*, ed. John J. Walsh. Westport, Conn.:
      Microform Review, Inc., 1979. I. *Author*; II. *Subject*.

      A non-critical list of nearly all microforms, classified in
      two volumes according to author or subject.

513   Hale, Richard Walden, Jr. *Guide to Photographed Historical Mate-
      rials in the U.S. and Canada*. Ithaca, N.Y.: Cornell University
      Press, 1961.

      Sponsored by the American Historical Association and designed
      primarily for post-eighteenth-century historians, this guide also
      contains a list of microfilm and other resources relevant to
      earlier historical studies in Great Britain, pp. 16-18.

514   Library of Congress. *National Register of Microform Masters*.
      Washington, D.C.: Library of Congress, 1976-.

      This periodical register lists American library materials which
      have been filmed and for which master negatives exist. Volumes
      published in 1976 cover the period 1965-75. Arrangement is al-
      phabetical under author or title, with the libraries indicated.

515   Modern Language Association. *Reproductions of Manuscripts and
      Rare Printed Books*. Menasha, Wis.: George Banta, 1942; *PMLA*,
      65 (1950), 289-338.

      A short-title list of microfilms on deposit in the Library of
      Congress. These may be borrowed on inter-library loan.

516   National Microfilm Association. *Buyer's Guide to Microfilm and
      Equipment, Products, and Services*. Silver Spring, Md.: The
      Association, 1971-.

      An annual list of general microfilm resources and technical
      equipment.

517   Philadelphia Bibliographical Center and Union Library Catalogue
      Committee on Microphotography. *Union List of Microfilms*, ed.
      Eleanor Este Campion. Ann Arbor, Mich.: 1951; *Cumulation*,
      1949-59; rev. ed. 2 vols., 1961.

A comprehensive list of available microfilms, excluding newspapers, in 215 libraries. Arrangement is alphabetical by author,
with title entries for serial and anonymous works.

518   Reichmann, Felix, Tharpe, Josephine M., *et al. Bibliographic
       Control of Microforms*. The Association of Research Libraries.
       Westport, Conn.: The Association, 1972.

       This useful bibliographic work surveys microform problems in
       terms of production and distribution, then gives descriptive
       lists of microform resources; these are divided into four groups:
       (1) Catalogs and Lists, pp. 59-110; (2) Collections and Series,
       pp. 112-65; (3) Manuscript and Archival Collections, pp. 168-
       230; and (4) Reference Books, pp. 232-5. There are indexes to
       the microform bibliography and to literature on the subject.

519   *Servicio Nacional de Microfilm*. Madrid: Dirección General, 1953-.

       A periodic guide to Hispanic microfilm resources from library
       and archival collections. For other international guides, see
       items 512, 515, 517.

See also item 1842.

                B. *COMMERCIAL DISTRIBUTORS: A SELECTION*

520   *American Library Compendium and Index of World Art*. New York,
       N.Y.: The American Library Association, 1961-.

       An index of slides available for purchase. The collection in-
       cludes illuminated manuscripts.

521   Colour Centre Slides, Ltd. Farnham Royal, Slough, Bucks., England.

       A firm which produces slide-sets of British illuminated manu-
       scripts, such as the Eton Apocalypse and Chad Gospels. Sales
       catalogue available.

522   Delaurier, Nancy, ed. *Slide Buyers' Guide 1976*. 3rd ed. New York,
       N.Y.: College Art Association, 1976.

       A directory, issued approximately biannually, of suppliers of
       slides on the international market; the quality of each repro-
       duction is usually rated.

523   General Microfilm Co., 100 Inmann St., Cambridge, Mass.

       This firm produces a large number of microfilm series and
       editions on a wide range of subjects, e.g., Italian Drama and
       Scandinavia. Catalogue available.

524   Inter-Documentation Co., Zug, Switzerland.

       A firm which publishes a series of catalogues to their own
       microform series; these include the History of Art, Law, Medi-
       cine, and Musicology.

525   Micro Methods, Ltd., Bradford Road, East Ardsley, Wakefield,
       West Yorks., England.

       A general selection of microform reproductions is offered by
       this firm on genealogy, heraldry, history, art and art history,
       and social history. Catalogue available.

See also item 1764 for commercial advertisements.

C. LIBRARIES, ARCHIVES, SPECIAL COLLECTIONS, AND PROJECTS

1. GENERAL

526   Olevnik, Peter P. *Selected Medieval and Renaissance Manuscript
       Collections in Microform.* University of Illinois School of
       Library Science. Occasional Papers, 133. Urbana, Ill.: Uni-
       versity Press, 1978.

       A general survey of collections, with location, address, hours,
       borrowing and copying facilities, and catalogues or other bibli-
       ography. These include the Pontifical Institute of Mediaeval
       Studies, Toronto; Library of Congress; Jerusalem; St. Catherine's
       Monastery, Mount Sinai; Knights of Columbus Vatican Library, St.
       Louis, Mo.; Center for Reformation Research, St. Louis, Mo.;
       Ambrosiana Library, Notre Dame, Ind.; Hill Monastic Library, St.
       John's University, Collegeville, Minn.; and the Medieval Micro-
       film Project.

2. INDIVIDUAL COLLECTIONS AND PROJECTS

527   Ambrosiana Library, Notre Dame, Ind.

       The present collection of microforms of over 1000 manuscripts
       is housed in the Frank M. Folsom Library of the Medieval Insti-
       tute. The project, begun in 1962, was to microfilm the entire
       manuscript and archival collections of Cardinal Borromeo's
       library in Milan, Italy. Although there is an emphasis upon
       scientific manuscripts, the collection includes many on history,
       philosophy, theology, and literature. More recently the library
       has acquired microforms of medieval and Renaissance manuscripts
       from the Franciscan Library in Dubrovnik and the Metropolitan
       Catholic Library in Zagreb. An account of the project is given
       by Astrik L. Gabriel in "The Ambrosiana Microfilming Project:
       E.A. Lowe, the Ambrosiana of Milan and the Experiences of a
       Palaeographer," *Folia Ambrosiana*, 1 (1965); he has also published
       *A Summary Catalogue of Microfilms of One Thousand Scientific
       Manuscripts in the Ambrosiana Library, Milan* (Notre Dame, Ind.:
       The Medieval Institute, 1968). The *Folia Ambrosiana*, published
       irregularly (1965-), provides articles and information on the
       collection, acquisitions, and related research. See also item
       343.

528   American Historical Association, Committee on Documentary Re-
       production. *Reports*, Washington, D.C.: Government Printing
       Office, 1952-.

       A series of reports on the project of microfilming medieval
       manuscripts in European libraries, which was begun in 1946
       following the destruction of many European manuscripts through
       war damage. For an account of the phases and progress of this
       project, see Loren MacKinney, "Post War Microfilming of Medieval
       Research Material," *Speculum*, 37 (1962), 492-6, and Lester K.
       Born, *Unpublished Bibliographical Tools in Certain Archives
       and Libraries of Europe. A Partial List* (Washington, D.C.:
       Library of Congress, 1952). See also item 549.

529   Bibliothèque Nationale, Département des Manuscrits. *Les Trésors
       de la Bibliothèque Nationale*. Paris: Bibliothèque Nationale,
       n.d.

       A series of slides available for purchase in sets with accom-
       panying handbooks; most are of illuminated French manuscripts.

       Born, Lester K. See items 528, 531.

530   British Library, Department of Manuscripts. *Register of Micro-
       films and Other Photocopies in the Department of Manuscripts*.
       List and Index Society, 9. London: Swift, 1976.

       A list of microfilms made from British Library manuscripts,
       with a general index.

531   *British Manuscript Project: A Checklist of the Microfilms Pre-
       pared in England and Wales for the American Council of Learned
       Societies 1941-45*, ed. Lester K. Born. New York, N.Y.: ACLS,
       1955/1968; Washington, D.C.: Library of Congress, 1955/1968.

       A list of the contents of 2,652 reels of microfilm from manu-
       scripts in the major public and private collections of England
       and Wales; listing is alphabetical by name of depository, then
       by collection.

       Brumbaugh, Robert S. See item 551.

532   Centre National de la Recherche Scientifique, Paris, Institut
       de Recherche et d'Histoire des Textes.

       Established in 1937 as a collection of microfilms from mainly
       literary manuscripts in France, the collection is continually
       expanding to include manuscripts from all genres and periods;
       the Centre issues periodical reports on the collection in item
       1869, and cf. 648.

533   Clagett, Marshall. "Medieval Mathematics and Physics: A Check-
       list of Microfilm Reproductions." *Isis*, 44 (1955), 371-81.

       The checklist is representative of periodic lists and reports
       appearing in this journal on early science manuscripts repro-
       duced in microform. See item 1822.

       Clark, Kenneth W. See items 537, 543.

534   Essex Record Office, Microfilm Service, County Hall, Chelmsford, Essex, England.

The office provides lists of archival records available on microfilm, with prices and other information.

Hassall, W.O. See item 539.

535   Hughes, Andrew. *Preliminary List of the Music Microfilms in the Possession of Professor A.H. Hughes*. Toronto: Pontifical Institute of Mediaeval Studies: Typescript, n.d.

See item 1262.

536   Institute of Research and Study in Medieval Canon Law. "Collection of Photographic Reproductions from Manuscripts." *Traditio*, 1942-.

An annual bibliography of acquisitions and a critical account of research in progress on all aspects of medieval canon law; there are periodic cumulative lists. See also item 936.

537   Jerusalem, Libraries of the Greek and Armenian Patriarchates, Library of Congress, Washington, D.C.

The filming of manuscripts began in these libraries in 1949. The *Checklist of Manuscripts in the Libraries of the Greek and Armenian Patriarchates in Jerusalem*, ed. Kenneth W. Clark (Washington, D.C.: Library of Congress, 1953) provides an index and description of 998 manuscripts from the Library of the Greek Orthodox Patriarchate and 32 from the Armenian Patriarchate; the manuscripts were selected for reproduction under the auspices of the American School of Oriental Research.

538   Knights of Columbus Vatican Film Library, St. Louis University, St. Louis, Mo.

Begun in 1951, the collection now includes over 10,000 rolls of microfilm selected from manuscripts in the Vatican Library, Rome, and over 10,000 additional rolls microfilmed from printed books and other manuscripts; reproductions from Vatican Library manuscripts not included in this collection may be ordered; a slide library from illuminated manuscripts in the Vatican Library now consists of over 48,000 slides. A general description is by Charles J. Ermatinger, *The Knights of Columbus Vatican Film Library* (St. Louis, Mo.: Pius XII Memorial Library, Pamphlet, n.d.), and "Projects and Acquisitions in the Vatican Library," *Manuscripta*, 12 (1968), 170-75. Checklists of manuscripts have appeared in *Manuscripta*, 1957-. See items 390 and 1835.

Library of Congress, Washington, D.C. See item 550.

MacKinney, Loren. See items 528, 545.

539   *Medieval Manuscripts in Microform*. Toronto: University Press, 1979-.

A series of illuminated manuscripts on microfiche accompanied by a set of bibliographic microfiches. The first series, selected and introduced by W.O. Hassall, provides ten manuscripts from the Bodleian Library, Oxford.

540   Medieval Microfilm Project, Charles Patterson Van Pelt Library,
          University of Pennsylvania, Philadelphia, Pa.

          A project begun in 1972 under the chairmanship of Ruth J. Dean,
          which has created an archive, based upon specific requests, of
          medieval manuscript sources. The collection of approximately
          650 manuscripts includes Latin and most vernacular languages,
          with manuscripts dating from the twelfth century. A typescript
          inventory, *Three Inventories*, ed. Thomas Waldman (Philadelphia,
          Pa.: University of Philadelphia, n.d.), is available for the
          collection up to 1975.

541   Monastic Manuscript Microfilm Project, St. John's Abbey and
          University, Collegeville, Minn.

          The photographing of manuscripts in monastic collections began
          in 1964 under the direction of Oliver L. Kapsner, O.S.B.; it
          has now been nearly completed for the "Austrian Phase," see
          Julian G. Plante, *Monastic Manuscript Project: Progress Reports*
          (Collegeville, Minn.: St. John's College Press, 1966-74), and
          Checklist of Microfilms for the Monastic Microfilm Library,
          2 vols. (1967). Included among the nearly 30,000 microfilms are
          collections from Nonnberg (Abtei Salzburg), Kremünster, and
          Sankt Peter (Erzabtei Stiftsbibliothek, Salzburg), with some
          manuscripts from Maltese and Spanish collections recently added.
          See also item 724.

542   Mount Athos Manuscript Project, Library of Congress, Washington,
          D.C.

          The microfilms of select manuscripts from the monasteries of
          Mount Athos, Greece, have been filmed for the Library of Congress
          and the International Greek New Testament Project, 1952-53.
          A Descriptive Checklist has been compiled by Ernest W. Saunders
          and Charles G. LaHood, Jr. (Washington, D.C.: Library of Congress
          Photoduplication Services, 1957) in two parts: part 1 lists and
          describes the manuscripts, while part 2 lists photocopies and
          where these are available. See item 550, and cf. item 379.

543   Mount Sinai, Saint Catherine's Monastery, Library of Congress,
          Washington, D.C.

          This collection forms part of the Jerusalem project begun in
          1950 (see item 537) and includes manuscripts from the fourth to
          sixteenth centuries. They are listed by Kenneth W. Clark in
          *Checklist of Manuscripts in Saint Catherine's Monastery, Mount
          Sinai* (Washington, D.C.: Library of Congress, 1952). See also
          item 550.

544   National Library of Medicine. *A Summary Checklist of Medical
          Manuscripts on Microfilm Held by the National Library of Medi-
          cine*. Bethesda, Md.: U.S. Department of Health, Education and
          Welfare, n.d.

          The medieval medical manuscripts in this collection are also
          listed and described in item 394.

545 North Carolina, University of, Manuscript Division, Ackland Art
     Library, Wilson Library, Chapel Hill, N.C.

     A microfilm and slide collection of mainly medieval, illuminated
     manuscripts, originally compiled by Loren C. MacKinney; a *Check-
     list* has been prepared by Michael McVaugh, available in the li-
     brary; see also item 1156.

546 Ohlgren, Thomas C., with pref. by W.O. Hassall. *Illuminated
     Manuscripts: An Index to Selected Bodleian Library Color Re-
     productions*. New York, N.Y.: Garland Publishing, Inc., 1977.

     A catalogue and index of 500 slide sets of manuscripts and
     books in the Bodleian Library, Oxford, with information about
     the subjects and indications whether slides may be purchased
     directly or rented from Purdue University, Lafayette, Ind.
     *Illuminated Manuscripts and Books in the Bodleian Library: A
     Supplemental Index* (1979) provides an extended reference cata-
     logue. See also item 539 and cf. 1092.

     Pennsylvania, University of. See item 540.

     Plante, Julian G. See items 541, 724.

     Plato Microfilm Project. See item 551.

547 Pontifical Institute of Mediaeval Studies, Toronto, Canada.

     The Gordon Taylor Microfilm Collection, part of the library
     of the Pontifical Institute and housed in the St. Michael's
     College Library, contains some 4,500 reels of microfilm repre-
     senting nearly 4,000 manuscripts and 500 books. The emphasis
     is upon theological and philosophical works, but the collection
     includes liturgical, historical, legal, and literary manuscripts.
     About 10% of the items are listed in the PIMS *Catalogue*, item
     401, while all items are represented in the card catalogue in
     the library; listing is by author, title, library, and incipit.
     For an account of the development and principles of selection
     see R.J. Scollard, "A List of Photographic Reproductions of
     Medieval Manuscripts in the Library of the Pontifical Institute
     of Mediaeval Studies," *Mediaeval Studies*, 4 (1942), 126-38, and
     5 (1943), 51-74; periodic reports appear in subsequent issues.

548 Public Record Office, London, England.

     The PRO issues periodic catalogues of available microfilms from
     documents in this repository. Some descriptive details about
     date, provenance, and bibliography are included.

     Purdue University, Lafayette, Ind. See item 546.

     Saunders, Ernest W. See item 542.

     Scollard, R.J. See item 547.

549 Ullmann, B.L. "Liaison Committee on Microfilming Manuscript
     Catalogues." *Renaissance News*, 7 (1954), 156-60.

A report on microfilms of library catalogues from Italian and Austrian libraries. These are now located in, or obtainable from, the Library of Congress, Washington, D.C. See item 550.

Vatican Library, St. Louis, Mo. See item 538.

Waldman, Thomas. See item 540.

550   Washington, D.C., Library of Congress, Microform Reading Room.

In addition to the microfilms of items 537 and 542-3, this collection includes microforms from manuscript and archival collections from the British Manuscript Project (item 531) and inventories of Latin manuscript books from German, Austrian, and Italian libraries, including the Pandects of the Notaries of Genoa to 1300. Further information appears periodically in the *Quarterly Journal of the Library of Congress*, 1943-. See also item 549.

Wells, Rulon. See item 551.

551   Yale University Library, New Haven, Conn., Plato Microfilm Project.

A project undertaking the microfilming of all pre- and post-1600 Plato manuscripts; for a description see Robert S. Brumbaugh and Rulon Wells, eds., *Plato Manuscripts: A Catalogue of Microfilms in the Plato Microfilm Project, Yale University Library*, 2 vols. (New Haven, Conn.: Yale University Press, 1962), and *The Plato Manuscripts: A New Index* (1968). The listing is by country, then city and library, then manuscript in order within collection; entries are numbered, with reference provided to film and reel number; a cumulative index by *Dialogues* is provided in the *Catalogue*, pt. II; supplementary indexes for the 1968 *New Index* refer to collated manuscripts and papyri. See also items 561, 588.

See also item 388.1.

IV. INCIPITS

The books, articles, and separates cited in this section contain *incipits* or *initia* of published and unpublished manuscripts. While many of the library catalogues
cited in Section II also include *incipits/explicits*,
the works listed here establish the initial line or
phrase of a text as a means of identification or generic
grouping.

CONTENTS

A. BIBLIOGRAPHICAL MATERIALS

552 Pelzer, Auguste. *Répertoire d'incipit pour la littérature latine philosophique et theologique du moyen âge*. 2nd ed. Rome: Edizioni di Storia e Letteratura, 1951.

This work is the only critical bibliography to appear thus far of books and articles devoted to *incipits*. Arrangement is alphabetical by topic, Adam de Bocfeld to Thomas Aquinas.

B. INDIVIDUAL COLLECTIONS

553 Barre, Henry. *Les Homeliaires carolingians de l'école d'Auxerre: authenticité-inventaire-tables comparatifs-initia*. Studi i Texti, 225. Rome: Vatican, 1962.

A list of Carolingian homilaries, localized in the School of Auxerre, with a list of sermon *incipits*, pp. 137-344.

554 Bloomfield, Morton W.; Guyot, Bertrand-Georges; Howard, Donald R.; and Kabealo, Thyra B. *Incipits of Latin Works on the Virtues and Vices, 1100-1500 A.D.: Including a Section of Incipits of Works on the Pater Noster*. Mediaeval Academy of America Publications, 88. Cambridge, Mass.: The Academy, 1979.

The incipits are arranged alphabetically, with serial numbers. Listed are manuscripts, editions, and cross references to alternate forms. Provided are extensive author/title/subject/location indexes.

555 Brown, Carleton. *Register of Middle English Religious Verse*. 2 vols. The Index Society. New York, N.Y.: Columbia University Press for the Society, 1916.

Vol. 1 contains descriptive lists of manuscripts containing Middle English verse, arranged by library collection; incipits are provided for each poem. Vol. 2 is a first-line index of Middle English verse, arranged alphabetically by first word. See also items 556 and 624.

556 ————, and Robbins, Rossell Hope. *The Index of Middle English Verse*. The Index Society. New York, N.Y.: Columbia University Press for the Society, 1943. *Supplement*, ed. Rossell Hope Robbins and J.L. Cutler. Lexington, Ky.: University of Kentucky Press, 1965.

A continuation of the preceding item, which adds about 900 more manuscripts. Arrangement is by first-line verse, in alphabetical order. Included are brief descriptions of the work and some bibliographical references. The indexes include works and lists of manuscripts.

557   Bursill-Hall, G.L. "A Check-List of Incipits of Medieval Latin Grammatical Treatises: A-G." *Traditio*, 34 (1978), 439-74.

The first in a series of checklists, which specify manuscript and bibliographical references. See also item 655.

558   Carboni, Fabio. *Inciptario della Livica italiana dei secoli XIII e XIV*. I. *Biblioteca Apostolica Vaticana*. Studi e Testi, 277. Rome: Vatican, 1977.

The first volume of this proposed survey of Livy manuscripts lists the manuscripts in the Vatican Library. Given are item number, incipit, manuscripts, and bibliographical references.

559   Clement, J.-M. *Initia Patrum Latinorum*. Turnhout: Typographi Brépols, 1971.

This work represents volume 2 in the *Corpus Christianorum* series. It provides an invaluable aid to the identification of Patristic texts, especially those edited in the series; incipits are listed in alphabetical order following a general index of authors and the volumes of the series in which they appear.

Glorieux, P. See item 566.

560   Hauréau, J.B. *Initia Operam Scriptorum Latinorum*. 6 vols. *Appendices*. Turnhout: Typographi Brépols, 1974.

An anastatically reprinted edition of the 4,600pp. of the Vatican copy, ca. 1880. Hauréau's handwritten entries, arranged alphabetically with notes on manuscripts and bibliography, have been supplemented with the incipits of manuscripts in Munich, Göttingen, and Brussels by A.G. Schmeller and G. Meyer.

561   Heusde, Philips Willem van. *Initia Philosophiae Platonicae*. 5 vols. Rhenum: J. Altheer, 1827-36.

A comprehensive index to the incipits of all Platonic dialogues. For a more up-to-date version, see item 551.

562   Kantorowicz, H. *Copy of a Card Index of Law Manuscripts*. Oxford: Bodleian Library, Typescript, n.d.

This brief, typescript list available in the Bodleian Library provides an alphabetical list of incipits from legal texts, mainly in that library. See also item 638.

563   Långfors, Artur. *Les Incipit des poèmes français antérieurs au XVIe siècle*. Paris: 1918/Geneva: Slatkine Reprints, 1977.

A detailed, critical list of incipits to French poems before 1500, exclusive of lyrics and *chansons de geste*. Arrangement is alphabetical by first word, separate lists of manuscripts are provided.

564   Little, A.G. *Initia Operum Latinorum Quae Saeculis XIII, XIV,*
      XV Attribuntur Secundum Ordinem Alphabeticum Deposita. Man-
      chester: University Press, 1904.

      This work lists over 9,000 incipits based upon manuscript
      collections in Oxford and Cambridge libraries.

565   Migne, J.-P. *Patrologiae Cursus Completus. Series Graeca.* 166
      vols. Petit-Montrouge: J.-P. Migne, 1857-66; *Indexes*, 3 vols.,
      1912-39.

      This standard and well-known series of Patristic texts has
      been concluded by three volumes of first-line and other indexes,
      including author and subject. References are to volume number
      and column.

566   ————. *Patrologiae Cursus Completus. Series Latinae.* 221 vols.
      Paris: J.-P. Migne, 1844-64.

      The Latin Patristic series concludes with four volumes of
      indexes for first lines and subjects, 1862-64, and reprinted
      separately as the *Index Alphabeticus* (Farnborough: Gregg Press,
      1965). For critical commentary on this index see P. Glorieux,
      Pour revaloriser Migne: tables rectificatives, Mélanges de
      Science Religieux, Cahier Suppl. (Lille: Facultés Catholiques,
      1952).

567   Mohan, Gaudens, E. "Incipits of Logical Writings of the XIIIth-
      XVth Centuries." *Franciscan Studies*, 12 (1952), 349-89.

568   ————. "Incipits of Philosophical Writings in Latin of the
      XIIIth-XVth Centures." St. Bonaventure, N.Y.: The Franciscan
      Institute, Typescript, n.d.

      Both works provide lists of incipits of Latin writings on
      Logic and Philosophy for this period, with some bibliographical
      references. See item 570.

569   Schaller, Dieter, and Konsgen, Ewald. *Initia Latinorum Saeculo*
      Undecimo Antiquorum: Bibliographisches Repertorium für die
      lateinische Dichtung der antike und des früheren Mittelalters.
      Göttingen: Vandenhoeck and Ruprecht, 1977.

      An invaluable first-line index of pre-eleventh-century Latin
      verse, with bibliographical references. No indexes are provided.

570   Schelling, Friedrich Wilhelm Joseph von. *Initia Philosophiae*
      Universae. 5th ed. (from 1820) by Horst Fuhrmans. Bonn:
      H. Bouvier, 1969.

      A comprehensive list of incipits to philosophical manuscripts,
      with bibliographical references. See also item 568.

571   Silvestre, H. "Les *Incipits* des oeuvres scientifiques latines
      du moyen âge, à propos du nouveau Thorndike-Kibre." *Scriptorium*,
      19 (1965), 273-8.

      A significant review of item 574, which suggests additions
      and further bibliography.

572   Sonet, Jean, S.J. *Répertoire d'incipit de prières en ancien
       français.* Société de Publications Romanes et Françaises, 54.
       Geneva: E. Droz, 1956.

       A list of incipits to French poems to ca. 1500. Indexes are
       provided for authors/titles/subjects. See items 632-3 for
       corrections and additions.

573   Tenneroni, Annibale. *Inizii di antiche poesie italiane religiose
       e morali, con prospetto dei condici ehe le contengono e
       introduzione alle 'Laudi Spirituali.'* Florence: Leo S. Olschki,
       1909.

       A first-line index of medieval Italian religious and moral
       poetry, preceded by a table of manuscripts and followed by a
       survey of manuscripts containing the *Laudi Spirituale.*

574   Thorndike, Lynn, and Kibre, Pearl. *Catalogue of Incipits of
       Mediaeval Scientific Writings in Latin.* Cambridge, Mass.:
       Mediaeval Academy of America, 1937; rev. ed. 1963.

       An invaluable alphabetical list of incipits, with manuscripts,
       of all medieval scientific Latin works. After its original publi-
       cation and subsequent revision, Thorndike added the following:
       "Additional *Incipits* of Mediaeval Scientific Writings in Latin,"
       Speculum, 14 (1939), 93-105; "Further *Incipits* of Mediaeval
       Scientific Writings in Latin," *Speculum,* 26 (1951), 673-95;
       "Additional Addenda," *Speculum,* 40 (1965), 116-22; and "Further
       Addenda and Corrigenda," *Speculum,* 43 (1968), 78-114. See also
       item 571.

575   Viveil, Coelestinus, O.S.B. *Initia Tractatuum Musices ex Codici-
       bus Editionis.* Graz: J. Meyerhoff, 1912.

       An alphabetical, first-line index of musical treatises; some
       bibliographical references to printed editions. Indexes are
       provided.

576   Walther, Hans, and Hilka, Alfons, eds. *Initia Carminum ac Versum
       Medii Aevi Posterioris Latinorum: Alphabetisches Verzeichnis
       der Versanfänoe mittellateinischer Dichtungen.* Carmina Medii
       Aevi Posterioris Latina, 1. Göttingen: Vandenhoeck and Ruprecht,
       1959.

577   ――――. *Ergänzungen und Berichtigungen zur 1. Auflage von 1959.*
       Göttingen: Vandenhoeck and Ruprecht, 1969.

       The *Initia* contains incipits from over 22,000 Latin poems, both
       edited and unedited, with bibliographical references to manu-
       scripts, editions, and other related poems. The general bibliog-
       raphy which concludes the work and the author/subject index are
       valuable assets, and the *Ergänzungen* adds additional references
       and corrections; for more of these, see R.W. Hunt, "Additions,"
       Oxford: Bodleian Library, Typescript, 1960, and "Nachträge,"
       Mittellateinisches Jahrbuch, 7 (1972), 273-344, and 9 (1973),
       320-44.

V. SPECIAL SUBJECTS: INDEXES, LISTS, CATALOGUES, AND REPERTORIA

The following items are lists, catalogues, or other types of *repertoria* of manuscripts selected on the basis of subject rather than library collection. In these some critical commentary and bibliography may be included, possibly first-line indexes as well, but the object of such works is to cite all known manuscripts of an individual text, of a particular *corpus*, or on a special subject. Obviously there is some overlap with certain titles in Sections II and IV, but the selections here are made for the convenience of the paleographer who might wish to check, for example, the possible (and indeed probable) existence of manuscripts within a similar textual tradition. Obviously some titles cannot be considered indexes or *repertoria* strictly speaking, but for the sake of convenience they are included for those areas in which no adequate *repertorium* of manuscripts exists.

CONTENTS

A. GENERAL AND LATIN

578   Faider, Paul. *Répertoire des éditions de scolies et commentaires d'auteurs latins.* Paris: Société d'Edition Les Belles-Lettres, 1931; Toronto: PIMS, 1974.

A brief (48pp.) bibliography of scolia, which lists manuscripts and edition.

579   Number deleted.

See also item 43.

B. GREEK

580   Aland, Karl, ed. *Repertorium der griechischen christlichen Papyri.* I. *Biblische Papyri.* Patristische Texte und Studien, 18.1. Berlin: De Gruyter, 1975-.

This series of descriptive catalogues for papyrus manuscripts includes bibliographical references. Arrangement is by generic group. An index is provided.

581   *Berichtegungsliste der griechischen Papyrusurkunden aus Ägypten,* ed. Friedrich Preisigke, *et al.* Vols. 1-3. Berlin: De Gruyter, 1922-33; vols. 3-6, Leiden: E.J. Brill, 1958/1976.

A descriptive catalogue for Egyptian papyri. Arrangement is by collection and bibliographical references to editions are provided.

582   Coles, Revel A. *Location-List of the Oxyrhynchus Papyri and of Other Greek Papyri.* The Egypt Exploration Society. London: The Society, 1974.

This work amalgamates information provided in *The Oxyrhynchus Papyri,* with corrections and supplements. It lists institutions (with addresses) holding published Oxyrhynchus and other papyri. The papyri are listed with reference to location and catalogue.

583   Gardthausen, Viktor. *Sammlungen und Kataloge griechischer Handschriften.* Byzantinisches Archiv, 3. Leipzig: Teubner, 1903/Aalen: Scientia Verlag, 1974.

A descriptive catalogue of Greek manuscripts from various
periods and provenances. Arrangement is by library. Bibliographical references and indexes are provided.

584   Lietzmann, Johannes, ed. *Tabulae in Usum Scholarum*. Bonn: Marcus
      and Weber, 1911-30.

      A series of catalogues by different hands on specific groups
      of Greek manuscripts, e.g., I. *Specima Codicum Graecorum Vatican-
      orum*, ed. P. Franchi de Cavalieri and Johannes Lietzmann (1929).

585   Lobel, E. *The Greek Manuscripts of Aristotle's 'Poetics.'*
      Supplement to the Transactions of the Bibliographical Society,
      10. London: The Society, 1935.

      A survey of manuscripts containing the *Poetics*, with critical
      commentary and bibliographical references.

586   Moraux, Paul, *et al.*, eds. *Aristotles Graecus: Die griechischen
      Manuskripte des Aristotles*. Berlin: De Gruyter, 1976.

      This important descriptive catalogue of the Greek texts of
      Aristotle's works is arranged alphabetically by location of
      library, Alexandria-London; an index of Aristotle's works with
      lists of manuscripts is included. The Aristotle Archives, Berlin,
      of which Moraux is director, publishes widely on the Aristo-
      telian textual tradition; see pp. xxi-xxxii of this item; for
      Latin manuscripts, see below, items 680, 682, and cf. item 591.

587   O'Callaghan, J. "Las colecciones españolas de papiros." *Studies
      in Papyrology*, 15 (1976), 95-102.

      A bibliographical survey of papyri in Spanish libraries. The
      article is representative of periodical lists appearing in this
      journal on special subjects.

588   Post, L.A. *The Vatican Plato and Its Relations*. Middletown,
      Conn.: The American Philological Association, 1934.

      This survey was used as one of the bases for the Plato Micro-
      film Project; see item 551.

      Preisgke, F. See item 581.

589   Richard, Marcel. *Répertoire des Bibliothèques et des catalogues
      de manuscrits grecs*. 2nd ed. Paris: CNRS, 1958.

      A comprehensive survey of all Greek manuscripts, arranged
      geographically by location. Bibliographic references include
      other manuscript catalogues. A concordance of entry numbers
      refers to the first edition of 1948. A general index is provided.

590   Turyn, Alexander. *Dated Greek Manuscripts of the Thirteenth and
      Fourteenth Centuries in the Libraries of Italy*. 2 vols. Urbana,
      Ill.: University of Illinois Press, 1972.

      This is a fully descriptive catalogue of dated Greek manuscript
      in Italian libraries, which indicates criteria for dating and

offers some bibliographical reference. Arrangement is alphabetical by city and collection; see also item 353.

591   Wartell, André. *Inventaire des manuscrits grecs d'Aristote et de ses commentateurs.* Collection d'Etudes Anciennes. Paris: Société d'Edition Les Belles-Lettres, 1963.

A list of manuscripts with brief descriptions and bibliography. Arrangement is alphabetical by geographical location of library. Indexes are provided for works and commentaries. See item 586.

See also items 45, 224, 265, 268, 335, 345, 353, 366, 433, 505, 537, 542-3, 551, 689, 691, 871-2, 1424.

C. PATRISTIC

592   Hoste, Anselm. *Bibliotheca Aelrediana: A Survey of the Manuscripts, Old Catalogues, Editions and Studies Concerning St. Aelred of Rievaulx.* Instrumenta Patristica, 2. The Hague: M. Nijhoff, 1962.

This work was compiled as a preface to the *Opera Omnia*, ed. F.M. Powicke, C.H. Talbot, and C. Dumont. It includes a classified bibliography, list of manuscripts with incipits/explicits, and general indexes.

593   Laistner, M.L.W., and King, H.H. *A Hand-List of Bede Manuscripts.* Ithaca, N.Y., Cornell University Press, 1943.

For a list of additions, corrections, and revisions to this work see W.F. Bolton, "A Bede Bibliography: 1935-1960," *Traditio*, 18 (1962), 438.

594   Lambert, Bernard. *Bibliotheca Hieronymiana Manuscripta. La Tradition manuscrite des oeuvres de Saint Jérôme.* Instrumenta Patristica, 4. 4 vols. Steenburgh: M. Nijhoff, 1969-70.

A descriptive list, with bibliographical references, of manuscripts containing the work of St. Jerome. For an extensive expansion, see Johannes D.-F. Römer, "Ergänzungen zur *Bibliotheca Hieronymiana Manuscripta*," *Scriptorium*, 30 (1976), 85-113.

595   Schenkl, Heinrich. *Bibliotheca Patrum Latinorum Britannica.* Sitzungsberichte der Philosophisch-historischen Klasse Kaiserlichen Akademie der Wissenschaften. Vienna: The Academy, 1891-1905.

A descriptive list of works and manuscripts of Patristic writings in British libraries. It is arranged by library, beginning with the Bodleian, Oxford. Bibliography is not included. A list of incipits and title/author index conclude.

See also items 573-4, 1676-81.

D. RELIGIOUS

1. BIBLICAL

596   Lampe, G.W.H., ed. *The Cambridge History of the Bible.* 3 vols.
       I. *From the Beginnings to Jerome*; II. *The West from the Fathers
       to the Reformation*; III. *The West from the Reformation to the
       Present Day.* Cambridge: University Press, 1963-69.

       This massive textual history of the Bible provides descriptive
       lists of manuscripts and accounts of their transmission. A
       bibliography for interpretive and exegetical studies is also in-
       cluded.

597   McGurk, Patrick. *Latin Gospel Books from A.D. 400 to A.D. 800.*
       Les Publications de Scriptorium, 5. Paris/Brussels: Editions
       Erasme, 1961.

       A careful account of the "architecture," i.e., the script, for-
       mat, contents, of Latin Gospel books of the period. Nearly all
       are of insular origin. Included are an invaluable catalogue of
       manuscripts and a list of incipits.

598   Metzger, Bruce M. *The Text of the New Testament. Its Transmission,
       Corruption, and Restoration.* 2nd ed. (from 1964). Oxford:
       Clarendon Press, 1968.

       A general, textual history of the Bible with reference to
       manuscripts. Metzger has published many studies and reference
       works on biblical manuscripts and studies, see the biblical
       bibliographies listed in Section I.6.

599   Stegmüller, F. *Repertorium Biblicum Medii Aevi.* Consejo Superior
       de Investigaciones Científicas, Inst. Francisco Suarez. 7 vols.
       Madrid: The Institute, 1950-61.

       A list of all medieval works both biblical and related to
       biblical studies; volume 1 gives *initia biblica*, *apocrypha*, and
       prologi; volumes 2-5 list *commentaria: auctores*; volumes 6-7
       commentaria: anonyma; arrangement is alphabetical by place of
       publication; included are incipits/explicits, editions, manu-
       scripts, and bibliographies. A detailed list of commentators on
       Rom. 13.1-7, with manuscripts and bibliographical references,
       is found in Werner Affeldt's "Verzeichnis der Römerbriefkommen-
       tare der lateinische Kirche bis zu Nikolaus von Lyra," *Traditio*,
       13 (1957), 369-406, with correlations to Stegmuller's *Repertorium.*

2. LITURGICAL

600   Amiet, Robert. *Repertorium Liturgicum Augustanum: Les témoins
       de la liturgie du diocèse d'Aoste.* Monumenta Liturgica Ecclesiae
       Augustannae, 1-2. Aoste: Typo-Offset Musumeci, 1974.

       A descriptive catalogue of manuscripts to the Diocese of Aosta,
       Italy, which contain liturgy. Includes some bibliographical
       references.

601   Austin, Gerard. "Liturgical Manuscripts in the United States and
       Canada." *Scriptorium*, 28 (1974), 82-100.

       A general introduction summarizes genres and their distribu-
       tion throughout North America; this is followed by a descriptive
       catalogue of manuscripts by library collection, arranged chrono-
       logically for the eighth to twelfth centuries.

602   Chevalier, Ulysse. *Repertorium Hymnologicum: Catalogue des chants,
       hymnes, proses, sequences, tropes en usage dans l'église latine
       depuis les origines jusqu'à nos jours.* Subsidia Hagiographica,
       4. 6 vols. Louvain: Lefèvres, 1892-1921/1959.

       A descriptive catalogue of the types of liturgical music,
       arranged by category and with reference to manuscripts. Indexes
       are provided.

603   Eizenhöfer, Leo, and Knaus, Hermann. *Die liturgischen Hand-
       schriften der Hessischen Landes- und Hochschulbibliothek
       Darmstadt.* Wiesbaden: Harrassowitz, 1968.

       Volume 2 of the Darmstadt Series, see items 625-6. This work
       describes liturgical manuscripts in the regional libraries and
       includes a useful table of manuscripts classified by generic
       type, e.g., sacramentary.

604   Gamber, Klaus, ed. *Codices Liturgici Latini Antiquiores.*
       Spicilegii Friburgensis, Subsidia 1. Fribourg: University
       Press, 1968.

       A descriptive catalogue of liturgical manuscripts, arranged
       according to generic type, e.g., the *Sacramentaria Gregoriana*.
       It includes bibliographies, notes, and indexes.

605   Leisibach, Josef. *Die liturgischen Handschriften der Kantons-
       und Universitätsbibliothek Freiburg.* Fribourg: University
       Press, 1976.

       This work provides a descriptive catalogue of liturgical manu-
       scripts from Canton Fribourg. Arrangement is by canton library,
       genre, and date. Included are *incipits* and a name/subject index.

606   Leroquais, Victor. *Les Bréviares manuscrits des bibliothèques
       publiques de France.* 6 vols. Paris: Prôtat Frères, 1934.

       This series includes the following two items. The introduc-
       tion to each volume gives an historical account of types of

service books. Arrangement within the catalogue proper is by
location and collection. A portfolio of plates is included for
each volume. Other volumes in the series include item 229.

607   ————. *Les Psaultiers manuscrits latin des bibliothèques
       publiques de France.* 3 vols. Macon: Prôtat Frères, 1940-41.

       See preceding item.

608   ————. *Les Sacramentaires et les missels manuscrits des
       bibliothèques publiques en France.* 4 vols. Paris: Prôtat
       Frères, 1924; *Supplément*, 1943.

       See item 606.

609   McRoberts, David. *Catalogue of Scottish Medieval Liturgical
       Books and Fragments.* Glasgow: John S. Burns and Sons, 1953.

       A revised and augmented catalogue reprinted from the *Innes
       Review*, 3 (1952), which provides a short, descriptive list with
       some illustrations. Arrangement is by genre, e.g., service books,
       inventories, then chronological by date of manuscript.

See also items 229, 283, 336, 344, 350, 1184, 1263, 1278-9, 1688,
and 1699.

3. HOMILETIC AND PENITENTIAL

610   Caplan, Harry. *Medieval Artes Praedicandi: A Handlist.* Cornell
       Studies in Classical Philology, 24. Ithaca, N.Y.: Cornell
       University Press, 1934; *A Supplementary Handlist*, 1936.

       A handlist of treatises on preaching, their manuscripts, and
       brief bibliography. For reference to and expansion of many of
       these entries, see the author's collected essays, *Of Eloquence*,
       ed. A. King and H. North (Ithaca, N.Y.: Cornell University
       Press, 1970).

611   Casutt, Laurentius. *Die Handschriften mit lateinischen Predigten
       Bertholds von Regensburg.* Freiburg: University Press, 1961.

       A list of manuscripts containing homiletic writings by
       Berthold von Regensburg with brief notes. Arrangement is by city
       and library.

612   Grégoire, Réginald. *Les Homiliares du moyen âge. Rerum ecclesi-
       asticarum documenta*, fontes 6. Rome: Herder, 1966.

       This work provides an invaluable introduction to homiletics,
       their rhetorical techniques and sources, as well as lists of
       manuscripts and indexes of incipits.

613   Hudson, Anne, ed. *Selections from English Wycliffite Writings.*
       Cambridge: University Press, 1978.

While primarily a collection of edited texts from sermons and other material, the work also gives a list of manuscripts, manuscript catalogues, and other works relating to Wycliff studies.

614   McNeill, J.T., and Gamer, Helena M. *Medieval Handbooks of Penance.* New York, N.Y.: Columbia University Press, 1938.

A translation of the principal *libri poenitentiales* and selections from related documents: those omitted but considered important are listed pp. 432-50. A list of manuscripts, select bibliography, and indexes are included.

615   Michaud-Quantin, Pierre. *Sommes de casuistique et manuels de confession au moyen âge (XII-XVI siècles).* Analecta Mediaevalia Namurcensia, 13. Louvain: Nauwelaerts, 1962.

This work provides a general introduction and summaries of works by Alain de Lille, Raymond de Pennafort, Jean de Fribourg, and others. The notes are especially rich with reference to medieval canon law, and a bibliography, first-line index, and general index are included.

616   Mosher, Joseph A. *The Exemplum in the Early Religious and Didactic Literature of England.* New York, N.Y.: Columbia University Press, 1911/New York, N.Y.: AMS Press, 1966.

Mosher defines the genre with a survey of documents to ca. 1500. Bibliography and indexes are provided.

617   Owst, Gerald K. *Literature and Pulpit in Medieval England. A Neglected Chapter in the History of English Letters and of the English People.* 2nd rev. ed. (from 1933). Oxford: Basil Blackwell, 1966.

An expansion of the next item, which provides further study of homiletic works, based upon a survey of extant manuscripts, many of them unpublished and all of them listed in the footnotes.

618   ————. *Preaching in Medieval England: An Introduction to Sermon Manuscripts of the Period, c. 1350-1450.* Cambridge: University Press, 1926/New York, N.Y.: Russell and Russell, 1965.

An account, documented from manuscripts and other sources, of the techniques of medieval preaching in England, their manuals and treatises. Manuscripts are listed in the footnotes and again in the index.

619   Pfander, H.G. "Some Medieval Manuals of Religious Instruction in England and Observations on Chaucer's Parson's Tale." *JEGP*, 35 (1936), 243-58.

A general survey of the more important manuals, such as the *Templum Domini, Oculus Sacerdotis, Speculum Christiani, Poor Caitif,* and others, with reference to manuscripts and printed editions.

Schmitt, J.-C. See item 623.

620   Schneyer, Johann Baptist. *Repertorium der lateinischen Sermones
       des Mittelalters für die Zeit von 1150-1350.* Freiburg-im-
       Breisgau/Münster: Aschendorffsche Verlagsbuchhandlung, 1969-75.

       A series of sermons, cited by author in alphabetical order,
       with manuscripts and bibliography.

621   ————. *Wegweiser zu lateinischen Predigtreihen des Mittelalters.*
       Bayerische Akademie der Wissenschaften, 1. Munich: C.H. Beck
       for the Academy, 1965.

       This and the preceding item provide excellent guides to medi-
       eval Latin sermons. After a general introduction, an index of
       themata follows (mostly the initial biblical text), then incipits
       alphabetically arranged to individual sermons. All four cate-
       gories of sermons are included (*sermones de tempore, de sanctis,
       de communi sanctorum,* and *de quadragesima*). When possible, details
       of authorship, editions, and secondary matter are included.

622   Tubach, Frederic C. *Index Exemplorum: A Handbook of Medieval
       Religious Tales.* Helsinki: Suomalainen Tiedeakatemia, 1969.

       An alphabetical index to common exempla, with bibliographical
       details on manuscripts, editions, and studies.

623   Welter, J.-T. *L'Exemplum de la littérature religieuse et didac-
       tique du moyen âge.* Paris: 1927/Geneva: Slatkine Reprints,
       1973.

       A descriptive account of representative *exempla* collections,
       with an inventory of manuscripts, bibliography of printed edi-
       tions, index, and a *Tabula exemplorum secundum ordinem alphabeti*
       edited from a thirteenth-century manuscript. Providing useful
       chronological and geographical tables in connection with this
       work is J.-C. Schmitt, "Recueils françiscains d'Exempla,"
       Bibliothèque de l'Ecole de Chartes, 135 (1977), 5-21.

624   Wenzel, Siegfried. *Verses in Sermons: Fasciculus Morum and Its
       Middle English Poems.* Mediaeval Academy of America Publica-
       tions, 87. Cambridge, Mass.: Mediaeval Academy of America,
       1978.

       After a general introduction and bibliography on the *Fasciculus
       Morum,* a Franciscan preachers' manual from the first half of
       the fourteenth century, Wenzel describes the 28 manuscripts and
       provides an edition of the Middle English verses. Included are
       a subject/author index, an index of first lines in Middle
       English and Latin, and a list of manuscripts.

See also items 141, 1701

4. DEVOTIONAL

625   Achten, Gerard, and Kraus, Hermann. *Deutsche und Niederländische
       Gebetbuchhandschriften, der Hessischen Landes- und Hochschul-
       bibliothek Darmstadt.* Darmstadt: Eduard Roetner, 1959.

This work is a descriptive catalogue of vernacular manuscripts of German and Netherlandic provenance which contain prayers. The incipits are listed, and the index includes names and churches. The volume represents the first of a series; see items 603, 626.

626 ————, and Eizenhofer, Leo. *Die lateinischen Gebetbuch*. Wiesbaden: Harrassowitz, 1972.

A survey of Darmstadt manuscripts containing Latin prayers.

627 Allen, Hope Emily. *Writings Ascribed to Richard Rolle, Hermit of Hampole*. MLA Monograph Series, 3. New York, N.Y.: MLA, 1927/Kraus Reprint, 1966.

A résumé of devotional works ascribed to Rolle, with some discussion of specific manuscripts. For some suggested revisions to attribution and manuscripts, see Joliffe, item 629.

628 Axters, Stephan G., O.P. *De Imitatione Christi: Een Handschriften Inventaris bij het vijfhonderdste verjaren van Thomas Hemerken van Kempen 1471*. Kempen: Niederrhein, 1971.

A brief descriptive list of manuscripts containing Thomas a Kempis' devotional works. Arrangement is by library collection, with a good bibliography.

629 Jolliffe, P.S. *A Check-List of Middle English Prose Writings of Spiritual Guidance*. Toronto: Pontifical Institute of Mediaeval Studies, 1974.

An invaluable checklist of Middle English religious prose writings which include, e.g., works by Richard Rolle, Walter Hilton, and Wycliffite writers. Arrangement is alphabetical by incipit, with lists of other manuscripts, editions, and bibliographical references. Provided are separate lists of manuscripts, titles, authors, and acephalous items, and these partly facilitate use of the somewhat complex system of classification into which the alphabetical incipits are placed, i.e., "A. Long Compilations of Spiritual Instruction," "B. *Pore Caitif*," "C. Forms of Confession," etc.

630 Kirchberger, C. "Bodleian Manuscripts Relating to the Spiritual Life, 1500-1750." *Bodleian Library Record*, 3 (1950-51), 155-64.

Although this descriptive list is for later devotional manuscripts, it does include a few late medieval manuscripts.

631 Revell, Peter. *Fifteenth Century English Prayers and Meditations: A Descriptive List of Manuscripts in the British Library*. New York, N.Y.: Garland Publishing, Inc., 1975.

A descriptive list of late Middle English prayers and meditations in some 350 manuscripts. Provided are fairly long incipits and explicits, with many bibliographical references and cross-references to other manuscripts. Name and manuscript indexes conclude.

632   Sinclair, Keith Val, comp. *French Devotional Texts of the Middle
       Ages: A Bibliographic Manuscript Guide.* Westport, Conn.: Green-
       wood, 1979.

       A descriptive list of manuscripts containing French devotional
       matter, with some bibliographical references. See also next item.

633   ————. *Prières en ancien français; nouvelles references, ren-
       seignements complementaires, indications bibliographiques,
       corrections et tables des articles du 'Répertoire' de Sonet.*
       Hamden, Conn.: Archon Books, 1978.

       Using the incipit numbers from Sonet's *Répertoire*, item 572,
       the author adds corrections and new manuscripts containing
       prayers in Old French. Bibliographical references are expanded
       and updated.

See also item 1690.

                              5. HAGIOGRAPHIC

634   Bollandist Institute. *Bibliotheca Hagiographica Latina Antiquae
       et Mediae Aetatis.* 2 vols. Brussels: The Institute, 1898-1901;
       Supplement, 2 vols. 1911/1949.

635   ————. *Bibliotheca Hagiographica Graeca.* 2nd ed. (from 1895).
       Brussels: The Institute, 1909.

       Both works provide *repertoria* for saints' legends, their manu-
       scripts and related documents. Arrangement is alphabetical by
       saint to the sixteenth century. A further volume, published
       in 1910, includes hagiographic sources and manuscripts in
       Arabic, Armenian, Coptic, and other Eastern languages.

636   ————. *Catalogus Codicum Hagiographicorum: Latinorum.* Brussels:
       The Institute, 1948.

       A catalogue of hagiographic manuscripts in Namur, Gand, and
       other Belgian libraries. Periodical additions are made in item
       1749.

637   Straeten, Joseph van der. *Les Manuscrits hagiographiques de
       Charleville, Verdun et Saint Mihiel.* Subsidia Hagiographica,
       56. Brussels: Bollandist Institute, 1974.

       A descriptive catalogue of local hagiographical collections,
       arranged by city and library.

See also items 212, 661, 1683-6, and 1749.

E. HISTORICAL AND LEGAL

638   Dolezalek, Goro. *Verzeichnis der Handschriften zum römischen Recht bis 1600: Materialsammlung, System und Programm für elektronische Datenverabeitung.* 4 vols. Frankfurt-am-Main: Max Planck Institute, 1972.

A computerized handlist for Roman law manuscripts to 1600, which is fully indexed. See also items 642 and 2046.

639   Garcia y Garcia, Antonio. *Los manuscritos jurídicos medievales de la Hispanic Society of America.* New York, N.Y.: The Society, 1964.

A descriptive list of Spanish legal manuscripts preserved in the Society's library, New York City.

640   Hardy, Thomas Duffus. *Descriptive Catalogue of Materials Relating to the History of Great Britain and Ireland to the End of the Reign of Henry VII.* 3 vols. London: Longman, Green, Longman, and Roberts, 1862-71.

The standard, early catalogue for British historical documents is still a useful starting point for further manuscript research in this area. Vol. 1 covers the period from the Romans to the Norman invasion, vol. 2 from A.D. 1066 to 1200, and vol. 3 to 1327. The work is fully indexed and filled with bibliographical information.

641   Number deleted.

642   Kuttner, S. *Repertorium der Kanonistik* (1140-1234). Studi e Testi, 71. Rome: Vatican, 1937.

A descriptive catalogue of canon law manuscripts, arranged by genre, e.g., decretals, glosses, and compilations, then by collection. Indexes are provided for incipits and manuscripts.

643   Leroquais, Victor. *Les Pontificaux manuscrits des bibliothèques publiques de France.* 4 vols. Paris: Prôtat Frères, 1937.

A descriptive catalogue of pontifical manuscripts, arranged by library and collection. The fourth volume provides illustrating plates.

644   Major, K., comp. *A Handlist of the Records of the Bishops of Lincoln and Archdeacons of Lincoln and Stow.* London/New York, N.Y.: Oxford University Press, 1953.

A list of the principal classes of records, e.g., administrative, court, visitation, and so on. Arrangement is by registration number in more of less chronological order. Included are brief descriptions of manuscripts and an index.

645   McCall, John P. "The Writings of John of Legano with a List of
      Manuscripts." *Traditio*, 23 (1967), 415-37.

      A non-descriptive list of manuscripts, arranged alphabetically
      by work, beginning with the *Concordancie Canonum*, ca. 1355
      (earliest manuscript dated 1396). Included are Legnano's works
      on science and theology.

646   *Typology of the Sources of the Western Middle Ages*. L. Genicot,
      gen. ed. Turnhout: Brépols for the Catholic University of
      Louvain, Institut d'Etudes Médiévales, 1972-.

      A proposed series of fascicles, to total 200, listing the
      sources for Western medieval history, A.D. 500-1500. After a
      major division into written and unwritten sources, e.g., monu-
      ments, the written sources are further divided into nine groups
      which include narrative, epistolary, and judicial; epistolary
      lists, e.g., have now been published as no. 17 by Giles Constable
      (1976). These invaluable bibliographies provide, in effect,
      methodological guides to kinds of evidence (*Gattungsgeschichte*)
      and the principles of interpretation for each.

See also items 58-94, 310, 334, 944, 1001, 1090, 1643-55, and 1877.

                              F. HUMANISTIC

647   Kristeller, Paul O. *Iter Italicum: A Finding List of Uncatalogued
      and Incompletely Catalogued Humanistic Manuscripts of the
      Renaissance in Italian and Other Libraries*. 2 vols. Warburg
      Institute. London: E.J. Brill, 1963-67.

      As the title explains, this work is a finding list for Human-
      istic manuscripts which may not appear in library catalogues.
      The fact that uncatalogued manuscripts for Petrarch alone occupy
      some 200pp. suggests the instrinsic value of this highly detailed
      and accurate repertory. Vol. 1 lists manuscripts from Agrigento
      to Novara, covering the period 1300-1600, while vol. 2 is devoted
      to the libraries of Orvieto to Voltarra and the Vatican. In-
      dexes are provided.

See also items 55-57, 1656-75.

G. LINGUISTIC AND LITERARY

648   Brayer, Edith. "Manuscrits de romans bretons photographies à l'Institut d'Histoire des Textes." *Bulletin Bibliographique de la Société Internationale Arthurienne*, 6 (1954), 79-84.

A descriptive list of one group of manuscripts photographed and forming part of the microform collection at the IHT, Paris; see item 532.

649   Brunel, Clovis. *Bibliographie des manuscrits littéraires en ancien provençal*. Société de Publications Romanes et Françaises, 13. Paris: E. Droz, 1935.

A descriptive list of manuscripts, arranged by country, location, and collection, then chronologically. A place/author/title index and table of manuscripts are provided.

650   Guddat-Figge, Gisela. *Catalogue of Manuscripts Containing Middle English Romances*. Texte und Untersuchungen zur englischen Philologie. Munich: W. Fink, 1976.

Originally the author's thesis (Bonn, 1973), the slightly expanded version provides a descriptive catalogue of manuscripts in the major British libraries. The bibliography is extensive.

651   Haelst, Joseph van. *Catalogue des papyrus littéraires juifs et chrétiens*. Paris: Sorbonne University Press, 1976.

A descriptive catalogue with plates and maps fully indexed.

652   Hofmann, Theodore, and Horden, John, eds. *Index of English Literary Manuscript Sources*. Institute of Bibliography and Textual Criticism. 5 vols. in 8. Leeds: University Press, forthcoming 1979.

An index to literary manuscript, exclusive of letters, by British and Irish authors, 1450-1900; volume 1, parts i-ii, will list manuscript sources for 1450-1625, and a general index will appear in volume 5.

653   Legry-Rosier, J. "Manuscrits de contes et de fabliaux." *Bulletin d'Information de l'Institut de Recherche et d'Histoire de Textes*, 4 (1955), 37-47.

A descriptive list of mainly French manuscripts, which contain *contes* and *fabliaux*; indexed.

654   Pellégrin, Elisabeth. *Manuscrits de Petrarque dans les bibliothèques de France*. Padua: Antenore, 1966.

An index of Petrarch's works in Latin and the vernacular, found in French manuscript collections. Originally published in *Italia Medioevale e Umanistica*, 4 (1961), 6 (1953), and 7 (1964). Pellégrin also lists authors mentioned by Petrarch, copyists, and original owners.

655   Thomson, David. *A Descriptive Catalogue of Middle English
      Grammatical Texts*. New York, N.Y.: Garland Publishing, Inc., 1979

      A description of 36 Middle English grammatical texts, 28 of
      which are versions of one of four main treatises, the *Accedence*
      (adapted from Donatus' *Ars Minor*); the *Comparacio*; the *Informacio*;
      and the *Formula*. The author provides a summary description of
      each type with a list of manuscripts and some extracts. This
      is followed by a fully descriptive catalogue of manuscripts and
      bibliography. See also item 557.

656   Thorndike, Lynn. "Copyists' Final Jingles in Medieval Manuscripts."
      Speculum, 12 (1937), 268; "More Copyists' Final Jingles."
      Speculum, 31 (1956), 321-8.

      Thorndike selects a group of representative final jingles
      from various Latin manuscripts and arranges them according to
      theme, e.g., Praise of Christ or Request for Drink; bibliograph-
      ical notes.

657   Vatasso, Marco. *I Codici Petrarcheschi della Biblioteca Vaticana*.
      Studi e Testi, 20. Rome: Vatican, 1908.

      A descriptive catalogue of Petrarchan manuscripts in the
      Vatican Library, arranged in collection sequence. Indexes in-
      clude works, manuscripts, and names.

See also items 585, 1641, 1691-1706.

H. LINGUISTIC AND NATIONAL

      The titles listed in this group define linguistic or
national origin for manuscripts found in more than one
library; manuscripts of similar linguistic or national
origin contained in a single library are cited among
the manuscript catalogues of Section II. Greek manuscripts
found in more than one library, which should theoretically
be cited here, are listed separately in V.B because of
their large number and their obvious relationship to
Classical, Byzantine, and Patristic manuscripts (Sections V.A and C).

658   Bergmann, Rolf. *Verzeichnis der althochdeutschen und altsächsi-
      schen Glossenhandschriften. Mit Bibliographie der Dialekt-
      bestimmungen*. Arbeiten zur Frühmittelalterforschung der Uni-
      versität Münster, 6. Berlin: De Gruyter, 1973.

      A list of over 1023 items in alphabetical order according to
      library; dialect, subject, and manuscript indexes are provided.
      The work is largely an updating of L. Steinmeyer and E. Sievers,
      Althochdeutsche Glossen, with additional bibliography, pp.
      xix-xxxiv.

659   Deschamps, J. *Middelnederlandse Handschriften uit Europese en Amerikaanse Bibliotheken.* 2nd ed. Leiden: E.J. Brill, 1972.

A descriptive catalogue of 125 manuscripts with some facsimiles; for suggestions about the limitations and possible future ex- pansion of this work, see Webber, item 671. Arrangement is alphabetical by author or title, with lists of places and manu- scripts.

660   Diaz y Diaz, M.C. *Index Scriptorum Latinorum Medii Aevi His- panicorum.* Consejo Superior de Investigaciones Científicas. 2 vols. Madrid: Menendez Pelayo, 1959.

A descriptive list of Latin manuscripts of Spanish provenance, arranged by century. The work includes an index of authors, in- cipits, manuscripts, editors, and quotations.

661   Genicot, L., and Tombeur, P. *Index Scriptorum Operumque Latino- Belgicorum Medii Aevi. Nouveau répertoire de oeuvres medio- latines belges.* Pt. I. *VIIe-Xe siècles.* Pt. III. *XIIe siècle.* Vol. I. *Oeuvres hagiographiques.* Comité National du Diction- naire du Latin Médiéval. Brussels: Academie Royale, 1973-77.

This represents the initial stage of a comprehensive index of Latin manuscripts of Belgian provenance. The descriptive index in vol. 1 cites Latin hagiographical works by Belgian writers. Anonymous works are listed by title.

662   Historical Manuscripts Commission. *Report on Manuscripts in the Welsh Language Made for the Historical Manuscripts Commission,* ed. John Gwenogvryn Evans. 7 pts. in 2 vols. London: HMSO, 1898-1910.

A descriptive list of manuscripts in Welsh, now in Cardiff, the British Library, Oxford, the National Library, and other Welsh collections.

663   Keller, Adelbert von. *Verzeichnis altdeutscher Handschriften.* ed. Eduard Sievers. Hildesheim/New York, N.Y.: G. Olms, 1974.

A descriptive catalogue, with bibliographical notes, of German manuscripts from A.D. 1050 to 1700. Reprinted from the original edition of 1890.

664   Ker, N.R. *Catalogue of Manuscripts Containing Anglo-Saxon.* Oxford: Clarendon Press, 1957. "Supplement," in *Anglo-Saxon England,* 5 (1976), 121-31.

A fully descriptive catalogue of Old English manuscripts and others containing Old English, numbering some 200 and written before 1200; arrangement is alphabetical by present location and library. There is a descriptive list of lost and untraced manuscripts and those copied by foreign scribes. The indexes list manuscripts, the contents of Aelfric's *Sermones Catholici,* and former owners. Plates provide facsmilies of different hands, and there is a valuable bibliography of editions and secondary works.

665   MacKinnon, Donald. *A Descriptive Catalogue of Gaelic Manuscripts
      in the Advocates' Library, Edinburgh, and Elsewhere in Scot-
      land*. Edinburgh: W. Brown, 1912.

      A descriptive catalogue of all manuscripts in Gaelic in Scot-
      land. Arrangement is by present library collection. Biblio-
      graphical notes and index are provided.

666   Menendez y Pelayo, Marcelino. *Bibliografía hispano-latina
      clasica. Codices, ediciones, comentarios, influencia de cada
      lino de los clasicos latinos en la literatura española*. 4 pts.
      Santander: Aldus, 1950-53.

      A descriptive catalogue of Classical Latin works used in
      Spanish literature; these are listed according to manuscript,
      edition, translation, and subject. Arrangement is alphabetical
      by Latin author. The work is updated by item 669.

667   Priebsch, Robert. *Deutsche Handschriften in England*. 2 vols.
      Erlangen: F. Junge, 1896-1901.

      This work provides a fully descriptive catalogue of German
      manuscripts, i.e., those of German provenance, in the libraries
      of Oxford, Cambridge, London, and Cheltenham. Bibliographical
      notes, index are provided.

668   Skulerud, Olai. *Catalogue of Norse Manuscripts in Edinburgh,
      Dublin, and Manchester*. Oslo: E. Moesteus, 1918.

      A list of manuscripts containing Old Norse with brief descrip-
      tions of contents and incipits. It includes an author/subject
      index.

669   Vallejo, José. *Papeletas de bibliografía hispano-latina*. Madrid:
      Instituto Antonio de Nebrija, 1967.

      A supplement to and updating of item 666 above. The items are
      arranged in four groups: manuscripts, editions, translations,
      and studies.

670   Vizkelety, Andras. *Beschreibendes Verzeichnis der altdeutschen
      Handschriften in ungarischen Bibliotheken*. 2 vols. Wiesbaden:
      Harrassowitz, 1969-73.

      A descriptive catalogue of Old High German manuscripts found
      in the five major Hungarian libraries; indexed.

671   Webber, P.E. "The Need for a Closer Description of the Medieval
      Netherlandic Manuscripts in American Libraries: Specific Cases
      in Point." *Archives et Bibliothèques de Belgique*, 46 (1975),
      283-7.

      Basing assumptions about the large number of manuscripts con-
      taining Dutch texts on Ricci and Wilson's *Census* and its *Supple-
      ment*, Webber outlines possible categories of contents and lists
      some manuscripts not included. See item 659.

See also items 43, 208, 221, 230, 309, 315, 362, 365, 367, 384.

I. MONASTIC

672 Axters, Stephan, O.P. *Bibliotheca Dominicana. Neerlandica Manuscripta 1224-1500*. Bibliothèque de la Revue d'Histoire Ecclésiastique, 49. Louvain: University Press, 1970.

A descriptive catalogue of manuscripts of Netherlandic, Dominican provenance. The two parts include, first, Dutch authors, then others. Arrangement is alphabetical by author, with a list of manuscripts and index of names.

673 Kaeppeli, Thomas, O.P. *Scriptores Ordinis Praedicatorum Medii Aevi*. 2 vols. Rome: Sabina, 1970-.

An alphabetical index of Dominican authors, which lists works, manuscripts, and bibliography. The fascicles thus far extend to "Johannes."

674 Talbot, C.H. "A List of Cistercian Manuscripts in Great Britain." *Traditio*, 8 (1952), 402-18, and Offprint.

An alphabetical author or work list, from Adam of Aldersbach to *Vita Sancti Bernardi*. Manuscripts are listed by collection and number, with dates. Omitted are Saint Bernard and Ailred of Rievaulx.

675 Troeyer, Benjamin de. *Bio-Bibliographia Franciscana Neerlandica ante Saeculum XVI*. I. *Pars Biographica. Auctores editionum qui Scripserunt ante Saeculum XVI*. Nieukoop: B. de Graf, 1974-.

A proposed series constituting a descriptive and bibliographical index to Franciscan writers in the Netherlands to the sixteenth century. The first volume cites manuscripts which have been published.

676 Zumkeller, Adolar, O.S.A. *Manuskripte von Werken der Autoren des Augustiner-Eremitenordens in mitteleuropäischen Bibliotheken*. Cassiciacum, 20. Würzburg: Augustinum, 1966.

An alphabetical index of Augustinian writers, with anonymous works cited by title. Bibliographical references are provided along with a table of manuscripts.

See also items 62, 1646-7, 1651.

J. PHILOSOPHICAL AND THEOLOGICAL

677   Garcia Pastor, Jesus; Hillgarth, J.N.; and Perez Martinez,
      Lorenzo. *Manuscritos Lulianos de la Biblioteca Publica de
      Palma*. Mallorca: Biblioteca Publica, 1965.

      A fully descriptive catalogue of Raymond Lull manuscripts in
      the Public Library of Palma. The information given includes
      bibliographical references, lists of incipits, secondary works,
      and a list of manuscripts classified according to date.

678   Glorieux, P. *Répertoire des maîtres en théologie de Paris au
      XIIIe siècle*. Paris: J. Vrin, 1933.

      A descriptive account of manuscripts and bibliography; included
      are indexes and a table of manuscripts. For general background
      on this subject, see Glorieux, item 1554.

679   Ker, N.R. "The English Manuscripts of the Moralia of Gregory
      the Great," in *Kunsthistorische Forschungen Otto Pächt zu
      seinem 70. Geburtstag*, ed. A. Rosenauer and G. Weber. Salz-
      burg: Residenz, 1972; pp. 77-89.

      A discussion and descriptive list of these manuscripts as
      found in various library collections.

680   Lacombe, Georges, *et al.*, eds. *Aristoteles Latinus. Pars Prior*.
      Corpus Philosophorum Medii Aevi, Union Academique Internationale.
      Bruges/Paris: Desclée de Brouwer, 1957; *Pars Posterior*. Cam-
      bridge: University Press, 1955.

      A descriptive catalogue of Latin Aristotelian manuscripts,
      arranged alphabetically by library location. Listed are the
      works, manuscripts, and editions. For Greek manuscripts, see
      items 585-6, 591.

681   Lefèvre, Yvres. *L'Elucidarium et les lucidaires; Contribution,
      par l'histoire d'un texte, à l'histoire des croyances religi-
      euses en France au moyen âge*. Paris: E. De Boccard, 1954.

      A detailed study and edition, in appendix, of the catechetical
      Summa by Honorius of Autun, ca. 1110. Chapter 1 examines the
      60 manuscripts extant in France, with classification and obser-
      vations on provenance; chapter 2 analyses the contents; chapter
      3 deals with sources and general theological and historical
      context, while the final chapters outline the work's later in-
      fluence.

682   Lohr, C.H. "Medieval Latin Aristotle Commentaries." *Traditio*,
      23 (1967), 313-413; 24 (1968), 149-245; 26 (1970), 135-216;
      27 (1971), 251-351; 28 (1972), 281-396; 29 (1973), 93-197;
      30 (1974), 119-44. "Addenda et corrigenda." *Bulletin de
      Philosophie Medievale*, 14 (1972), 116-26.

      An alphabetical, descriptive list of commentaries, with bio-
      graphical notes, manuscripts, incipits, and bibliographical
      references; the final issue provides additions and corrections.

683   Munari, Franco. *Mathei Vindocinensis: Opera*. Rome: Edizioni di
      Storia e Letteratura, 1977.

      An excellent and detailed descriptive catalogue of manuscripts
      attributed to Matthew of Vendome, arranged alphabetically by
      location. Classified lists of manuscripts indicate period and
      owners. An author/title index is provided.

684   Pedersen, Olaf. *Petrus Philomena de Dacia: A Problem of Identity
      with a Survey of the Manuscripts*. Cahiers de l'Institut du
      Moyen Âge Grecque et Latin. Copenhagen: The Institute, 1976.

      A descriptive list of manuscripts, with extracts. Arrangement
      is by individual work.

685   Spade, Paul Vincent. *The Mediaeval Liar: A Catalogue of the
      "Insolubilia"-Literature*. Subsidia Mediaevalia, 5. Toronto:
      Pontifical Institute of Mediaeval Studies, 1975.

      A descriptive catalogue of medieval manuscripts and other
      literature on *insolubilia*, from the early thirteenth century to
      the early fifteenth. It provides lists of manuscripts with their
      locations and offers new information on the identity of the
      authors and nature of their works. Entries are arranged by author
      and incipit; anonymous texts are listed first by incipit.

686   Stegmüller, F. *Repertorium Commentariorum in Sententias Petri
      Lombardi*. 2 vols. Würzburg: F. Schöningh, 1947; *Commentaires
      sur les sentences, Supplement*, by Victorin Doucet. Florence:
      St. Bonaventure College, 1954.

      A fully descriptive list of commentaries, arranged alphabet-
      ically by author, with incipit/explicit for each work and list
      of manuscripts, bibliographical references. Volume 2 provides
      indexes for incipits, manuscripts, chronology, and author. The
      Supplement, extracted from *Archivum Franciscanum Historicum*,
      47 (1954), provides additional works and manuscripts, with
      numerical reference to Stegmüller.

See also items 1676-82.

K. SCIENTIFIC AND MEDICAL

687   Agrimi, Jole. *Tecnica e scienza nella cultura medievale: inven-
      tario dei manoscritti relativi alla scienza e alla tecnica
      medievale (saec. XI-XV): Biblioteche di Lombardia*. Florence:
      La Nuova Italia, 1976.

      A descriptive list of scientific and technical manuscripts
      found in the libraries of Lombardy; arrangement is by library
      and subject, with bibliographical references. A subject/place/
      manuscript index is provided.

688   Beccaria, Augusto. *I Codici di medicina del periodo presalernitano*
      (secoli IX, X e XI). Studi e Testi, 53. Rome: Studi e Testi,
      1956.

      A fully descriptive catalogue, arranged by country, of early
      manuscripts. Arrangement is by country, city, and manuscript
      number. The work provides an index of incipits and an author/
      work index.

689   Bidez, J.; Cumont, F.; Delatte, L.; Kenyon, F.; and Falco, V. de,
      eds. *Catalogue des manuscrits alchemiques grecs.* 2 vols.
      Brussels: M. Lamertin, 1924-35.

690   ————. *Catalogue des manuscrits alchemiques latins.* Union
      Academique Internationale. 3 vols. Brussels: UAI, 1939-51.

      These descriptive catalogues of alchemical manuscripts are
      arranged by library location, first those in the public libraries
      of Paris, then in departmental public libraries. Manuscripts
      are listed by collection and chronology. See also item 703.

691   Cumont, F.; Boll, F.; and Kroll, W., eds. *Catalogus Codicum*
      Astrologorum Graecorum. 12 vols. Brussels: M. Lamertin, 1898-
      1953.

      A survey of extant Greek astrological manuscripts, preserved
      in European libraries; these also include Byzantine or modern
      copies of Byzantine manuscripts. Arrangement is by national
      location.

692   Goldberg, Ada, and Saye, Hyman. "An Index to Mediaeval French
      Medical Receipts of the Middle Ages That Have Been Published."
      Bulletin of the Institute of the History of Medicine, 1 (1933),
      435-66.

      An alphabetical bibliography of published editions appearing
      in periodicals.

693   Jayawardene, S.A. "Western Scientific Manuscripts before 1600:
      A Checklist of Published Catalogues." *Annals of Science*, 35
      (1978), 143-72.

      A list of printed catalogues by topic, e.g., general science,
      computus, then by city or chronological order, although the
      arrangement is somewhat confused. Name and city indexes are
      provided.

694   Kibre, Pearl. "*Hippocrates Latinus*: Repertorium of Hippocratic
      Writings in the Latin Middle Ages." I, *Traditio*, 31 (1975),
      99-126; II, 32 (1976), 257-92; III, 33 (1977), 253-95; IV,
      34 (1978), 193-226.

      A list of known sixth to sixteenth-century Latin translations
      of Hippocratic writings, with brief manuscript histories. Kibre
      gives an excellent account of textual traditions, both within
      and outside the established canon.

695   Lindberg, David C. *A Catalogue of Medieval and Renaissance
      Optical Manuscripts*. Subsidia Mediaevalia, 4. Toronto: Pontif-
      ical Institute of Mediaeval Studies, 1975.

      A descriptive catalogue of manuscripts on optics, excluding
      opthalomology, e.g., the translation of Abhomadi Malfegeyr by
      Gerard of Cremona; these are followed by manuscripts containing
      opthalmological treatises. There are good indexes of incipits,
      manuscripts, authors, and translators.

696   McGurk, Patrick. *Catalogue of Astrological and Mythological
      Illuminated Manuscripts of the Latin Middle Ages. IV. Astro-
      logical Manuscripts in Italian Libraries (Other Than Rome)*.
      London: The Warburg Institute, University of London Press,
      1966.

      This work represents vol. IV of the series of descriptive and
      illustrated catalogues begun by Säxl, item 700. It contains an
      introduction on the general nature and scope of these manuscripts,
      then a descriptive list arranged by city and library.

697   Robbins, Rossell Hope. "English Almanacks of the Fifteenth
      Century." *Philological Quarterly*, 18 (1939), 321-31.

      Robbins looks at those popular calendars which preceded the
      printed almanacks of the sixteenth century. These are based
      mainly on prognosticary works such as the lunary. Individual
      manuscript traditions are studied for, e.g., the *Erra Pater* or
      Prognostications of Esdras. The bibliographical references cite
      many manuscripts.

698   ————. "Medical Manuscripts in the Middle English." *Speculum*,
      45 (1970), 393-415.

      A discussion of Middle English manuscripts containing medical
      treatises or other matter, in British libraries; lists of manu-
      scripts occur in the notes. For a brief bibliography of relevant
      catalogues, see p. 407n.

699   Saint-Lager, Jean Baptiste. *Recherches sur les anciens herbaria*.
      Paris: J. Bailliere, 1886.

      A survey of the major herbals, especially those in manuscripts
      of French provenance, with lists of manuscripts, editions, and
      studies.

700   Säxl, Fritz. *Verzeichnis astrologischer und mythologische illus-
      trierter Handschriften des lateinische mittelalters. I. Röm-
      ischen Bibliotheken*. Heidelberg: 1915; II. *National-Bibliothek
      in Wien*, 1927; III. *Catalogue of Astrological and Mythological
      Illuminated Manuscripts of the Latin Middle Ages: Manuscripts
      in English Libraries*, with Hans Meier, ed. Harry Bober. London:
      Warburg Institute, 1953.

      These volumes constitute a comprehensive and lavishly illustrated
      catalogue of astrological and mythological manuscripts, with the
      fourth volume edited by McGurk, item 696. In his introductory

essay Säxl traces the oriental influence upon illustrated astrological manuscripts and its ultimate fusion with the Classical
imagery of Duns Scotus. The volumes are issued by geographical
location of libraries, with vol. 3 listing manuscripts from
London, Oxford, Cambridge, and Durham. All volumes are fully
indexed.

701   Singer, Dorothea Waley. "Survey of Medical Manuscripts in the
       British Isles Dating from before the Sixteenth Century." *Pro-
       ceedings of the Royal Society of Medicine, History of Medicine
       Section*, 12 (1918-19), 96-107.

       Singer is the first and last scholar to attempt a comprehensive
       listing of all medical manuscripts in British libraries. On the
       inevitable limitations of such a survey see Rossell Hope Robbins,
       "A Note on the Singer Survey of Medieval Manuscripts in the
       British Isles," *Chaucer Review*, 5 (1969), 66-70.

702   ————, and Anderson, Annie. *Catalogue of Latin and Vernacular
       Plague Texts in Great Britain and Eire in Manuscripts Written
       before the Sixteenth Century*. Collection de Travaux de l'Aca-
       demie Internationale d'Histoire des Sciences, 5. London: The
       Academy, 1950.

       A descriptive catalogue of treatises on and descriptions of
       the plague in Latin and English, mainly in fourteenth and fif-
       teenth-century manuscripts. Arrangement is by collection, with
       an index provided. Several have been printed by Singer in "Some
       Plague Tractes," *Proceedings of the Royal Society of Medicine*,
       19 (London: 1916), 159-212.

703   ————; Anderson, Annie; and Addis, Robina. *Catalogue of Latin
       and Vernacular Alchemical Manuscripts in Great Britain and
       Ireland, Dating from before the Sixteenth Century*. 3 vols.
       Brussels: M. Lamertin for UAI, 1928-31.

       A descriptive catalogue with format similar to Bidez, item
       689. Vol. 3 provides an appendix with table of corrections,
       lists of incipits, and an index of authors.

704   Thorndike, Lynn. "Latin Manuscripts of Works by Rasis at the
       Bibliothèque Nationale, Paris." *Bulletin of the History of
       Medicine*, 32 (1958), 54-67.

       Thorndike offers notes on some astronomical, astrological, and
       mathematical manuscripts by Rasis to be found at the Bibliothèque
       Nationale. Reprinted from the *Journal of the Warburg and Courtauld
       Institutes*, 20 (1957), 112-72.

705   ————, ed. *Latin Treatises on Comets Between 1238 and 1368*.
       Chicago, Ill.: University Press, 1964.

       An edition with descriptions of manuscripts, of works by
       Albertus Magnus, Thomas Aquinas, Gerard de Silteo, and others.
       Indexes for manuscripts and incipits are provided.

706   ————. "Some Unpublished Minor Works Bordering on Science
        Written in the Late Fifteenth Century." *Speculum*, 39 (1964),
        85-95.

        A critical list of manuscripts from the Vatican Library by
        mainly Humanist authors; they include, e.g., Giovanni Pietro
        Gonzaga's *Dactylotheca Iovis*, a poem on precious stones. Thorn-
        dike also makes useful references to related manuscripts in
        other libraries.

707   Toomer, G.I. "A Survey of the Toledan Tables." *Osiris*, 15 (1968),
        5-174.

        A comprehensive list, arranged by collection, of the manuscripts
        of the Toledan astronomical tables; bibliographical references
        are provided.

708   Wickersheimer, E. *Les Manuscrits latins de medicine du haut
        moyen âge dans les bibliothèques de France*. Documents, Etudes
        et Répertoires Publiés par l'Institut de Recherche et d'Histoire
        des Textes, 11. Paris: CNRS, 1966.

        A descriptive list of a wide variety of Latin medical texts
        in French libraries, arranged by city, library, and manuscript
        number. An author/person/subject index is provided.

See also items 167-79, 213, 330, 351, 371, 404, 1707-28.

VI. PALEOGRAPHY: WRITING AND SCRIPTS

The first part of this section cites general works on paleography as a discipline. These include introductory essays and practical handbooks on how to read and transcribe manuscripts. The second part presents individual sections on the major scripts. Problems in terminology for scripts and hands are, of course, implicit in all the classifications presented here. I have therefore kept to the simplest and broadest categories, and these are Greek, Roman, Runic, Uncial and Insular, Caroline, Gothic, National, Humanistic, Book, Court, and Cursive. Titles cited under some scripts may refer to individual hands or those with national features, but most references which have to do with *scriptoria* in specific monasteries have been cited under "Scribal Practice and Formulas" in Section XI. The third part of this section offers a highly select list of facsimile editions and facsimile collections. These are intended as additional aids in the recognition and reading of scripts and as representative of different periods and countries. Facsimile editions of mainly illuminated manuscripts are cited in Section IX.C.

CONTENTS

A. BIBLIOGRAPHICAL MATERIALS

709   Bischoff, B. "Deutsches Schriftum zur lateinischen Paläographie
       und Handschriften Forschung, 1945-52." *Scriptorium*, 7 (1953),
       298-318.

       An especially significant survey of scholarship for this
       period. Such accounts appear periodically in this journal, see
       item 1877, of varying quality and scope.

710   Bonacini, Claudio. *Bibliografia delle arti scrittorie e della
       calligrafia*. Florence: Sansoni, 1953.

       A general, non-critical bibliography on the history of writing.

711   Lacombe, P. *Bibliographie des travaux de M. Léopold Delisle,
       membre de l'institut, adminstrateur général de la Biblio-
       thèque Nationale*. 2 vols. Paris: Imprimérie Nationale, 1902-11.

       While this bibliography is ostensibly on the writings of Delisle,
       his books and articles cover many aspects of paleography and
       textual criticism over the last quarter of the nineteenth cen-
       tury. The focus is upon the French and Latin manuscripts of
       the Bibliothèque Nationale.

712   Mateu Ibars, Josefina, and Mateu Ibars, Dolores. *Bibliografia
       Paleografica*. Universidad de Barcelona, Facultad de Filosofia
       y Letras, Departamento de Paleografia y Diplomatica. Barcelona:
       University Press, 1974.

       A comprehensive but non-discriminatory bibliography of inter-
       national titles, arranged alphabetically within three major
       parts: writing, scripts, and libraries. The focus is upon
       Spanish works and resources, which represent the most detailed
       and accurate portions of this work. Indexes for authors, titles,
       places, and subjects are provided.

713   Nelis, H. *L'Ecriture et les scribes*. Brussels: G. van Oest, 1918.

       A very general and summary bibliography of Latin paleography,
       with some emphasis upon archival material of the late nineteenth
       century.

714   Sattler, P., and Selle, G. von. *Bibliographie zur Geschichte der
       Schrift bis in das Jahr 1930*. Archiv für Bibliographie, Beiheft
       17. Linz: F. Winkler, 1935.

       An annotated bibliography of the general history of writing
       from ancient to modern times. The emphasis is upon German works.

715   Wilks, John, and Lacey, A.D. *Catalogue of Works Dealing with*
       the Study of Western Palaeography in the Libraries of the
       University of London. London: University of London Press,
       1921.

       A descriptive list of works on paleography available in these
       libraries. Although this bibliography is now out of date and
       somewhat weak in international references, it does offer a con-
       venient guide to a basic core of significant early twentieth-
       century works.

See also items 1751, 1779, 1789, 1795-6, 1835-6, 1839, 1849, 1853,
       1869, 1871-2, 1877-8, 1892.

                     B. FESTSCHRIFTEN AND COLLECTIONS

716   Gumbert, J.P., and Haan, M.J.M. de, eds. *Litterae Textuales:*
       A Series on Manuscripts and Their Texts: Essays Presented to
       G.I. Lieftinck. 4 vols. Amsterdam: A.L. van Gendt, 1972-76.

       A *Festschrift* in four annual issues, dedicated to G.I. Lief-
       tinck, formerly Professor of Palaeography at Leiden, with an
       appended bibliography of his many publications on the subject.
       The essays, on all aspects of paleography and codicology, have
       been contributed by an international group of scholars. Vol. 1
       is devoted to Caroline and Gothic manuscripts; see item 815.
       When the series ceased publication in 1976, it was continued
       in the same attractive format but under a different name; see
       next item.

717   ————, and Gruys, A., eds. *Codicologica.* Leiden: E.J. Brill,
       1976-.

       A continuation of the preceding item, which has appeared
       annually and must now be considered a journal.

718   Lowe, E.A. *Palaeographical Papers*, ed. Ludwig Bieler. 2 vols.
       Oxford: Clarendon Press, 1972.

       A collection of Lowe's excellent papers on every aspect of
       paleography. It concludes with a bibliography of Lowe's many
       publications, 1907-69.

719   *Medieval Learning and Literature: Essays Presented to Richard*
       William Hunt, ed. J.J.G. Alexander and M.I. Gibson. Oxford:
       Clarendon Press, 1976.

       A collection of essays by leading paleographers and codicol-
       ogists, accompanied by a bibliography of Hunt's many publica-
       tions; the essays include B. Bischoff, "Die Hofbibliothek unter
       Ludwig dem Frommen"; N.R. Ker, "The Beginnings of Salisbury
       Cathedral"; G. Pollard, "Describing Medieval Bookbindings";

R.H. Rouse and M.A. Rouse, "The *Florilegium Angelicum*"; M.B.
Parkes, "The Influence of the Concepts of *Ordinatio* and *Com-
pilatio* on the Development of the Book"; B.C. Barker-Benfield,
"A Ninth-Century Manuscript from Fleury: *Cato de Senectute cum
Macrobio*"; T. Silverstein, "The Graz and Zurich Apocalypse of
Saint Paul: An Independent Witness to the Greek"; A.B. Scott,
Some Poems Attributed to Richard of Cluny"; Anonymous, "La
Tradition manuscrite des 'Questiones Nicolai Peripatetici'";
A.C. de la Mare, "The Return of Petronius to Italy"; R.W.
Southern, "Master Vacarius and the Beginning of the English
Academic Tradition"; E. Rathbone, "Peter of Corbeil in an
English Setting"; B. Smalley, "Oxford University Sermons 1290-
93"; R.J. Dean, "Nicholas Trivet, Historian"; A.B. Emden, "Ox-
ford Academical Halls in the Later Middle Ages"; M. Labowsky,
"An Unnoticed Letter from Bessarion to Lorenzo Valla"; L.E.
Boyle, "*E Cathena et Carcere*: the Imprisonment of Amaury de
Montfort, 1276"; W.A. Pantin, "Instructions for a Devout and
Literate Layman."

720   *Medieval Scribes, Manuscripts and Libraries: Essays Presented
      to N.R. Ker*, ed. M.B. Parkes and Andrew G. Watson. London:
      Oxford University Press, 1978.

      The twelve papers by different hands on aspects of paleography
      and codicology are introduced by an assessment of Ker's contri-
      butions as Oxford Reader in Palaeography, 1946-68, and concluded
      by a lengthy and useful bibliography by Joan Gibbs of Ker's many
      publications. The essays include Pierre Chaplais, "The Letter
      from Bishop Wealdhere of London to Archbishop Brihtwold of
      Canterbury: the Earliest Original 'Letter Close' Extant in the
      West"; John C. Pope, "Palaeography and Poetry: Some Solved and
      Unsolved Problems of the Exeter Book"; T.A.M. Bishop, "The
      Prototype of *Liber Glossarum*"; J.J.G. Alexander, "Scribes as
      Artists: The Arabesque Initial in Twelfth-Century Manuscripts";
      R.M. Thompson, "The 'Scriptorium' of William of Malmesbury";
      Graham Pollard, "The *Pecia* System in Medieval Universities";
      A.I. Doyle and M.B. Parkes, "The Production Copies of the *Canter-
      bury Tales* and the *Confessio Amantis* in the Early Fifteenth
      Century"; A.J. Piper, "The Libraries of the Monks of Durham";
      R.W. Hunt, "The Library of the Abbey of St. Albans"; Andrew
      Watson, "Thomas Allen of Oxford and His Manuscripts"; A.G. Rigg,
      "Antiquarians and Authors: The Supposed Works of Robert Baston,
      O. Carm."; Richard H. Rouse and Mary A. Rouse, "The Medieval
      Circulation of Cicero's 'Posterior Academics' and the *De Fini-
      bus Bonorum et Malorum*." Included in this volume are indexes
      of manuscripts and printed books.

721   *Medieval Studies: An Introduction*, ed. James M. Powell. New
      York, N.Y.: Syracuse University Press, 1976.

      This collection of general, introductory essays covers
      historical and literary topics, but one especially useful for
      the paleographer is John James' "Latin Paleography," pp. 1-68,
      which also includes a good bibliography.

722 *Nomenclature des écritures livresques du IXe au XVIe siècle.*
     Premier Colloquie International de Paléographie Latine. Paris:
     CNRS, 1954 for 1953.

     Three papers, each illustrated with facsimiles: I.B. Bischoff,
     "La Nomenclature des écritures livresques du IXe au XIIIe
     siècle," pp. 7-14 (Caroline bookhands); II. G.I. Lieftinck,
     "Pour une nomenclature de l'écriture livresque de la periode
     dite gothique," pp. 15-34 (Gothic bookhands, especially of
     Netherlandic provenance); and III. G. Batelli, "Nomenclature
     des écritures humanistiques," pp. 35-44 (includes facsimiles
     of Humanist/Chancery hands). The whole monograph provides a
     lucid attempt by three outstanding Continental paleographers
     to deal with difficult distinctions among certain bookhands
     and to provide a standardized terminology. Unfortunately bibli-
     ographical references are few.

723 O'Meara, John L., and Naumann, Bernd, eds. *Latin Script and
     Letters A.D. 400-900: Festschrift Presented to Ludwig Bieler
     on the Occasion of His 70th Birthday.* Leiden: E.J. Brill,
     1976.

     This collection of papers focuses upon different scripts, but
     it also includes items on individual manuscripts and aspects of
     textual criticism plus a bibliography. See item 1928.

724 Plante, Julian G., ed. *Translatio Studii. Manuscript and Library
     Studies Honoring Oliver L. Kapsner, O.S.B.* The Monastic Micro-
     film Library. Collegeville, Minn.: St. John's University Press
     for the Library, 1973.

     A collection of essays on mainly manuscript libraries and
     individual manuscripts. The bibliographical references cover
     all aspects of paleography. See also item 541.

C. PALEOGRAPHY AS A DISCIPLINE

725 Batelli, G. *Lezioni di paleografia.* 3rd ed. (from 1936). Rome:
     Vatican, 1949/1968.

     A general introduction to paleographical studies, with emphasis
     upon Italian resources. The organization and documentation leave
     much to be desired.

726 Bischoff, Bernhard. *Paläographie des römischen Altertums und
     des Abendländischen Mittelalters.* Grundlagen der Germanistik,
     24. Berlin: E. Schmidt, 1979.

     A lucid and attractively produced introduction to paleography,
     based on earlier work by Bischoff (1955-56). Sections are on
     materials, format, scripts, and the role of manuscripts in cul-
     tural history from Roman times to the Renaissance. Indexes are
     provided for works, authors, names, topics, and manuscripts cited.
     The focus is upon German resources and practices.

727   Bonenfant, Paul. *Syllabus du cours de paléographie du moyen
       âge.* 2nd ed. (from 1938). Liège: Editions Desoer, 1947.

       An excellent but brief handbook in outline form of the major
       scripts and periods, designed originally for the Faculty of
       Philosophy and Lettres at the Free University of Brussels. Not
       illustrated.

728   Bretholz, B. *Lateinische Paläographie.* 3rd ed. (from 1905).
       Leipzig/Berlin: Teubner, 1926.

       A general handbook to the study of manuscripts, with some
       emphasis upon historical documents. Not illustrated.

729   Brown, T.J. "Latin Palaeography Since Traube," in item 716, 1,
       pp. 58-74.

       A lucid résumé of the difficulties in defining such terms as
       "paleography," "diplomatics," and "codicology," with an account
       of their historical development in the context of earlier scholar-
       ship represented by Traube and his contemporaries; originally
       Brown's inaugural lecture in the Chair of Palaeography, Uni-
       versity of London, Nov. 1962. See items 720, 755.

730   Concetti, G. *Lineamenti di storia della scrittura latina.
       Paleografia e diplomatica.* Bologna: R. Patron, 1956 for 1954.

       A general introduction to paleography and diplomatics, with
       emphasis upon Italian resources; not well documented.

731   Dain, Alphonse. *Les Manuscrits.* 3rd ed. (from 1949). Paris:
       Les Belles Lettres, 1975.

       A general introduction to the subject devoted to mainly Byzan-
       tine paleographical studies; provides an account of materials,
       scripts, major documents, and textual criticism, with full
       indexes and bibliography.

732   Deuel, Leo. *Testaments of Time: The Search for Lost Manuscripts
       and Records.* New York, N.Y.: Knopf, 1965; London: Secker and
       Warburg, 1966.

       An account of mainly archaeological research on manuscripts,
       with a discussion of their conservation and restoration. It
       provides a useful bibliography.

733   Foerster, Hans. *Abriss der lateinischen Paläographie.* Bern: P.
       Haupt, 1949.

       To date the most valuable study of the discipline. Foerster
       discusses in four successive sections the development of scripts.
       He includes accounts of the practice of *notae* and punctuation
       and provides excellent bibliographical notes, although unfortu-
       nately of pre-1938 items.

734   Gardthausen, V. *Griechische Paläographie.* 2nd ed. (from 1879).
       2 vols. Leipzig: Veit, 1911-13.

       Vol. 1 introduces the subject of Greek book production and
       their distribution from Classical antiquity to the Byzantine

period, while vol. 2 analyzes the different scripts in more or less chronological sequence. Useful documentation, although now out of date.

735 Groningen, B.A., van. *Short Manual of Greek Palaeography*. Leiden: A.W. Sijthoff, 1967.

A clear, concise introduction to the history of Greek writing, writing materials, codices, numbering, accentuation, punctuation, glosses, and *scholia*. Plates with descriptive notes are provided, as well as a select bibliography.

736 ———, "Ursprung und Entwickelung der griechisch-lateinischen Schrift." *Germanisch-romanische Monatschrift*, 1 (1909), 273-83. Offprint.

An earlier and more concise version of item 735 above.

737 Haselden, R.B. *Scientific Aids for the Study of Manuscripts*. Bibliographical Society. Oxford: Oxford University Press for the Society, 1935.

An introduction to the study of paleography, with an account of scripts, early book production, and library resources. A short bibliography concludes each chapter.

738 Hector, L.C. *The Handwriting of English Documents*. 2nd ed. (from 1958). London: Arnold, 1966.

This brief introduction is more comprehensive than its title implies. It introduces the hands of mainly archival documents, but also discusses language, abbreviations, scribal conventions, and provides illustrative material through plates.

739 Helgason, Jon. *Handritaspjall*. Reykjavik: Mal og Menning, 1958.

An account of mainly Icelandic manuscripts and their special features; useful even for non-Scandinavian scholars for the general references and bibliography.

740 Hunt, R.W. "Paleography." *Chambers Encyclopaedia*. Vol. 10. London: W. and R. Chambers, 1952.

A summary but lucid description of the nature and scope of the discipline by one of Great Britain's early leading scholars in the field.

741 Jakó, Sigismund, and Manolescu, Radu. *Scierea latină în evul mediu*. Bucharest: Editura Stiintifica, 1971.

A well-designed general introduction to paleography, which discusses scripts, *scriptoria*, libraries, archives, and other aspects of the subject. Although in Roumanian, the illustrations and bibliography are international and résumés are provided in German, French, and Russian.

742 Kirchner, Joachim. *Germanistische Handschriftenpraxis: Ein Lehrbuch für die Studierenden der deutschen Philologie*. Munich: C.H. Beck, 1950.

A practical introduction to the study of medieval German paleography. The author discusses medieval libraries, types of scripts, catalogues, describing manuscripts, editing, and the care and preservation of manuscripts in library collections. The work is lacking in organization and documentation.

743 Lehmann, Paul. *Lateinische Paläographie, bis zum Siege der Karolingischen Minuskel*. Leipzig: Teubner, 1925.

A brief (31pp.) introduction and survey of paleography to the tenth century.

744 Löffler, Karl. *Einführung in die Handschriftenkunde*. Leipzig: Hiersemann, 1929.

The author of this useful introduction focuses upon paleographical methods rather than specific features. He considers German medieval manuscripts in more detail. For a companion volume on manuscript catalogues and their use, see item 197.

745 Madan, Falconer. *Books in Manuscript: A Short Introduction to Their Study and Use*. London: 1893: 2nd ed. New York, N.Y.: Empire State Book Co., 1927.

After a general introduction to the basic paleographical issues, the author provides a useful series of appendices which contain lists of public libraries with more than 4,000 manuscripts and their catalogues. These include, among others, the British Library, the Bodleian Library, and the Oxford and Cambridge college libraries.

746 Millares Carlo, Augustin. *Tratado de paleografia española*. 2nd ed. (from 1929). 2 vols. Madrid: Hernando, 1932.

An introduction to Spanish paleography, especially national hands; accompanied by facsmiles in vol. 2, with lists of Visigothic manuscripts and an atlas. Continued by next item.

747 ————. *Nuevos estudios de paleografia española*. Mexico City: La Casa de España en Mexico, 1941.

This work represents an expansion of the preceding item, with additional lists of Visigothic manuscripts.

748 Prou, M., and Bocard, A. de. *Manuel de paléographie latine et française*. 4th ed. (from 1890) with Alain de Böuard. Paris: A. Picard, 1924.

A general introduction, illustrated with plates; the work also includes the diplomatic abbreviations first listed by J.L. Walther, *Lexicon Diplomaticum Abbreviationes Syllabarum et Vocum in Diplomatibus et Codicibus* (Göttingen: 1745-47; Ulm: 1756).

749 Reusens, Edmond H.I. *Eléments de paléographie*. Louvain: The Author, 1899/1963.

An introductory handbook; although superseded by later studies in coverage, detail, and bibliographical references, the section on foliation (pp. 459ff.) is still useful for its lucid presentation of this complex subject.

750 Reynolds, L.D., and Wilson, N.G. *Scribes and Scholars: A Guide to the Transmission of Greek and Latin Literature*. 2nd ed. (from 1965). Oxford: Clarendon Press, 1974.

An indispensable handbook for the undergraduate; an introduction with select bibliography provides an account of the processes
by which Classical literature has been preserved by the transmission of texts through Hellenistic libraries to medieval *scriptoria*
and ultimately to the Humanist editors of the Renaissance. Subsequent chapters discuss various scripts and the final chapter
outlines the basic premises of textual criticism.

751   Seip, Didrik Arup. *Palaeografi*. Nordiskultur, 288. Stockholm:
      Bonnier, 1954.

      This concise and well-designed book offers a useful introduction
      to Scandinavian methodology and resources; illustrated with a
      selection of facsimiles.

752   Stiennon, Jacques. *Paléographie du moyen âge*. Paris: A. Colin,
      1973.

      An introduction to paleography as a discipline, with some
      emphasis upon French resources and bibliography. The accompany-
      ing paleographical maps are especially useful. Chapter III is
      on Codicology, and facsimile illustrations are included with
      transcriptions, pp. 181-283.

753   Strubbe, E. *Grondbegrippen van de Paleografie du Middeleeuwen*.
      3rd ed. (from 1932). 2 vols. Ghent: Wetenschappenijke Uitg.
      en Boekhandel, 1961.

      A general introduction to Netherlandic paleography, accompanied
      by bibliography and facsimile illustrations in vol. 2.

754   Thompson, E.M. *An Introduction to Greek and Latin Palaeography*.
      Oxford: Clarendon Press, 1912; New York, N.Y.: Burt Franklin,
      1964.

      This work is considered the best English introduction to ancient
      manuscripts and their interpretation. It incorporates the author's
      earlier *Handbook*, 3rd ed. 1906.

755   Traube, Ludwig. *Vorlesungen und Abhandlungen*. 3 vols. Munich:
      C.H. Beck, 1965. I. *Zur Paläographie und Handschriftenkunde*,
      ed. Paul Lehmann, with introd. by Franz Boll, from the 1st ed.
      of 1909; II. *Einleitung in die Lateinische Philologie des
      Mittelalters*, ed. Paul Lehmann, from the 1st ed. of 1911; III.
      Kleine Schriften, ed. Samuel Brandt, from the 1st ed. of 1920.

      Of Traube's three original volumes the first is specifically
      devoted to the study of manuscripts; it includes the history of
      scripts, the nature of materials, and the problems of textual
      criticism. The bibliographies are excellent for that period. On
      Traube's contributions to the study of paleography, see item
      729.

756   Wattenbach, Wilhelm. *Das Schriftwesen im Mittelalter*. 4th ed.
      (from 1896). Graz: Akademische Druck- und Verlagsanstalt,
      1958.

      An introduction to the study of mainly medieval German manu-
      scripts. The work includes the development of scripts, types of
      materials, and book production.

757 ——. *Anleitung zur lateinische Paläographie.* 4th ed. (from 1876). Leipzig: Hirzel, 1886.

A general introduction to Latin paleography, intended as a companion volume to *Griechische Paläographie*, 1888.

758 Widding, Ole. *Handskriftanalyser.* Bibliotheca Arnamagnaeana, 20. Copenhagen: The Institute, 1960; pp. 51-112; 327-49; offprint.

An elementary introduction to the paleography of mainly Old Norse manuscripts, with bibliographical references to Scandinavian resources.

759 Zazo, Alfredo. *Paleografia Latina e Diplomatica.* 7th ed. (from 1946). Naples: Pellerano, 1950.

This work is useful primarily as a general introduction to the study of manuscripts of Italian provenance and to the use of Italian library resources.

D. WRITING AND SCRIPTS

1. GENERAL STUDIES

760 Bretholz, Bertold. *Lateinische Paläographie.* 3rd ed. (from 1905). Grundriss der Geschichtswissenschaft, I.1. Liepzig/Berlin: Teubner, 1926.

In this work a short account is given of the development of Latin writing. Arrangement is by period and script.

761 Cameron, Angus. *English Handwriting in the Dark Ages.* University of Toronto, Centre for Medieval Studies. Video-tape Series. Toronto: Media Centre, n.d.

A 19-minute black-and-white video-tape cassette, available for rental or purchase from the University of Toronto Media Centre. It traces the early development of rustic capitals, uncial, and insular majuscule and minuscule in a visually attractive introduction to paleography and its early scripts in England.

762 Cohen, Marcel. *La Grande invention de l'écriture et son évolution.* 3 vols. Paris: Imprimérie Nationale, 1958.

Vol. 1 contains a general introduction to the evolution of the alphabet, vol. 2 offers a bibliography and indexes, while vol. 3 provides illustrative facsimiles.

763 Denholm-Young, N. *Handwriting in England and Wales.* Cardiff: University Press, 1954.

This book provides a general introduction to the major types of English and Welsh hands, especially to the development of bookhands. Illustrated.

764   Eis, Gerhard. *Altdeutsche Handschriften*. Munich: C.H. Beck, 1949.

A work which introduces a collection of facsimiles illustrating German scripts from Runic characters to Luther's New Testament. Each is accompanied by a transcription and descriptive notes. A bibliography is provided.

765   Fichtenau, H. *Mensch und Schrift im Mittelalter*. Institut für österreichische Geschichtsforschung, 5. Vienna: Universum, 1946.

A general study, orginally the author's *Habilitattionschrift*, Vienna, of the development of writing during the Middle Ages; arrangement is by different script and hand, with a full bibliography.

766   Frels, Wilhelm. *Deutsche Dichterhandschriften von 1400 bis 1900*. Rev. ed. (from 1934). Stuttgart: Hiersemann, 1970.

A facsimile collection and study of representative German poetic manuscripts from the late Middle Ages to the present. Autograph manuscripts have been selected when possible.

767   Jensen, Hans. *Die Schrift in Vergangenheit und Gegenwart*. 2nd ed. (from 1935). Berlin: Deutscher Verlag der Wissenschaften, 1958.

A general and fairly popular study of the development of all scripts, but the bibliographical notes are of some value.

768   Kapr, Albert. *Deutsche Schriftkunst*. Dresden: Verlag der Kunst, 1959.

An illustrated survey of German scripts and hands, especially from the early period.

769   Lange, Wilhelm H. *Schriftfibel. Geschichte der Abendländischen Schrift von den Anfängen bis zur Gegenwart*. 3rd ed. Wiesbaden: F. Steiner, n.d.

This introductory book provides a general but well-documented history of all Western scripts to the present time.

770   Lowe, E.A. *Handwriting, Our Medieval Legacy*. Rome: Edizione di Storia e Letteratura, 1969.

A good, general introduction to the development of script, reprinted with facsimiles and transcriptions from the original edition in C.G. Crump and E.F. Jacob, *The Legacy of the Middle Ages* (Oxford: Clarendon Press, 1926).

771   Mabillon, Jean. *De Re Diplomatica Libri Sex*. Paris: L. Billaine, 1681: *Librorum De Re Diplomatica Supplementum*. C. Robustel, 1704.

Mabillon, called the "father of scientific paleography," established in these works the basic distinctions between the major scripts: "*litteratoria, diplomatica, romana, gothica*, and *francogallica seu merovingica*." For an evaluation of Mabillon's contributions to the study of paleography and history of scripts, see item 938.

772 Mallon, Jean. *Ecriture latine de la capitale romaine à la minuscule.* Paris: Arts et Metiérs Graphiques, 1939.

A general survey of writing from Roman capitals to a manuscript dated A.D. 1470; the descriptive text is accompanied by a portfolio of 85 facsimiles.

773 Morison, Stanley. *Notes on the Development of the Latin Script from Early to Modern Times.* Cambridge: University Press, 1949.

Morison provides an introductory account of the main features of Rustic capitals, uncial, Carolingian, minuscule, Gothic, Humanist, and Chancery scripts, with several illustrative plates. He also gives some account of "universal modern Latin script."

774 Schulze-Delitzsch, H. *Geschichte der abendländischen Schreibschriftformen.* Leipzig: Teubner, 1933.

A general, introductory history of the major Western scripts, illustrated by plates and figures.

775 Spehr, Harald. *Der Ursprung der isländischen Schrift und ihre Weiterbildung bis zur Mitte des 13. Jahrhunderts.* Halle: Max Niemeyer, 1929.

Originally an inaugural dissertation and never subsequently provided with much documentation, this work nevertheless constitutes a lucid, descriptive history of the earliest Icelandic scripts.

776 Spunar, Pavel. "Palaeographical Difficulties in Defining an Individual Script," item 720, 4, pp. 62–68.

This essay is too brief to be of essential value, but it is worth citing here for its methodological approach to the question of distinguishing individual hands on the basis of certain graphical signs.

777 Tassin, R., and Toustain, C. *Nouveau traité de diplomatique ou l'on examine les fondemens de cet art ... par deux religieux benedictines de la congregation de S. Maur.* 6 vols. Paris: G. Desprez, 1750-65.

While primarily concerned with diplomatic documents and their historicity, this very important work also establishes for the first time the script distinctions "capital," "uncial," "half-uncial," and "cursive."

778 Ullman, B.L. *Ancient Writing and Its Influence.* New York, N.Y.: Longmans, 1932/1969.

An invaluable introduction to early Latin scripts and their later adaptations by Caroline and Humanist scribes, illustrated with 48 facsimiles. Ullman's theories are more fully developed and documented in item 848. The latest reprint (1969) is prefaced by an introduction by Julian Brown, who also expands and updates the original bibliography.

779 Wright, C.E. *English Vernacular Hands from the Twelfth to the Fifteenth Centuries.* Oxford Palaeographical Handbooks, 2. Oxford: Clarendon Press, 1960.

This important descriptive study presents representative
examples from manuscripts datable 1155-1469, with plates, transcriptions, and analyses of scripts. The author's useful introduction discusses the survival of vernacular manuscripts and the
paleographical features of English vernacular hands. See Roberts,
item 790, and Parkes, item 856, for other volumes in this series.
A valuable assessment with corrections may be found in the review by A.I. Doyle, *Medium Aevum*, 30 (1961), 117-20.

2. SPECIFIC STUDIES

(a) Greek

780   Bataille, André. *Les Papyrus. Traité d'Etudes Byzantines*, 2.
      Paris: Presses Universitaires de France, 1955.

      A general introduction to papyrus studies, with 14 plates from
      various periods beginning with the reign of Diocletian. The four
      chapters include (1) the papyrological document: materials,
      writing, dating, facsimiles; (2) interpretation; (3) collections
      of texts; and (4) problems such as chronology and the occult.
      Appendexes list Greek-Egyptian months with their Julian equiva-
      lents and a table of leading Egyptian officials. The index of
      Greek words for proper names and subjects is a valuable aid.
      This volume actually represents the first in a series called
      Traité d'Etudes Byzantines, ed. Paul Lemerle.

781   Bell, Sir H.I. *Egypt from Alexander the Great to the Arab Con-
      quest*. Oxford: Clarendon Press, 1948.

      This work provides a general but useful background to Greek
      scripts and the rule of papyrus documents.

782   Carlson, Arthur. *The Orthography and Phonology of the Latin
      Papyri*. Ann Arbor, Mich.: University of Michigan Press, 1950.

      Although specifically on Latin papyri, this work is also of
      some value for Greek papyrus studies, especially in its biblio-
      graphical references.

783   David, Martin, and Groningen, B.A. van. *Papyrological Primer*.
      3rd ed. Leigen: E.J. Brill, 1952.

      A general handbook for the beginner, with a select bibliography.
      The illustrating plates and maps are useful.

784   Jeffrey, Lilian. *The Local Scripts of Archaic Greece: A Study
      of the Origin of the Greek Alphabet and Its Development from
      the Eighth to the Fifth Centuries B.C.* Oxford Monographs on
      Classical Archaeology. Oxford: Clarendon Press, 1961.

      Although this work is primarily on inscriptions, with a list
      of catalogues in pt. 3, the comprehensive bibliography contains
      references to later scripts in manuscripts.

785   Lake, Kirsopp, and Lake, Silva, eds. *Monumenta Paleographica*

Vetera. Ser.1. Boston, Mass.: American Academy of Arts and
Science, 1934-.

A series of fascicles, issued by country, containing facsimile
reproductions and bibliographical notes on dated Greek minuscule
manuscripts to the year 1200.

786   Mayser, E. *Grammatik der Griechischen Papyri aus der Ptolemäerzeit*.
       2nd ed. (from 1906). Leipzig/Berlin: Teubner, 1938.

       Although this work is primarily concerned with the history of
       the Greek language and its grammar, it does include some dis-
       cussion of paleography and provides relevant bibliography.

787   Mioni, Elpidio. *Introduzione alla Paleografia Greca*. Universita
       di Padova, Studi Bizantini e Neogreci, 5. Padua: Liviana Edi-
       trice, 1973.

       A well-organized students' manual, with sections on codicology,
       writing instruments, codices, scripts, description of manuscripts.
       Included are 30 plates, with a final bibliography and index.

788   Mitteis, Ludwig, and Wilcken, Ulrich, eds. *Grundzüge und Chresto-
       mathie der Papyruskunde*. 2 vols. in 4. Leipzig: Teubner, 1912.

       A standard, early work on papyrology, with valuable bibliog-
       raphies for the nineteenth-century. Vol. 1 lists the principal
       papyrus collections.

789   Powell, John V., and Barber, Eric A., eds. *New Chapters in the
       History of Greek Literature: Recent Discoveries in Greek
       Poetry and Prose of the Fourth and Following Centuries, B.C.*
       Oxford: Clarendon Press, 1921.

       A discussion and edition of new fragments from Egyptian papyri,
       which includes a valuable bibliography and appendixes listing the
       major papyrus collections.

790   Roberts, Colin H. *Greek Literary Hands 350 B.C. - A.C. 400*.
       Oxford Palaeographical Handbooks, 1. Oxford: Clarendon Press,
       1955.

       The first in the new series of Oxford handbooks and significant
       for establishing the general format and methodology. Sixty
       different texts are here reproduced in collotype plates, with
       paleographical analyses and transcriptions on facing pages.

791   Schubart, Wilhelm. *Einführung in die Papyruskunde*. 2nd ed. (from
       1918). Berlin: Weidmann, 1920.

       A general introduction to the study of Greek papyrus manuscripts
       of the Graeco-Roman period, with a good bibliography; cf. the
       author's catalogue of Erlangen papyri, item 238.

792   ———. *Griechische Paläographie*. Munich: C.H. Beck, 1925.

       A re-edition of an earlier section in Von Müller's *Handbuch*,
       1624, which provides an introduction to all periods of Greek
       writing and an account of individual scripts.

793   Turner, Eric. *Greek Papyri: An Introduction*. Oxford/Princeton:
       University Press, 1968.

       This recent introduction to the subject is of special value
       for the paleographer in its lucid presentation of scripts and
       other matters; bibliographical references are included in the
       section on notes to chapters.

794   Wilson, Nigel G. *Mediaeval Greek Bookhands. Examples Selected
       from Greek Manuscripts in Oxford Libraries*. 2 vols. I. *Text*;
       II. *Plates*. Mediaeval Academy of America Publications, 81.
       Cambridge, Mass.: Mediaeval Academy, 1973.

       An introduction to medieval Greek paleography, originally
       designed as a seminar held at Harvard, Summer, 1972. The manu-
       scripts represent specimens of majuscule, cursive, and medieval
       minuscule from the fourth to the sixteenth centuries. The fac-
       similes are introduced in vol. 1 with paleographical comments
       and a general introduction to Greek bookhands.

795   Youtie, Herbert. *Scriptunculae*. 3 vols. Amsterdam: Hakkert,
       1973-75.

       A major collection of writings on all aspects of Greek papyri
       and their scripts; the range of bibliography is correspondingly
       large.

See also items 296, 734-6, 754, 757.

                                (b) Roman

796   Hoesen, Henry B. van. *Roman Cursive Writing*. Princeton, N.J.:
       University Press, 1915.

       A general introduction to all forms of Roman cursive; the
       bibliography is comprehensive for nineteenth-century items.

797   Mallon, Jean. *Paléographie romaine*. Consejo Superior de In-
       vestigaciones Científicas, Instituto Antonio de Nebrija de
       Filologia. Madrid: The Institute, 1952.

       An introduction to Roman writing to the second century A.D.
       The work discusses papyrus manuscripts, inscriptions, and the
       latest forms of script. Illustrated with figures and annotated
       plates.

See also item 778.

                            (c) Runic or Futhark

798   Arntz, Helmut. *Bibliographie der Runenkunde*. Leipzig: Otto
       Harrassowitz, 1937.

       A non-critical bibliography, arranged according to works and
       studies, titles, periodicals, index of editors, and lists of
       manuscripts grouped according to linguistic origin. An invalu-
       able list of nineteenth-century secondary works mainly in German.

799 Derolez, R. *Runica Manuscripta. The English Tradition.* Rijksuniversiteit to Gent. Werken uitgeven door de Faculteit van
de Wijsbegeerte en Letteven, 118. Ghent: The University, 1954.

An introduction to runes and their manuscripts, with emphasis
upon those of known English provenance.

800 Elliott, Ralph W.V. *Runes: An Introduction.* Manchester: University
Press, 1963.

To date this work represents the best English study of runic
manuscripts; it includes a select bibliography.

801 Krause, Wolfgang, ed. *Bibliographie des Runenischriften nach
Fundorten.* Abhandlungen der Akademie der Wissenschaften in
Göttingen philologischhistorische Klasse, 48. Göttingen: Vanden-
hoeck and Ruprecht, 1961-. I. *Die Runenischriften der Britischen
Inseln,* ed. Hertha Marquardt, 1961.

A list of editions and works on runic inscriptions, which also
includes indication of relationships to manuscript sources.
Arranged alphabetically by geographical location.

802 Musset, Lucien. *Introduction à la runologie. En partie d'après
les notes de Fernand Mossé.* Bibliothèque de Philologie German-
ique, 20. Paris: Aubier-Montaigne, 1965.

A comprehensive and detailed study of runic letters, which
owes much to an unfinished work by Mossé. The bibliography is
useful in its citation of many lesser known French studies in
runology.

803 Page, R.I. *An Introduction to English Runes.* London: Methuen/
New York: Harper and Row, 1973.

This work provides a general survey of the background to runic
letters and gives an account and bibliography for runes found
in English literary texts.

804 Paues, A.C. "Runes and Manuscripts." *The Cambridge History of
English Literature,* I. Cambridge: University Press, 1907.

A brief account of runic letters in manuscripts. A brief
bibliography is provided.

(d) Uncial and Insular

805 Bieler, Ludwig. "Insular Palaeography: Present State and Problems."
Scriptorium, 3 (1949), 267-94.

A detailed, critical summary of the state of scholarship,
perhaps the best example of similar and periodical statements
appearing in this journal. Bieler presents his bibliographical
references according to location and chronology.

806 Branner, R. "The Art of the Scriptorium at Luxeuil." *Speculum,*
29 (1954), 678-90.

An analysis more of paleographical features associated with

the Merovingian manuscripts produced at Luxeuil (a *coenobia* founded by Saint Columban, ca. A.D. 590) than of the activities of the *Scriptorium* itself. Branner describes and illustrates through plates the types of manuscripts produced, their scripts, and their decoration; he also provides a good, critical bibliography of related items.

807   Hatch, W.H.P. *Principal Uncial Manuscripts of the New Testament.* Chicago, Ill.: Chicago University Press, 1939.

An introduction to the script and a descriptive list of manuscripts with illustrating facsimiles; a companion volume (Cambridge, Mass.: Harvard University Press, 1951) provides commentary and facsimiles for select minuscule manuscripts of the New Testament.

808   Lindsay, W.M. *Contractions in Early Latin Minuscule Manuscripts.* Oxford: J. Parker and Co., 1908.

A discussion on and dictionary of early minuscule abbreviations and the manuscripts in which they are found.

809   ———. *Early Irish Minuscule Script.* St. Andrew's University Publications, 6. Oxford: J. Parker and Co., 1910.

A general account of the development of this script, with 12 illustrating plates and a select bibliography.

810   Lowe, E.A. "A Hand-list of Half-Uncial Manuscripts." *Miscellanea Francesco Ehrle*, 4, Studi e Testi, 40 (1924), 34–61.

This early study provides one of the bases for the more complete study published in 1960; see next item.

811   ———. *English Uncial.* Oxford: Clarendon Press, 1960.

The standard introduction to the development of *scriptura uncialis* in late seventh century England, and an analysis of its characteristics. Lowe provides paleographical comments on many individual manuscripts and illustrates his text with 40 plates.

812   ———. "'The Script of Luxeuil,' a Title Vindicated." *Revue Bénédictine*, 63 (1953), 132–42.

The author uses 'display scripts' as a criterion for localizing the home of this script.

813   Rand, E.K., and Jones, Leslie Webber. *The Earliest Book of Tours: with Supplementary Descriptions of Other Manuscripts of Tours.* Studies in the Script of Tours, 2. Cambridge, Mass.: The Mediaeval Academy of America, 1934.

An account of the Paris Eugippius (A.D. 700–750), with detailed analyses of the varieties of script it contains. Indexes and plates are provided. For a study of slightly later manuscripts, see Rand, item 821.

814   Wright, David H. "Some Notes on English Uncial," *Traditio*, 17 (1961), 441–56.

Taking Lowe as his starting point, Wright re-examines the
chronology, localization, and sources of English uncial. He
concludes that the capitulary script of the Codex Amiatinus
developed from different, older models. Illustrated by six plates.

See also item 1157.

(e) Caroline

815 Autenrieth, J. "Problems der Lokalisierung und Datierung von
Spätkarolingischen Schriften (10. und 11. Jahrhundert)." in
item 716, 1, pp. 67-74.

Problems in regard to this script are considered under such
headings as "nature of script," "scriptoria," "dating," and
"text."

816 Bischoff, B. "Frühkarolingische Handschriften und ihre Heimat."
Scriptorium, 22 (1968), 306-14.

The author discusses the development of early Caroline script,
wiᴛh reference to that of St. Amand. For a more detailed analysis,
see item 1330.

817 ————. "Paläographische Fragen deutschen Denkmäler der
Karolingerzeit," *Frühmittelalterliche Studien.* 5 (1971), 101-
34.

See item 816.

818 Bishop, T.A.M. *English Caroline Minuscule.* Oxford: Clarendon
Press, 1971.

The author divides the script into periods within 950-1100
and discusses its features chronologically. These are related
to the 24 plates, which are also accompanied by transcriptions
and paleographical notes. Bishop examines the script of Corbie
in item 716, 1, pp. 9-16.

819 Jones, Leslie W. *The Script of Cologne, from Hildebald to Hermann.*
Cambridge, Mass.: Mediaeval Academy of America, 1932.

This excellent study describes the development of an early
Caroline hand associated with Cologne. It is illustrated with
over 100 plates.

820 Lindsay, W.M. *Early Welsh Script.* Oxford: J. Parker and Co.,
1912.

A general history of Welsh Caroline and Gothic scripts, illustrated by 17 facsimiles and transcriptions.

821 Rand, E.K. *A Survey of the Manuscripts of Tours. I. Text; II.
Plates.* Studies in the Script of Tours, 1. Cambridge, Mass.:
The Mediaeval Academy of America, 1929.

A fully descriptive account of slightly later manuscripts,
from the ninth to the twelfth centuries, with reference to their
paleographical and historical background. Indexes are provided
for manuscripts, authors, works, and subjects. See item 813.

(f) Gothic

822   Boussard, J. "Influences insulaires dans la formation de l'écri-
      ture gothique." *Scriptorium*, 5 (1951), 238-64.

      A detailed analysis of certain features (breaking, ligatures,
      etc.) in view of straight and oblique writing instruments, with
      examples in the letters *a*, *e*, *o*, *r*, and *s* compared from insular
      and caroline miniscule. A fusion of insular and continental ele-
      ments appears to suggest the origins of Gothic script.

823   Boyle, L.E. "The Emergence of Gothic Handwriting." *The Journal
      of Typographical Research*, 4 (1970), 307-16.

      A general account of the development of Gothic script as a
      result of the growing market for writings during the late twelfth
      century. Illustrations, taken from H. Meyer's *Die Schriftenwicklung*
      (Zurich: Graphis Press, 1958), show the main lines of change
      and adaptation from late Roman cursive to fifteenth-century
      textura.

824   Crous, E., and Kirchner, J. *Die gotischen Schriftarten*. Leipzig:
      Klinkhardt and Biermann, 1928.

      Illustrates the development of Gothic scripts from mainly
      German examples, especially from the fourteenth and fifteenth
      centuries. Full bibliography, indexes.

825   Heinemeyer, Walter. *Studien zur Geschichte der gotischen Urkunden-
      schrift*. Cologne: Böhlau, 1962.

      A carefully documented study of the development of Gothic
      script as represented chiefly in diplomatic documents. It also
      attempts to localize certain features. Facsimiles, bibliography,
      and indexes are provided.

826   Ker, N.R. "The Date of the 'Tremulous' Worcester Hand." *Leeds
      Studies in English*, 6 (1937), 28-29.

      Ker offers paleographical notes on the thirteenth-century
      gloss found in MSS. Hatton 115 and Corpus Christi College Cam-
      bridge 198.

827   Kirchner, Joachim. *Scriptum Gothica Libraria a saeculo 12 usque
      ad finem medii aevi*. Munich/Vienna: Oldenbourg, 1966.

      This work appears to be the best and most fully documented
      study of Gothic scripts, especially those of German provenance.
      It provides 87 illustrations of dated manuscripts, with tran-
      scriptions and paleographical/codicological discussion. The
      plates form two series: *litterae textuales*, then *litterae notulae*,
      bastardae, and *cursivae*.

828   Simon, Georg. *Gotisk Scrift: laesning af slaegts-og lokal-
      historiske kilder*. Copenhagen: Dansk Historisk Handbogsforlag,
      1977.

      A detailed study of Gothic scripts as found in Danish medieval
      manuscripts, mainly archival. The work provides an invaluable
      and up-to-date bibliography on Scandinavian studies for this script.

(g) National Hands

829   Brown, Virginia. "A Second New List of Beneventan Manuscripts
      (1)." *Mediaeval Studies*, 40 (1978), 239-89.

Continuing E.A. Lowe's "New List" in *Collectanea Vaticana in
Honorem Anselmi M. Card. Albareda a Biblioteca Apostolica Edita*,
Studi e Testi, 220 (Rome: Vatican, 1962), 211-44, itself an
addenda to the next item, Dr. Brown adds about 275 separate
entries, of which all but about 25 are fragmentary. These are
listed alphabetically by present location, Agnone-Zagreb, with
an appendix of presumed Beneventan manuscripts. She provides
valuable bibliographical notes for other Beneventan manuscript
lists and studies.

830   Lowe, E.A. *The Beneventan Script: A History of the South Italian
      Minuscule*. Oxford: Clarendon Press, 1914.

An important initial study of the script associated with Monte
Cassino and the Duchy of Benevento, from the eleventh to the
fifteenth centuries. Among other topics the author discusses
origins, morphology, abbreviations, punctuation, and materials.
Indexes list scribes and manuscripts. For a collection of illustrating facsimiles, see item 907. A forthcoming second edition
has been prepared and enlarged by Dr. Brown (Rome: Edizioni di
Storia e Letteratura, 1980?); see also her article, item 829.

See also item 350.

(h) Humanistic and Renaissance

831   de le Mare, A.C. *The Handwriting of the Italian Humanists*, I.
      London: Oxford University Press, 1973.

An accurate and detailed analysis and study of eight major
Florentine Humanists and their hands: Petrarch, Boccaccio,
Salutati, Niccoli, Bracciolini, Aragazzi, Sozomeno, and Vespucci.
Arrangement is by individual with biography, and an account of
extant manuscripts, bibliography, and facsimile examples. Volume
II is in progress.

832   ————. "Humanist Script: The First Ten Years," in *Das Verhält-
      nis der Humanisten zum Buch*, ed. F. Krafft and D. Wuttke.
      Deutsche Forschungsgemeinschaft, Kommission für Humanismus-
      forschung, Mitteilung 4. Boppard: 1977, pp. 89-110.

A study of several of the earliest (1406) Humanist manuscripts,
among them Florence Laurenziana MS. conv. sopp. 131.

833   Elder, J.P. "Clues for Dating Florentine Humanistic Manuscripts."
      Studies in Philology, 44 (1947), 136-9.

After a brief introduction on the general nature of these
manuscripts, the author lists dated manuscripts by such Humanists as di Mario, Civiagio, and Sinibaldi. For additions and
corrections to this article, see Ullman, item 848.

834   Fairbank, A.J., and Wolpe, B.L. *Renaissance Handwriting: An
      Anthology of Italic Scripts.* Cleveland: World Publishing Co.,
      1960.

      This work constitutes a general introduction and a collection
      of 96 plates. Each is accompanied by paleographical notes and
      there is a select bibliography.

835   ————, and Hunt, R.W. *Humanistic Script of the Fifteenth and
      Sixteenth Centuries.* Bodleian Picture Book, 12. Oxford: Bodleian
      Library, 1960.

      This attractively printed book provides a brief introduction
      to types of Humanistic scripts by means of a series of facsimile
      illustrations; these range in place and date from Florence,
      1412, to Scotland, 1603. Some interesting comparisons are made
      between Caroline minuscule of the early ninth century and select
      nineteenth-century imitations, e.g., William Morris' *Odes of
      Horace* (1875-76).

836   ————, and Dickins, Bruce. *The Italic Hand in Tudor Cambridge.*
      Cambridge Bibliographical Society, Monographs, 5. Cambridge:
      The Society, 1962.

      A general discussion with analyses of select illustrations of
      sixteenth-century Cambridge documents, both public and private.

837   Hessel, Alfred, "Die Entstehung der Renaissanceschriften." *Archiv
      für Urkundenforschung,* 13 (1933), 1-14.

      An introduction to Renaissance scripts in mainly archival
      documents.

838   Hirsch, Hans. *Gotik und Renaissance in der Entwicklung unserer
      Schrift.* Vienna: Hölder-Pichler-Tempsky, 1932.

      A brief and general discussion of the development of modern
      writing from late Gothic and early Renaissance scripts. Not
      documented.

839   Judge, Cyril B. *Specimens of Sixteenth-Century English Hand-
      writing.* Cambridge, Mass.: Harvard University Press, 1935.

      A collection of specimens from public and private records,
      with some paleographical and contextual discussion.

840   Kristeller, Paul O. "A New Work of the Origin and Development
      of Humanistic Script." *Manuscripta,* 5 (1961), 35-40.

      This article and the following two items survey scholarship
      on the development of Humanistic scripts.

841   ————. "A New Work on the Origin and Development of Humanistic
      Script—Addenda." *Manuscripta,* 5 (1961), 171.

842   ————. "Tasks and Experiences in the Study of Humanistic
      Manuscripts." *Renaissance News,* 7 (1954), 75-84.

      See item 840.

843   Meiss, Millard. "Towards a More Comprehensive Renaissance Palae-
       ography." *The Art Bulletin*, 42 (1960), 97-112.

       The author proposes that the use of capital letters modeled on
       Roman Imperial inscriptions was due to the influence of the
       painter Mantegna in Padua. Bibliographical notes are provided.

844   Mentz, Georg. *Handschriften der Reformationzeit*. Bonn: A. Marcus
       and E. Weber, 1912.

       A discussion and collection of plates, each with descriptive
       notes, of handwriting samples from Erasmus to Leonhard von Eck,
       1541.

845   Morison, Stanley, "Early Humanist Script and the First Roman
       Type." *The Library*, 24 (1943), 1-30.

       A study of localized Humanistic scripts, which focuses upon
       the calligraphy of Niccolò Niccoli and its adaptation to print-
       ing type.

846   Piepkorn, Arthur Carl, ed. *Reproductions of Sixteenth-Century
       Handwriting: Reformation Essays and Studies Paleography Manual*.
       Foundation for Reformation Research, St. Louis, Mo.: The
       Foundation, 1972.

       Designed as a manual to provide illustrative material for a
       paleography course at Concordia Seminary, St. Louis, Mo. The
       photocopied documents date from 1524 to 1601.

847   Thomas, D. "What is the Origin of the 'Scrittura umanistica'?"
       La Bibliofilia, 53 (1951), 1-10.

       In an analysis of MS. Florence, Laur. 48.22, the author vindi-
       cates Novati's early dating and proposes that the manuscript
       was transcribed by Poggio in Rome, 1403, and emended by Coluccio
       in 1428.

848   Ullman, B.L. *The Origin and Development of Humanistic Script*.
       Rome: Edizioni di Storia e Letteratura, 1960.

       This represents one of the major and most influential works
       on Humanistic script. Beginning with Coluccio Sallutati (1395),
       whom Ullman considers the originator of *littera antiqua*, he goes
       on to trace the development of Humanistic calligraphy throughout
       the Renaissance. In successive chapters he discusses the con-
       tributions of Coluccio, Poggio, Niccolò, and Florentine callig-
       raphers such as Aretino and di Mario. The bibliographical docu-
       mentation is of considerable value to paleographers working in
       this period.

849   Wardrop, James. *The Script of Humanism: Some Aspects of Human-
       istic Script, 1460-1560*. Oxford: Clarendon Press, 1963.

       These were originally lectures delivered at King's College,
       University of London, in March, 1952. The 58 facsimiles and
       bibliographical references have been subsequently added to pro-
       vide a survey of select aspects of the mainly later develop-
       ment of this script. See also item 778.

See also items 1396, 1401-2, 1406.

(i) Bookhands

850   Bischoff, B. "Paläographie der abendländischen Buchschriften
       vom V. bis zum XII. Jahrhundert," *Relazioni del X Congresso*
       Internazionale di Science Storiche, Roma (Sept. 4-11, 1955).
       6 vols. Firenze: G.C. Sansoni, 1955. Vol. 1, pp. 385-406.

       A summary of the development and main features of early book
       hands.

851   Thompson, S. Harrison. *Latin Bookhands of the Later Middle Ages*
       1100-1500. Cambridge: University Press, 1969.

       With 132 manuscripts represented in facsimile extracts, nearly
       all of fixed date and provenance, the author attempts to trace
       the development of various regional bookhands. This is an
       attractively produced folio volume which includes bibliographical
       references.

See also item 722.

(j) Court Hands

852   Jenkinson, Sir Charles Hilary. *The Later Court Hands in England*
       from the Fifteenth to the Seventeenth Centuries. Cambridge:
       University Press, 1927.

853   ————. *Palaeography and the Practical Study of Court Hand.*
       Cambridge: University Press, 1915.

       The latter of these two works constitutes a general introduc-
       tion to the main features of court hands (it was originally a
       paper read before the International Congress of Historical
       Studies, April, 1913), with plates accompanied by paleographical
       notes; the first work is a continuation of the second and fo-
       cuses upon later court hands.

854   Johnson, Charles, and Jenkinson, Sir Charles Hilary. *English*
       Court Hand, A.D. 1066 to 1500. 2 vols. Oxford: Clarendon
       Press, 1915/New York: F. Ungar, 1967.

       Volume 1 of this significant study includes a discussion of
       court hand and its development, while the second volume pro-
       vides facsimile examples, many from public records.

For chancery hands, see Section VII.

(k) Cursive Hands

855   Federici, Vicenzo. *Esampi di corsiva antica dal secolo I dell'era*
       moderna al IV. Rome: Arti Grafiche e Fotomeccaniche Sansaini,
       1968.

A general introduction to the development of early cursive hands, accompanied by a portfolio of 19 plates.

856 Parkes, M.B. *English Cursive Book Hands, 1250-1500*. Oxford Palaeographical Handbooks, 3. Oxford: Clarendon Press, 1969.

A history of cursive hands (*littera cursiva*) used in English books, with an account of their origins and latest medieval forms; Parkes recognizes two major types: *Anglicana* and *Secretary*; *Anglicana* in turn presents two variant hands, *Anglicana Formata* (or bookhand) and *Bastard Anglicana* (*Anglicana* and *Textura* combined). Each of the 48 manuscripts used to illustrate one form or another is transcribed and analyzed for distinctive features.

857 Poulle, Emmanuel. *Paléographie des écritures cursives en France du XVe au XVIIe siècle*. Geneva: Droz, 1966.

A brief introduction to late cursive features as seen in manuscripts of Parisian provenance; each of the 32 facsimiles is transcribed and annotated.

3. FACSIMILES

(a) Bibliographical Materials

858 Zotter, Hans. *Bibliographie faksimilierter Handschriften*. Graz: Akademische Drück- und Verlagsanstalt, 1976.

A bibliography for all facsimiles of medieval manuscripts, arranged alphabetically by city and library. It contains descriptions of manuscripts and notes printed facsimile editions. Included are subject/work, period, place, and editor/author indexes.

(b) General Collections

859 Arndt, Wilhelm. *Schrifttafeln zur Erlerhnung der lateinischen Paläographie*. 3 vols. 4th ed. (from 1874). Berlin: Grote, 1904-29.

A series of facsimiles from Latin manuscripts dating from the second to the fourteenth centuries. It is designed to serve as a series of practical exercises for the beginning student.

860 Batelli, G., Bischoff, B., *et al.*, eds. *Umbrae Codicum Occidentalium*. Societas Codicum Mediaevalium Studii Promovendis. Amsterdam: North Holland Publishing Co., 1960-.

A series of complete facsimiles of manuscripts mainly from the earlier period, e.g., IV, *Saint Dunstan's Classbook from Glastonbury*, ed. R.W. Hunt, 1961. The volumes contain some introductory and bibliographical matter.

861   *Codices Graeci et Latini Photographice Depicti.* Leiden: A.W.
      Sijthoff, 1897-; *Supplementum*, 1902-.

      A series of manuscripts in facsimile, ed. by such paleographers
      as W.N. Rieu (vol. 1, 1897), S. de Vries (vols. 2-19), and
      most recently, G.I. Lieftinck.

862   *Codices Latini Antiquiores*, ed. E.A. Lowe. 11 vols. Oxford:
      Clarendon Press, 1934-66; *Supplement*, 1971; Pt. II, *Great
      Britain and Ireland*, 2nd ed. by Virginia Brown, 1972.

      This extensive collection contains one facsimile each of repre-
      sentative Latin manuscripts before the ninth century, classified
      by country and area; each volume is prefaced by an introduction.
      Paleographical indexes are now in preparation by J.J. John.
      Brown has added a bibliographical supplement, pp. 56-60.

863   *Codices Selecti.* Graz: Akademische Druck- und Verlagsanstalt,
      1960-.

      A series of well-printed facsimile editions in four groups:
      Illuminated Manuscripts, Texts, Middle American Manuscripts,
      and Oriental Manuscripts. The medieval examples range from a
      fourth-century Vergil to various sixteenth-century texts. Vol 1:
      Sacramentarium Leonianum (Cod. Veronensis 85, olim 80), ed. F.
      Sauer (1960). Extra-series editions appear occasionally.

864   Degering, Hermann. *Die Schrift. Atlas der Schriftformen des
      Abendlandes vom Altertum bis zum Ausgang des 18. Jahrhunderts.*
      3rd ed. (from 1929). Tübingen: E. Wasmuth, 1952.

      A series of illustrations for the development of Western
      scripts to the eighteenth century.

865   Hatch, W.H.P. *Facsimiles and Descriptions of Minuscule Manuscripts
      of the New Testament.* Cambridge, Mass.: Harvard University
      Press, 1951.

      Over 100 facsimiles of biblical manuscript leaves, each
      illustrating a minuscule variant.

866   Kirchner, Joachim. *Scriptura Latina Libraria a Saeculo Primo
      Usque ad Finem Medii Aevi.* Munich: R. Oldenburh, 1955.

      A collection of facsimiles, primarily of bookhands, with
      descriptive annotation and bibliography; the manuscripts are
      located in 20 major libraries, including the Vatican, British
      Library, and Bibliothèque Nationale.

867   Monaci, Ernesto. *Esempi di Scrittura latina del secolo I di
      Cristo al XVIII.* Rome: Domenico Anderson, 1906.

      A limited collection (52pp.) of facsimiles designed to intro-
      duce beginning paleographers to the major scripts.

868   Prou, M. *Manuel de paléographie: Recueil de fac-similes d'écri-
      tures du Ve au XVIIe siècle.* 3 vols. Paris: A. Picard et fils,
      1892-1904.

A collection of early Latin, French, and Provençal manuscripts, each transcribed and annotated.

869 *Recueil des facsimiles à l'usage de l'Ecole des Chartes.* 5 vols. Paris: Ecole des Chartes, 1880-1900.

A wide selection of facsimiles from every period and provenance.

870 Steffens, F. *Lateinische Paläographie. 100 Tafeln mit einer systematischen Darstellung der lateinischen Schrift.* 2nd rev. ed. (from 1903). Berlin/Leipzig: De Gruyter, 1929; trans. from 1st ed. R. Coulon, *Paléographie latine*, Trier: Schaar & Dathe, 1910.

An excellent selection of attractively printed facsimiles; each receives full paleographical commentary and bibliography.

871 Turyn, Alexander. *Codices Graeci Vaticani Saeculis XIII e XIV Scripta Annorumque Notis Instructi.* Rome: Bibliotheca Vaticana, 1964.

A folio-size collection of plates, each accompanied by a half-page of paleographical notes. Name/subject indexes are provided.

872 Wattenbach, G. *Scripturae Graecae Specimina.* 4th ed. Berlin: Berolini, 1936.

A portfolio collection of 35 plates, with transcriptions and commentary.

(c) Collections or Individual Manuscript
Facsimiles of National Origin

The following items are intended as merely a select group of individual or collective facsimile editions, either representative in nature or of special interest for the manuscripts they reproduce. For specific manuscripts in facsimile editions, see item 858.

i. Belgium

873 Cheyn, J. van den. *Album belge de paléographie. Recueil de specimens d'écritures, d'auteurs et de manuscrits belges (VIIe - XVIe siècles).* Jette/Brussels: Vandamme and Rosignol, 1908.

A collection of examples from 32 manuscripts, most of them dated. Some paleographical commentary is included.

See also item 914.1.

ii. Czechoslovakia

874 Friedrich, C. *Acta Regum Bohemiae Selecta.* 2 vols. Prague: The University, 1908-30.

Approximately 30 facsimiles selected from royal charters of the (mainly) medieval period.

875 ———. *Monumenta Palaeographica Bohemiae et Moravia*. Prague: The University, 1904.

A small collection of eight facsimiles from various medieval manuscripts. Paleographical annotations are provided.

iii. France

876 Champion, Pierre, ed. *Le Manuscrit autographe des poésies de Charles d'Orléans*. Geneva: Slatkine Reprints, 1975.

A facsimile of the early fifteenth-century manuscript; of some significance as one of the few medieval autograph manuscripts. Reprinted from the 1907 edition, originally issued as vol. 3 of the *Bibliothèque du quinzieme siècle*. See also item 455.

877 Lauer, P., and Samaran, C. *Les Diplômes originaux des Merovingiens*. Paris: E. Leroux, 1908.

A small collection of Merovingian (to A.D. 987) documents, with a preface by Maurice Prou.

878 Lemps, Michel de, ed. *Trésors de la Bibliothèque Municipale de Reims*. I. *Manuscrits*; II. *Imprimés*, ed. Roger Laslier. Reims: Bibliothèque Municipale, 1978.

A collection of facsimiles from the seventh to sixteenth centuries, each with full description; photographs of some bindings are included. A useful introduction prefaces the work, which includes a bibliography of French library catalogues. Also useful is a small dictionary of terms, e.g., "antiphonaire."

879 Lot, F.; Lauer, P.; and Tessier, G., eds. *Diplomatica Karolinorum. Recueil de reproductions en facsimile des actes originaux des souvereins carolingiens conservés dans les archives et bibliothèques de France*. 5 vols. Paris: H. Didier/Toulouse: E. Privat, 1936-38.

An extensive group of diplomatic documents of royal provenance; some paleographical annotations; bibliography.

880 Omont, H. *Listes des recueils de fac-similés et ses reproductions de manuscrits conservés à la Bibliothèque Nationale*. 3rd ed. by P. Lauer. Paris: Bibliothèque Nationale, 1935.

A descriptive catalogue, arranged alphabetically by author or genre. It contains a general index.

iv. Germany

881 Baesecke, G. *Lichtdrucke nach althochdeutsche Handschriften*. Halle/Salle: Max Niemeyer, 1926.

A portfolio of 38 plates from five Old High German manuscripts; paleographical notes.

882 Duft, Johannes, ed. *Das Nibelungenlied und Die Klage, MS. B. (Cod. Sangall. 857).* Cologne/Graz: Böhlau, 1962.

A succinct introduction on manuscript and script, followed by facsimiles of pp. 291-451 of the St. Gall manuscript, dated ca. 1260.

883 Enneccerus, M. *Die ältesten deutschen Sprachdenkmaler in Lichtdrucken.* Frankfurt-am-Main: The Author, 1897.

A collection of facsimiles from early German manuscripts, including the *Hildebrandslied*, 1-4, and *Strasbourg Oaths*, 34-36.

884 Gallee, J.H. *Altsächsiche Sprachdenkmaler. Faksimilesammlung.* Leiden: E.J. Brill, 1895.

A small collection of Old Saxon manuscripts, which includes a facsimile sample from the *Heliand*.

885 Koennecke, G. *Bilderatlas zur Geschichte der deutschen Nationalliteratur.* 2nd ed. Marburg: Elwert, 1912.

A somewhat eclectic series of plates illustrating the history of German literature; a few represent the medieval period, e.g., the *Hildebrandslied* and *Lucidarius*.

886 *Monumenta Palaeographica. Denkmaler der Schreibkunst des Mittelalter*, ed. Anton Chroust. Munich: F. Bruckmann, 1902-17/ Leipzig: Harrasowitz, 1927-40.

A series of volumes of facsimiles illustrating Latin manuscripts. The first (1902-06) offers examples of Latin and German manuscripts.

887 Petzet, E., and Glauning, O., eds. *Deutsche Schrifttafeln des IX. - XVI. Jahrhunderts aus Handschriften der Konl. Hof- und Staatsbibliothek in München.* 5 vols. Munich: C. Kuhn, 1910-12; Leipzig: Hiersemann, 1924-30.

A facsimile-illustrated history of Old High and Middle High German scripts of mainly Bavarian provenance.

See also item 914.

v. Great Britain and Ireland

888 *Book of Kells. Evangeliorum quattuor Codex Cenannensis.* Auctoritate Collegii Sacrosanctae et Endividuae Trinitatis Juxta Dublin- auxilioque Bibliothecae Confederationis. Helveticae Totius Codicis similitudinem Accuratissime De Pecti Exprimendam Curavit Typographaeum Urs Graf. Introd. by Ernest Henry Alton and Peter Meyer. Berne/New York: Graf, 1950-51.

A full size and beautifully printed facsimile of the complete *Book of Kells*; the introduction gives descriptive analyses of the manuscript, art, and cultural background. See also item 1144.

889   Chaucer Society. *Autotypes of Chaucer Manuscripts*. Series 1,
      nos. 48, 56, 62, and 74. London: The Society, 1876–86/New York,
      N.Y.: Johnson, 1967.

      Facsimiles (16) of Chaucer's works from manuscripts in British
      libraries such as the Bodleian and British Library.

890   Croft, P.J. *Autograph Poetry in the English Language: Facsimiles
      of Original Manuscripts from the Fourteenth to Twentieth
      Centuries*. 2 vols. London: Cassell, 1973.

      A beautifully reproduced folio-sized collection of facsimile
      pages. Vol. 1 (for the earlier period) includes pages from
      William Herbert, John Shirley, Thomas Hoccleve, John Capgrave,
      John Skelton, Thomas Wyatt, and Thomas Sackville. Each plate is
      introduced by paleographical notes and a full transcription.

891   *Early English Manuscripts in Facsimile*, ed. Peter Clemoes,
      Bertram Colgrave, Kemp Malone, and Knud Schiltsbye. Copenhagen:
      Rosenkilde and Baggar, 1951-. Baltimore, Md.: Johns Hopkins
      Press, 1951-.

      The series includes such manuscripts as *The Leningrad Bede*,
      ed. O Arngart (1952). Detailed and documented introductions
      preface each facsimile edition.

892   Early English Text Society, Director, N. Davis. London: Oxford
      University Press, 1883-.

      The Society primarily publishes editions of texts, but
      occasionally issues a facsimile volume. The first was the *Fac-
      simile of the Epinal Glossary*, ed. H. Sweet, EETS. OS. 79 (1883).
      Other facsimile editions include *Beowulf* (1958/1967); MS. Harley
      2253 (1964); and MS. Bodley 34 (1959). The introductory matter
      varies in scope and detail.

893   Ellis, R. *Specimens of Latin Palaeography from Manuscripts in
      the Bodleian Library*. Oxford: University Press, 1903.

      A small collection of 20 plates from Latin manuscripts in this
      library.

894   Greg, Walter W. *Facsimiles of Twelve Early English Manuscripts
      in the Library of Trinity College Cambridge*. Oxford: Clarendon
      Press, 1913.

      This collection provides facsimiles of extracts from eleventh-
      century homilies to a fifteenth-century manuscript of Chaucer's
      Canterbury Tales. Transcriptions and notes are included.

895   *Lindisfarne Gospels, The. Evangeliorum Quattuor Codex Lindis-
      farnei Musei Britannici Codex Cottonianus Nero D. IV*, ed. with
      introd. T.D. Kendrick, *et al*, 2 vols. Oltun/Lausanne: Urs
      Graf, 1956–60.

      An attractively reproduced facsimile of the manuscript, with
      an introductory study and bibliography. The earlier facsimile
      edition by Eric George Millar (London: Trustees of the British
      Library, 1923), provides plates from two related manuscripts and
      a detailed study of the decoration.

896 New Palaeographical Society. *Facsimiles of Ancient Manuscripts*, ed. J.P. Gilson, E.M. Thompson, and G.F. Warner. *First Series*, London: The Society, 1903 12; *Second Series*, 1913-32; *Indices*, 1914, 1932.

897 Palaeographical Society. *Facsimiles of Manuscripts and Inscriptions*, ed. E.A. Bond, E.M. Thompson, and G.F. Warner. *First Series*, London: W. Clowes and Sons, 1873-83; *Second Series*, London: 1884-94, *Indices*, 1901.

Both series present folio-sized facsimiles in chronological arrangement, from an inscription of 432 B.C. (item 997); each is accompanied by paleographical notes and transcription. The useful indexes are divided into sections according to chronology, author/subject, country, script, ornamentation, and owners past and present.

898 Petti, Anthony G. *English Literary Hands from Chaucer to Dryden*. London: Edward Arnold, 1977.

A collection of facsimiles from fourteenth to seventeenth-century English literary manuscripts, with transcriptions and notes on facing pages. The summary introduction also provides lists of punctuation signs and abbreviations. An important review appeared in *The Library*, 5th ser., 33 (1978), 343-9.

899 *Scolar Press Facsimile Series*. London: Scolar Press, 1975-.

A series of attractively printed facsimile editions of the more important Middle English manuscripts. The first to appear was *The Thornton Manuscript* (ca. 1440), ed. D.S. Brewer and A.E.B. Owen (1975); subsequent vols. include the Findern (1977), Bannatyne (1979), Fairfax (1979), and Cambridge University Library MS. Ff 2. 3B (1979).

900 Skeat, W.W. *Twelve Facsimiles of Old English Manuscripts*. Oxford: Clarendon Press, 1892.

This collection includes a general paleographical introduction and 12 plates from MS. Hatton 20 (ca. 900) to MS. Rawlinson Poet. 163 (late fifteenth century). Transcriptions are included.

vi. Hispanic Countries

901 Buelow, Kenneth, and Mackenzie, David. *A Manual of Manuscript Transcription for the Dictionary of the Old Spanish Language*. Madison, Wis.: Hispanic Seminary of Medieval Studies, 1977.

A collection of facsimiles from medieval Spanish manuscripts, with paleographical notes, bibliography, and indexes. See item 143.

902 Burnam, John Miller. *Palaeographia Iberica: fac-similes de manuscrits espangnols et portugais (IXe-XVe siècles)*. 3 pts. in 2 vols. Paris: H. Champion, 1912-25.

A collection of one-page facsimiles from representative Spanish and Portuguese medieval manuscripts; transcriptions and paleographical notations accompany each.

903   Clark, Charles Upson. *Collectanea Hispanica*. Transactions of
       the Connecticut Academy of Arts and Sciences, 24. Paris:
       H. Champion, 1920.

       Facsimiles of Spanish manuscripts representing a wide range
       of medieval scripts.

904   Ewald, Paul, and Loewe, G., eds. *Exempla Scripturae Visi-Goticae
       XL Tabulis Expressa*. Heidelberg: G. Koesler, 1883.

       The 40 full-page facsimiles of Latin and Spanish manuscripts
       cover the sixth to eleventh centuries.

vii. Italy

905   Ehrle, Franz, and Liebaert, Paul. *Specimina Codicum Latinorum
       Vaticanorum*. 2nd ed. (from 1912). Berlin/Leipzig: De Gruyter,
       1932.

       Designed mainly for the use of students, the 50 loose fac-
       simile sheets are transcribed on separate sheets with paleo-
       graphical and bibliographical notes.

906   Katterbach, B.; Pelzer, A.; Silva-Tarouca, C.; and Batelli, G.,
       eds. *Exempla Scripturarum Edita Consilio et Opera Procuratorum
       Bibliothecae et Tabularii Vaticani. I. Codices Latini Saeculi
       XIII*; II. *Epistolae et Instrumenta Saeculi XIII*; III. *Acta
       Pontificum*. Rome: Vatican, 1929-30.

       Similar in format to item 905 above, this varied collection
       of facsimile portfolios includes examples from many different
       Gothic hands and documents. The bibliographical notes, following
       each transcription, are mainly limited to edtions.

907   Lowe, E.A. *Scriptura Beneventura. Facsimiles of South Italian
       and Dalmatian Manuscripts*. 2 vols. Oxford: Clarendon Press,
       1929.

       A collection of facsimile pages from sixth- to fourteenth-
       century manuscripts, with transcriptions and both paleographical
       and bibliographical notes. The collection is intended to accom-
       pany Lowe's study of this script; see item 830 above.

908   Monaci, E., ed. *Facsimili di antichi manoscritti*. Archivio
       Paleografico Italiano. Rome: A. Mattelli, 1881-92.

       A collection of facsimiles in four groups, arranged by period
       and provenance. It includes bibliographical notes.

909   ————. *Facsimili di documenti per la storia delle lingue e
       delle letterature romanza*. 2 vols. Rome: D. Anderson, 1910.

       A small portfolio of 65 facsimiles from medieval French and
       Italian manuscripts. Some paleographical and bibliographical
       notes are included.

910   Ruggieri, R.M. *Testi antichi romanzi*. 2 vols. Modena: Societa
       Tipografica Modenese, 1949.

A facsimile collection of folios from medieval vernacular
texts. Vol. 1 provides plates, while vol. 2 gives transcriptions
and paleographical commentary. Some bibliographical notes are
included.

911   Ugolini, Francesco A. *Atlante paleografico romanzo*. Turin:
      Libreria de 'La Stampa,' 1942-.

      A continuing series of facsimile collections, which are in-
      tended to provide an atlas for Italian paleography illustrating
      the chronological development of scripts.

viii. Netherlands

912   Brouwer, H. *Atlas voor Nederlandsche Paleographie*. Amsterdam:
      Van Kampen and Zoon, 1944.

      A facsimile collection of documents dating 1290-1670, mainly
      from the state papers in The Hague, although other representative
      manuscripts are included.

913   Brugmans, H., and Oppermann, O. *Atlas der nederlandische paleo-
      graphie*. The Hague: A.D. Jager, 1910.

      A portfolio of facsimiles from representative manuscripts.
      Included are paleographical notes and transcriptions.

914   Hulshof, A. *Deutsche und lateinische Schrift in den Niederlanden
      (1350-1650)*. Bonn: A. Marcus and E. Weber, 1918.

      A collection of 50 facsimiles of manuscripts of German proven-
      ance in Netherland collections. The brief introductions to each
      include paleographical notes and transcriptions.

914.1 *Medieval Manuscripts from the Low Countries in Facsimile*.
      J. Deschamps, gen. ed. Copenhagen: Rosenkilde and Bagger, 1971-.
      I. *The Vienna Manuscript of the "Second Part" of the "Spiegel
      Historiel*," ed. J. Deschamps. 1971.

      This attractively produced series proposes to present the
      more important Netherlandic manuscripts in facsimile. The first
      vol., ed. Deschamps, includes an extensive introduction in English
      on the codex, its editions, contents, dating, copyist, and
      history of the manuscript.

ix. Poland

915   Krzyzanowski, S. *Album Palaeographicum*. 4th ed. Crackow:
      Sumptibus Universitatis Iagellonicae, 1959.

916   ————. *Monumenta Poloniae Palaeographica*. Crackow: Sumptibus
      Universitatis Iagellonicae, 1959.

      Both volumes form a collection of facsimiles from medieval
      Polish manuscripts, including archival matter. A *Supplement*
      provides additional texts, ed. S.K. and Sophia Budkowa (2nd
      ed., 1960).

x. *Scandinavia*

917   Benediktsson, Hreinn. *Early Icelandic Script, as Illustrated in*
       the Vernacular Texts from the Twelfth to the Thirteenth Cen-
       turies. Icelandic Manuscripts, Series in Folio II. Reykjavík:
       The Manuscript Institute, 1965.

       A collection of sample facsimiles, transcribed. They are in-
       troduced by a general outline of the main features of Icelandic
       paleography, in which the author traces relationships between
       Icelandic scripts and Continental Caroline and Insular British
       scripts.

918   Brøndum-Nielsen, J., ed. *Corpus Codicum Danicorum Medii Aevi.*
       Copenhagen: E. Munksgaard, 1960-.

       A series of facsimile editions with critical introductions,
       from medieval manuscripts of Danish provenance.

919   *Early Icelandic Manuscripts in Facsimile.* Copenhagen: Rossen-
       kilde and Baggar, 1958-.

       A series of individual manuscripts published in facsimile.
       Introductory matter, notes, and bibliography are included.

920   Haarstad, Kjell, ed. *Gotisk Skrift: en Tekstamling.* Trondheim:
       Tapir, 1975.

       A facsimile collection of leaves serving to illustrate the
       development of Norwegian Gothic hands.

921   Helgason, Jon, ed. *Manuscripta Islandica.* Copenhagen: Rosenkilde
       and Baggar, 1954-.

       A facsimile series of individual manuscripts, e.g., *The Saga*
       Manuscript 9. 10 Aug. 4to in the Herzog-August Library Wolfen-
       büttel, ed. Jon Helgason, 1956.

922   Kalund, K. *Palaeografisk Atlas. Oldnorsk-Islandsk Afdeling.*
       3 vols. Copenhagen: Arnamaegnaean Commission, 1903-07.

       Facsimiles (132) illustrating chronologically the development
       of Icelandic scripts.

923   Manuscript Institute of Iceland (Handritastofnum Íslands).
       Islenzk Handrit. Series, 1956-. Superseded by Stofnum Arna
       Magnússonar Íslandi. Reykjavík: The Institute, 1969-.

       A series of facsimile editions of early Icelandic manuscripts
       reproduced in full with critical and bibliographical matter.

924   Munksgaard, E., ed. *Corpus Codicum Islandicorum Medii Aevi.*
       20 vols. Copenhagen: E. Munksgaard, 1930-56.

       This series consists of editions of individual manuscripts
       of Icelandic provenance, each with paleographical notes and
       bibliographical references.

925   Nielsen, L. *Danmarks middelalderlige Haandskriften.* Copenhagen:
       Gyldendal, 1937.

A large facsimile collection of 1500 examples from select medieval Danish manuscripts; introductory, paleographical, and bibliographical material is included.

926   Royal Library, Copenhagen, *Islanddke Handskrifter og Dansk Kultur*. Copenhagen: Kongelige Bibliotek, 1965.

Five articles by different hands on mainly Icelandic collections in Danish libraries; illustrated by facsimiles in colour and black and white, with accompanying descriptions.

927   Seip, D.A., ed. *Corpus Codicum Norvegicorum Medii Aevi*. Oslo: Selskapet til Utgivelse av Gamle Norske Handskrifter, 1950–; 1952–.

Editions of individual Old Norse manuscripts, issued in quarto from 1950, in folio from 1952. A companion series to next item.

928   Wessén, E., ed. *Corpus Codicum Suecicorum Medii Aevi*. Copenhagen: E. Munksgaard, 1943–.

Editions of individual medieval Swedish manuscripts.

xi. Switzerland

929   Bieler, L., ed. *Psalterium Graeco-Latinum, Codex Basiliensis A. VII. 3. Griechischen Psalter mit lateinischer Interlinearversion vom 9. Jahrhundert*. Umbrae Codicum Occidentalium, 5. Amsterdam: North Holland Publishing Co., 1960.

A facsimile edition of a Greek psalter with Latin glosses, presumably of St. Gall provenance.

930   Bruckner, Albert, ed. *Scriptoria Medii Aevi Helvetica. Denkmäler Schweizerischer Schreibkunst des Mittelalters*. Geneva: Roto-Sadag, 1935–.

A series of facsimile editions with full paleographical descriptions, issued by diocese. Indexes are combined in one volume.

931   Kocher, Alois, ed. *Mittelalterliche Handschriften aus dem Staatsarchiv Solothurn*. Veröffentlichungen des Solothurner Staatsarchives, 7. Solothurn: Staatsarchiv, 1974.

A paleographical album of facsimiles of scripts dating eighth to fifteenth centuries. Many are contained in fragments taken from seventeenth-century bindings in the Solothurn civic library.

932   Pfister, Arnold. *De Simplici Medicina. Kräuter-Handschrift aus dem letzten Viertel des 14. Jahrhunderts im Besitz der Basler Universitats-Bibliothek*. Basel: University Press, 1961.

Facsimile edition of a late fourteenth-century herbal, with full paleographical introduction and notes.

933   Rith, K., and Schmidt, P., eds. *Handschriftenproben zur Basler Geistgeschichte des XV. und XVI. Jahrhunderts*. Basel: Helbing and Lichtenhal, 1926.

A representative collection of facsimiles from late religious manuscripts, with analyses of paleographical features. Intended as a companion volume to next item.

934   Thommen, Rudolf. *Schriftproben aus Basler Handschriften des XIV-XVI Jahrhunderts*. 2nd ed. Basel: Helbing and Lichtenhal, 1908.

A portfolio collection of localized German-Swiss manuscripts.

VII. DIPLOMATICS AND ARCHIVES

The manuscripts, scripts, and nature of repositories for diplomatic and archival material constitute on the whole an area of research distinctly different from that for historical, literary, religious, or scientific documents. I have therefore kept them within a separate section, even though this has meant an artificially contrived classification in some cases, perhaps a rigidly enforced distinction in others. As many cross-references as possible have been made to facilitate the use of the various categories and as well to illustrate the fact that archival documents can be used in the service of other disciplines.

The references of this section include two basic groups of manuscripts: general, historical documents and those official or semi-official documents issued by chanceries, parochial administrators, courts, and other administrative bodies. The main criterion for including both groups in one section is that both are generally classed as public documents and stored under official supervision. Cartularies, or the register of muniments, constitute a large and varied group of documents in that they represent title-deeds, charters of privilege, and other documents retained by landowners as personal or corporate records of legal transactions. Both groups, moreover, tend to make use of a common body of scripts, abbreviations, and writing materials.

Because every church has its register or other parochial body of records, and because every county or other recognized administrative district has its central record office, the following represent only a selection from the total number available. I have included for the most part only those titles which would the more readily facilitate location, identification, and reading of public materials. Obviously many documents of this nature will also be found in manuscript collections not generally considered archival. The student is therefore advised to consult the sections above on *Libraries* under the appropriate country, or *Special Subjects* under the most likely finding list, see especially, "Historical and Legal," items 638-46.

CONTENTS

A. BIBLIOGRAPHICAL MATERIALS

935   Ellis, Robin, ed. *Work in Archives, 1939-47*. Repr. from *The Year's Work in Librarianship, 1947*. British Records Association. London: The Association, 1950.

A survey of scholarship representative of critical bibliographies appearing annually in this periodic bibliography; some critical annotation is provided.

935.1   Evans, Frank B., comp. *Modern Archives and Manuscripts: A Select Bibliography*. n.p.: The Society of American Archivists, 1975.

A non-critical bibliography for North American archival administrators. Many of the categories, however, have relevance to earlier material, e.g., sections 2 (General Bibliography) and 3.2 (European Background).

936   Institute of Research and Study in Medieval Canon Law. "Select Bibliographies." *Traditio* (1942-).

Annotated bibliographies of the year's work in canon law and related subjects appear annually in this journal. Arrangement is alphabetical by author. Separate bulletins are issued in the form of offprints. See item 536 for manuscript reproductions in the Institute's collection.

See also items 638-46, 713.

B. METHODOLOGY AND STUDIES

1. GENERAL STUDIES

937   Barraclough, G. *Public Notaries and the Papal Curia: A Calendar and a Study of Formularium Notariorum from the Early Years of the Fourteenth Century*. London: Macmillan, 1934.

An introduction discusses the formulary as a product of the curia, its manuscripts, origins, and later history. The Formulary edited by Barraclough is based upon six manuscripts from the fourteenth to the eighteenth centuries.

938   Bergkamp, Joseph Urban. *Dom Jean Mabillon and the Benedictine
       Historical School of Saint-Maur*. Diss. Catholic University
       of America. Washington, D.C.: 1928.

       An important but still unpublished thesis outlining Mabillon's
       contribution to diplomatics (the term derives from his major
       work, *De Re Diplomatica*, 1681) and the establishment of princi-
       ples for determining the date and authenticity of early charters.
       The bibliography is valuable for further study. See item 771.

939   Bompaire, Jacques. "Les Sources diplomatiques byzantines et,
       en particulier, les actes de la chancellerie impériale, de
       1025 à 1118." *Travaux et Memoires du Centre de Recherche
       d'Histoire et de Civilization de Byzance*, 6 (1976), 153-8.

       The author describes the characteristics of diplomatic writings
       and the acts of the Imperial Chancery, 1025-1118. Tables of
       statistics are listed for each monarch.

940   Boüard, A. de. *Manuel de diplomatique française et pontificale*.
       3 vols. Paris: A. Picard, 1929-48.

       A general introduction to French and Pontifical diplomatics.
       Volume 1 considers the characteristic features of official docu-
       ments, volume 2 discusses the nature of private documents, and
       volume 3 provides a collection of illustrative facsimiles.

941   Bresslau, H. *Handbuch der Urkundenlehre für Deutschland und
       Italien*. 3rd ed. (from 1912). 3 vols. Leipzig/Berlin: Teubner,
       1958.

       A general handbook on methodology and resources, with special
       reference to Pontifical documents in Germany.

942   Bruckner, Albert, and Marichal, Robert, eds. *Chartae Latinae
       Antiquiores. Facsimile Editions of the Latin Charters Prior
       to the Ninth Century*. 7 vols. Dietikon/Zurich: Urs Graf,
       1969-; 1976-.

       A series of editions of early charters, including papyri. The
       excellent introductions and commentary have wider applications
       for the general study of the subject.

943   Caenegem, C.R. van, with Ganshof, F.L. *Guide to the Sources of
       Medieval History*. Amsterdam: North Holland Publishing Co.,
       1978/1979.

       An English translation of the original Dutch (1962) and German
       (1964) survey of source material for medieval history, fifth
       to sixteenth centuries. Described are types of narrative and
       non-narrative texts, and there is a valuable bibliography of
       reference works.

944   Feenstra, R. *Repertorium Bibliographicum Institutorum et Sodali-
       tatum Iuris Historiae*. Leiden: E.J. Brill, 1969.

       A directory, arranged alphabetically by country, of libraries
       and institutes devoted to the study of the history of law. Manu-
       script catalogues and other important publications are listed
       for each, with a bibliography of periodicals in the subject,
       pp. 167-77.

945 Fichtenau, Heinrich. *Beiträge zur Mediävistik ausgewählte Aufsätze.* 2 vols. I. *Allgemeine Geschichte*; II. *Urkunden-forschung.* Stuttgart: Hiersemann, 1975-77.

A collection of Fichtenau's articles on historical and archival documents. Vol. 2 includes topics such as formularies and chanceries. A general index is provided, as well as an extensive bibliography of the author's publications on these subjects.

946 Foerster, Hans. *Urkundenlehre in Abbildungen mit Erlaüterungen und Transkriptionen.* Bern: P. Haupt, 1951.

947 ───. *Urkundenlesebuch für akademischen Gebrauch.* Bern: P. Haupt, 1947.

Both works by Foerster provide an authoritative introduction to the study of archives. The *Lesebuch* offers facsimiles of a wide selection of archival documents to be used as practical exercises in transcription.

948 Giry, A. *Manuel de diplomatique.* Rev. ed. (from 1894). 2 vols. Paris: F. Alcan, 1925.

This essential handbook on methodology uses exhaustive examples from French sources, but is useful in a general way for its admirable résumé of chronological and other computistical documents. An onomasticon of French proper names and a list of formulary collections conclude, pp. 482-4.

949 *Guide International des Archives:* I. *Europe.* Paris/Rome: Société des nations, 1934; *Supplément*, 1934.

A list of the major collections, compiled by different national contributors. A further *Supplément* was provided by Robert Henri Bautier and Charles Samaran in "Bibliographie sélective des guides d'archives," *Journal of Documentation*, 19 (1953), 1-41.

950 Mazzoleni, Jole. *Le fonti documentarie e bibliografiche dal sec. X al sec. XX.* 2 vols. Naples: Archivio di Stato di Napoli, 1978.

One of the best introductions to appear thus far on archival studies and resources. Well-presented and documented, although dependent upon Italian libraries.

951 ───. *Lezioni di archivistica.* Scuola di paleografia diplomatica e archivista dell'archivo di stato di Napoli. Naples: Stato di Napoli, 1954.

A handbook for the study of archives. A good bibliography for Italian resources is provided.

952 ───. *Paleografia e diplomatica e scienze ausiliarie.* 2nd ed. (from 1955). Naples: Libreria Scientifica Editrice, 1970.

General introduction to diplomatics, with focus upon South Italian chanceries. The chapters on coinage and sigillography provide good surveys of Italian resources. A select bibliography concludes each chapter. The work incorporates much of Mazzoleni's earlier *Lezioni di diplomatica* (Naples: 1950). Intended as a companion to item 951.

953   Plöchl, W.M. *Geschichte des Kirchenrechts*. 5 pts. in 2 vols. Vienna/Munich: Herold, 1953-69.

Pt. 1 gives the history of canon law from its beginnings to the great Schism; pt. 2 covers the period 1055 to 1517, and pts. 3-5 modern canon law. An invaluable bibliography makes this introductory work especially useful.

954   Sägmüller, J.B. *Lehrbuch des katholischen Kirchenrechts*. 4th ed. (from 1900). Freiburg-im-Breisgau: Herder, 1925.

A handbook on the sources of canon law and its relationship to ecclesiastical politics. Good bibliographies are provided.

955   Svornos, Nicolas G. *Recherches sur la tradition juridique à Byzance: La Synopsis Major des Basiliques et ses Appendices*. Bibliothèque Byzantine, 4. Paris: Presses Universitaires de France, 1964.

A collection of tenth-century Byzantine legal texts, the *Synopsis Basilicorum Maior*, with a study of the manuscripts and their relationship to legislative work of the period.

956   Thomas, Daniel H., and Case, Lynn M., eds. *Guide to the Diplomatic Archives of Western Europe*. Philadelphia, Pa.: University of Pennsylvania Press, 1959.

A descriptive account of the major countries, Austria-Vatican. It includes comments on systems of classification and a bibliography of catalogues for each country. Out of date but indispensable for earlier references.

957   Wallach, Luitpold. *Diplomatic Studies in Latin and Greek Documents from the Carolingian Age: Collected Essays*. Ithaca, N.Y.: Cornell University Press, 1977.

Collected articles reprinted from journals; perhaps the best known is on the *Libri Carolini*.

See also items 1921, 1944, 1972, and 2030.

2. INDIVIDUAL COUNTRIES

(a) Austria

958   Fichtenau, Heinrich. *Das Urkundenwesen in Österreich vom 8. bis zum frühen 13. Jahrhundert*. Mitteilungen den Instituts für österreichische Geschichtsforschung, 23. Vienna: Böhlaus, 1971.

The best guide thus far to Austrian official documents. A critical summary of the characteristics of various types of

documents, e.g., *carta, notitia, libri traditionum*, etc., is
given by way of introduction along with a survey of the nine
districts in which they may be found. The bibliography includes
lists of editions and secondary matter. Author/place/subject
indexes are provided.

See also items 206-10.

(b) Belgium

959 Ganshof, F.L. *Wat Waren de Capitularia?* Verhandelingen van de
     Koninklijke Vlaamse Academie voor Wetenschappen, Letteren en
     Schone Kunsten van Belgie, Klasse der Letteren, 22. Brussels:
     Palais der Academiën, 1955.

     Also published in a French translation as *Les Recherches sur
     les capitulaires*. Société d'Histoire du Droit (Paris: Sirey,
     1958). A brief but lucid account of capitularies in three parts:
     (1) the capitularies and their editorial problems; (2) the nature
     of the capitularies; and (3) their promulgation. The period
     covered extends from Charlemagne to Charles the Bald.

960 Gysseling, Maurits, and Koch, A.C.F., eds. *Diplomatica Belgica
     ante Annum Millesium Centesimum Scripta*. 2 vols. Brussels:
     Inter-Universitaircentrum voor Neerlandistiek, 1950.

     A study and collection of facsimile examples dating pre-1500.

961 Pirenne, H., ed. *Album Belge Diplomatique: Recueil de facsimiles
     pour servir à l'étude de la diplomatique des provinces belges
     au moyen âge*. Jette-Brussels: Vandamme and Rossignol, 1909.

     A collection of 32 facsimiles, representing different periods
     and geographical provenance. Paleographical and other annota-
     tions are provided.

(c) Egypt

See items 238, 265, 268, 303, 780-95, and 1639.

(d) France

962 Carolus Varré, Louis. *Les Plus ancienne chartes en langue
     française*. Paris: C. Klincksieck, 1974-. I. *Problèmes généraux
     et recueil des pièces originales conservées aux archives de
     l'Oise, 1241-1286*. Paris: C. Klincksieck, 1974.

     A general introduction, to be followed by individual editions,
     e.g., vol. I on the Oise. The nature and scope of local archival
     material is described, with bibliography and indexes provided.

962.1 Fawtier, Robert, gen. ed. *Registres du trésor des chartes; in-*
      ventaire analytique établi par les archivistes aux archives
      nationales. Paris: Imprimérie Nationale, 1958-.

      A periodical inventory of archival documents in the national
      archives collections; indexed.

963   Gandilhorn, R., and Hourlier, J. *Inventaire sommaire de frag-*
      ments de manuscrits et d'imprimés conservés aux archives de
      la Marne. Chalons-sur-Marne: Archives de la Marne, 1956.

      One of many such inventories for French regional collections,
      usually published by the "Archiviste en Chef." See also the
      Union Catalogues under appropriate geographical heading.

964   Gasparri, Françoise. *L'Ecriture des actes de Louis VI, Louis VII*
      et Phillippe Auguste. Centre de Recherches d'Histoire et de
      Philologie de la IVe Section de l'Ecole Pratique des Hautes
      Etudes, 20. Geneva: E. Droz/Paris: Minare, 1973.

      A beautifully printed book, divided into two sections: (1)
      introduction, with reproduced alphabets from documents of differ-
      ent periods, 1018-1223; and (2) a collection of facsimile leaves
      upon which the alphabets are based. A full bibliography is in-
      cluded.

965   Langlois, C.V., and Stein, H. *Les Archives de l'histoire de*
      France. Paris: A. Picard, 1891-93.

      A description of principal archival deposits in France. The
      three parts include French internal historical archives; histor-
      ical archives related to France but deposited in other countries;
      and historical archives in general manuscript collections, e.g.,
      the Bibliothèque Nationale.

965.1 Molinier, Auguste. *Les Sources de l'histoire de France des*
      origines à la fin du XVe siècle, rev. ed. Robert Fawtier
      (from 1901-6). 5 vols. Paris: Editions A. and J. Picard, 1971.

      A descriptive bibliography of mainly historical documents,
      arranged chronologically from the Merovingian period to the
      fifteenth century, with grouping according to genre, e.g.,
      chronicles and saints' legends. Fawtier's updating of archival
      matter is especially useful.

966   Stein, H. *Bibliographie générale des cartulaires français ou*
      relatifs à l'histoire de France. Manuels de Bibliographie
      Historique, 4. Paris: Hachette, 1907.

      A general guide to the major documents, now out of date but
      still useful for its historical notes and nineteenth-century
      bibliography.

See also items 84, 87, 130, 136, 1752, 1765-6, 1770, 1794, 1836, 1847,
1852, 1863-4, 1868-75, 1877-8, and 1892.

(e) Germany

967 Oesterley, Hermann. *Wegweiser durch die Literatur der Urkunden Sammlungen.* 2 vols. Berlin: Georg Reimer, 1885-86/Hildesheim: Georg Olms, 1969.

A general guide to cartulary and other collections in Europe, with emphasis upon Germany. Arrangement is alphabetical by location within country. A bibliography of older catalogues from the seventeenth to the nineteenth centuries appears on pp. 1-3. The section on formularies, letters, and crusade documents is a useful bibliography for further study, see pp. 3-46.

968 Thommen, Rudolf. *Diplomatik. Die Lehre von den Königs- und Kaiserkunden.* Leipzig: Teubner, 1905.

An introduction to the study of medieval and modern German diplomatics, designed primarily for undergraduates.

969 ———. *Urkundenlehre.* 2nd ed. Leipzig/Berlin: Teubner, 1913.

An expanded version of the preceding item, with a more complete bibliography included.

970 Wentzcke, P., and Lüdtke, G. *Die Archiven.* Berlin: De Gruyter, 1932.

A guide to mainly German archives, pp. 1-385. The remaining pages summarize archival resources in the Low Countries, Austria, Switzerland, and Scandinavia.

See also items 88-90, 234-6.

(f) Great Britain and Ireland

i. Bibliographical and General Works

971 British Records Association. *General Report of a Committee on the Classification of English Archives.* Reports from Committees, 1. London: The Association, 1936.

A short (31pp.) guide to classification and probable location of types of archival documents in England. The Association issues periodic publications on all aspects of the subject; see next item.

972 ———. *Record Repositories in Great Britain.* 3rd ed. London: HMSO, 1968.

An indispensable guide to the location of public documents and their classification. It represents an expanded and updated version of the first ed. of 1964 and replaces the *List of Records* (1956). Over 250 repositories are listed.

973   Cheney, C.R. *Notaries Public in England in the Thirteenth and
       Fourteenth Centuries*. Oxford: Clarendon Press, 1972.

       Cheney discusses the practice of notaries public and gives
       an account of the types of legal documentation. He considers
       the use of notarial fragments in later bindings, and concludes
       that notarial instruments were less widely used in England than
       on the continent. Appended are representative facsimiles from
       a variety of documents.

974   Cox, J. Charles. *The Parish Registers of England*. London:
       Methuen, 1910.

       An historical account of parish registers after 1538, with
       some reference to earlier formulas and practices. Appendices
       include names of parishes with dates. The index gives places
       and names.

975   Flower, C.T. "On Indexing Mediaeval Record Works." *Indian
       Archives*, 4 (1950), 142-9.

       A short guide to the methodology of handling various classi-
       fications of documents. Some bibliographical references are
       included.

976 · Galbraith, V.H. *An Introduction to the Use of Public Records*.
       London: Nelson, 1934; 2nd ed. London: 1952/1963.

       A guide to the use and location of materials, mainly in the
       Public Record Office, London. See also 1001.

977   Hall, Hubert. *A Repertory of British Archives: (1) England*.
       London: The Royal Historical Society, 1920.

       A general survey with some description; only part 1 has been
       published. Brought up to date by Corbett, item 249, and Downs,
       item 250; see also Pemberton, item 986. Especially useful are
       references to local official documents not in the PRO. Classi-
       fication of documents is by type, e.g., judicial or state papers.
       A *Special Supplement* (1932) provides additional information.

978   Hepworth, Philip. *Archives and Manuscripts in Libraries*. 2nd ed.
       Library Association Publications, 18. London: The Association,
       1964.

       A brief (40pp.) bibliography of printed catalogues and guides
       to local collections. Arrangement is geographical, London-Ireland.

979   ————. "Manuscripts and Non-Book Materials in Libraries."
       Archives, 9 (1969), 90-97.

       A paper originally given at the College of Librarianship in
       Wales, Feb. 13, 1969, in which the work of the librarian is
       distinguished from that of the archivist. The author also describes
       the work of the Library Association and the Manuscripts Sub-
       Committee, with some reference to the Maud Commission and archival
       work in the United States.

Historical Manuscripts Commission. See Royal Commission on Historical Manuscripts, item 987.

980   Institute for Historical Research. *Guide to the Accessibility of Local Records of England and Wales*. Bulletin for the Institute of Historical Research, Special Supplement, 1.1. 2 vols. London: The Institute, 1932-34.

Vol. 1 contains records of counties, boroughs, dioceses, cathedrals, archdeaconries, and probate offices; vol. 2 includes the resources for the Inns of Court, collegiate churches, educational foundations, repositories approved by the Master of the Rolls, and local societies. Although now out date, this work nevertheless still represents an essential starting point for research in local records.

981   ————. "Historical Manuscripts: Accessions and Migrations." *Bulletin of the Institute for Historical Research*, 1- (1923-).

Periodic and bibliographical accounts of documents and repositories, including accessions to the PRO and British Library. See items 987, 1787.

982   Jenkinson, Sir Charles Hilary. *A Manual of Archive Administration*. Rev. ed. (from 1922). London: P. Lund, Humphries and Co., 1965.

A useful handbook on the classification and care of archives with focus upon British documents. An introduction and updated bibliography are provided by Roger H. Ellis.

983   Kitson Clark, G., and Elton, G.R. *Guide to Research Facilities in History in the Universities of Great Britain and Ireland*. 2nd ed. Cambridge: University Press, 1965.

A brief (55pp.) summary of library holdings and other resources, relating to historical documents.

984   Library Association. "The Place of Archives and Manuscripts in the Field of Librarianship." *Library Association Record*, 71 (1969), 12-15.

A succinct statement of policy on the distinctions between the two types of documents and their classification.

985   Newton, K.C. "Reading Medieval Local Records." *Amateur Historian*, 3 (1956), 81-93.

Not designed for the scholar, but still useful for its outline of some common problems in locating and interpreting local records.

986   Pemberton, John E. *British Official Publications*. Oxford: Pergamon Press, 1971.

Chapter 16 gives a full description of the location, holdings, and publications relevant to the National archives.

987   Royal Commission on Historical Manuscripts. 1869-, 1959-.
        Publications. London: HMSO, 1883-. *Bulletins*. 1904-.

        The Commission publishes information regularly on the archives,
        records, and documents held by individuals and institutions,
        and issues an annual *List of Accessions to Repositories*. For a
        full description of the Commission and list of its publications,
        see the preceding item. Among the most important is *A Guide to
        the Reports on Collections of Manuscripts of Private Families,
        Corporations, and Institutions in Great Britain and Ireland*.
        I. *Topographical Guide* (London: HMSO, 1914); II. *Guide to the
        Reports of the Royal Commission on Historical Manuscripts* (1870-
        1957). 2nd ed. (1966). See also item 662.

988   Sawyer, P.H. *Anglo-Saxon Charters: An Annotated List and Bibliog-
        raphy*. Royal Historical Society Guides and Handbooks, 8. Lon-
        don: The Society, 1968.

        A critical list of charters to ca. 1100, with a summary of
        contents and bibliographies.

989   Tate, W.E. *The Parish Chest: A Study of the Records of Parochial
        Administration in England*. 2nd ed. Cambridge: University Press,
        1951.

        An introduction to the search for and interpretaion of parish
        records. A bibliography and index are provided.

See also items 81-82, 640-1, 646, 971-1013, 1751, 1764, 1770, 1782,
        1787, 1807, 1809, 1821, 1823, 1827, 1830, 1854, 1873, 1878.

ii. England: Individual Collections and Studies

990   Bishop, T.A.M. *Scriptores Regis: Facsimiles to Identify and
        Illustrate the Hands of Royal Scribes in Original Charters
        of Henry I, Stephen and Henry II*. Introd. V.H. Galbraith.
        Oxford: Clarendon Press, 1955.

        A collection of facsimiles of the personal hands of regularly
        employed scribes identified in royal charters, 1100-89. The
        author describes paleographical features and discusses general
        practices in the royal chancery.

991   ————, and Chaplais, P., eds. *Facsimiles of English Royal Writs
        to A.D. 1000. Presented to Vivian Hunter Galbraith*. Oxford:
        Clarendon Press, 1957.

        A small collection of 30 plates with paleographical descrip-
        tions and a general introduction.

992   British Library, Department of Manuscripts. *Facsimiles of Ancient
        Charters in the British Museum*. 4 vols. London: Trustees of
        the British Library, 1876-8.

        A collection of facsimiles from representative charters; each
        is transcribed on the facing page.

993   Ellis, Henry J., and Bickley, Francis B., eds. *Index to the Charters and Rolls in the Department of Manuscripts, British Museum.* 2 vols. London: Trustees of the British Library, 1900-12.

    The two volumes comprise: I. *Index Locorum*; II. *Religious Houses and Other Corporations*, and *Index Locorum for Acquisitions from 1832-1900.* The list is alphabetical, with manuscripts, place of origin, and dates.

994   Fawtier, Robert, *et al.*, eds. *Hand-List of Charters, Deeds, and Similar Documents in the Possession of the John Rylands Library.* Manchester: The Library, 1925-37. 3 vols. Repr. from *Bulletin of the John Rylands Library*, 7-18 (1922-33).

    A descriptive list of documents, with bibliographical references.

995   Grieve, Hilda E.P. *Examples of English Handwriting 1150-1750.* I. *Essex Parish Records.* II. *Other Essex Archives.* Essex Records Office Publications, 21. n.p.: Essex Records Office, 1954/1966.

    An attractively reproduced collection of documents with transcriptions, translations, and notes on facing pages.

996   Hollaender, A.E.J. "The Muniment Room of Manchester Cathedral." *Archives*, 1 (1951), 3-10.

997   Hull, F. *Guide to the Kent County Archives Office.* Maidstone: The County of Kent, 1958.

    This work is not only a brief guide to local archives, but it also contains a section by M.B. Parkes on the nature and type of fragments found within archival collections.

998   Major, Kathleen. "Original Papal Documents in the Bodleian Library." *Bodleian Library Record*, 3 (1951), 242-56.

    A brief, descriptive list, with bibliographical references.

999   Martin, Charles Trice. *Catalogue of the Archives in the Muniment Rooms of All Souls' College.* London: Spottiswoode, 1877.

    See item 423.

1000   Peek, Heather E., and Hall, Catherine P. *The Archives of the University of Cambridge: An Historical Introduction.* Cambridge: University Press, 1962,

    An historical account of the Cambridge University archives, from the thirteenth century to the present. It offers a survey of the present classes of documents, a tabular outline of University muniments, and a bibliography of historical literature about the University. See also item 259.

1001   Public Record Office. *Guide to the Contents of the Public Record Office.* 3 vols. London: HMSO, 1963-68.

A revision of earlier guides by Scargill (1891, and see item 1005) and Giuseppi (1923). Vol. 1 includes medieval and legal records, while vol. 3 lists documents transferred 1960-66 to the present holdings. The guide describes state papers, legal records, and other documents in the PRO and concludes each vol. with a name/place/subject index. The PRO has also published a series of individual handbooks, among them a *Guide to Seals*, 2nd ed. (1968) and *Domesday Rebound* (1954). Other publications include *Lists and Indexes Calendars*, *Chronicles*, and other guides to official papers in the collection. For a bibliography, see item 986. See also item 976.

1002   Salter, H.E. *Facsimiles of Early Charters in Oxford Muniment Rooms*. Oxford: John Johnson at the University Press, 1929.

A folio-sized collection of collotypes, which includes transcriptions with notes on facing pages. Most of the documents date from the twelfth century. A name index is provided.

1003   Sayers, Jane E. *Estate Documents at Lambeth Palace Library: A Short Catalogue*. Leicester: University Press, 1965.

A descriptive list of papers from archepiscopal estates, Christ Church estates, and others. Included are dates, some bibliographical notes, and indexes.

1004   ————. *Original Papal Documents in the Lambeth Palace Library*. London: University of London, Athlone Press, 1967.

In addition to providing a catalogue of papal documents, the author offers interesting historical notes on the decreasing importance of papal bulls in England from the fourteenth century and the fate of surviving bulls in bindings after 1536.

1005   Scargill Bird, Samuel R. *A Guide to the Principal Classes of Documents Preserved in the Public Record Office*. London: HMSO, 1891; 3rd ed. 1908.

Published as part of the Rolls Series, this guide to the PRO lists legal records and state papers. While it has been largely updated by item 1000, some of its descriptive matter is still valuable.

1006   Warner, George F., and Ellis, Henry J. *Facsimiles of Royal and Other Charters in the British Museum. I. William I-Richard I*. London: Trustees of the British Library, 1903.

A collection of facsimiles with transcriptions and paleographical notes.

See also item 644.

iii. Ireland and Northern Ireland

1007   Griffith, M. "A Short Guide to the Public Record Office of Ireland." *Irish Historical Studies*, 8.29 (1952), 45-58.

1008   Northern Ireland Public Record Office. *Reports*. Belfast: HMSO, 1952-.

A periodic list of the contents and recent acquisitions, issued by the PRO of Northern Ireland through the Keeper of Records.

See also items 79-83, 309-15, 640-1.

iv. Scotland

1009   Dell, R.F. "Some Fragments of Medieval Manuscripts in Glasgow City Archives." *The Innes Review*, 18 (1967), 112-7.

An account of manuscript fragments, most of which have gone into sixteenth and seventeenth-century bindings.

1010   Livingstone, Matthew. *Guide to the Public Records of Scotland Deposited in H.M. General Register House, Edinburgh*. Edinburgh: HMSO, 1905.

A classified list without descriptive matter; updated by items 1011 and 1013 below.

1011   Scottish Record Office. *Official Guide to the Documents Exhibited in the Historical Museum of the Register House*. Edinburgh: HMSO, 1952.

This brief work (31pp.) constitutes a guide to early documents in the Register House.

1012   Simpson, Grant G. *Scottish Handwriting, 1150-1650: An Introduction to the Reading of Documents*. Edinburgh: Bratton, 1973/ Aberdeen: University Press, 1977.

This is a valuable handbook for the reading of Scottish archival documents. It includes bibliography and facsimile illustrations, as well as a list of manuscripts.

1013   Somerville, Sir R., ed. *Handlist of Scottish and Welsh Record Publications*. British Record Association Publications, 4. London: The Association, 1954.

A classified list of documents, with brief histories and descriptive notes.

See also items 80, 83, 316-9, 640.

v. Wales

See items 78, 80-3, 320-3, 662.

(g) Hispanic Countries

1014   Cortada, James W. "Libraries and Archives of Barcelona."
        Library Chronicle, 42 (1978), 98-112.

        This descriptive list focuses upon holdings in Barcelona, but
        some of the bibliographical references are useful for Spanish
        archives in general.

1015   Frank, I. "Les 'Varia codicum fragmenta' des archives capitu-
        laires de la Cathedral de Barcelone." *Scrinium*, 1 (1951),
        13-17.

        A descriptive list of archival fragments in the Cathedral
        Library of Barcelona; bibliographical notes are included.

1016   González Palencia, Ángel. *Los archivos españoles y las in-
        vestigaciones histórico-literarias*. Madrid: Dirección General,
        1926.

        A descriptive guide to official, historical archives and
        miscellaneous documents; bibliographical references are fairly
        comprehensive.

1017   Hoenerbach, Wilhelm, ed. and trans. *Spanische-Islamische
        Urkunden aus der Zeit der Nasriden und Moriscos*. 2 vols.
        University of California Publications, Near Eastern Studies,
        3. Berkeley and Los Angeles, Calif.: University of California
        Press, 1965-.

        While this work is primarily an edition of Spanish-Arabic
        notarial documents, a general preface outlines the categories
        of Spanish notaries and provides photocopies of the edited texts.
        Vol. 1 contains 13 marriage documents with their notarial in-
        structions; vol. 2 contains 46 items on public and private
        laws. An invaluable bibliography is included.

1018   Mateu Ibars, Josefina, and Lapresa Molina, Eladio de, *et al*.,
        eds. *Paleográfia de Andalucia Oriental*. I. *Album*. II. *Tran-
        scripciones*. Universidad de Granada, Departamento de Paleo-
        gráfia y Diplomática. Granada: University Press, 1973-77.

        A collection of mainly archival documents from the fourteenth
        century to the eighteenth. The descriptive matter includes a
        facsimile dictionary of abbreviations derived from the docu-
        ments.

1019   Millares Carlo, Augustin. *Notas bibliográficas de archivos
        municipáles*. Madrid: Dirección Servicio de Publicaciones del
        Ministerio de Educación Nacional, 1952.

        A general guide to archival collections in Spain, with a
        bibliography of further publications on contents and location.

1020   Muñoz y Rivero, Jesus. *Chrestomathia Paleographica: Scripturae
        Hispanae Veteris Specimena*. Madrid: G. Gernando, 1891.

A collection of diplomatic texts (*Scriptura Chartarum*) in facsimile. The proposed second part, containing other documents, was never published. For the manual to be used in conjunction with this work, see next item.

1021 ————. *Manual de paleográfia diplomática española de los siglos XII al XVII*. 2nd ed. (from 1880). Madrid: Daniel Jorro, 1917.

An introduction to Spanish diplomatics, illustrated with over 240 facsimiles to be used in conjunction with the preceding item. A bibliography is provided.

See also items 91-92, 143-7, 324-6, 639, 1030, 1815.

(h) Italy

1022 Boyle, Leonard E. *A Survey of the Vatican Archives and of its Medieval Holdings*. Subsidia Mediaevalia, 1. Toronto: Pontifical Institute of Mediaeval Studies, 1972.

A comprehensive guide to the Vatican archives, which supersedes item 1026 below. It is divided into three parts: (1) introduction and history, with reference to research aids; (2) a detailed survey of the original *archivo segreto vaticano*; and (3) notes on select medieval holdings, e.g., the Vatican and Avignon Registers. See also items 538, 1029.

1023 Caserta, Aldo. *Archivi Ecclesiastici*. Naples: D'Agostino, 1961.

A short (77pp.) guide to the archives of Naples. Being limited to a precise area, it presents the archival holdings of that region with clarity and accuracy. Arrangement is by collection, then by materials and genre within each. Excellent bibliographical references are provided for each collection.

1024 Denifle, H., and Palmieri, G., eds. *Specimina Paleographica Registorum Romanorum*. Rome: Vatican, 1888.

A large folio-sized collection of leaves from papal registers, Innocent III to Urban V (1198-1370). Most are from the Vatican Library, but several are included from elsewhere, e.g., the Bibliothèque Nationale.

1025 Federici, Vicenzo. *La Scrittura delle cancellerie italiane dal secolo XII al XVII*. Rome: P. Sansaini, 1934.

This work represents a collection of facsimiles from Italian state archives of the twelfth to seventeenth century. Paleographical features are discussed and some bibliography is provided.

1026 Fink, K.A. *Das vatikanische Archiv*. 2nd ed. Bibliothek des deutschen historischen Institut in Rom, 20. Rome: The Institute, 1951.

Now largely superseded by item 1022 above.

1027   Hoepli Publishers. *Archivo storico civico*. Milan: Hoepli, 1950-.

A series of catalogues of local archival collections. They
are issued approximately biannually, and each lists the holdings
of an individual city, e.g., Milan.

1028   Lemut, Maria L. Ceccavelli, ed. *Repertorio delle fonti docu-
mentarie edite del medioevo: Italia-Toscana*. Biblioteca del
"Bollettino Storio Pisano," Collana Storica, 17. Pisa: Pacini
Editore, 1977.

A descriptive and detailed account of archival repositories
in Tuscany. A list of references to local archives, which includes general bibliographical references to other parts of
Italy, is found on pp. 11-18.

1029   Macfarlane, Leslie. *The Vatican Archives, with Special Reference to Sources for British and Irish Medieval History*.
London: British Records Association, 1959. Repr. from *Archives*,
4 (1959), 29-44, 84-101.

A descriptive summary of 12 classes of documents within the
working records of the Papal curia, from "Inventories and Indices" to "Various Additional Collections." Details given include number of vols., general nature of contents, and bibliographical references to printed catalogues and other descriptions. Specific references are made to material relevant to
British history. Part 2 (pp. 84-101) lists transcripts and
microfilms available in the PRO, BL, and other British repositories from Vatican sources, also repositories in Rome other
than the Vatican.

1030   Mallon, Jean. *L'Ecriture de la chancellerie impériale romaine*.
Acta Salamanticensis, Filosofia y Letras, 4.2. Salamanca:
University Press, 1948.

A brief (35pp.) descriptive guide to scripts in documents
of the Royal Chancery, Salamanca, with illustrating facsimiles.

1031   Omont, H. *Bulles pontificales sur papyrus, IXe-XIe siècle*.
Bibliothèque de l'Ecole des Chartes, 65. Paris: L'Ecole des
Chartes, 1904.

A descriptive catalogue of papyrus documents, arranged by
collection.

1032   Ufficio Centrale degli Archivi di Stato. *Gli Archivi di Stato*.
Bologna: Ufficio Centrale, 1944.

A brief description of each library and collection in Italy,
with a bibliography of printed catalogues. The work is kept up
to date by *Notizie degle Archivi di Stato* (Rome: 1941-).

1033   ————. *Le pubblicazioni degli Archivi di Stato, 1951-71*.
Spoleto: Ufficio Centrale, 1972.

A catalogue with full descriptions of archival publications

for the major Italian cities in 1951-71. Indexes are provided for curators and locations.

See also items 148-50, 340-54, 1768-9, 1776, 1778, 1789, 1839, 1851, 1859, 1879, 1884, 1888, 1889.

(i) Netherlands

1034   Fruin, R. *De provincie Zeeland en hare rechterlijke indeeling voor 1795*. Middelburg: J.C. and W. Altorffer, 1933.

A survey of Zealand archives, with good bibliographical references, including those to other areas of the Netherlands. For the author's explanation of his chronological systems, see item 1528.

1035   Miller, S.; Feith, J.A.; and Fruin, R. *Handleiding voor het ordenen en beschrijven van archieven*. 2nd ed. (from 1898). Leipzig: Harrassowitz, 1920; trans. Arthur H. Leavitt, *Manual for the Arrangement and Description of Archives*. New York, N.Y.: H.W. Wilson, 1944.

A brief descriptive account of the classification of mainly Belgian archives, their scope and chronology. Earlier French and Italian editions were published in 1910 and 1908 respectively.

See also items 151, 355-8, 912-3, 1766, 1863, 1893-4.

(j) Poland

See items 915-6.

(k) Scandinavia

1036   Macray, William Dunn. *Report on the Royal Archives of Denmark*. Reports of the Deputy Keeper of Public Records, 45. London: HMSO, 1885. *Appendix*, 1886. *Appendix*, 1887.

A descriptive survey of archival material in Denmark. Arrangement is by district and library within each.

1037   Ottervik, G.; Mohlenbrock, S.; and Anderson, I. *Libraries and Archives in Sweden*. Swedish Institute for Cultural Relations with Foreign Countries. Stockholm: For the Institute, 1953.

A general survey of the major archival collections in Sweden. Bibliographical references include published catalogues and other lists.

1038   Sjörgren, Paul, gen. ed. *Svensk historisk bibliografi*. Uppsala: Alqvist and Wiksell, 1956-.

A periodic bibliography devoted to historical and archival
resources in Sweden, which is actually a continuation of the
earlier *Bibliografi* (1771-1920). Both provide important reference works to the many Scandinavian publications on local
Swedish repositories.

See also items 93-94, 359-67, 1758, 1763, 1818.

(1) Switzerland

1039   Largiader, Anton. *Die Papsturkunden des Staatsarchivs Zürich
        von Innocenz III. bis Martin V.: Ein Beitrag zum Censimentum
        Helveticum.* Zurich: Schulthess and Col, 1963.

        A descriptive catalogue of the civic archives for medieval
        papal documents. Some illustrations are provided, as well as
        a good bibliography.

1040   Stelling-Michaud, S. *Catalogue des manuscrits juridique (droit
        canon et droit romain) de la fin du XIIe au XIVe siècle con-
        servés en Suisse.* Geneva: E. Droz, 1954.

        A catalogue of manuscripts currently in Swiss repositories,
        which include canon law (nos. 1-125) and civil law (nos. 126-
        87). Each is described in some detail and identified when pos-
        sible, e.g., nos. 1-4 are copies of the *Decretum Gratiani*,
        while the last eight manuscripts represent exemplars of an
        Ars Dictaminis, *Notaria*, and *Formularia*. Stelling-Michaud re-
        veals here and elsewhere (see the bibliography) the influence
        of Bologna upon Swiss legal studies and practice.

See also items 368-75.

C. SIGILLOGRAPHY

1041   Brugmans, H. *Corpus Sigillorum Neerlandicorum.* The Hague:
        M. Nijhoff, 1937-40.

        A descriptive catalogue of pre-1300 seals of Dutch provenance.
        Provided are bibliographical references and an index.

1042   Ellis, Roger H., comp. *Catalogue of Seals in the Public Record
        Office.* London: HMSO, 1978-. I. *Personal Seals.* 1978.

        An excellent, descriptive catalogue of personal seals in the
        PRO, arranged alphabetically by name of owner. There is a
        section for seals of uncertain ownership. Most descriptions
        are accompanied by a photograph. For a more general account
        of PRO seals, see item 1045.

1043 Ewald, W. *Siegelkunde*. Munich/Berlin: Oldenburgh, 1914.

A general introduction to types and characteristic features of seals and their use in archival documents. The information on criteria for dating is especially useful.

1044 Gandilhorn, René. *Sigillographie des universités de France*. Paris: Editions Delmas, 1952.

A critical description of some 204 seals used by the faculties, nations, rectors, deans, chancellors, proctors, and receptors of French universities to 1793. A general introduction on, e.g., the heraldic elements used in seals, makes the work a valuable guide to sigillography in general. A bibliography and some plates are provided.

1045 Jenkinson, Sir Hilary. *Guide to Seals in the Public Record Office*. London: HMSO, 1954.

A very general work which considers the use and users of seals, their materials and colors, methods of attaching seals, devices, and classes of design. It is illustrated with 12 plates. For a descriptive catalogue of PRO seals, see item 1042 above.

1046 Roman, J. *Manuel de sigillographie française*. Paris: A. Picard, 1912.

A general introduction to types of French seals and their dates. For specific studies and references to individual collections, see the author's bibliography listed in this work.

1047 Tonnochy, A.B. *Catalogue of British Seal-dies in the British Museum*. London: Trustees of the British Library, 1952.

A descriptive catalogue of seals from documents of all historical periods and geographical areas which include Scotland, Ireland, Wales, and the Commonwealth.

VIII. FRAGMENTS, BOOKLETS, AND RELATED PROBLEMS

Many catalogues of the preceding sections list fragments, often separately, and some discuss problems of identification, description, and cataloguing. Normally these catalogues have been so indicated in my annotations. The items of this section represent a selection of specialized lists and studies of fragmentary manuscripts and "booklets."

1048   Butzmann, Hans. "Gedankend und Erfahrungen bei Katalogisierung
        von Handschriftenfragmenten." *Litterae Textuales*, 1 (1972),
        87-98.

        The author offers suggestions on the cataloguing of such
        sample fragments as he presents in facsimile.

1049   Duft, Johan, and Meyer, Peter. *The Irish Miniatures in the
        Abbey Library of St. Gall*. Olten/Berne/Lausanne: Urs Graf,
        1954.

        Duft's inventory describes the role of some fragments in the
        reconstruction of the history of the Irish liturgy and rites,
        pp. 68ff.

1050   Parkes, M.B. "The Palaeography of the Parker Manuscript of the
        Chronicle, Laws and Sedulius, and Historiography at Winchester
        in the Late Ninth and Tenth Centuries." *Anglo-Saxon England*,
        5 (1976), 149-71.

        A detailed description of the Parker manuscript, Corpus
        Christi College MS. 173, which illustrates the format and some
        paleographical features of "booklets" in complete manuscripts.

1051   Rickert, Margaret. *The Reconstructed Carmelite Missal: An
        English Manuscript of the Late XIVth Century in the British
        Museum (Additional 29704-5, 44892)*. London: Faber and Faber,
        1952.

        A well-documented account, illustrated by 56 plates, of the
        methodology employed in the reconstruction of a manuscript.
        In this case the fragments were contained in five scrapbooks
        of mounted cuttings acquired from different sources.

1052   Number deleted.

1053   Robinson, P.R. "Self-Contained Units in the Composite Manuscripts
        of the Anglo-Saxon Period." *Anglo-Saxon England*, 7 (1978),
        231-8.

        A descriptive analysis of two manuscripts, Meresburg Stifts-
        bibliothek 105, ff. 85-105 (Alcuin's *Vita S. Vedasti*), and St.
        Gall Stiftsbibliothek 567, pp. 135-53 (*Vita S. Lucii*) as exam-
        ples of "booklets."

1054   Thiel, H. van. "Die liturgischer Bücher des Mittelalters: ein
       kleines Lexikon zur Handschriftenkunde." *Borsenblatt für den
       deutschen Buchhandel*, 83 (1967), 2379-95.

       An analysis in considerable detail of the general nature and
       frequent survival of liturgical fragments found in later bind-
       ings.

1055   Watson, Rowan. *A Descriptive List of Fragments of Medieval
       Manuscripts in the University of London Library*. London:
       University of London, Typescript, 1976.

       A brief list (pp. xvii-40) of 56 fragments, grouped by subject.
       Watson includes books in London libraries which contain frag-
       ments of medieval manuscripts in their bindings.

1056   ————. "Medieval Manuscript Fragments." *Archives*, 13 (1977),
       61-73.

       A discussion of the main problems relevant to manuscript
       fragments. The author discusses their identification, classifi-
       cation, and preservation, with bibliographical notes.

1057   Wilson, R.M. *The Lost Literature of Medieval England*. 2nd ed.
       London: Methuen, 1970.

       In addition to discussing works presumed lost, Wilson also
       describes those surviving in single manuscripts, many of which
       are fragmentary in nature. These are listed in the index by
       collection.

See also items 664, 997.

IX. DECORATION AND ILLUMINATION

Although the items of this section will be of interest primarily to the art historian, many will be of
some value to the paleographer who seeks clues to the
dating, identification, and provenance of a manuscript
through its decoration and illumination. In some cases,
scribe and decorator may be one and the same, a situa-
tion of considerable importance for the paleographer
and one studied in items 1101 and 1211.

Many original medieval treatises are extant on both
the practical art of producing pigments for colouring
manuscripts and the theoretical art of illumination.
Since their number and invaluable contents would appear
to justify their inclusion here, they are accordingly
grouped under "Primary Sources," Section IX.D.

CONTENTS

A. BIBLIOGRAPHICAL MATERIALS

1058   Allen, J.S., ed. *Literature on Byzantine Art (1882-1967)*.
        2 vols. London: Mansell for the Dumbarton Oaks Center,
        Washington, D.C.: 1973-76.

        A bibliography especially rich in items on Byzantine iconog-
        raphy. Arrangement is by topographical location and media.
        Author/subject indexes are provided. Entries in the *Byzantinische
        Zeitschrift*, vols. 1-60, are listed.

1059   *Annual Bibliography of the History of British Art*. Cambridge:
        University Press, 1934-.

        This annual bibliography provides annotated items on subjects
        arranged according to media or subject, e.g., painting and
        iconography. Indexed.

1060   *Annuario Bibliografico di Storia dell'Arte, Instituto Nazionale
        d'Archeologia e Storia dell'Arte*. Modena: 1954-.

        An international, periodical bibliography, with critical
        entries and indexes; arrangement is by artist and country.

1061   *Art Index. A Cumulative Author and Subject Index*. New York,
        N.Y.: H.W. Wilson, 1929-.

        A bibliography of items in art and art history periodicals,
        with book review citations. It appears twice annually and is
        fully indexed.

1062   Besterman, T. *A World Bibliography of Bibliographies*. 4th ed.
        Lausanne: Societas Bibliographica, 1965.

        This basic bibliography for most subjects (see item 9) in-
        cludes a section on art, vol. 1, cols. 519-52. It also lists
        catalogues of illuminated manuscripts.

1063   *Bibliographic Guide to Art and Architecture*. Boston, Mass.:
        G.K. Hall, 1975-.

        A comprehensive, subject bibliography which draws upon
        publications catalogued by the New York Public Library with
        additional entries from Library of Congress union lists. Non-
        descriptive, with a general section on illuminated manuscripts,
        then citations by individual country.

1064   *Bibliographie zur Kunst und Kunstgeschichte*, ed. Gisela Krienke.
        Leipzig: Karl-Marx Universität, 1956-.

        A list of publications, vol. 1 for 1945-53, mainly in the
        DDR.

1065   *Bibliothèque d'Art et d'Archéologie*. Fondation Jacques Doucet.
        Nendeln: Kraus Thompson, 1972-.

        A non-critical, periodic bibliography for art and art history,
        with emphasis upon French periodical resources.

1066   Chamberlain, M.W. *Guide to Art Reference Books*. Chicago, Ill.:
        University of Chicago Press, 1959.

        A comprehensive and descriptive bibliography for reference
        works on the history of art. It lists reference materials,
        periodicals, and studies, with indexes; updated by Ehresmann,
        item 1069.

1067   Courtauld Institute. *Bibliography of the History of British
        Art*. Cambridge: University Press, 1936-57.

        A classified bibliography, which includes Celtic and Viking
        art in Britain.

1068   Donati, Lamberto, ed. *Bibliografia della miniatura*. 2 vols.
        Florence: L.S. Olschki, 1972.

        The two volumes of this bibliography are devoted to (1)
        country and century, and (2) topics, e.g., Nicholas of Lyra,
        Books of Hours, and Iconography. Reviews of works are usually
        cited, although no index is provided.

1069   Ehresmann, D.L. *Fine Arts. A Bibliographic Guide to Basic
        Reference Works, Histories, Handbooks*. Littleton, Colo.:
        Libraries Unlimited, 1975.

        While this bibliography is basically an updating of Chamber-
        lain's, item 1066 above, it presents classified material in a
        more useable form. Indexed.

1070   Goldman, Bernard. *Reading and Writing in the Arts: A Handbook*.
        Rev. ed. (from 1972). Detroit, Mich.: Wayne State University
        Press, 1978.

        A handbook of critical bibliography and general information
        on the history of art, designed primarily for the undergraduate
        but providing a useful and readable introduction to basic
        materials. For medieval manuscript illumination and decoration,
        see "Medieval Manuscripts" in the Reference Key. Also useful
        are lists of art history dictionaries and encyclopedias, pp.
        65-73, art history catalogues, pp. 73-74, and iconography, pp.
        107-14 (the last contains references to hagiography and Eastern
        sources).

1071   Lucas, Edna. *Art Books: A Basic Bibliography on the Fine Arts*.
        Greenwich, Conn.: Graphic Society, 1968.

        A bibliography based upon the author's *The Harvard List of
        Books on Art* (Cambridge, Mass.: Harvard University Press, 1952).
        It lists works under the major categories of painting, iconog-
        raphy, illumination, and individual artists.

1072   *Répertoire d'art et d'archéologie.* Continued from the *Biblio-
       thèque d'art et archéologie.* Paris: University of Paris
       Press, 1910–; Paris: CNRS, 1956–.

       An annotated, classified annual bibliography, with sections
       on art history, iconography, and libraries. A more specialized
       version is published as *Bibliographie d'histoire de l'art*
       (1956–).

1073   *RILA. Répertoire internationale de la littérature de l'art.*
       n.p.: College Art Association, 1975–.

       An annual, fully critical bibliography on all aspects of art
       history and criticism. Classification is by general work, then
       period, collection, and exhibition.

1074   *Repertorium voor de Geschiedenis der Nederlandsche Schilderen
       Graveerkunst sedert het Begin der 12de Eeuw.* ed. H. van Hall.
       2 vols. The Hague: Nijhoff, 1936–49.

       A classified bibliography, which includes many items on
       illuminated manuscripts from the thirteenth century. First
       augmented, then continued by the *Bibliography of the Nether-
       lands Institute for Art History* (The Hague: Nijhoff, 1943–).

1075   Wulff, Oskar. *Bibliographisch-kritischer Nachtrag zu alt
       christliche und byzantinische Kunst.* Handbuch der Kunstwissen-
       schaft. Potsdam: Athenaion, 1939.

       A classified, critical bibliography and handbook for early
       Christian and Byzantine art, issued as a supplement to *Alt-
       christliche und byzantinische Kunst* (1916), see Wulff, item
       1258.

1076   *Zeitschrift fur Kunstgeschichte. Neue Folge von Repertorium
       für Kunstwissenschaft.* Berlin/Leipzig: W. de Gruyter, 1932–.

       An annual bibliography for the history of western European
       art. Indexed.

See also periodical bibliographies in items 1790, 1792–3, 1877–8, and
1892.

B. *CATALOGUES AND LISTS OF COLLECTIONS*

Most library catalogues listed in Section II cite
illuminated manuscripts or indicate those which contain
some decoration. The following titles are specialized
catalogues for illuminated or decorated manuscripts.
Catalogues for exhibitions have generally been omitted
in this list, although they often provide detailed information on groups of manuscripts either from a single
collection or brought together on the basis of style,
period, or topic. Such catalogues or *repertoria* are
listed in union lists, e.g., the Library of Congress
Subject Catalogue under year, "illuminated manuscripts,"
and individual country; see also *RILA*, item 1073.

1077   Alexander, J.J.G., gen. ed. *A Survey of Manuscripts Illuminated
         in the British Isles*. I. *Insular, Sixth to Ninth Centuries*,
         J.J.G. Alexander; II. *Anglo-Saxon, 960-1066*, Elzbieta Temple;
         III. *Romanesque Manuscripts, 1066-1190*, C.M. Kaufmann: IV.
         Early Gothic, 1190-1300, N.J. Morgan; V. *Gothic, Fourteenth
         Century*, Lucy Freeman Sandler; and VI. *Fifteenth Century*,
         Kathleen Scott. London: Harvey Miller/New York: Graphic
         Society, 1975-76.

         This series, published as a chronological study of illuminated
         British manuscripts, provides in each volume a general introduc-
         tion followed by a descriptive catalogue of manuscripts. Manu-
         scripts are listed in chronological order and grouped generi-
         cally. For a valuable assessment of the scope and content of
         this series, see Brownrigg, item 1080 below, and the review
         by T.H. Ohlgren, *Speculum*, 55 (1980), 178-80.

1078   Barker-Benfield, B.C. *Illuminated Manuscripts in the Bodleian*.
         A Concordance of Shelfmarks. Oxford: Bodleian Library, Xeroxed
         from Manuscript Copy, 1974.

         A concordance to manuscripts described by Pächt and Alexander,
         item 1092.

1079   Bibliothèque Nationale. *Les Manuscrits à peintures en France
         du VIIe au XVIe siècle*. Preface by André Malraux. Paris:
         Bibliothèque Nationale, 1954-.

         A series of descriptive catalogues of illuminated manuscripts
         in French libraries. Arrangement is by geographical location
         and collection. Some introductory matter and bibliography are
         provided

1080   Brownrigg, Linda L., "Manuscripts Containing English Decora-
         tion 871-1066, Catalogued and Illustrated: A Review." *Anglo-
         Saxon England*, 7 (1978), 239-66.

         A critical review of item 1077, vol. II, which discusses the
         scope of the series in general and provides a useful bibliog-
         raphy of related works.

1081   Calkins, Robert G., comp. "Medieval and Renaissance Illuminated
        Manuscripts in the Cornell University Library." *Cornell
        Library Journal*, 13 (1972), 3-93.

        A fully descriptive catalogue of the 54 illuminated manuscripts
        in this collection, dating from the late thirteenth to early
        sixteenth centuries, with a facsimile illustration from each.

1082   Demus, Otto, gen. ed. *Corpus der byzantinischen Miniatur-
        handschriften*. Österreichische Akademie der Wissenschaft zu
        Wien. Vienna: The Academy, 1976-.

        A beautifully printed series of descriptive catalogues for
        Byzantine illuminated manuscripts. The volumes are issued by
        library or collection, e.g., volume 2 for the Bodleian Library,
        Oxford, ed. Irmgard Hutter (Stuttgart: Hiersemann, 1978).

1083   Gengaro, Maria Luisa, ed. *Inventario dei Codici decorato e
        miniati (saec. VII-XIII) della Biblioteca Ambrosiana*.
        Florence: L.S. Olschki, 1968.

        This descriptive catalogue has been issued as volume 3 in
        the series *Storia della miniatura, Studi e documenti*. Indexed
        and illustrated.

1084   Grabar, Andre. *Les manuscripts grecs enluminés de provenance
        italienne IXe-XIe siècles*. Paris: Klincksieck, 1972.

        A descriptive catalogue of Byzantine manuscripts from ninth-
        to eleventh-century Italy, with bibliographical references.

1085   Homburger, Otto. *Die illustrierten Handschriften der Burger-
        bibliothek Bern: Die vorkarolingischen und karolingischen
        Handschriften*. Bern: Burgerbibliothek, 1962.

        A descriptive list and analysis of the Bongars manuscripts
        (named after Jacques Bongars, a sixteenth-century Humanist).
        The description includes script, ornamentation, illumination,
        and contents.

1086   Köllner, Herbert. *Die illuminierten Handschriften der Hessischen
        Landesbibliothek Fulda*. Stuttgart: Hiersemann, 1976-. I.
        Handschriften 6.-13. Jahrhunderts. 1976.

        One of the most recent publications in the project sponsored
        by the Forschungsinstitut für Kunstgeschichte, Marburg/Lahn.
        It provides a detailed, descriptive catalogue of illuminated
        manuscripts in the library collection, with many facsimile
        illustrations. Arrangement is by groups of manuscripts accord-
        ing to provenance, e.g., the Codices Bonifatiam.

1087   Number deleted.

1088   Lutze, Eberhard, ed. *Die Bilder-handschriften der Universitäts-
        bibliothek Erlangen*. 2nd ed. (from 1936). Wiesbaden: Harrasso-
        witz, 1971.

        This fully descriptive catalogue with bibliography lists the
        illuminated manuscripts from all periods in the Erlangen Uni-
        versity Library.

1089   McGrath, Robert L., ed. *Illuminated Manuscripts in the Dart-
        mouth College Library*. Hanover, N.H.: The Library, 1972.

        The Dartmouth College collection of illuminated manuscripts
        is described in this catalogue. The 70 manuscripts are arranged
        by country of origin, and illustrated with many facsimiles.

1090   Melnikas, Anthony. *The Corpus of the Miniatures in the Manu-
        scripts of the Decretium Gratiani*. 3 vols. Studia Gratiani,
        16-18. Rome: Studia Gratiani, 1975.

        A descriptive catalogue, with study, of miniatures in manu-
        scripts of Gratianus the Canonist, with facsimile illustrations.

1091   Pächt, O., gen. ed. *Die illuminierten Handschriften und In-
        kunabeln der Nationalbibliothek in Wien*. Vienna: Verlag der
        Österreichischen Akademie der Wissenschaften, 1974-.

        A series of fully descriptive catalogues for the different
        schools of illuminated manuscripts in the National Library,
        Vienna; see item 1093 below.

1092   ————, and Alexander, J.J.G. *Illuminated Manuscripts in the
        Bodleian Library, Oxford*. 3 vols. Oxford: Clarendon Press,
        1973.

        The volumes of this descriptive catalogue are organized by
        national origin of manuscript: German, Dutch, Flemish, Spanish,
        and Italian. A concordance of shelf-marks has been compiled
        by Barker-Benfield, item 1078. Given are a general history of
        each collection and brief accounts of style and special features;
        there are many illustrating facsimiles and eight separate in-
        dexes on texts, authors, artists, and scribes. For a later
        index, see 546.

1093   ————, and Jenni, Ulrike. *Die illuminierten Handschriften und
        Inkunabeln der österreichische Nationalbibliothek. Hollandische
        Schule*. 2 vols. Österreichische Akademie der Wissenschaften,
        Philosophische-Historische Klasse. Vienna: The Academy, 1975.

        This illustrated and annotated catalogue represents one of
        the best in the series. The manuscripts include the work of
        Dutch miniaturists from the mid-fourteenth to the sixteenth
        century. The first volume provides facsimile illustrations and
        the second the descriptive text and bibliography. See also item
        1091.

1094   Pierpont Morgan Library. *Medieval and Renaissance Manuscripts:
        Major Acquisitions, 1924-74*. New York: The Library, 1974.

        A descriptive catalogue of manuscripts, many illuminated,
        in the collection. A brief bibliography of related items is
        provided.

1095   Swarzenski, Hanns. *Die lateinischen illuminierten Handschriften
        des 13. Jahrhunderts in den Landern an Rhein, Main, und Donau*.
        Deutscher Verein für Kunstwissenschaft. Berlin: Denkmäler
        Deutscher Kunst, 1936.

A general survey, limited to examples in Latin manuscripts of the fourteenth century. Many plates illustrate the descriptive text.

1096   UNESCO. *Dismembered Illuminated Manuscripts--European Art.* Paris: UNESCO, 1974.

A descriptive list of mainly medieval illuminated manuscripts which are extant in fragments.

1097   Vikan, Gary, ed. *Illuminated Greek Manuscripts from American Collections in Honor of Kurt Weitzmann.* Princeton, N.J.: Princeton University Press, 1973.

An important catalogue for an exhibition held at the University of Princeton Art Museum, April 14-May 20, 1973. It also refers to other manuscripts in American collections not displayed at the exhibition.

1098   Weinberger, Wilhelm. *Beiträge zur Handschriftenkunde.* Sitzungsberichte de. phil.- hist. Kl. der östereichische Akademie der Wissenschaften. Vienna: The Academy, 1909.

A general, descriptive catalogue of the major Austrian collections of illuminated manuscripts.

See also items 379, 397, 696, 700, and 712.

C. REPRODUCTIONS OF ILLUMINATED MANUSCRIPTS; GENERAL AND SPECIFIC STUDIES

Most of the items in the preceding section contain reproductions of illuminated and decorated manuscripts. Items below offer facsimiles and other illustrations in support of a particular aspect or study of medieval painting. They may also present a single, complete manuscript in facsimile. The list is necessarily select. For further titles see the bibliographical materials listed at the beginning of this section, or the national collections listed in Section VI.

1099   Alexander, J.J.G. *Italian Renaissance Illumination.* London: Chatto and Windus, 1977.

A study, illustrated with plates, of illuminated manuscripts and printed books from fifteenth- and sixteenth-century Italy.

1100   ————. *Norman Illumination at Mont St. Michel, 866-1100.* Oxford: Clarendon Press, 1970.

A study with illustrations of select Carolingian manuscripts from Mont St. Michel.

1101   ———. "Scribes as Artists," in item 720, pp. 87–116.

A well-documented account, with many facsimiles and bibliographical notes, of scribal decoration. The focus is upon
mainly twelfth-century manuscripts and the arabesque initial.

1102   ———. "Some Aesthetic Principles in the Use of Colour in
Anglo-Saxon Art." *Anglo-Saxon England*, 4 (1975), 145–54.

A discussion of Anglo-Saxon painting, based mainly upon manuscript illuminations of the eighth to eleventh centuries, which
considers two innovative techniques: the use of precious metals
in manuscript illumination (e.g., in the Benedictional of St.
Aethelwold) and colored ink drawings (e.g., in the Junius MS.).
There was an increasing tendency to use color in an abstract,
expressionistic manner, and a manifest parallel in the use of
light and dark colors with poetic imagery.

1103   Ancona, Mirella Levi d', et al. *Storia della miniatura, studi e
documenti*. 4 vols. Florence: L.S. Olschki, 1962-70. I. *Miniatura e miniatori e Firenze dal XIV al XVI secolo*, 1962. II.
Lineamenti di Storia della miniatura in Sicilia, 1965. III.
*Gemma villa Guglielmetti: Inventario dei codici decorati e
minati (sec. VII-XIII) della Biblioteca Ambrosiana*, 1968. IV.
The Wildenstein Collection of Illuminations. The Lombard School,
1970.

These four volumes contain inventories and studies of different
Italian collections of illuminated manuscripts. All are illustrated with many facsimiles but less well provided with bibliographical references.

1104   Alcona, Paolo D', and Aeschlimann, Erhard. *Die Kunst der Buchmalerei. Eine Anthologie illuminierter Handschriften vom 6.
bis zum 16. Jahrhunderts*, trans. Karl Berisch. Cologne/Marien-
burg: Phaidon, 1967.

A representative anthology; trans. by Alison M. Brown as *The
Art of Illumination* (London: Phaidon, 1969), with additional
notes on the plates by M. Alison Stones.

1105   Anker, Peter, and Andersson, Aron. *The Art of Scandinavia*.
2 vols. London: Hamlyn, 1971.

A comprehensive history of medieval art in Scandinavia, illustrated with plates and diagrams and includes bibliographical
notes. Trans. from *La Pierre-qui-vire* (Paris: Zodiaque, 1968-69).

1106   Avril, François. *Manuscript Painting in the Court of France:
Introduction and Commentary; The Fourteenth Century (1319-1380)*,
trans. Ursule Molinaro, with Bruce Benderson. London: Chatto
and Windus, 1978.

A collection of facsimiles from Gothic illuminated manuscripts,
with an introductory study and bibliography.

1107   Baumann, Felix Andreas. *Das Erbario carrarese und die Bildtradi-
tion das Tractatus de herbis: Ein Beitrag zur Geschichte der
Pflanzen Darstellung im übergang von Spätmittelalter zu Früh-

renaissance. Berner Schriften zur Kunst, 12. Bern: Benteli, 1974.

A study, illustrated by facsimiles, of botanical illustration for manuscripts in the *Tractatus de Herbis* tradition to the sixteenth century. A bibliography is included.

1108   Beckmann, Josef Hermann, and Schroth, Ingeborg, eds. *Deutsche Bilderbibel aus dem späten Mittelalter: Handschrift 334 der Universitätsbibliothek Freiburg im Breisgau und M. 719-720 der Pierpont Morgan Library, New York.* Constance: J. Thorbecke, 1960.

An introduction to late medieval picture Bibles, especially in Germany, with a detailed analysis of and facsimiles extracts from two exemplars. A bibliography is provided.

1109   Beckwith, John. *The Art of Constantinople: An Introduction to Byzantine Art, 330-1453.* London: Phaidon, 1965.

An introductory survey of Byzantine manuscript illumination, with facsimile illustrations.

1110   ————. *Early Medieval Art, Carolingian, Ottonian, Romanesque.* World of Art Library. London: Phaidon, 1964.

A general survey, illustrated partly from illuminated manuscripts, of ninth- to twelfth-century schools and styles.

1111   Berg, Knut. *Studies in Tuscan Twelfth-Century Illumination.* Oslo: Universitetsforlaget, 1968.

A demonstration that both professional and monastic scribes and illuminators combined activities in the same manuscripts.

1112   Bland, D. *A History of Book Illumination.* Rev. ed. (from 1958). Berkeley and Los Angeles, Calif.: University of California Press, 1969.

The first two chapters of this history survey the techniques and provide examples of medieval manuscript painting. A general bibliography is included.

1113   Blum, Pamela Z. "The Cryptic Creation Cycle in MS. Junius XI." *Gesta*, 15 (1976), 211-26.

A new interpretation for Anglo-Saxon drawings in *Genesis A* representing the Creation; Blum maintains that the artist has arranged all six days in a schematized format in the tradition of Eastern Octateuchs. In many of the illustrations there appears a conflation of iconography and suggested relationships with Patristic exegesis, possibly to Aelfric's *Exameron Anglice*.

1114   Boeckler, Albert. *Abendländische Miniaturen.* Berlin/Leipzig: De Gruyter, 1930.

An illustrated, general history of miniatures in Western manuscripts. More specialized but summary studies are provided by the two following items.

1115   ———. *Deutsche Buchmalerei der Gotik.* Die Blauen Bücher.
        Königstein im Taunus: H. Köster, 1966.

1116   ———. *Deutsche Buchmalerie vorgotischer Zeit.* Die Blauen
        Bücher. Königstein im Taunus: K.R. Langeweische, 1963.

        An introduction to Romanesque illumination with facsimile
        illustrations and bibliography.

1117   Bohigas Balaguen, Pedro. *La ilustracion y la decoración del libro
        manuscrito en Catalunia.* 2 vols. Barcelona: Asociación de
        Bibliofilos de Barcelona, 1960-67.

        A study of illuminated manuscripts and their schools in Cata-
        lonia from the early Romanesque period to the Renaissance.
        Facsimiles and bibliography are included.

1118   Branner, Robert. *Manuscript Painting in Paris During the Reign
        of Saint Louis: A Study of Styles.* California Studies in the
        History of Art, 18. Berkeley, Calif.: University of California
        Press, 1977.

        An illustrated study of thirteenth-century painting techniques
        as reflected in the moralized Bible ateliers and the Sainte
        Chapelle group, with reference to ateliers in Vienna and Oxford.
        An appendix lists the Canonic Parisian Order of Bible books
        and prologues, illuminators, parchmenters, scribes and book-
        sellers. Bibliography and index are provided.

1119   British Library. *Schools of Illumination: Reproductions from
        Manuscripts in the British Museum.* 4 vols. London: Trustees
        of the British Library, 1914-22. I. *Hiberno-Saxon and Early
        English Schools, A.D. 700-1100,* 1914. II. *English, Twelfth and
        Thirteenth Centuries,* 1915. III. *English, A.D. 1300-1350,*
        1921. IV. *English A.D. 1350-1500,* 1922.

        A chronological survey of English manuscript illumination,
        reproduced in facsimile from manuscripts in the British Library
        collection. See also item 1077.

1120   Buchtal, Hugo. *The Miniatures of the Paris Psalter: A Study in
        Middle Byzantine Painting.* Studies of the Warburg Institute,
        2. London: Warburg Institute, 1938/Nendeln, Liechtenstein:
        Kraus, 1968.

        A detailed study of techniques and iconography in this manu-
        script. Bibliographical references and facsimile illustrations
        are included.

1121   ———. *Historia Troiana: Studies in the History of Mediaeval
        Secular Illustration.* Studies of the Warburg Institute, 32.
        Leiden: E.J. Brill, 1971.

        A survey of the extant Troy manuscripts by Benoit and Guido,
        with an analysis of their illumination and decoration. The
        author demonstrates historic development of style and schools
        of illumination within the manuscript traditions. A bibliog-
        raphy and a large collection of plates conclude.

1122   Clark, James Midgley. *The Abbey of St. Gall as a Centre of Literature and Art*. Cambridge: University Press, 1926.

An introduction to the manuscripts and their features. The author includes facsimile examples, a list of insular manuscripts at St. Gall and those from St. Gall now in other libraries. A useful bibliography is found pp. 305-13. See also item 1160.

1123   Dembowski, Hermann. *Initium Sancti Evangelii*. Kassell: Lometsch, 1959.

A brief study of Romanesque initials from select Gospel books, illustrated with plates. A bibliography is provided.

1124   Diringer, David. *The Illuminated Book, Its History and Production*. Rev. ed. (from 1958). New York, N.Y.: Philosophical Library, 1967.

A comprehensive and encyclopedic work on all aspects of book production and illumination. Arrangement is chronological, from the Ancient Egyptian Book of the Dead to the sixteenth-century Grimani Breviary. Each chapter is devoted to one or a group of countries. Illustrated by 100 plates and over 254 figures; bibliography and index.

1125   Dodwell, C.R. *The Canterbury School of Illumination 1066-1200*. Cambridge: University Press, 1954.

The author considers the influence of a pre-Conquest school of illumination upon the Norman school and also analyses English hands from that of the Utrecht Psalter to early Gothic manuscripts. An appendix lists manuscripts illuminated at Canterbury, 1050-1200. The bibliography cites many items of general historical interest for the period.

1126   Duft, Johannes. *Der Bodensee in Sanktgaller Handschriften: Texte und Miniaturen aus der Stiftsbibliothek Sankt Gallen*. Zurich: Carta Verlag, 1958.

A small collection of plates with introduction on representative illuminated manuscripts from the St. Gall Library.

1127   Ebersolt, Jean. *La Miniature byzantine*. Paris/Brussels: Van Oest, 1926.

An analysis of over 140 Byzantine miniatures with illustrating facsimiles. The manuscripts are mainly from collections in Berlin and Paris. The author's interest is in the Oriental influence upon early Western medieval art.

1128   Egbert, Virginia Wylie. *The Mediaeval Artist at Work*. Princeton, N.J.: Princeton University Press, 1967.

A brief account of manuscript initials and other decoration which represents scribes and their instruments; facsimile examples illustrate.

1129   Evans, Joan. *Art in Medieval France 987-1498*. Bibliography
       added 3rd impression. Oxford: Clarendon Press, 1969.

       A general study of French art in its cultural context, espe-
       cially that produced in monastic *scriptoria*. Plates and bibli-
       ography are provided.

1130   ————. *Cluniac Art of the Romanesque Period*. Cambridge:
       University Press, 1950.

       A study of Cluniac manuscripts and architecture; bibliography.

1131   Evans, Michael Wingfield. *Medieval Drawings*. Feltham: Hamlyn,
       1969.

       This work constitutes primarily a collection of plates (132)
       from medieval manuscripts of all periods, but a short intro-
       ductory study with bibliographical references is included.

1132   Focillon, Henri. *Art d'occident*. Paris: 1938; trans. Donald
       King, *The Art of the West in the Middle Ages*, ed. Jean Bony.
       2 vols. New York, N.Y.: Phaidon, 1963.

       Although the author's main interest is medieval architecture,
       he discusses briefly painting in manuscripts and attempts some
       interpretation of its developing forms. Bibliographies are
       provided.

1133   Folda, Jaroslav. *Crusader Manuscript Illumination at Saint-
       Jean d'Acre, 1275-1291*. Princeton, N.J.: Princeton University
       Press, 1976.

       A detailed study of the eleven illuminated manuscripts from
       this *scriptorium* with regard to style, iconography, and paleog-
       raphy; they show a conflation of French Gothic style with Italo-
       Byzantine and well demonstrate the work of the "Hospitaller
       Master." Illustrations, bibliography, and index are provided.

1134   Garrison, Edward B. *Studies in the History of Medieval Italian
       Painting*. 4 vols. Florence: L'Impronta, 1953-62.

       A comprehensive history of medieval Italian painting, which
       includes a study of manuscript illumination from the Carolingian
       period to the Renaissance. Illustrated and documented.

1135   Gerstinger, Hans. *Die griechische Buchmalerei*. Vienna: Staats-
       druckerei, 1926.

       A study of Greek illuminated manuscripts, with selected plates
       from manuscripts in the Vienna National Library.

1136   Grabar, A., and Nordenfalk, C. *Early Medieval Painting*. Lausanne:
       Skira, 1957.

       An account of the development of manuscript illumination in-
       ferred on the basis of historical and geographical lines.

1137   ————. *Romanesque Paintings*. New York, N.Y.: Skira, 1958.

       Along with a general study of the development of Romanesque
       manuscript painting, this useful work also includes a detailed
       analysis of types of initials such as the arabesque.

1138   Grieve, Hilda, and Roberts, F. *Ornament and Decoration in Essex
       Records.* Essex Records Office Publications, 12. Chelmsford:
       Essex Country Council, 1950.

       A brief study (22pp.) with illustrations in facsimile.

1139   *Grimani Breviary, The.* trans. from Italian by Simon Pleasance,
       Linda Packer, and Geoffrey Webb; pref. by Giorgio E. Ferrari,
       introd. by Mario Salmi, commentaries by Gian Lorenzo Mellini.
       Woodstock, N.Y.: Overlook Press, 1974.

       A re-edition and translation of *Breviario Grimani*, with
       facsimile reproductions of this Flemish Breviary in the Biblio-
       teca Nazionale Marciana, Venice. A bibliography is provided for
       related items in the same collection and on the breviary itself.

1140   Guilmain, Jacques. "Zoomorphic Decoration and the Problem of
       the Sources of Mozarabic Illumination." *Speculum*, 35 (1960),
       17-38.

       A significant article on this aspect of Mozarabic manuscripts
       in Spain, richly annotated and illustrated with plates and
       drawings.

1141   Gutbrod, Jürgen. *Die Initiale in Handschriften des achten bis
       dreizehnten Jahrhunderts.* Stuttgart: Kolhhammer, 1965.

       A study, with many facsimile examples from medieval German
       manuscripts from the Romanesque and early Gothic periods, of
       initials and their development.

1142   Hassall, W.O., ed. *The Holkham Bible Picture Book.* 2nd ed.
       London: Dropmore Press, 1954.

       An attractively reproduced facsimile edition of the illustrated
       Middle English Bible, ca. 1330, with introduction and bibliog-
       raphy.

1143   ————, and Hassall, A.G., eds. *The Douce Apocalypse.* New York,
       N.Y.: T. Yoseloff, 1961.

       A facsimile edition of MS. Douce 108 in the Bodleian Library.
       Introduction and bibliography are provided.

1144   Henry, Françoise, ed. *The Book of Kells.* London: Thames and
       Hudson/New York, N.Y.: Knopf, 1974.

       A full-sized facsimile edition from the Trinity College,
       Dublin, manuscript; the editor's extensive introduction gives
       an account of the manuscript, its relationship to other Gospel
       Books of the same school of illumination and period, and many
       bibliographical references. For another facsimile edition see
       item 888.

1145   Herbert, J.A. *Illuminated Manuscripts.* London: Methuen, 1911;
       repr. with additional bibliography by Joyce I. Whalley. Bath:
       Cedric Chivers, 1974.

       A general study of mainly English illuminated manuscripts from
       various periods with facsimile illustrations.

1146   Hindman, Sandra. *Text and Image in Fifteenth-Century Illustrated Dutch Bibles*. Leiden: E.J. Brill, 1977.

A study of relations between text and illustration in late Dutch illuminated Bible manuscripts. An extensive bibliography is provided; indexed.

1147   ————, and Farquhar, James Douglas. *Pen to Press: Illustrated Manuscripts and Printed Books in the First Century of Printing*. College Park, Md.: University of Maryland Press, 1977.

Although an exhibition catalogue for September–October, 1977, this work presents a well-documented study of relations between late manuscript illumination and the illustration of early printed books.

1148   Hinks, Roger. *Carolingian Art; a Study of Early Medieval Painting and Sculpture in Western Europe*. Ann Arbor, Mich.: University of Ann Arbor Press, 1935/1962.

While this study is more interested in aesthetical implications than historical, it does contain references to specific Carolingian illuminated manuscripts and a good bibliography; indexed.

1149   Holmqvist, Wilhelm. *Germanic Art During the First Millennium A.D.* Stockholm: Kungl. Vitterhets., historie- och antikvitels Akademien, 1955.

A work which discusses in some detail the origins of Germanic zoomorphic decorations, many of which found their way into manuscript decoration and illumination. The author considers such designs derived initially during the fifth century from zoomorphic decorations on the edges of provincial Roman chip carvings, and were first adopted by the tribes of the Danubian basin and eventually brought into Scandinavia from there. A full bibliography and index are provided.

1150   Jones, Leslie Webber. *The Miniatures of the Manuscripts of Terence prior to the Thirteenth Century*. 2 vols. Princeton, N.J.: Princeton University Press, 1930-31.

A well-illustrated and documented study of extant illuminated Terence manuscripts. Vol. 1 contains a series of plates, while vol. 2 the text.

1151   Katzenellenbogen, A. *Allegories of the Virtues and Vices in Medieval Art*. Studies of the Warburg Institute, 10. London: Warburg Institute/University of London Press, 1939.

A translation of *Die Psychomachie in der Kunst des Mittelalter von den Anfängen bis zum 13. Jahrundert* (Hamburg: 1933). The author surveys illuminated manuscripts of Prudentius' *Psychomachia* and related texts from the fifth century, with illustrating facsimiles. A bibliography is included.

1152   Klein, Peter K. *Der altere Beatus-Kodex, Vitr. 14.1 der Biblioteca Nacional der Madrid: Studien zur Beatus-Illustration und der Spanischen Buchmalerei des 10. Jahrhunderts*. Hildesheim/New York: Georg Olms, 1976.

A detailed study of a Beatus commentary on the apocalypse, from a north-Spanish manuscript of the eleventh century. The facsimiles are included as volume 2; full bibliography, pp. 605-31. This important work provides a useful starting-point in methodological and factual matter for further studies on apocalyptic illumination.

1153   Kluckert, Ehrenfried. *Die Erzäulformendes spätmittelalterlichen Simultanbildes*. Ph.D. Diss., Ancient and Liberal Arts. Tübingen: University Press, 1974.

A study, from select manuscripts, of fourteenth- and fifteenth-century pictorial narratives and the use of simultaneous scenes within a single illuminated picture. A bibliography is included.

1154   Koehler, W., *et al.*, eds. *Die karolingische Miniaturen*. Deutschen Vereins für Kunstwissenschaft. Berlin: B. Cassirer, 1930-63. 4 vols.: I. *Die Schule von Tours*. II. *Die Hofschule Karl des Grossen*. III. *Die Gruppe des Wiener Krönungs-Evangeliars*. IV. *Die Hofschule Kaiser Lothars*.

Each of these comprehensive and detailed studies, focusing upon a particular school and period, is illuminated with many plates and a full bibliography. See Zimmermann, item 1224, for a pre-series volume.

1155   Lowrie, Walter. *Art in the Early Church*. 2nd ed. New York, N.Y.: Harper, 1965.

A general survey of early Christian art and architecture, with a brief account of manuscript illumination. A work useful mainly for its chronological tables and bibliography.

1156   MacKinney, Loren. *Medical Illustrations in Medieval Manuscripts*. Wellcome Historical Medical Library, Publications, n.s., 5. London: The Library, 1965; Berkeley, Calif.: University of California Press, 1965.

Part 1 of this work introduces various areas of medieval medicine, e.g., hospitals, clinics, phlebotomy, relevant to the 106 miniatures reproduced mostly from the author's own microfilm collection and consequently little known; part 2 (pp. 105-183) is a check list, compiled with the assistance of Thomas Fherndon, of medieval miniatures in pre-1550 manuscripts. A large number of inaccuracies are noted in Florence McCulloch's review, *Speculum*, 41 (1966), 755-7. Some of Mac-Kinney's many microfilms and slides remain in the Ackland Library, University of North Carolina; see item 545.

1157   Masai, F. *Essai sur les origines de la miniature dite Irland-aise*. Publications de Scriptorium, 1. Gand: Editions Scientifiques, 1947.

The author maintains that only insular minuscule derives from Irish scribes, while majuscule and insular illumination originate in Northumbria.

1158   Meiss, Millard. *Andrea Mantegna as Illuminator: An Episode in Renaissance Art, Humanism, and Diplomacy*. New York, N.Y.: Columbia University Press, 1957.

A study of the work of Andrea Mantegna (1431-1506), with
reference to the extant manuscripts. A bibliography and index
are included.

1159   ———. *French Painting in the Time of Jean de Berry: The
        Limbourgs and Their Contemporaries.* 2 vols. London: Thames
        and Hudson, 1974.

        The author examines late fourteenth- and early fifteenth-
        century manuscript illumination, especially that by the Lim-
        bourgs for the Hours of Jean, Duc de Berry. Vol. 1 contains
        the text and extensive bibliography, and vol. 2 the plates.

1160   Merton, Adolf. *Die Buchmalerei in St. Gallen von neunten bis
        zum elften Jahrhundert.* 2nd ed. (from 1917). Leipzig: Hierse-
        mann, 1923.

        An introduction to the work of the St. Gall school, cf. Clark,
        item 1122 above.

1161   Micheli, G.L. *L'Enluminure du haut moyen âge et les influences
        irlandaises.* Brussels: Editions de la Connaissance, 1955.

        A study of select Breton *scriptoria* and those illuminated
        manuscripts which show Irish influence.

1162   Millar, E.G. *English Illuminated Manuscripts from the Xth to
        the XIIIth Century.* Paris/Brussels: G. van Oest, 1926.

1163   ———. *English Illuminated Manuscripts of the XIVth and XVth
        Centuries.* Paris/Brussels: G. van Oest, 1928.

        Both works survey the major illuminated manuscripts found in
        British libraries, e.g., the Lindisfarne Gospels and the Luttrell
        Psalter. Millar provides a general study of school and style,
        illustrated with plates.

1164   ———. *The Lutrell Psalter.* London: Trustees of the British
        Library, 1931.

        A collection of 185 plates from this manuscript, accompanied
        by a brief introduction and notes.

1165   Moé, E.A. van. *La Lettre ornée dans les manuscrits du VIIIe au
        XIIe siècle.* Paris: Editions du Chêne, 1943.

        An historical account of the development of illuminated ini-
        tials, illustrated with 80 plates. Trans. by Joan Evans as
        Illuminated Initials in Mediaeval Manuscripts, pref. by Francis
        Wormald (London: Thames and Hudson, 1950).

1166   Muterich, Florentine, and Gaehde, Joachim E. *Carolingian Paint-
        ing.* New York, N.Y.: Braziller, 1976.

        An illustrated introduction to book painting from the late
        eighth to late ninth centuries; full descriptions and commentary
        for each plate (54) from 29 representative manuscripts. For
        other volumes in the Braziller series see items 1172, 1216,
        1220.

1167   Narkiss, Bezalel. *Hebrew Illuminated Manuscripts*. Jerusalem:
        Encyclopaedia Judaica, 1969.

        A collection of manuscripts and fragments from Egyptian times
        through the nineteenth century, represented in 60 colored
        plates. The glossary and bibliography, however, contain many
        related items significant for the study of illumination in
        Western manuscripts.

1168   Neuss, Wilhelm. *Die Apokalypse des Hl. Johannes in der alt-*
        spanischen Bibelillustration. Münster-in-Westfalen: Aschen-
        dorff, 1931.

1169   ————. *Die katalanische Bibelillustration um die Wende des*
        ersten Jahrtausends und die altspanische Buchmalerei. Bonn/
        Leipzig: K. Schroeder, 1922.

        Both works discuss the development of illumination and
        calligraphy during the early tenth century, especially as
        exemplified in the work of Magius and Florentius. See also
        Klein, item 1152.

1170   Nolan, Barbara. *The Gothic Visionary Perspective*. Princeton,
        N.J.: University Press, 1977.

        A history of apocalyptic commentaries from Bede to Alexander
        of Bremen and their influence upon later styles of illumination.
        Many facsimile illustrations are included, as well as a bibliog-
        raphy and index.

1171   Nordenfalk, Carl. "Before the Book of Durrow." *Acta Archaeo-*
        logica, 18 (1947), 141-74.

        This article examines early insular developments in the
        decorated initial.

1172   ————. *Celtic and Anglo-Saxon Painting. Book Illumination*
        in the British Isles, 600-800. London: Chatto and Windus/
        New York, N.Y.: Braziller, 1977.

        A study of selected early British manuscripts and their
        decoration and illumination. Facsimile illustrations and a
        bibliography are included. See also items 1166, 1216, 1220.

1173   ————. *Die spätantiken Kanontafeln. Studien über die euse-*
        bianische Evangelien-Konkordanz in den vier ersten Jahr-
        hunderts ihrer Geschichte. Göteborg: Isaacson, 1938.

1174   ————. *Die spätantiken Zierbuchstaben*. Stockholm: Egnellska,
        1970.

        Both books offer detailed and well-illustrated studies, the
        first of the Eusebian Canon Tables in early manuscripts, the
        second of the earliest initial letters (from the fourth cen-
        tury) which appear to combine both script and decoration. One
        of the author's theses is the effect of change resulting from
        the replacement of professional, Classical decorators by
        monastic scribes, whose more individual styles demonstrate
        greater freedom and personalization in decoration.

1175   Oakeshott, W. *Sigena: Romanesque Paintings in Spain and the
        Winchester Bible Artists.* London: H. Miller and Metcalf, 1972.

        A comparative study of styles, based in part upon the author's
        earlier work on *The Artists of the Winchester Bible* (London:
        Faber and Faber, 1945).

1176   ————. *The Sequence of English Medieval Art.* London: Faber
        and Faber, 1950.

        A study of English illumination in manuscripts from 650 to
        1450. A bibliography is included.

1177   Ohlgren, Thomas H. "Some New Light on the Old English *Caedmonian
        Genesis.*" *Studies in Iconography,* 1 (1975), 38–73.

        The author attributes MS. Junius 11 to Fleury, ca. 970, on
        the basis of the iconographical analysis of certain scenes,
        the relationship to Beatus' commentary, and to certain archi-
        tectural features such as capitals.

1178   *Oxford History of English Art, The.* Oxford: Clarendon Press.
        II. *English Art, 871-1100,* David Talbot Rice, 1952. III.
        English Art, 1100-1216, T.S.R. Boase, 1953. IV. *English Art,
        1216-1307,* Peter Brieger, 1957. V. *English Art, 1307-1461,*
        J. Evans, 1949.

        This excellent series offers a history of art and architecture
        from the ninth century. Each volume discusses development within
        a chronological framework, with individual chapters devoted to
        the major monuments, schools, and manuscripts. Each includes
        a bibliography as well as illustrations.

1179   Pächt, O. *The Rise of Pictorial Narrative in Twelfth-Century
        England.* Oxford: Clarendon Press, 1962.

        The author traces pictorial illustrations in illuminated manu-
        scripts as they developed through the historiated initial and
        considers some relationships between illustration and text. A
        bibliography and index are provided.

1180   Pearsall, Derek. "Hunting Scenes in Medieval Illuminated Manu-
        scripts." *Connoisseur,* 196.789 (1977), 170–81.

        A thematic study of the symbolism of hunting and falconry in
        psalters, Books of Hours, and hunting manuals, with some con-
        sideration of their painting techniques and styles. Biblio-
        graphical references are included.

1181   Pelekanides, S.M., *et al.,* eds. *The Treasures of Mount Athos:
        Illuminated Manuscripts, Miniatures, Headpieces, Initial
        Letters.* Athens: Ekdotike Athenon for the Patriarchal Insti-
        tute for Patristic Studies, 1974.

        A collection of facsimiles from illuminated manuscripts in
        the Protaton and monasteries of Dionysiou, Koutloumousiou,
        Keropotamou, and Gregoriou. Some descriptive annotation and
        bibliography are provided.

1182   Pickering, F.P. *Literature and Art in the Middle Ages.* Coral
        Gables, Fla.: University of Miami Press, 1970.

A revised edition and translation of the author's *Literatur und darstellende Kunst im Mittelalter* (Berlin: 1966). His main interests are the general aesthetics of medieval manuscript illumination and aspects of relationships between text and illustration; he also gives a close analysis of such topics as typology and source books. Although the work is not organized for efficient reference, the indexes of biblical quotations, subjects, and names can be so used.

1183   Ploss, Ernst. *Ein Buch von alten Farben. Technologie der Textilfarben im Mittelalter mit einem Ausblick auf die festen Farben.* Heidelberg/Berlin: Moos, 1962.

A well-illustrated analysis of the manufacture and use of colored dye and pigment in the Middle Ages.

1184   Plummer, John. *The Book of Hours of Catherine of Cleves*, foreword by Frederick B. Adams, Jr., *et al.* New York, N.Y.: Pierpont Morgan Library, 1964.

Although relatively short (83pp., plus 32 plates), this work represents a detailed description of one of the more significant illuminated manuscripts in North America. The miniatures are related to their iconographical traditions and a catalogue is provided for the exhibition of miniatures from the *Cleves Hours*, held at the Pierpont Morgan Library.

1185   Randall, Lillian M.C. "Exempla as a Source of Gothic Marginal Illumination." *Art Bulletin*, 39 (1957), 97-107.

An analysis of one type of marginalia found in thirteenth- to fifteenth-century manuscripts. For a more general survey, see next item.

1186   ――――. *Images in the Margins of Gothic Manuscripts.* California Studies in the History of Art, 4. Berkeley/Los Angeles, Calif.: University of California Press, 1966.

A general survey of marginalia, thirteenth to fifteenth century, illustrated with nearly 750 black and white reproductions. See also items 1185 and 1187.

1187   ――――. "The Snail in Gothic Marginal Warfare." *Speculum*, 37 (1962), 358-67.

See items 1185-6.

1188   Réau, L. *L'Art gothique en France.* Rev. ed. Paris: Le Prat, 1968.

A concise history of Gothic art in France, which outlines the main features of architectural styles as well as the Gothic schools of manuscript illumination. The author provides a useful glossary of terms and a general bibliography.

1189   ――――. *Histoire de la peinture au moyen âge: La Miniature.* Melun: Librairie d'Argences, 1946.

This introductory study, with facsimile illustrations and bibliography, constitutes vol. 1 of a proposed series on medieval, mainly French, art.

1190   Robb, David M. *The Art of the Illuminated Manuscript.* Cranbury,
        N.J.: A.S. Barnes, for the Philadelphia Art Alliance, 1973.

        This work is a useful introduction to methods of production
        and nomenclature. It discusses painting in medieval codices to
        the fifteenth century, although the later manuscripts are not
        treated in as much detail as the earlier in regard to stylistics
        and iconography. A full bibliography is included.

1191   Ross, J.D.A. *Alexander Historiatus: A Guide to Medieval Illus-
        trated Alexander Literature.* Warburg Institute, Surveys, 1.
        London: Warburg Institute/University of London Press, 1963.

        For a study of this manuscript tradition, see next item.

1192   ————. *Illustrated Medieval Alexander Books in England and
        the Netherlands: A Study in Comparative Iconography.* Cam-
        bridge: Modern Humanities Research Association, 1971.

        An analysis of English and Dutch illuminated manuscripts,
        with an extensive bibliography on Alexander romances and litera-
        ture.

1193   Salmi, Mario. *Italian Miniatures.* 2nd ed. trans. from *La Mini-
        atura Italiana* (1956) by Elisabeth Borgese-Mann. New York,
        N.Y.: H.N. Abrams, 1956/London: Collins, 1957.

        A facsimile collection of 95 color plates and 99 in mono-
        chrome from Italian miniatures of various periods, with an
        historical introduction and bibliography.

1194   Saunders, O.E. *English Illumination.* 2 vols. Florence: Pantheon,
        1928.

        A survey of English illuminated manuscripts for the medieval
        period. A bibliography is provided.

1195   Schapiro, Meyer. "The Decoration of the Leningrad Manuscript
        of Bede." *Scriptorium*, 12 (1958), 191-207.

        The author presents some initials from this manuscript as
        the first extant examples of the historiated initial.

1196   ————. *Words and Pictures; On the Literal and Symbolic in the
        Illustration of a Text.* Approaches to Semiotics, 11. The
        Hague: Mouton, 1973.

        Derived from lectures presented in 1960 and 1969, this work
        demonstrates one of the first applications of semiotics to
        medieval manuscript illumination. Schapiro uses mainly Old
        Testament imagery in fifth- to thirteenth-century manuscripts
        and considers, first, the artist's reading of a text, second,
        themes of state and of action, and finally, front and profile
        as symbolic forms.

1197   Schardt, Alois. *Das Initial. Phantasie und Buchstabenmalerei
        des frühen Mittelalters.* Berlin: Rembrandt, 1938.

        A study of early medieval initials. Illustrations are drawn
        mainly from eighth-century Merovingian and insular manuscripts.

1198 Scheller, R.W. *A Survey of Medieval Model Books.* Harlaam:
      Erven and Bohm, 1963.

      A descriptive account of selected manuscripts used as pattern
      books by illuminators. Organization is by theme, e.g., fortune's
      wheel, beasts, and saints.

1199 Schmidt, G. *Die Armenbibeln des XIV Jahrhunderts.* Graz/Cologne:
      H. Böhlaus, 1959.

      A study of the illustrations for and iconography of fifteenth-
      century picture Bibles such as the Vienna *Biblia Pauperum.* A
      bibliography and index are provided.

1200 Schrade, Hubert. *Vor- und frühromanische Malerei. Die Karol-
      ingische, Ottonische und frühsalische Zeit.* Cologne: M.
      Dumont Schauberg, 1958.

      A comprehensive, illustrated study of early Carolingian and
      Ottonian illumination, with plates and maps.

1201 Stemmler, Theo. *The Ellesmere Miniatures of the Canterbury
      Tales.* 2nd ed. Mannheim: English Department, Medieval Section,
      University of Mannheim, 1977.

      A reproduction of the miniatures from the Ellesmere manuscript
      in the Huntingdon Library, accompanied by the General Prologue.

1202 Strange, Alfred. *Deutsche Buchmalerei der Gotik,* ed. August
      Fink, 11 vols. Munich/Berlin: Deutsche Kunstverlag, 1951-69.

      A series of volumes, each presenting the style of a particular
      region at a certain period and beginning with 1250-1350.

1203 Tailhan, Jules. "Appendice sur les bibliothèques espagnoles du
      haut moyen âge," in *Nouveaux mélanges d'archéologie, d'histoire
      et de littérature sur le moyen âge,* ed. Charles Cahier. 4
      vols. Paris: Firmin-Didot, 1874-77, pp. 217-346.

      An early but still valid essay on Mozarabic *scriptoria.* The
      author discusses in particular the abrupt transition in Spain
      from the Mozarabic style to the Romanesque.

1204 Thompson, Daniel V. *The Materials and Techniques of Medieval
      Painting,* with a foreword by Bernard Berenson. London: Allen
      and Unwin, 1936/1956.

      An introductory chapter discusses the importance of book-
      painting, and this is followed in Chapters II-IV by descriptions
      of techniques for making parchment, vellum, pigments, ink,
      and for the use of metals. Much of the material derives from
      Cennini's fifteenth-century treatise; see item 1230; bibliog-
      raphy is limited and there are no footnotes.

1205 Tikkanen, Johan Jakob. *Die Psalterillustration in Mittelalter.*
      1 vol. in 3 pts. Helsinki: University Press, 1895-1900.

      After a general introduction, the author discusses Byzantine
      and monastic psalters, with a detailed study of the Utrecht
      Psalter.

1206   ————. *Studien über die Farbengebung in der mittelalterlichen Buchmalerei*. Helsinki: Central-Tryckeriet, 1933.

A technical study of pigments and other materials used in medieval manuscript decoration and illumination.

1207   Turner, D.H. *Romanesque Illuminated Mansucripts in England*. London: Trustees of the British Library, 1965.

A small collection of representative manuscripts, mainly from the British Library, with facsimile extracts; brief introduction and bibliography; this work constitutes vol. 1 of the series *English Book Illustration 966-1846* (1965-), and is succeeded by *Gothic Illuminated Manuscripts* (1965).

1208   UNESCO. *Irish Illuminated Manuscripts of the Early Christian Period*, introd. by James Johnson Sweeney. Mentor-UNESCO Art Books. New York, N.Y.: New American Library, 1965.

A highly select survey (24pp.) of early, representative Irish manuscripts, with 28 plates in color.

1209   Unterkircher, Franz. *Die Buchmalerei: Entwicklung, Technik, Eigenart*. Vienna/Munich: Schroll, 1974.

An introductory study of the development of manuscript illumination, with extensive bibliography and index.

1210   ————. *La Miniature autrichienne*. Milan: Electa Editrice, 1954.

The author selects representative illuminated manuscripts of Austrian provenance and studies the characteristic features of different periods. Illustrated, with brief bibliography.

1211   Valentine, L. *Ornament in Medieval Manuscripts. A Glossary*. London: Faber and Faber, 1965.

This study of decoration and illumination provides an especially good account of what the author calls "calligraphic initials," i.e., those made by the scribe.

1212   Number deleted.

1213   Watson, Bruce. "The Calligrapher as Artist: A Note on Bodley MS. Auct. D.3.2." *Scriptorium*, 28 (1974), 281-5.

The author analyses decorations by the scribe of this thirteenth-century English Bible.

1214   Weitzmann, Kurt. *Ancient Book Illumination*. Cambridge, Mass.: Harvard University Press, 1959.

Originally the Martin Classical Lectures, this series of studies considers various aspects of early illumination. Some bibliographical notes are provided.

1215   ————. *Die Byzantinische Buchmalerei des 9. und 10. Jahrhunderts*. Berlin: Gebr. Mann, 1935.

A brief study with plates of Byzantine books and manuscripts;
select bibliography. More detailed studies are the following
items.

1216 ————. *Late Antique and Early Christian Book Illumination.*
New York, N.Y.: Braziller, 1977.

A descriptive introduction, bibliography, and collection of
66 plates from early medieval manuscripts. For other volumes
in this series see items 1166, 1172, 1220.

1217 ————. *Studies in Classical and Byzantine Manuscript Illumina-*
tion, introd. by Hugo Buchtal, pref. by Herbert Kessler.
Chicago, Ill.: University Press, 1971.

This volume contains twelve essays, reprinted from journals,
on such topics as the Tabula Odysseaca, the Greek sources of
Islamic scientific illustrations, and Septuagent illustrations.
The collective bibliographical references represent a wide
variety of topics.

1218 ————, gen. ed. *Studies in Manuscript Illumination.* Princeton,
N.J.: Princeton University Press, 1940–.

A series of excellent studies on aspects of illumination,
thus far in seven volumes, which include: I. Adolph Goldschmidt,
An Early Manuscript of the Aesop Fables of Avianus and Related
Manuscripts; II. Kurt Weitzmann, *Illustrations in Roll and*
Codex: A Study of the Origin and Method of Text Illustration.
2nd ed. (from 1947) (1970); and VII. Herbert L. Kessler, *The*
Illustrated Bibles from Tours (1977).

1219 ————; Loerke, William C.; Kitzinger, Ernst; and Buchtal,
Hugo. *The Place of Book Illumination in Byzantine Art.* The
Art Museum, Princeton University. Princeton, N.J.: Princeton
University Press, 1975.

Four essays on different aspects of Byzantine book illustra-
tion; the last, by Buchtal and entitled "Toward a History of
Palaeologan Illumination," traces the lines of development in
Byzantine manuscript illumination to the fourteenth century.
Included are bibliographies and index.

1220 Williams, John. *Early Spanish Illumination.* New York, N.Y.:
Braziller, 1977.

A collection of facsimiles from fourteen manuscripts, ninth
to twelfth century, which include among the earliest the Bible
of Danila. In addition to the commentaries, the work includes
an introduction to the illumination of the Visigothic, Asturian,
and pre-Romanesque period. Bibliography. For other items in
this series, see 1166, 1172, 1216.

1221 Wilson, David Mackenzie, ed. *The Architecture of Anglo-Saxon*
England. London: Methuen, 1976.

Although this comprehensive work is primarily on Anglo-Saxon
architecture, the author considers its relationship to manuscript
illumination. A bibliography and index are provided.

1222   Wormald, Francis. *English Drawings of the Tenth and Eleventh
        Centuries*. London: Faber and Faber, 1952.

        An introduction to the finely sketched and occasionally
        colored outline drawings in such Anglo-Saxon manuscripts as
        the Junius 11, Corpus Christi College Cambridge 9, Harley 2904,
        and others. All manuscripts are listed and described in the
        catalogue on pp. 59-80. Plates and index are provided.

1223   ————. *The Miniatures in the Gospels of St. Augustine, Corpus
        Christi College MS. 286*. Cambridge: University Press, 1948.

        The Sandars Lectures in Bibliography, 1948, in which the author
        analyses style and technique in this illuminated, Romanesque
        manuscript.

1224   Zimmermann, E. Heinrich. *Vorkarolingische Miniaturen*. Deutsche
        Verein für Kunstwissenschaft. Berlin: B. Cassirer, 1916.

        A collection of four portfolios of pre-Carolingian miniatures,
        with notes and commentary. For later portfolio volumes in this
        series, see item 1154.

See also item 1688.

D. PRIMARY SOURCES FOR DECORATION AND ILLUMINATION

1. INDIVIDUAL TREATISES

1225   Adam of Dore. *Pictor in Carmine*, ed. M.R. James. *Archaeologia*,
        94, n.s. 44 (1951), 141-66.

        A treatise written *ca.* 1200 according to the Cistercian prin-
        ciples of restraint and significant "message" in art. Adam
        gives a program of subjects, 646 in all, which he considers
        worthy of treatment. His emphasis is upon typological subjects
        from the Old and New Testaments.

1226   Anonymous. *De Arte Illuminandi*, ed. A. Lecoy de la Marche as
        L'Art d'enluminer. Paris: E. Leroux 1890; pp. 8-81.

        This anonymous treatise (from Naples?) is more than a tech-
        nical manual; the author, using such sources as Bartholomaeus
        Anglicus' *Liber de Proprietatibus Rerum*, links the seven
        "natural colours" to the seven planets and, in a tradition
        going back to Isidore of Seville's *Etymologiae* and Pliny's
        De Rerum Natura, distinguishes between natural and artificial
        colors. For a more recent edition see Franco Brunello, ed.
        (Vicenza: N. Pozza, 1975).

1227   Anonymous. *Liber de Coloribus Illuminatorum Siue Pictorum*, ed.
        Daniel V. Thompson, Jr. *Speculum*, 1 (1926), 280-307.

From London, British Library, MS. Sloane 1754. In a later
note, pp. 448-50, Thompson corrects date and provenance of
the manuscript to early fourteenth century, English, and adds
many corrections to the Latin text.

1228   Anonymous. *Liber Illuministrarum Pro Fundamentis Auri et Color-*
        ibus, ed. Ludwig Rockinger in *Zum baierischen Schriftwesen*
        in Mittelalter. Abhandlungen der historischen Klasse der
        königlichen bayerischen Akademie der Wissenschaft, 12. Munich:
        The Academy, 1872.

        An anonymous treatise on the making of pigments and goldleaf,
        here summarized rather than edited. Written near Tebernsee, *ca.*
        1500.

1229   Boltz, Valentin. *Illuminierbuch, wie man allerley farben*
        bereitte, mischen schattieren unnd [sic] *ufftragen soll.*
        Basel: J. Kündig, 1549; ed. C.J. Benziger, in *Sammlung mal-*
        technischer Schriften, vol. 4. Munich: C.D.W. Callway, 1913.

        This treatise by Boltz, also called "von Ruffach," represents
        the earliest printed version in Benziger's collection.

1230   Cennini, Cennino d'Andrea. *Il Libro dell'arte*, trans. Daniel
        V. Thompson, Jr., in *The Craftsman's Handbook: The Italian*
        "Il Libro dell' Arte." New York, N.Y.: Dover Publications,
        1933/1954.

        Originally written in Florence, 1437, this work is rich in
        information not only on painting materials and techniques, but
        also on mosaics, coloring parchment and leather, making goat-
        glue, and the personal life of the artist. Thompson's transla-
        tion sustains a high degree of accuracy, and there is much
        bibliographical matter in the notes. See also item 1204.

1231   Dionysios of Mount Athos. *Painter's Handbook*, trans. Gotehard
        Schäfer as *Maler Handbuch des Malermönches Dionysios vom*
        Berge Athos. Munich: The Slavic Institute, 1960.

        Although this treatise deals explicitly with eighteenth-cen-
        tury icons, the techniques are based upon the traditions of
        early Byzantine painting.

1232   Dunstan, St. *Classbook*. Facsimile edition, ed. R.W. Hunt.
        Umbrae Codicum Occidentalium, 4. Amsterdam: Hakkert, 1961.

        For a summary and reference to other writings associated with
        St. Dunstan, see Lehmann-Brockhaus, item 1236.

1233   *Göttingen Model Book, The. A Facsimile Edition and Translation*
        of a Fifteenth-Century Illuminator's Manual, ed. and trans.
        H. Lehmann-Haupt. Columbia, Mo.: University of Missouri Press,
        1972.

        This attractively produced color facsimile edition pro-
        vides an introduction on the Niedersächsische Staats- und
        Universitäts-bibliothek manuscript (Cod. Offenb. 51) and an
        English translation of the Rhenish Franconian dialect text.
        The model book embodies features not found in other such works,

e.g., it contains both verbal instruction and pictorial
models; it is also important insofar as it can be identified
as the direct source for the illumination of a large group of
manuscripts and early printed books, e.g., the Giant Bible of
Mainz. The editor includes plates from several of these works
for comparison.

1234   Honnecourt, Villard de. *Sketch Book*, ed. Theodore Bowie as *The*
        Sketch Book of Villard de Honnecourt. 2nd ed. Bloomington,
        Ind.: Indiana University Press, 1959/New York, N.Y.: G.
        Wittenborn, 1962.

        A thirteenth-century pattern-book, which contains architectural
        and other drawings used in decoration and illumination. Arrange-
        ment is not according to the manuscript, Paris B.N. fr. 19093,
        but by subject.

1235   Mure, Conrad von. *Libellus de Naturis Animalium*, ed. F.J. Bendel.
        Mitteilungen des Instituts für Österreichische Geschichts-
        forschung, 30 (1909), 51-101.

        A treatise offering detailed instruction on the manufacture
        of materials used in bookmaking, e.g., parchment. See also
        item 1435.

                        2. COLLECTED TREATISES

1236   Lehmann-Brockhaus, O. *Lateinische Schriftquellen zur Kunst in*
        England, Wales und Schottland von Jahre 901 bis zum Jahre
        1307. 5 vols. Veröffentlichungen des Zentralinstitut für
        Kunstgeschichte in München, 1-2. Munich: Prestel, 1955-60.

        A study with editions of such scribes and artists as Saint
        Dunstan and the eleventh-century Worcester master, Ervenius.
        Vols. 1-2 arrange the texts topographically in alphabetical
        order. Vol. 3 lists types of sources, e.g., allegorical. Vols.
        4-5 contain registers and indexes. See also item 1232.

        E. ICONOGRAPHY AND GENERAL REFERENCE WORKS

1237   Ancona, Mirella Levi D'. *The Iconography of the Immaculate Con-*
        ception in the Middle Ages and Renaissance. Monographs on
        Archaeology and Fine Arts, Archaeological Institute of America
        and College of Art Association, 7, in conjunction with *The*
        Art Bulletin. New York, N.Y.: The Association, 1957.

        A general survey of the major illuminated manuscripts, with
        some study and bibliography. A series of plates illustrate the
        development and variation of the theme of the Immaculate Con-
        ception.

1238   Aurenhammer, Hans. *Lexikon der christlichen Ikonographie.*
         5 vols. Vienna: Brüder Hollinek, 1959-65.

         An iconographical lexicon, arranged alphabetically by Christian
         topic, e.g., *Christus.*

1239   *Bibliographie zur Symbolik, Ikonographie und Mythologie,* ed.
         M. Lurker. Internationales Referateorgan. Baden-Baden: Heitz,
         1968-.

         Thus far only one volume has appeared in this projected
         periodic bibliography for all areas of symbolism, iconography,
         and mythology.

1240   Brault, G.J. *Early Blazon, Heraldic Terminology in the Twelfth
         and Thirteenth Centuries with Special Reference to Arthurian
         Literature.* Oxford: Clarendon Press, 1972.

         An illustrated dictionary of medieval blazons and explana-
         tion of some heraldic terms. A bibliography is included.

1241   Cirlos, J.E. *A Dictionary of Symbols,* trans. from the Spanish
         by Jack Sage. New York, N.Y.: Philosophical Library, 1962.

         A convenient and useful dictionary for both Eastern and
         Western symbolism, but one which reveals some unevenness in the
         detail and documentation of its entries. The bibliography, pp.
         367-77, provides many valuable references and there is a general
         index.

1242   Eliade, Mircea. *Images and Symbols: Studies in Religious Sym-
         bolism,* trans. from the French ed. of 1952 by Philip Marvet.
         New York, N.Y.: Sheed and Ward, 1969.

         A general, theoretical discussion of symbolism, psychoanal-
         ysis, and the survival of images; the last chapter (V) is
         devoted to the Christian symbolism of water and the cosmic
         tree. There is a general index, but only scattered biblio-
         graphical notes.

1243   Fox-Davies, A. *The Art of Heraldry: An Encyclopaedia of Armory.*
         New York, N.Y.: T.C. and E.C. Jack, 1904/1967.

         An historical introduction to and dictionary of heraldry,
         with many illustrations of motifs and symbols.

         Index of Christian Art. See item 1251.

1244   Künstle, Karl. *Ikonographie der christlichen Kunst.* 2 vols.
         Freiburg-im-Breisgau: Herder, 1926-28.

         An excellent reference work on the iconography of Christian
         art. Arrangement is alphabetical by subject, with vol. 2
         devoted to the iconography of hagiography. A bibliography and
         index are provided.

1245   *Larousse Encyclopedia of Byzantine and Medieval Art,* gen. ed.
         René Huyghe, trans. Dennis Gilbert *et al.* New York, N.Y.:
         Prometheus Press, 1965.

This encyclopedia of medieval art and architecture contains over 1,000 illustrated entries (photographs, manuscript facsimiles, and drawings), with discussion and select bibliography. This and the following item constitute two of the six volumes in the series.

1246   *Larousse Encyclopedia of Pre-historic and Ancient Art*, gen. ed. René Huyghe, trans. Michael Heron *et al.*; rev. ed. from the French ed. of 1958 and the 1st English ed. of 1963. New York, N.Y.: Prometheus Press, 1968.

See preceding item.

1247   *Lexikon der christlichen Ikonographie*, ed. Engelbert Kirschbaum, *et al.* Freiburg-im-Breisgau: Herder, 1968-.

To date the standard dictionary on iconography of the Christian church. A comprehensive reference work on all aspects of Christian iconography, arranged alphabetically in signed articles on each topic, with a bibliography included in each.

1248   Marle, R. van. *Iconographie de l'art profane au moyen âge et à la renaissance: La Vie quotidienne.* 2 vols. The Hague: M. Nijhoff, 1931-32.

An iconographical survey of such themes as Fortuna, illustrated from frescoes, miniatures, furniture, and other domestic articles.

1249   Millet, Gabriel. *Recherches sur l'iconographie de l'Evangile aux XIVe, XVe, et XVIe siècles d'après les monuments de Mistra, de la Macédoine et du Mont-Athos.* 2nd ed. (from 1916). Paris: Editions E. de Boccard, 1960.

An initial "sommaire" outlines the contents of this extensive study of the iconography of Gospel manuscripts produced in Mistra, Macedonia, and Mt. Athos; see also the author's index of subjects which concludes the work. He considers narrative cycles, programs of decoration, types of miniatures, and schools of art, especially in relation to sources. His illustrating plates derive not only from manuscripts, but also from wall paintings and sculpture.

1250   Panofsky, Erwin. *Studies in Iconology: Humanistic Themes in the Art of the Renaissance.* London: Oxford University Press, 1939.

Focusing upon such images as Father Time and Blind Cupid, Panofsky illustrates his theories of intrinsic meaning or iconographical significance. Although his examples are drawn mainly from Renaissance art, there are many references to earlier literature, e.g., the Ovide moralisé, and to medieval manuscripts. These are cited in the index. The bibliography numbers some 413 items on all aspects of medieval and Renaissance iconography.

1251   Princeton University. *Index of Christian Art.*

A collection of over 100,000 photographs of examples of Christian art, arranged by subject, medium, and location. The

locations to date are the Princeton University Library, Princeton, N.J.; Dumbarton Oaks Research Library, Washington, D.C.;
University of California Library, Los Angeles, Calif.; Biblioteca Vaticana, Rome; and the Kunsthistorische Instituut of the
Rijksuniversiteit, Utrecht. A catalogue of over 500,000 cards
provides a systematic analysis of the subject matter, and a
Handbook was compiled by H. Woodruff (1942).

1252   *Reallexikon zur byzantinische Kunst.* Stuttgart: Hiersemann,
        1963–.

        This and the following item are useful lexica for tracing
        the pictorial representations of medieval themes in art, espe-
        cially manuscript illumination, e.g., the heroic figure of
        Alexander. Arrangement is by topic, theme, or object.

1253   *Reallexikon zur deutschen Kunstegeschichte*, ed. Otto Schmidt,
        Ernst Gall, and L.H. Heydenreich. Stuttgart: Hiersemann,
        1937.

        See preceding item.

1254   Réau, Louis. *Iconographie de l'art chrétien.* 3 vols. in 6 pts.
        Paris: Presses Universitaires de France, 1955–59.

        Each volume of this comprehensive study is devoted to some
        aspect of medieval iconography: vol. 1 offers a general intro-
        duction on sources and media, while vols. 2 and 3 study in some
        detail the iconographical background for the Testaments and
        hagiography respectively.

1255   Schiller, Gertrud. *Iconography of Christian Art*, trans. from
        the 2nd ed., 1969, by Janet Seligman. 2 vols. Greenwich,
        Conn.: New York Graphic Society, 1971.

        This massive work studies the changes in presentation in the
        iconography of Christian art, especially as represented in
        manuscripts of the Bible and the liturgy. She considers, e.g.,
        the question of theological typology and the pre-figuring of
        New Testament persons and events in Old Testament iconography.
        Extensive indexes render the work a useful dictionary on the
        subject.

1256   Timmers, J.J.M. *Symboliek en Iconographie der christelijke
        Kunst.* Roermond/Massiek: Romen and Zonen, 1947.

        Although this work is merely a general study, it does provide
        an analysis of early medieval treatises on the symbolism of
        the liturgy, e.g., Beleth and Durand. There is a subject/per-
        son/place index.

1257   Worsley, Alice Feeney. "An Index of the Visual Content of Five
        Thousand Medieval Manuscript Illuminations in the Bodleian
        Library," in *Three Medieval Studies.* Unpublished Doctoral
        Dissertation, University of California. Santa Cruz: 1973.
        DA, 34, 5130A.

        A computerized index for manuscript items dating from the
        second to the sixteenth centuries. These are categorized under

21 headings, e.g., abstractions such as allegorical figures,
biblical personages and events, science, music, and so on. An
index gives information on the manuscripts and makes cross-
references whenever possible to the Princeton *Index of Christian
Art*, item 1251.

1258 Wulff, Oskar. *Altchristliche und byzantinische Kunst*. 2 vols.
Berlin: F. Burger, 1914-18.

A manual on Byzantine art which serves to indicate much of
the oriental derivation of early Christian art. For the bibliography associated with this work, see Wulff, item 1075.

See also item 126.

X. MUSIC

This section is intended primarily as a convenient reference guide for those paleographers or codicologists who may be faced with the problem of medieval musical manuscripts only in the context of historical, literary, or other studies. The presence of musical notation in a manuscript may be a useful guide to its date and provenance, perhaps to its generic identification. Music may also be an important ancillary to the main contents of a manuscript, e.g., the liturgical music which accompanies dramatic texts such as the Fleury Herod play. It is hoped that for all such problems the bibliographical references given in this section will lead to those works suggesting the most plausible and the most specific solutions.

The selection and arrangement of items have been much facilitated by Andrew Hughes' admirable bibliography for medieval music, item 1262. To items selected from that work which obviously relate to paleographical concerns, I have added several which were either omitted or which appeared after 1974.

CONTENTS

A. BIBLIOGRAPHICAL MATERIALS

1259   Gerboth, Walter, comp. "An Index of Festschriften and Some
        Similar Publications," in *Aspects of Medieval and Renaissance
        Music: A Birthday Offering to Gustave Reese*, ed. Jan LaRue.
        New York, N.Y.: Norton, 1966, pp. 183-307.

        This article provides indexes of Festschriften, then works
        by period and composer, with a general index. For a later re-
        vision, see next item.

1260   ———. *An Index to Music Festschriften and Similar Publica-
        tions*. New York, N.Y.: Norton, 1969.

        A revised and enlarged bibliography based upon the preceding
        item, which includes an author/subject index.

1261   Heyer, Ann H., ed. *Historical Sets, Collected Editions and
        Monuments of Music*. 2nd ed. (from 1957). Chicago, Ill.:
        American Library Association, 1969.

        A list, uncritical, of a series of editions, mainly of music.
        A composer/subject/author index is provided.

1262   Hughes, Andrew. *Medieval Music: The Sixth Liberal Art*. Toronto
        Medieval Bibliographies, 4. Toronto: University Press, 1974.

        Thus far the most complete and up-to-date bibliography on
        the subject of medieval music. Entries usually have some critical
        comment, and arrangement is by type of work, e.g., bibliographies,
        general reference, studies, then type of music, e.g., plain-
        song, lyric, polyphony, Renaissance. Much of the confusion
        created by multiple divisions is compensated for by extensive
        indexes and cross-references. For reference to Hughes' micro-
        film collection, see item 535.

1263   Jenkins, G., comp. *A Short-title Liturgical Bibliography*. London:
        Sold for the Author by Duckett, 1951.

        A short (16pp.) list of liturgical items, both texts and
        music.

1264   Lesure, F. "La Musicologie médiévale d'après des travaux
        récents." *Rom*, 74 (1953), 271-8.

        A brief, annotated survey of recent scholarship in musicology
        for the preceding three years.

1265   *Music Article Guide. A Comprehensive Quarterly Reference Guide
        to Signed Feature Articles in American Music Periodicals*.
        Philadelphia, Pa.: 1964-.

A quarterly bibliography to periodical literature in music,
with brief summaries. Arranged alphabetically by author.

1266   *Music Index, The: Annual Cumulation.* Detroit, Mich.: Informa-
        tion Service, Inc., 1949-.

        Lists books and articles by subjects, authors, and composers
        in alphabetical order, with cross-references. Appears monthly
        with annual cumulations. Recordings and performances are also
        listed.

1267   *Répertoire internationale de littérature musicale.* Flushing,
        N.Y.: 1967-.

        A quarterly bibliography, with abstracts of books, articles,
        reviews, dissertations, catalogues, and other works. Annual
        cumulations and a complete computerized index.

1268   Schmieder, Wolfgang, *et al.*, comp. *Bibliographie des Musik-*
        schriftums. Institut für Musikforschung Berlin, Frankfurt-
        am-Main: Friedrich Hofmeister, 1954-.

        A periodic bibliography for international resources in music
        and music history. It contains sections on bibliographies,
        periodicals, instruments, and other categories. A subject/name/
        place index is provided.

1269   Waesberghe, J. Smits, comp. "Das gegenwartige Geschichtsbild
        der mittelalterlichen Musik." *Kirchenmusikalisches Jahrbuch,*
        42 (1962-).

        An annual, annotated bibliography of articles on medieval
        music from all published sources; there is a special section
        on the paleography of music. A cumulative index arranged by
        subject, area, manuscript, name, and author appeared in vol.
        53 (1969).

See also item 1307.

B. MANUSCRIPT LISTS AND CATALOGUES

1270   Arkwright, G.E.P. *Catalogue of Music in the Library of Christ*
        Church, Oxford. London: Oxford University Press, 1915/1971.

        An annotated list of all music manuscripts of which author-
        ship is known. The collection includes several late medieval
        items.

1271   Bannister, Henry M., ed. *Monumenti Vaticani di Paleografia*
        Manuscripta Latina. 2 vols. Leipzig: Teubner, 1913; reprinted
        Westmead: Gregg International, 1969.

        Vol. 1 of this work represents a catalogue of sources and
        notations for plainsong, with incipits and indexes. Vol. 2

represents a portfolio of 206 reproductions from manuscripts of the ninth to fourteenth centuries.

1272   Corbin, Solange, gen. ed. *Répertoire de manuscrits médiévaux contenant des notations musicales*. 3 vols. Paris: CNRS, 1965-74.

The first three volumes of a proposed series of music catalogues. Each volume gives a descriptive list of manuscripts containing musical notations, grouped according to library: I. *Bibliothèque Sainte-Geneviève-Paris*, ed. Madeleine Bernard (1965); II. *Bibliothèque Mazarine-Paris*, ed. Madeleine Bernard (1966); III. *Arsenal, Bibliothèque Nationale, Université, Ecole des Beaux-Arts-Paris*, ed. Madeleine Bernard (1974).

1273   Gajard, Dom Joseph, ed. *Les Principaux manuscrits du chant. Gregorien, ambrosien, mozarabe, gallican, publiés en facsimiles phototypeques*. 1st series. Vols. 1-14. Solesmes: Abbaye Saint-Pierre, 1889-1931; 2nd series. Vols. 1-2, 1900-24.

A collection of representative facsimiles from several periods and countries; each is accompanied by a transcription and commentary; general introductions and bibliographies are given for each.

1274   Gottwald, Clytus. *Die Musikhandschriften der Staats- und Stadbibliothek Augsburg*. Wiesbaden: Harrassowitz, 1974.

This volume represents no. 1 in the series of manuscript catalogues for Augsburg, see item 243. Arrangement is by codex number; full descriptions, index of incipits and titles.

1275   Hughes, Anselm. *Medieval Polyphony in the Bodleian Library, Oxford*. Oxford: The Library, 1951.

A brief (63pp.) descriptive list of manuscripts containing polyphonic music from the late middle ages.

1276   Hughes-Hughes, Augustus, ed. *Catalogue of Manuscripts of Music in the British Museum*. 3 vols. London: Trustees of the British Library, 1906-09.

A fully descriptive catalogue in three volumes: vol. 1 lists polyphonic sacred vocal music; vol. 2 lists secular vocal music; and vol. 3 lists instrumental music and includes treatises, histories, dictionaries, drawings, and instruments. Each is accompanied by indexes of titles, incipits, names, subjects, and manuscripts.

1277   Mixter, Keith E. *An Introduction to Library Resources for Music Research*. Columbus, Ohio: Ohio State University, College of Education, School of Music, 1963.

A useful, introductory guide to classifications of works on music and their contents. An index is provided.

1278   Reaney, G. *Manuscripts of Polyphonic Music, Eleventh to Early*
        Fourteenth Centuries. Duisburg: Henle, 1966; *Manuscripts of*
        Polyphonic Music, c. 1320-1400. Munich/Duisburg: Henle, 1969.

        Published as vol. B.IV, pts. 1-2, of *Répertoire International*
        des Sources Musicales; for an account of this project, see Wayne
        D. Shirley, *International Inventory of Music Sources: Report*
        of the Joint U.S. Committee on Activities, Washington, D.C.:
        1966, I.v-vi. The volumes are descriptive catalogues, arranged
        by location and chronology. Reaney provides an introduction
        and thematic incipits.

1279   Stenzl, J. *Repertorium der liturgischen Handschriften der*
        Diozese Sitten, Lausanne und Genf. I. Sitten. Fribourg:
        University Press, 1972.

        A proposed survey of liturgical manuscripts in Swiss Diocesan
        collections. Full descriptions, many facsimiles, and indexes
        are provided.

See also items 600-9.

C. GENERAL AND SPECIFIC STUDIES, INCLUDING FACSIMILES

1280   Apel, Willi. *The Notation of Polyphonic Music, 900-1600.* 5th
        ed. Cambridge, Mass.: Mediaeval Academy of America, 1961.

        The standard, general work on notation in medieval manuscripts,
        with facsimile illustrations. It does not include plainsong
        notations.

1281   Blanc, Maurice J. *Introduction to Gregorian Paleography.* Toledo,
        Ohio: Gregorian Institute of America, 1951.

        An introductory study of Gregorian notation in early manu-
        scripts. Illustrations, map, index, and bibliography are pro-
        vided.

1282   Carapetyan, A. "A Preface to the Transcription of Polyphonic
        Music." *Musica Disciplina*, 5 (1951), 3-14.

        A general editorial on the principles of editing early music
        manuscripts.

1283   Corbin, S. "Les Notations neumatiques en France à l'epoque
        carolingienne." *Revue d'Histoire de l'Eglise de France*, 38
        (1952), 225-32.

        A discussion of the origin of Carolingian notational style,
        especially the so-called "Lorraine" notation.

1284   Frere, W.H. "The Palaeography of Early Medieval Music," in
        Walter Howard Frere: A Collection of His Papers. Alcuin Club
        Collections, 35 (1940), 90-106.

A general introduction to the principles of early musical notation as demonstrated in select manuscripts; bibliography.

1285   Handschin, Jacques. "Eine alte Neumenschrift." *Acta Musicologica*, 22 (1950), 69-97; 25 (1953), 87-88.

An illustrated discussion on the origin of neumes and their interpretation in early manuscripts.

1286   Higginson, J.V. "The Monastic Scriptorium." *Catholic Choirmaster*, 36 (1950), 53-55.

A brief survey of the major features in the production of early music manuscripts.

1287   Hourlier, J. "Le Domaine de la notation messine." *Revue Gregorienne*, 30 (1951), 96-113, 150-8.

A discussion of the form of notation thought to have originated in Metz and eventually replaced by the type of square notation called "Lorraine."

1288   Hughes, Anselm, ed. *Early Medieval Music up to 1300*. Rev. ed. The New Oxford History of Music, 2. London: Oxford University Press, 1955.

A general survey of medieval music, with a good bibliography, indexes, and illustrative plates. The discussion of techniques of musical notation is introductory, but a useful starting point for further studies; see next item.

1289   ————, and Abraham, Gerald, eds. *Ars Nova and the Renaissance, 1300-1540*. The New Oxford History of Music, 3. London: Oxford University Press, 1960.

A continuation of the preceding item.

1290   Huglo, M. "Reglement du XIIIe siècle pour la transcription des livres notés," in *Festschrift für Bruno Stäblein zum 70. Geburtstag*, ed. Martin Ruhnke. Kassel: Bärenreiter-Verlag, 1967; pp. 121-33.

An account, with bibliographical references, of plainsong notation and the use of *custos*.

1291   Jammers, Ewald. *Tafeln zur Neumenschrift*. Tutzing: H. Schneider, 1965.

A collection of plates illustrating early musical notation in manuscripts. Each is fully described, with bibliographical references.

1292   Parrish, C. *The Notation of Medieval Music*. New York, N.Y.: W.W. Norton, 1958.

An introduction to the musical notation of medieval manuscripts; illustrated by extracts in facsimile. Select bibliography, index.

1293   Reese, Gustave. *Music in the Middle Ages*. 2nd ed. (from 1940).
       London: J.M. Dent, 1941/New York, N.Y.: W.W. Norton, 1948.

       This work discusses, among other matters, the development
       and spread of square notation from the Ile de France; useful
       bibliography and notes.

1294   Sachs, C. "Some Remarks about Old Notation." *Musical Quarterly*,
       34 (1948), 365-70.

       A brief but condensed discussion of notation and tempo, with
       transcriptions from manuscripts. There is some criticism of
       early twentieth-century editorial practices and bibliographical
       references.

1295   Seebass, Tilmann. *Musikdarstellung und Psalterillustration in
       früheren Mittelalter*. Bern: Francke, 1973.

       A study in musical iconography, which attempts to relate
       representations of musical instruments to sources and the nature
       of the manuscripts in which they are found. Indexes provide
       an excellent catalogue of material. A 30pp. bibliography is
       included.

1296   Strunk, William Oliver. *Essays on Music in the Byzantine World*.
       New York, N.Y.: W.W. Norton, 1977.

       A collection of essays on aspects of Byzantine Church music.
       The bibliography is comprehensive. Indexes are provided.

1297   Suñol, Gregorio Maria. *Introduction à la paléographie musicale
       grégorienne*, trans. from Catalan. Paris: Desclée, 1935.

       This important work provides a general introduction to
       Gregorian notation, with a classification of regional systems.
       It includes 154 facsimiles, an exhaustive bibliography, and
       invaluable indexes of neumes, notations, scripts, places,
       persons, and manuscripts.

1298   Thibaut, Jean-Baptiste. *Origine byzantine de la notation
       neumatique de l'église latine*. Bibliothèque musicologique,
       3. Paris: A. Picard, 1907.

       The history of early Byzantine notation and its relation to
       Western neumes. Illustrated with 28 facsimiles, transcriptions,
       and diagrams.

1299   Wellesz, Egon. *A History of Byzantine Music and Hymnography*.
       2nd ed. Oxford: Clarendon Press/New York, N.Y.: Oxford Uni-
       versity Press, 1961.

       A discussion of historical and literary background to music
       styles and techniques. Although there appears to be some
       lacunae in the areas of psalmodic and ordinary chants and the
       liturgy in general, this work represents the best general
       history thus far of a most complex subject.

1300   Wolf, Johannes. *Handbuch der Notationskunde*. 2 vols. Leipzig:
       Teubner, 1913/Hildesheim, 1965.

Vol. 1 of this work discusses medieval notation, including
Byzantine, and manuscript transcription, richly annotated and
illustrated with transcriptions and facsimiles. Vol. 2 discusses
sixteenth- and seventeenth-century music.

1301 ————. *Geschichte de Mensural-Notation von 1250-1460.* 3 vols.
Leipzig: Teubner, 1904; vol. 1 repr. 1965.

A comprehensive account of notation for this period. The work
is well-documented and indexed. Vol. 3 provides transcriptions
of the 78 pieces in vol. 2.

D. REFERENCE WORKS

1302 Benton, Rita, comp. *Directory of Music Research Libraries.*
3 vols. International Association of Music Libraries, Commission of Research Libraries. Iowa City, Ia.: The Commission,
1967; 1970, 1972.

Individual volumes list library facilities in music for
different countries. Included are bibliographies for music manuscript collections.

1303 Blume, Friedrich, ed. *Die Musik in Geschichte und Gegenwart.*
14 vols. Kassel: Bärenreiter-Verlag, 1949-.

A dictionary with periodic supplements on all aspects of
musicology, especially medieval musical notation. It includes
references to European dissertations.

1304 Carter, Henry H. *A Dictionary of Middle English Musical Terms.*
Indiana University Humanities Series, 45. Bloomington, Ind.:
Indiana University Press, 1961/New York, N.Y.: 1968.

A dictionary of terms directly relevant to music, e.g.,
musical instruments, and those basically musical in meaning,
e.g., "blowen." Full entries give forms and extracts from
Middle English texts with dates. Some, e.g., "horn," constitute
short treatises on the subject. Included is a bibliography of
texts quoted and another for works cited.

1305 Padelford, Frederick M. *Old English Musical Terms.* Bonner
Beiträge zur Anglistik, 4. Bonn: P. Hanstein, 1899.

A general introduction to works on music in Old English,
followed by a glossary in which Latin terminology is also
included.

1306 Porte, Jacques, ed. *Encyclopedie des musiques sacrées.* 2 vols.
Paris: Editions Lagergine, 1968-69.

A detailed study, well-illustrated with facsimiles, with
contributions by different hands. Vol. 1 includes Eastern music,
while vol. 2 discusses Christian, mainly medieval traditions.
Bibliographies are provided.

1307   Spiess, Lincoln B., ed. *Historical Musicology, a Reference
        Manual for Research in Music*. Brooklyn, N.Y.: Institute of
        Mediaeval Music, 1963.

        An invaluable but non-critical survey of all areas of scholar-
        ship and scholars in musicology to 1960. The list of journals
        is especially useful toward further scholarship.

XI. CODICOLOGY: THE MANUSCRIPT BOOK

While it is not within the scope of this *Handbook* to
enter into the current debate over the precise nature
and province of "codicology," or indeed to attempt to
justify the existence of "codicology" as a separate
discipline (see item 1311), it does seem useful to define an area of research which includes the physical
features of early manuscripts or rolls and the processes
by which they became books. In this section I have accordingly listed general works on what is variously termed
"codicology," "Buchwesen," and "Boek-archeologie," and
followed these with bibliographical citations from the
more precise categories of production, materials, and
the preservation of manuscript books and documents. It
might be argued, of course, that decoration and illumination could also be an aspect of "codicology," or indeed
that script itself has physical features enough to qualify
its inclusion under this heading, but I have devoted separate sections to these on the grounds that their extensive
bibliographies and wide ramifications for manuscript study
set them apart from topics considered here.

Production and materials are especially relevant to the
identification and dating of manuscripts. Thus, for example, scribal practice at Lorsch and other *scriptoria*
might be characterized not only by particular hands but
also by methods of pricking, foliation, or parchment
production; similarly, a particular type of binding might
indicate that a certain manuscript could be traced in
its provenance at least to a well-known collector such
as Archbishop Laud. No physical feature of a manuscript
is without value either as a clue to its identity and
provenance or as representing one facet in the general
history of book production.

A small group of references have formed themselves into
a recognizable area of what might be called the "primary
sources" of "codicology." Listing them as such I do
so with the *caveat* that they are highly select and by
no means intended as anything near a complete list. They
are, nevertheless, of some interest insofar as they suggest
a medieval notion of "codicology": they describe a continued awareness of the need for clarity, precision, and
standardization among scribes in order to avoid the shame
of improfessionalism and the obscurity imposed by illeg-
ibility; they offer technical descriptions for the production of parchment and bindings; they discuss classification
and circulation; and, finally, they express some concern
for the preservation of books and documents. Certainly
they offer a rich area for future research, one which
would expand our knowledge of the manuscript book and
enlarge the investigations of "codicology" in general.

CONTENTS

A. GENERAL WORKS

1308   Bennett, H.S. "The Production and Dissemination of Vernacular
Manuscripts in the Fifteenth Century." *The Library*, 5th ser.,
1 (1946-47), 167-78.

A general discussion (originally a paper for the Bibliographical Society, December 17th, 1946) on the relationships between
genre and publication, whether through patrons or other means.
Bennett considers publication by individual scribes and professional scriveners, bibliographical notes refer to individual
manuscripts.

1309   Bühler, Curt F. *The Fifteenth-Century Book*. Philadelphia, Pa.:
University of Pennsylvania Press, 1960.

Originally three lectures for the University of Pennsylvania
in connection with the A.S.W. Rosenbach Fellowship in Bibliography. They discuss scribes, printers, and decorators; extensive
bibliographies have been added, especially for that area of
transition between manuscripts and printed books. In this the
author demonstrates the close relationship between the production of manuscripts and books and the fact that both materials
could be bound together, or that manuscripts could be copied
from printed books. See also item 1316.

1310   Dahl, Svend. *Histoire du livre de l'antiquité à nos jours*,
trans. from *Bogens Historie*, 1926. Paris: J. Lamavre, 1933.

A general account of manuscript and book production; discusses
materials and methods, with some bibliography, illustrations.
A German translation, *Geschischte des Buches*, appeared in 1928.

1311   Gruys, Albert. *Codicologie of boek-archeologie? Een vals dilemma*.
Nijmegen: Thoben, 1971.

A lecture given at the Catholic University of Nijmegen,
September, 1971, in which Gruys discusses the nature of codicology and the problems of terminology.

1312   Goldschmidt, E.P. *The Printed Book of the Renaissance*. 2nd ed.
Amsterdam: G.T. van Heusden, 1974.

Three lectures on type, illustration, and ornament, with
facsimile illustrations. The author demonstrates the influence
of late medieval manuscript books on early printing techniques.

1313   Johnson, Edward. *Writing, Illuminating, and Lettering*. 11th
ed. (from 1906). London/New York, N.Y.: Sir I. Pitman, 1920/
1932.

An introductory account of book production; included are the production of materials (the description of pen-cutting derives from a medieval source), writing techniques of the *scriptorium*, and illuminating. A select bibliography is provided.

1314   Kruitwagen, Bonaventura, O.F.M. *Laat-Middeleeuwische Paleografica, Paleotypica, Liturgica, Kalendalia, Grammaticalia.* The Hague: M. Nijhoff, 1942.

If the title seems somewhat "pompous," claims the author, p. iii, none could better describe this collection of essays in Dutch on late medieval scribes and manuscript production in the Netherlands: many were earlier published as articles in *Het Boek*, 1933–. The six essays and 15 appendix items cover a wide range of topics, from the fifteenth-century scribe, Herman Strepel (see item 1403 below) to an explanation of the word "Paleotype," i.e., the type faces of incunabula. An index facilitates use as a mine of information on many aspects of book production and scripts.

1315   Madan, Falconer. "The Localization of Manuscripts," in *Essays in History Presented to Reginald Lane Poole*, ed. H.W.C. Davis. Oxford: Clarendon Press, 1927/Freeport, N.Y.: Books for Libraries, 1967; pp. 5–29.

A somewhat generalized essay which discusses localized variants in abbreviations through suspension or contraction, forms of letters, gathering, and format. Madan provides a table of tests for localization in *Horae* manuscripts.

1316   Mazal, Otto. *Buchkunst der Gotik.* Graz: Akademische Drunk- und Verlaganstalt, 1975.

A general history of the Gothic book from the thirteenth to the sixteenth centuries, described in terms of general historical background, miniatures, scripts, and collation. The author also discusses the transition to early printed books. Full bibliography and indexes. For some important omissions, however, see Curt F. Bühler's review in *Speculum*, 52 (1977), 1022–4.

1317   Milkau, F. *Handbuch der Bibliothekswissenschaft.* 2nd ed. (from 1930). 3 vols. in 4. Stuttgart/Wiesbaden: Harrassowitz, 1950-61.

A thorough and detailed account of all aspects of manuscript book production, including materials, production, and binding. The emphasis is upon the resources of Germany and Scandinavia.

1318   Ouy, Gilbert. "Comment rendre les manuscrits médiévaux accessibles aux chercheurs." *Codicologica*, 4 (1978), 9–58.

A clear and well-documented account of methodological stages in cataloguing and describing early manuscripts, with a good classification of their physical features.

1319   Putnam, George H. *Books and Their Makers During the Middle Ages. A Study of the Conditions of the Production and Distribution of Literature from the Fall of the Roman Empire to the*

Close of the Seventeenth Century. 2 vols. New York, N.Y.:
Hillary House, 1896-97/1962.

A general survey of the manufacture and publication of manuscript books and early printed books, with some consideration
of their cultural contexts. The bibliography is outdated but
still useful for early items.

1320 Rigg, George. *The Making of A Manuscript.* University of Toronto,
Centre for Medieval Studies, Media Centre, Video-Tape Series.
Toronto: Media Centre, n.d.

A 23-minute colour video-tape cassette available for rental
or purchase, dealing with the physical history of the medieval
manuscript book. It describes both materials and production.

1321 Stokes, Roy, ed. *Esdailes' Manual of Bibliography.* 4th ed.
(from 1932). London: Allen and Unwin, 1967.

This useful manual contains articles on all aspects of book
production: materials, writing, collation, and binding. An
extensive bibliography is provided.

1322 Treu, Kurt, ed. *Studia Codicologica.* Berlin: Akademie Verlag,
1977.

A collection of 46 essays by different scholars, of which
several are on matters pertaining to codicology, e.g., J. Leroy,
"Quelques systemes de reglure des manuscrits grecs," pp. 291-
312.

1323 Turner, Eric G. *The Typology of the Early Codex.* Philadelphia,
Pa.: University of Pennsylvania Press, 1972.

An account of the papyrus and parchment manuscript book;
bibliography and index. See also *Codicologica*, 2 (1978), 9-14.

1324 Vervliet, H.D.L., ed. *The Book Through Five Thousand Years.*
London: Phaidon, 1972.

Essays by several hands on book production and binding.
Bibliographies are provided.

1325 Vreese, Willem de. *Over Handschriften en Handschriftenkunde:
Tien Codicologische Studien*, ed. P.J.H. Vermeeren. Zwolle:
W.E.J. Tjeenk Willink, 1962.

A collection of ten essays by Dutch scholars on manuscripts
and their production. Bibliographies are provided.

1326 Weise, Oskar. *Schrift und Buchwesen in alter und neuer Zeit.*
Leipzig: Teubner, 1899.

A general history of books and book production, with facsimile
illustrations. A bibliography is provided.

See also items 21, 29, 54, 1901.

B. *SCRIBES, SCRIPTORIA, AND BOOK PRODUCTION*

1327   Andrieu, J. "Pour l'explication psychologique des fautes de
        copiste." *Revue des Etudes Latines*, 28 (1950), 279-92.

        This article outlines the basic scribal errors and suggests
        reasons why they were made; he discusses, e.g., eyeskips pro-
        ducing a hiatus then doubling of letters, and analyzes the
        complexity of pen and eye movements combined with such psycho-
        logical phenomena as anticipation; his examples are drawn from
        Classical texts. See item 1351 for a more detailed account,
        and cf. items 1352, 1388, 1984.

1328   Autenrieth, J. *Die Domschule von Konstanz zur Zeit des Investi-
        turstreits. Die wissenschaftliche Arbeitsweise Bernolds von
        Konstanz und zweier kleriker dargestellt auf Grund von Hand-
        schriftenstudien.* Forschungen zur Kirchen- und Geistgeschichte.
        Neue Folge, 3. Stuttgart: W. Kohlhammer, 1956.

        Originally Autenrieth's Munich thesis, 1952, he studies the
        school and *scriptorium* of Constance during the Carolingian
        period. The focus is upon the work and writings of Bernold.
        An extensive bibliography is provided.

1329   Beeson, C.H. *Lupus of Ferrieres as Scribe and Text Critic: A
        Study of His Autograph Copy of Cicero's 'De Oratore.'* Boston,
        Mass.: Mediaeval Academy of America, 1930.

        This detailed study includes a facsimile of the manuscript
        and a bibliography.

1330   Bischoff, B. *Die südostdeutschen Schreibschulen und Bibliotheken
        in der Karolingerzeit.* 2nd ed. 2 vols. Wiesbaden: Harrasso-
        witz, 1960.

        Bischoff describes in some detail the *scriptoria* and libraries
        associated with St. Amand. Vol. 1 is devoted to Bavarian sources,
        and vol. 2 to Salzburg, Mondsee, and other areas. See also items
        816-7.

1331   ————. *Lorsch im Spiegel seiner Handschriften.* Munich: Arbeo-
        Gesellschaft, 1974.

        A study of the Carolingian *scriptorium* at Lorsch and the
        production of its manuscripts. Some lists of manuscripts and
        bibliography are provided.

1332   Blakey, B. "The Scribal Process," in *Medieval Miscellany Pre-
        sented to Eugene Vinaver*, ed. F. Whitehead. Manchester: Uni-
        versity Press, 1965; pp. 19-27.

        An essay discussing the transmissions of texts from authors
        to editing scribes; specific reference is to Old French texts.

1333   Carey, Frederick M. "The *Scriptorium* of Reims during the Arch-
        bishopric of Hincmar," in *Classical and Mediaeval Studies in*

Honor of E.K. Rand, ed. L.W. Jones. New York, N.Y.: 1938/ Freeport, N.Y.: Books for Libraries Press, 1968; pp. 41-60.

An account of all known manuscripts originally from the *scriptorium* of Reims bearing the *ex dono* of Hincmar, 845-82. Carey describes their special features and present locations.

1334   Clemoes, Peter. *Liturgical Influence on Punctuation in Late Old English and Early Middle English Manuscripts.* Cambridge, Department of Anglo Saxon. Occasional Papers, 1. Cambridge: University Press, 1952.

A brief (22pp.) conjectural account of the influence of Latin punctuation symbols, e.g., the *punctus elevatus*, upon English secular manuscripts.

1335   Davis, N. "Scribal variation in Late Fifteenth-Century English," in *Mélanges de linguistique et de philologie: Fernand Mossé in Memoriam.* Paris: Didier, 1959.

Evidence from the Paston letters illustrates the movement toward conformity and, at the same time, distinctively regional scribal usages. The six scribes are Gloys, Calle, Playter, Pampyng, Danbeney, and Wykes.

1336   Delaissé, L.M.J. "Towards a History of the Manuscript Book." *Codicologica*, 1 (1976), 75-83.

Notes on the construction of the codex.

1337   Destrez, J. *La Pecia dans les manuscrits universitaires du XIIIe et du XIVe siècle.* Paris: Editions Jacques Vautrain, 1935.

An account of the production of *pecia* (large parchment sheets folded to form folio or quarto leaves) in accordance with the need for rapid reproduction of books in the University of Paris from the thirteenth century. Destrez' theories are challenged by Pollard, see item 1373.

1338   Doyle, A.I. "The Shaping of the Vernon and Simeon Manuscripts," in *Chaucer and Middle English Studies in Honour of Rossell Hope Robbins*, ed. Beryl Rowland. London: Allen and Unwin, 1974, pp. 328-41.

Obervations on two of the largest anthologies of Middle English verse and prose. Doyle gives detailed descriptions of the contents, divisions, quires, etc. of these manuscripts, with some plausible conclusions about their compilation and manufacture. Full bibliographical notes are provided.

1339   ————. "An Unrecognized Piece of *Piers the Ploughman's Creed* and Other Work by its Scribe." *Speculum*, 34 (1959), 428-36.

A detailed analysis of f. 3 from MS. Harley 78 and portions of three others in terms of script, scribal practice, and other features. Doyle suggests they were produced by a London scribe in the reign of Edward IV (1460-83), possibly working in a *scriptorium* where at least two Shirley manuscripts were produced.

1340   ————. "The Work of a Late Fifteenth-Century English Scribe,
        William Ebesham." *John Rylands Library Bulletin* 39 (1957),
        298-325.

        A detailed study of the evidence of the work of this scribe,
        who undertook various scribal tasks for Sir John Paston the
        Elder; facsimile illustrations are included from MSS. British
        Library Addit. 43491, 10106, and Lansdowne 285; Rylands Latin
        395; St. John's College Oxford 147; and Durham University
        Library Cosin V.III.7. Extensive bibliographical notes are
        a useful source for further study.

1341   ————, and Parkes, M.B. "The Production of Copies of the
        Canterbury Tales and *Confessio Amantis* in the Early Fifteenth
        Century," in *Medieval Scribes, Manuscripts, and Libraries:
        Essays Presented to N.R. Ker*, item 720, 163-203.

        A detailed and well-documented account of the relationships
        between scribes copying English works in London during this
        period, based partly upon evidence from Trinity College Cam-
        bridge MS. R.3.2 (581). Bibliographical notes are provided.

1342   ————; Rainey, Elizabeth; and Wilson, D.B. *Manuscript to
        Print: Tradition and Innovation in the Renaissance Book.*
        Durham University Library Guides, special ser., 1. Durham:
        University Library, 1975.

        A brief (32pp.) introduction to the transition from manuscript
        to printed book in the fifteenth century, which actually con-
        stitutes a guide to the semi-permanent exhibition at the Uni-
        versity of Durham. Illustrated.

1343   Garand, Monique-Cecile. "Le *Scriptorium* de Guibert de Nogent."
        Scriptorium, 31 (1977), 3-29.

        An article providing a detailed account of scribal practices,
        with illustrations of scripts, decoration, and collation.

1344   Gasparri, Françoise. "Le Scriptorium de Corbie à la fin du
        VIIIe siècle." *Scriptorium*, 21 (1967), 86-93.

        A study of some early Caroline minuscule manuscripts produced
        at Corbie, with useful tables of facsimile extracts.

1345   Gilissen, Léon. "La Composition des cahiers, le pliage du
        parchemin et l'imposition." *Scriptorium*, 26 (1972), 3-33.

        The making of the manuscript book: folding, gathering, and
        assembling of quires; see also *Prolegomènes*, item 1347.

1346   ————. *L'Expertise des écritures médiévales: Recherche d'une
        méthode avec application à un manuscrit du XIe siècle: Le
        Lectionnaire de Lobbes, Codex Bruxellensis 18018.* Les Publica-
        tions de Scriptorium, 6. Gand: Editions Scientifiques E.
        Story-Scientia S.P.R.L., 1973.

        A beautifully printed and detailed analysis of scribal methods
        in the Lectionary of Lobbes, late eleventh century; these in-
        clude, among other aspects, angle of the quill, duct, and

morphology. Diagrams, enlarged photographs of individual letters, and full-page facsimiles from the manuscripts representing the work of different scribes are provided.

1347 ————. *Prolegomènes à la codicologie: Recherches sur la construction des cahiers et la mise en page des manuscrits médiévaux.* Publication de Scriptorium, 7. Gand: Editions Scientifiques, 1977.

1348 ————. "Un Élément codicologique trop peu exploité: La reglure." *Scriptorium,* 23 (1969), 150-62.

Both works explore related aspects of the making of the manuscript book, 400-1400. *Prolegomènes* is copiously illustrated with drawings, diagrams, and plates; it also includes full bibliography and lists of manuscripts, mainly from the Bibliothèque Royale, Brussels.

1349 Gumbert, J.P., and Haan, M.J.M. de, eds. *Litterae Textuales,* item 716, 1 (1972).

Essays by A.I. Doyle and others on manuscript book production. See especially Doyle's article "Further Observations on Durham Cathedral MS. A. IV. 34," pp. 35-47, which illustrates the method described by Samaran, item 1376 below.

1350 Hajnal, István. *L'Enseignement de l'écriture aux universités médiévales.* Studia Historica Academiae Scientiarum Hungaricae. Budapest: The Academy, 1954.

Hajnal discusses methods of teaching writing and their influence upon diplomatic practices, including those of the Hungarian court, to the Renaissance.

1351 Havet, Louis. *Manuel de critique verbale appliquée aux textes latins.* Paris: Hachette, 1911/Rome: L'Erma di Bretschneider, 1967.

While this manual is intended as an aid in textual criticism in its classification and explanation of scribal errors, its basis is in scribal practice and codicology. Section 1 describes the state of texts for mainly the Carolingian period to the Renaissance; section 2 analyses scribal faults, the influence of context, personality and education of the scribe, the work of the rubricators, etc. Updated in part by item 1327, and supplemented in item 1388. See also item 1956.

1352 Headlam, W. "Transposition of Words in Manuscripts." *Classical Review,* 16 (1902), 243-56.

An explanation of scribal, psychological error (see also item 1327) and an explanation of why scribes tend to use a simpler prose word order in copying.

1353 Hirsch, J.C. "Author and Scribe in *The Book of Margery Kempe.*" *Medium Aevum,* 44 (1975), 145-50.

A conjectural analysis of the work of the "second" scribe
and his contributions to *The Book* in terms of editing and interpolation. This article was prompted by Sanford Meech's
statement in the EETS edition of 1940 that Margery's "amanuenses"
were "faithful to her dictation." On the "first" scribe, see
Seymour, item 1380.

1354   Jeudy, Colette. "Signes de fin de ligne et tradition manuscrite.
        Le 'De Translatione Romani Imperii de Marsile de Padoue.'"
        Scriptorium, 27 (1973), 252-62.

        Jeudy considers the particular implications of line-fillers
        for establishing manuscript foliation.

1355   Jones, Leslie Webber. "Ancient Prickings in Eighth-Century
        Manuscripts." *Scriptorium*, 15 (1961), 14-22.

1356   ———. "Pricking Manuscripts: The Instruments and Their
        Significance." *Speculum*, 21 (1946), 389-403.

        Both articles provide detailed studies of the use of the
        circle, awl, toothed-wheel, and other instruments in marking
        manuscripts for writing. The author considers briefly the sig-
        nificance of such instruments for determining provenance and
        date, a subject studied in more detail in the next item.

1357   ———. "Prickings as Clues to Date and Origin: The Eighth
        Century." *Medievalia et Humanistica*, 14 (1962), 15-22.

        See preceding item.

1358   Keiser, George R. "Lincoln Cathedral Library MS. 91: Life and
        Milieu of the Scribe." *Studies in Bibliography*, 32 (1979),
        158-79.

        This manuscript was copied presumably by Robert Thornton,
        ca. 1420-50, in the North Riding of Yorkshire. Keiser makes
        many references to the sale and distribution of books for this
        period, then describes the contents of the manuscript in the
        context of public tastes and interests. He also considers
        Thornton's scribal habits and criteria for selection.

1359   Ker, N.R. "From 'Above top line' to 'Below top line': A Change
        in Scribal Practice." *Celtica*, 5 (1960), 13-16.

        A brief look with examples of a change in scribal practice
        which took place in the twelfth and thirteenth centuries.

1360   Lehmann, Paul. "Blatter, Seiten, Spalten, Zeilen." *Zentral-
        blatt für Bibliothekswesen*, 53 (1936), 333-61.

        A discussion of foliation and other gathering techniques from
        about 1300.

1361   Levine, Philip, "Historical Evidence for Calligraphic Activity
        in Vercelli from St. Eusebius to Atto." *Speculum*, 30 (1955),
        561-81.

A study of the Vercelli manuscripts for the period 370-960 against their historical background, e.g., the career of Luitward and the collection of the *Anselmo dedicata*.

1362   Lindsay, W.M. "Collectanea Varia." *Paleographia Latina*, 16 (1923), 10-14.

A brief article discussing some local traditions for corrections, marked passages, and related techniques.

1363   ————. *The Bobbio Scriptorium: Its Early Minuscule Abbreviations*. Zentralblatt für Bibliothekswesen, Separatabdruck, 26. Leipzig: Harrassowitz, 1909.

An illustrated account of abbreviations used during the Carolingian period; see Lindsay, item 1515.

1364   ————. "The (Early) Lorsch Scriptorium." *Paleographia Latina*, 3 (1924), 5-48.

1365   ————. "The Old Script of Corbie, Its Abbreviation Symbols (with two photographs of Montpellier, Bibl. univ. MS. 69)." *Revue des Bibliothèques*, 22 (1912), 405-29.

1366   ————, and Lehmann, Paul. "The (Early) Mayence Scriptorium." *Paleographia Latina*, 4 (1925), 15-37.

These three articles provide further studies of individual *scriptoria* during the Carolingian period with, collectively, a full set of bibliographical references on scribal practices and abbreviations for the period.

1367   Lucas, P.J. "John Capgrave, O.S.A. (1393-1464). Scribe and 'Publisher.'" *Transactions of the Cambridge Bibliographical Society*, 5 (1969), 1-35.

An attempt to resolve the conflicting views on Capgrave's "autograph" manuscripts. The two scripts are defined as "Y" and "Z," and attributed to Capgrave; the one is described as secretary-influenced and the other a modified textura. The attributable manuscripts are so grouped, with some relationship made to the hands of Ebesham and Werken. For an objection to this conclusion, see Edmund Colledge and Cyril Smetana, "Capgrave's Life of St. Norbert: Diction, Dialect and Spelling," *Mediaeval Studies*, 34 (1972), 422-34.

1367.1 McIntosh, Angus. "Towards an Inventory of Middle English Scribes." *Neuphilologische Mitteilungen*, 75 (1974), 602-24.

The author proposes an "ordered assemblage" of individual profiles towards the compilation of a dictionary of known or identifiable scribes. His criteria would be based upon what he considers three main characteristics of scribal practice. Cf. item 2015.

1368   McLachlin, Elizabeth Parker. "The *Scriptorium* of Bury St.-Edmunds in the Third and Fourth Decades of the Twelfth Century: Books in Three Related Hands and Their Decoration." *Mediaeval Studies*, 40 (1978), 328-48.

A study of the resources and bibliography for the monastic
scriptorium, with a list of possible manuscripts classified
into three groups according to hand; typical initials and orna-
ments are analyzed and reproduced in figures, along with facsimile extracts from seven manuscripts.

1369   Morley, H.T. "Notes on Arabic Numerals in Medieval England."
        Berkshire Archaeological Journal, 50 (1949 for 1947), 81-86.

        From an initial treatise, ca. 1300, by the Byzantine scholar
        Planudes, the use of Arabic numerals was gradually introduced
        into Western manuscripts, making a common appearance in English
        manuscripts from the early fifteenth century.

1370   Mynors, R.A.B. "A Fifteenth-Century Scribe: T. Werken." *Trans-
        actions of the Cambridge Bibliographical Society*, 1 (1950),
        97-104.

        A detailed account of the Dutch scribe, writing in Rome,
        Cologne, and finally London, with a description of the 17 manu-
        scripts attributable to him. Bibliographical references and
        facsimile extracts are provided.

1371   Orlandelli, Gianfranco. *Il libro a Bologna da 1300 al 1330*.
        Universita degli Studi di Bologna, Studi e ricerche di storia
        et scienze ausiliairie, 1. Bologna: Zanichelli, 1959.

        A detailed account of the production and distribution of
        Bolognese manuscript books. Discussed are contracts (*formulae*)
        and the role of the universities in production; indexes.

1372   Pfaff, Carl. *Scriptorium und Bibliothek des Klosters Mondsee
        im hohen Mittelalter*. Österreichische Akademie der Wissen-
        schaften, 2. Vienna: Böhlaus, 1967.

        The author surveys the *scriptorium* and libraries of the
        Abbey of St. Michael at Mondsee (upper Austria). Initial chap-
        ters trace its history from Carolingian times to 1791 and
        describe manuscript characteristics and known scribes; the final
        chapter assesses possible library holdings in the late Middle
        Ages. Appended is a descriptive catalogue of 59 manuscripts
        and a series of plates.

1373   Pollard, Graham. "The Pecia System in the Medieval Universities,"
        in item 720, pp. 145-61.

        An expansion and revision of some points originally made by
        Destrez, item 1337. Pollard disagrees that the *pecia* system
        began in Paris and instead attributes it to Bologna, ca. 1200.
        He then traces the spread of the system throughout the conti-
        nent.

1374   Roberts, C.H. "The Codex." *Proceedings of the British Academy*,
        40 (1954), 169-204, and Offprint.

        On the codex as it developed from the writing tablet and
        begun to replace the roll in Classical Antiquity. Especially
        useful are the author's detailed bibliographical references,
        including those to the first use of the word "codex," attri-

buted to Commodianus in the *Carmen Apologeticum*, 11, second
half of the third century.

1375   Russell, G.H., and Nathan, V. "A *Piers Plowman* Manuscript Now
        in the Huntington Library." *Huntington Library Quarterly*,
        26 (1963), 119-30.

        A detailed study of scribal practices as reflected in the
        spellings of this manuscript.

1376   Samaran, C. "Manuscrits imposés à la maniere typographique,"
        in *Mélanges en Hommage à la Memoire de Fr. Martroye*. Paris:
        Société Nationale des Antiquaires de France, 1940.

        See next item and cf. 1349.

1377   ———. "Manuscrits 'imposés' et manuscrits non-coupés--un
        nouvel exemple." *Codices Manuscripti*, 2 (1976), 38-42.

        In this and in 1376 the author describes the practice of
        writing a number of pages upon a large sheet of unfolded parch-
        ment, which is then folded to produce a number of bifolia in
        the manner of printed books. His evidence draws upon incomplete
        copies rejected by scribes before they were folded, cut, and
        passed to the binder in an open state.

1378   Schulz, H.C. "Thomas Hoccleve, Scribe." *Speculum*, 12 (1937),
        71-81.

        A study of Hoccleve's hand, illustrated with facsimiles; see
        also Doyle, item 720, and Lucas, item 1367.

1379   *Scriptorium Opus: Schrieber-Mönche am Werk. Prof. Dr. Otto Meyer
        zum 65 Geburtstag am 21 September 1971*. Wiesbaden: Reichert,
        1971.

        A brief dedicatory essay (31pp.) on the work of the monastic
        scriptorium; bibliographical references.

1380   Seymour, M.C. "A Fifteenth-Century East Anglian Scribe." *Medium
        Aevum*, 37 (1968), 166-73.

        A study of similar scribal features in MSS. Univ. Lib. Cam-
        bridge Gg. IV. 27 and Bodleian Library e Musaeo 116. Dialectical
        and scribal features suggest a connection with the "first" scribe
        of Margery Kempe's *Book*, see also Hirsch's article, item 1353.

1381   Skeat, T.C. "The Use of Dictation in Ancient Book Production."
        Proceedings of the British Academy, 42 (1956), 179-208.

        Skeat considers the theory that manuscripts produced on a
        commercial scale were dictated to a number of scribes simul-
        taneously, with application specifically to the Codex Sinaiticus.
        He provides good critical references to earlier works on the
        subject.

1382   Spang, Paul. *Handschriften und ihre Schreiber. Ein Blick in dem
        Scriptorum der Abtei Echternach, Luxemburg*. Editiones Ep-
        ternacenses. Luxemburg: Bourg-Bourger, 1967.

A brief study of scribal practices and book production in
monastic *scriptoria* of this area during the Carolingian and
Gothic periods. A bibliography is provided.

1383   Spendal, R.J. "The Manuscript Capitals in *Cleanness.*" *Notes and
        Queries*, 23 (1976), 340-1.

The observation is made that the capitals in the unique manuscript of the poem, MS. Cotton Nero A.X., divide thematic rather
than narrative sections of the poem and point to a network of
parallel passages that epitomize the central moral concerns.

1384   Steele, R. "The Pecia." *The Library*, 4 ser., 11 (1931), 230-4.

A brief historical account of the *pecia* as a unit-rate of
payment to scribes at the University of Bologna in the thirteenth century, with some specific references to *peciae* in
manuscripts containing works by Roger Bacon.

1385   Steinberg, S.H. "Medieval Writing Masters." *The Library*, 4th
        ser., 22 (1941), 1-24.

An account illustrated by plates of the few extant documents
associated with known writing-masters; these include handbooks
on writing, specimens of script, and advertisements. In the
last context Steinberg describes the development of a group
of itinerant writing-masters from the fourteenth century, who
offered to instruct *in diversis textibus et notulis*. Useful
references are made to manuscripts and editions. Some quotations are made from the writings of Hermann Strepel, see item
1403.

1386   Stewart, Z. "Insular Script Without Insular Abbreviations:
        A Problem in Eighth-Century Palaeography." *Speculum*, 25
        (1950), 483-90.

A study of the Harvard fragment, Jerome's *Epistula ad Helio-
dorum*, second half of the eighth century. Evidence for establishing provenance derives from the avoidance of abbreviations and
in some similarities with the *en-* type Corbie script, suggesting origin in a Continental *scriptorium*.

1387   Stockwell, Robert P., and Barritt, C. Westbrook. "Scribal
        Practice: Some Assumptions." *Language*, 37 (1961), 75-82.

A linguistic argument for scribal traditions in orthography
and a consistent use of certain allophones and allographes.
Bibliographical references are provided to earlier works by
these and other authors.

1388   Stoll, Jakob. "Zur Psychologie der Schreibfehler." *Fortschritte
        der Psychologie und ihrer Anwendung*, 2 (1914), 1-133.

The author attempts to duplicate writing conditions with his
own students and analyzes the resultant errors against common
medieval scribal errors. See Andrieu, item 1327.

1389 Thompson, E.M. "Calligraphy in the Middle Ages." *Bibliographica*, 3 (1897), 280-92.

A discussion of the practice of using writing desks and their various types as reflected in illustrations provided by manuscript illuminations.

1390 Thomson, R.M. "The 'Scriptorium' of William of Malmesbury," item 720, pp. 117-42.

An account of Malmesbury manuscripts associated with William during the twelfth century, illustrated with facsimiles; cf. William of Malmesbury, item 1418.

1391 Vezin, Jean. *Les Scriptoria d'Angers au XIe siècle.* Bibliothèque de l'Ecole des Hautes Etudes, IVe Section, Sciences Historiques et Philologique, 332. Paris: H. Champion, 1974.

An account of *scriptoria* at Saint-Aubin and Saint-Serge, based upon a close study of 53 eleventh-century manuscripts. Their present location is in the Angers municipal library or at Rouen.

1392 ————. "Observations sur l'emploi des réclames dans les manuscrits latins." *Bibliothèque de l'Ecole des Chartes*, 125 (1967), 15-33.

Vezin discusses the system of catchwords, developed after the twelfth century.

1393 Wagner, Leonhard. *Probo Centum Scriptuarum (Diversarum). Ein Augsburger Schriftmusterbuch aus dem Beginn der 16. Jahrhunderts.* 2 vols. Leipzig: Insel, 1963.

A facsimile edition (vol. 1) of a late medieval scribal handbook from Augsburg, with a study (vol. 2).

1394 Williams, S.J. "An Author's Role in Fourteenth-Century Book Production." *Romania*, 90 (1969), 433-54.

A study of select authors, including Chaucer, and their scribes; bibliographical references.

1395 Windeatt, B.A. "The Scribes as Chaucer's Early Critics." *Studies in the Age of Chaucer*, 1 (1979), 119-41.

A discussion of the scribal responses to Chaucer's poetry as a means of determining the extent and nature of early Chaucerian criticism.

See also items 721, 723-4, 731, 734-5, 737, 741, 749, 753, 754-6.

C. PRIMARY SOURCES

1. SCRIPTS

1396   Amphiareo, Vespasiano. *Copy* Book. Venice: 1548.

       Examples of calligraphic alphabets, with representative extracts.

1397   Anonymous. *Alphabet for Anglicana Formata.*

       Written in the margin of Oxford, Bodleian Library, MS. Douce 84, f. 30v. ca. 1400.

1398   Anonymous. *Alphabet for Gothic Bookhand.*

       An alphabet, degenerating into pen-trials, written in the margin and lower leaf of London, British Library, MS. Harley 3725, f. 66v, first half of fifteenth-century.

1399   Anonymous. *Script Sampler.*

       Described with illustrations by Martin Steinmann, "Ein mittelalterliches Schriftmusterblatt," *Archiv für Diplomatik, Schriftgeschichte, Siegel- und Wappenkunde*, 21 (1975), 450-8.

1400   Arrighi, Ludovico. *Regola da imparare scrivere.* Venice: 1533.

       On the calligraphic alphabets represented in this model book, see Stanley Morison, *The Calligraphic Models of Ludovico degli Arrighi surnamed Vicentino* (Paris: 1926).

1401   Moro, Francesco. *Copy Book.*

       Extant in London, Victoria and Albert Museum, MS. 1485, f. 29. On these and other calligraphic alphabets of the sixteenth century, see B.L. Wolpe, *Renaissance Handwriting* (London: 1960), and A.S. Osley, *Luminario: An Introduction to the Italian Writing-Books of the 16th and 17th Centuries* (Niewwkoop: 1972).

1402   'Oxford Master, The.' *Advertisement Sheet.*

       A placard or poster, hung at or near the scribe's workshop, with several examples of mainly Gothic scripts. This early fourteenth-century placard is thought to be the earliest thus far discovered. It is described, with illustrations, by Stephen John Peter van Dijk in "An Advertisement Sheet of an Early Fourteenth-Century Writing Master at Oxford," *Scriptorium*, 10 (1956), 47-64.

1403   Strepel, Herman. *An Advertising Folio.*

       An advertising folio for Gothic bookhands, illustrating both *fracta* and *rotunda* and some musical notation. It is described with two facsimiles and transcriptions by B. Kruitwagen, item 1314, pp. 1-22.

See also item 296.

2. SCRIBAL PRACTICE AND FORMULAS

(a) Anonymous Treatises and Writings

1404 Benedictines of Bouveret. *Colophons des manuscrits occidentaux des origines au XVIe siècle.* Fribourg: University Press, 1970-.

A collection of colophons, published by region and collection.

1405 Lenham, Carol D. *Salutatio formulas in Latin Letters to 1200: Syntax, Style, Theory.* Münchener Beiträge zur Mediaevistik und Renaissance Forschung, 22. Munich: Arbeo, 1975.

1406 Meiss, Millard. "Alphabetical Treatises in the Renaissance," adapted from *Andrea Mantegna as Illuminator. An Episode in Renaissance Art, Humanism, and Diplomacy* (New York, N.Y.: Columbia University Press, 1957), Chapt. IV; reprinted in *The Painter's Choice: Problems in the Interpretation of Renaissance Art: Selected Essays of Millard Meiss* (New York, N.Y./Hagerstown: Harper and Row, 1976). See also items 1401-2.

1407 Quain, E.Z. "The Medieval *Accessus ad Autores.*" *Traditio*, 3 (1945), 215-64.

An edition and discussion of representative extracts; bibliographical references.

1408 Rockinger, Ludwig von. *Briefsteller and Formelbücher des vierzehnten Jahrhunderts.* 2 vols. Quellen und Erörterungen zur bayerischen und deutschen Geschichte, 9. Munich: G. Franz, 1863.

A collection of *formularia* and *ars dictaminis* from several chancelleries and other manuscript sources.

1409 Wieruszowski, Helene. "A Twelfth-Century '*Ars Dictaminis*' in the Barberini Collection of the Vatican Library." *Traditio*, 18 (1962), 382-63.

A careful description of MS. Barberini Lat. 47, with an edition of the 18 "model" letters; bibliographical references to other works on the *ars*, including the important contributions by G. de Luca.

(b) Ascribed Works

1410 Bury, Richard de. *Philobiblon*, ed. and trans. E.G. Thomas. Oxford: Basil Blackwell, 1959/New York, N.Y.: Barnes and Noble, 1970.

A "Humanist" treatise written ca. 1345 on all aspects of book production and ownership; the bibliographical notes refer to sources and other related matters.

1411   Chaucer, Geoffrey. "To Adam Scryven," in *The Works of Geoffrey
        Chaucer*, ed. F.N. Robinson. 2nd ed. Cambridge, Mass.: Harvard
        University Press, 1957; p. 534.

        Chaucer refers to his scribe's "negligence and rape" and for
        the resulting need to "correcte and eek to rubbe and scrape";
        on Petrarch's similar concern, see item 1415.

1412   Durand, William. *Speculum Iudiciale*, ed. Peter Herde, in "Der
        Zeugen zwang in den Päpstlichen Delegationereskripten des
        Mittelalters." *Traditio*, 18 (1962), 282-4, with an anonymous
        formulary, 284-8.

        A treatise, ca. 1300, on *clausula* in use by the Roman curia.

1413   John of Tilbury. *Ars Notaria*, ed. Valentine Rose, in "*Ars
        notaria*: Tironischen Noten and Stenographie in 12. Jahr-
        hundert." *Hermes*, 8 (1874), 303-26.

        An edition of and commentary on John of Tilbury's treatise,
        ca. 1174, which describes the shorthand method for taking down
        dictated material, or *velocitatem scribendi docere*, and of
        substituting *figurae* for words or phrases, e.g., *C* for *centum*
        or *M* for *mille*.

1414   Langland, William. *Piers Plowman: The B. Version*, ed. G. Kane
        and E.T. Donaldson. London: University of London, Athlone
        Press, 1977; X, 337; and *Piers Plowman by William Langland,
        an Edition of the C. Text*, ed. Derek Pearsall. York Medieval
        Texts. 2nd Series. London: Edward Arnold, 1978; XI, 97.

        Both refer to the possibility that scribes may lie or copy
        texts inaccurately.

1415   Petrarca, Francesco. *De Librorum Copia*, in *Petrarch: Four
        Dialogues for Scholars*, ed. and trans. C.H. Rauski. Ashtabula,
        Ohio: Case Western Reserve University Press, 1967; pp. 34-37.

        Cf. Chaucer, item 1411.

1416   Samaritanus, Adalbertus. *Praecepta Dictaminum*, ed. F.J. Schmale.
        Quellen zur Geistgeschichte des Mittelalters, 3. Weimar:
        Harrasowitz, 1961.

1417   Trithemius, Johannes. *In Praise of Scribes (De Laude Scriptorum)*,
        ed. Klaus Arnold, trans. Roland Behrendt, O.S.B. Lawrence,
        Kansas: Coronado Press, 1974.

        A treatise by Johannes Trithemius of Sponheim, 1492, on the
        methods of scribes, the appropriateness of this occupation for
        monks, texts they should use (mainly biblical), training, books
        which libraries should contain, etc. The author mentions that
        scribes should not stop copying because of the invention of
        printing.

1418   William of Malmesbury. *Gesta regum*, ed. W. Stubbs. Rolls Series,
        1. London: 1887; *Gesta Pontificorum*, ed. N.E.S.A. Hamilton,
        R.S., 1870.

An account of William's reading, collecting, and writing, with reference to an autography copy in MS. Magdalen College Lat. 172; see R.M. Thompson, item 720, pp. 117–42, which includes bibliographical notes.

See also items 759, 937, 1225–36.

D. MATERIALS AND BINDING

1. PARCHMENT, PAPER, AND OTHER MATERIALS

1419   Bayley, H. *A New Light on the Renaissance*. London: J.M. Dent, 1909/1967.

An illustrated discussion of the development of emblems and watermarks on paper during the Renaissance. A bibliography is provided.

1420   Blanchet, Heou-Han-Chou. "Le Papier et sa fabrication à travers les âges." *La Bibliofilia*, 12 (1911), 45–66.

An account of the early production of paper, with special reference to China and the contributions of Ts'Ai Lun in the early third century.

1421   Churchill, W.A. *Watermarks in Paper in Holland, England, France, etc., in the XVII and XVIII Centuries and Their Interconnection*. Amsterdam: M. Hertzberger, 1935/1965.

The author traces the later development and descent of some medieval watermarks. A good bibliography is provided.

1422   Gerardy, Theodor. "Der Identitätsbeweis bei der Wasserzeichendatierung." *Archiv für Geschichte des Buchwesens*, 9 (1969), 733–78.

Some criteria are described for dating late medieval and early Renaissance watermarks, with reference to their principal emblems and locations.

1423   Glaister, Geoffrey Ashall. *Glossary of the Book: Terms Used in Papermaking, Printing, Bookbinding, and Publishing, with Notes on Illuminated Manuscripts, Bibliophiles, Private Presses, and Printing Societies*. London: Allen and Unwin, 1960.

A comprehensive reference work on all aspects of book production, although the focus is upon printed books of the post-Renaissance. It contains many illustrations. Republished as *An Encyclopedia of the Book* (Cleveland, Ohio: World, 1960).

1424   Harlfinger, D., and Harlfinger, J. *Wasserzeichen aus griechischen
        Handschriften*. Berlin: Mielke, 1974-.

        A series of illustrated fascicles, which give an account of
        the materials, with focus upon paper and watermarks, of Byzan-
        tine manuscripts. Some discussion is devoted to production and
        binding. Bibliographical references and indexes are provided.

1425   Heawood, E. "Sources of Early English Paper Supply." *The Library*,
        4th ser., 10 (1929), 282-307.

        Paper used in Britain before 1500 is classified by watermark,
        alphabetically, with reference to the corresponding number in
        Briquet. The watermarks are reproduced in figures, and conclu-
        sions are made about their distribution.

1426   Hunter, Dard. *Papermaking. History and Technique of an Ancient
        Craft*. 2nd ed. (from 1943). New York, N.Y.: A.A. Knopf, 1947.

        A general history of paper manufacture, watermarks, and
        distribution. A bibliography is provided.

1427   Karabacek, J. "Das arabische Papier. Eine historischantiquarische
        Untersuchung." *Mitteilungen aus der Sammlung der Papyrus
        Erherzog Rainer*, 2/3 (Vienna: 1887), 87-178; "Neue Quellen
        zur Papiergeschichte," 4 (1888), 75-122.

        A detailed study of paper produced from the ninth century in
        Syria, Charta Bambycina, with reference to paper manuscripts
        in the Erherzog Rainer collection.

1428   Labarre, E.J. *Dictionary and Encyclopaedia of Paper and Paper
        Making, with Equivalents of the Technical Terms in French,
        German, Dutch, Italian, Spanish, and Swedish*. 2nd ed. (from
        1937). Amsterdam: Swets and Zeitlinger/London: Oxford Uni-
        versity Press, 1952. *Supplement*, by E.G. Loeber, 1967.

        More than a dictionary of terms, this work also provides
        descriptive articles for many aspects of papermaking and its
        history. Indexes in languages listed in title.

1429   Leif, I.P. *An International Sourcebook of Paper History*. Hamden,
        Conn.: Archon/Folkestone: W. Dawson and Sons, 1978.

        A bibliography of paper history and watermark studies. A
        general section is followed by three continental sections, and
        these are subdivided by country with authors arranged alpha-
        betically. The final section covers the study and bibliography
        of paper history. Its many omissions, including Briquet's *Les
        Filigranes*, have prompted a most negative review by J.S.G.
        Simmons in *The Library*, 6th ser., 1 (1979), 173-4.

1430   *Monumenta Chartae Papyraceae Historiani Illustrantia*, Emile
        Joseph Labarre, gen. ed. Hilversum: Paper Publications So-
        ciety, 1950-.

        A series of monographs on all aspects of the history of paper,
        e.g., watermarks, paper mills, and distribution. Good indexes
        are provided.

1431   Reed, R. *Ancient Skins, Parchments and Leathers*. London/New
        York, N.Y.: Seminar Press, 1972.

        A scientific analysis of the physical properties of animal
        skins, illustrated with microscopic photographs. The chapter
        on the nature and manufacture of parchment, pp. 118-73, is of
        special interest for paleographers. See also item 1500.

1432   Renker, Armin. *Das Buch vom Papier*. 4th ed. (from 1929). Wies-
        baden: Insel-Verlag, 1951.

        A general introduction to the production of paper books, in-
        cluding the development of watermarks. A bibliography is pro-
        vided.

1433   Säxl, Hedwig. "Histology of Parchment," in *Technical Studies
        in the Field of Fine Arts*. Boston, Mass.: William Hayes Fogg
        Art Museum, 1939.

        The author discusses the difficulties in distinguishing
        identities of particular types of skins due to the practice
        of heavy scraping of membrane, especially during the thirteenth
        century, from which only the reticular layer of parchment may
        remain. Identity of material is therefore more accurate when
        based upon type, size, and method of preparation of the book
        itself. A bibliography is provided.

1434   *Short Guide to Books on Watermarks, A*. Paper Publications
        Series. Hilversum: The Society, 1955.

        A brief (16pp.) descriptive bibliography of watermarks.

1435   Thompson, Daniel V. "Medieval Parchment-Making." *The Library*,
        4th ser., 16 (1936), 113-7.

        Discussion and extracts from a thirteenth-century German
        treatise on parchment, extant in British Library MS. Harley
        3915, f. 148. Some references are made to related treatises,
        including those mentioned in items 1226 and 1235.

1436   Vezin, Jean. "La réalisation materielle des manuscrits latins
        pendant le haut moyen âge." *Codicologica*, 2 (1978), 15-51.

        A detailed and illustrated account of book production and
        materials, including writing desks, papyrus, parchment, the
        codex, pricking, binding, etc. Bibliographical references are
        provided.

1437   Weiss, Karl Theodor. *Handbuch der Wasserzeichenkunde*, ed.
        Wisso Weiss. Leipzig: VEB, 1962.

        A survey of the technique and major watermarks, with 66
        illustrations. A bibliography is provided.

2. BINDING

(a) Bibliographical Materials

1438   Hobson, Robert Alwyn. *The Literature of Bookbinding.* London:
        Cambridge University Press, 1954.

        A brief (15pp.) bibliographical introduction to bookbinding
        for all periods.

1439   Kyriss, Ernest. *Studies in the History of Bookbinding: A Bibli-
        ography of Books and Articles.* University of Kentucky Li-
        braries, Occasional Contributions, 72. Lexington, Ky.: 1955.

        A pamphlet (5pp.) of the major works and articles.

1440   Loubier, Hans, and Klette, Erhard, eds. *Jahrbuch der Einband-
        kunst.* 4 vols. Leipzig: Verlag für Einbandkunst, 1927-37.

        A comprehensive bibliographical survey of book binding of all
        periods. Indexed.

(b) General and Specific Studies

1441   Adam, Paul. *Der Bucheinband. Seine Technik und seine Geschichte.*
        Leipzig: Seemann, 1890.

        While this historical survey is out of date, it nevertheless
        provides a comprehensive bibliography for nineteenth-century
        items.

1442   Biddle, M., ed. *Winchester in the Early Middle Ages: An Edi-
        tion and Discussion of the Winton Doomsday.* Oxford: Clarendon
        Press, 1976.

        This work contains a careful description of a twelfth-century
        liturgical fragment used as a later binding, pp. 541ff., a
        representative case for many other bindings adapted from
        earlier folios.

1443   Bollert, Martin. *Lederschnittbände des XIV Jahrhundert.* Leipzig:
        Hiersemann, 1925.

        A brief account of fourteenth-century German leather bindings.
        A good bibliography is provided.

1444   Brassington, W. Salt. *Historic Bindings in the Bodleian Library
        Oxford.* London: Sampson Low and Co., 1891.

        A descriptive account of representative early bindings in
        the Bodleian Library, including some medieval and Renaissance
        examples.

1445   ———, ed. *A History of the Art of Bookbinding, with Some
        Account of the Books of the Ancients.* London: Eliot Stock,
        1894.

A general history of early bookbinding, illustrated with over 112 photographs of various types of examples. A bibliography is provided.

1446 Devaucheville, Roger. *La Reliure en France de ses origines à nos jours.* 3 vols. Paris: Rousseau-Girard, 1959-61.

Vol. 1 of this work surveys French binding from its early medieval origins to the seventeenth century. The author includes a bibliography.

1447 Gibson, S. *Early Oxford Bindings.* Bibliographical Society. Oxford: Oxford University Press, 1903.

A general survey, mainly of Bodleian Library bindings, illustrated by 40 plates. See also item 1454.

1448 Gottlieb, Theodor. *Englische Einbände des XII Jahrhunderts in franzosischen Stil.* Vienna: Krystall, 1926.

A brief descriptive account of several French-influenced English bindings, illustrated with two plates and supported with bibliographical references.

1449 Helwig, Hellmuth. *Das deutsche Buchbinder Handwerk. Handwerks- und Kulturgeschichte.* 2 vols. Stuttgart: Hiersemann, 1962-65.

A detailed history of German bookbinding, from the social position of the binder in the fifteenth century to individual binderies. A name/place/subject index is provided.

1450 ———. *Einführung in die Einbandkunde.* Stuttgart: Hiersemann, 1970.

A comprehensive introduction to all aspects of bookbinding, including its history, materials, and techniques. Illustrated and with a bibliography.

1451 Hobson, G.D. *Bindings in Cambridge Libraries.* Cambridge: University Press, 1929.

A collection of folio plates, each accompanied by a detailed description and full bibliography, of bindings from the twelfth century to the eighteenth. Some have detailed illustrations of individual stamps. Hobson also provides lists of similar bindings with present location and other references.

1452 ———. *Blind-Stamped Panels in the English Booktrade.* The Bibliographical Society, Supplement to the Bibliographical Society Transactions, 17. London: The Society, 1944.

An illustrated history of blind-stamping, from the fifteenth to the seventeenth centuries. See also preceding item, and items 1460-1.

1453 ———. *English Binding Before 1500.* Cambridge: University Press, 1925.

An historical account of all types of medieval bindings in England. Illustrated with 85 plates and provided with a good bibliography.

1454   Ker, N.R. *Fragments of Medieval Manuscripts Used in Pastedowns
        in Oxford Bindings, with a Survey of Oxford Binding, c. 1515-
        1620.* Oxford Bibliographical Society, n.s., 5. Oxford: A.T.
        Broome for the Society, 1954.

        From over 2,000 fragments in bindings, datable and attributable
        to particular workshops on the basis of stamped decoration and
        other features, Ker is able to make general observations about
        the history of Oxford bindings and the fates of some medieval
        manuscripts in the Renaissance. After a general introduction,
        Ker lists the manuscript fragments by stamps, i.e., the numer-
        ation of stamped bindings in Gibson, item 1447 above. Extensive
        indexes are based upon manuscripts, rolls, present owners,
        binders and booksellers, and guard books. Plates of rubbings,
        14 in all, are provided as illustration.

1455   Kyriss, Ernst. "An Esslingen Binder of the Late Gothic Period."
        Speculum, 25 (1950), 73-77.

        Kyriss traces 61 extant bindings to an Esslingen workshop,
        and gives a descriptive analysis with plates of their main
        features. Bibliographical references relate these to other
        German bindings.

1456   Loubier, Hans. *Der Bucheinband von seiner Anfängen bis zum
        Ende des 18. Jahrhunderts.* 2nd ed. Monographien des Kunst-
        gewerbes, 21/22. Leipzig: Klinckhardt und Biermann, 1926.

        This work offers a general history of bindings, mainly German,
        and is illustrated with 232 plates. The bibliography is useful
        for pre-1920 items.

1457   Marinis, Tammaro de. *Le legatura artistica in Italia nei secoli
        XV e XVI. Notizie ed elenchi.* Florence: Alinari, 1960-.

        A series of monographs on early regional bindings, e.g., vol.
        1: Naples, Rome, Urbino, and Florence.

1458   Mazal, Otto. *Europaische Einbandkunst am Mittelalter und
        Neuzeit.* Graz: Akademiedruck- und Verlag, 1970.

        A description with bibliographical references of 270 bindings
        from the Austrian National Library. Illustrations are included.

1459   Nixon, Howard, ed. *Five Centuries of English Bookbinding.*
        London: Scolar Press, 1978.

        A series of articles on various aspects of bookbinding from
        the fifteenth to the twentieth centuries. Of special interest
        for medieval specialists is the discussion of later bindings
        by such collectors as Archbishop Laud. A bibliography is pro-
        vided.

1460   Oldham, Basil. *Blind Panels of English Binders.* Cambridge:
        University Press, 1958.

1461   ————. *English Blind Stamped Bindings.* Cambridge: University
        Press, 1952.

These two works are intended as companion volumes for a
detailed study of English bindings of the sixteenth and seventeenth centuries. Studied are the techniques of manufacture,
sale, and circulation. A bibliography and index are provided.
See also item 1452.

1462   Oxford, Bodleian Library. *Gold-tooled Bookbindings*, introd. Jan
        Gilbert Philip. Bodleian Picture Books, 2. Oxford: The Library,
        1951.

        A popular book, but well-illustrated with photographs of
        representative examples from the Bodleian collection.

1463   Pollard, G. "Changes in the Style of Bookbinding, 1550-1830."
        The Library, 5th ser., 11 (1956), 71-94.

        In this short article Pollard demonstrates how the introduc-
        tion of bookshelves influenced binding materials, resulting
        in more decorative and less bulky bindings.

1464   ————. "The Construction of English Twelfth-Century Bindings."
        The Library, 5th ser., 17 (1962), 1-22.

        A detailed description of a style of binding found in a large
        number of English and some continental bindings of the twelfth
        century. These are characterized by a flat, prolonged spine
        with tabs at each end. Illustrated with photographs and dia-
        grams.

1465   ————. "Describing Medieval Bookbinding," in *Medieval Learn-
        ing and Literature*, item 719, pp. 50-65.

        The author establishes useful criteria for the description
        of medieval bindings, e.g., types of leather, methods of sewing,
        the use of boards, etc.

1466   ————. "The Names of Some English Fifteenth-Century Binders."
        The Library, 5th ser., 25 (1970), 193-218.

        Pollard attempts to present a coordinated picture of early
        English stamped binding, classifed by design, e.g., "all-over,"
        "central block," etc. Illustrated with plates. An appendix
        gives a table of designs for convenient reference.

1467   ————. "Some Anglo-Saxon Bookbindings." *The Book Collector*,
        24 (1975), 130-59.

        A detailed description of 21 Anglo-Saxon bindings, with dia-
        grams to illustrate how the boards were sewn. The manuscripts
        include the Victor Codex, Hatton MSS. 42 and 48, Bodleian
        Library MSS. 311 and 319, British Library MS. Additional 37517,
        and others. The study reveals that some books used by Saints
        Boniface, Dunstan, and Wulfstan still retain their original
        wooden boards and that, moreover, it is possible to recognize
        four books from binderies at Christ Church Canterbury of ca.
        A.D. 1000. Pollard has employed in his research an innovative
        method of X-Ray examination.

1468   Regemorter, B. van. "Evolution de la technique de la reliure
        du VIIIe au XIIe siècle." *Scriptorium*, 2 (1948), 275-85.

        A description of early bindings preserved in the libraries
        of Autun, Auxerre, and Troyes, illustrated with figures demon-
        strating techniques. Some comparisons are made with early Cop-
        tic bindings. See also next item.

1469   ————. "La Reliure des manuscrits de S. Cuthbert et de S.
        Boniface." *Scriptorium*, 3 (1949), 45-51.

        Some characteristics are described of ninth- and tenth-century
        Coptic manuscripts in the British Library and comparisons made
        with the Evangelary of St. Cuthbert at Stonyhurst College,
        Lancs., and three St. Boniface manuscripts from the Cathedral
        Library, Fulda.

1470   Schunke, Ilse. *Die Einbände der Palatina in der Vatikanischen
        Bibliothek*. 2 vols. in 3 parts. Studi e Testi, 216-8. Rome:
        Vatican, 1962.

        A detailed study of types of bindings, e.g., those from the
        Amberg and Fugger libraries. An extensive register lists bind-
        ings by classification. Illustrated with plates and some bibli-
        ographical references.

1471   Steenbock, Frauke. *Der kirchliche Prachteinband im frühen
        Mittelalter, von den Anfängen bis zum Beginn der Gotik.*
        Berlin: Deutscher Verlag für Kunstwissenschaft, 1965.

        A catalogue of ecclesiastical and liturgical bindings, ca.
        400-1350, with full descriptions and assessments of regional
        origins and characteristics. A bibliography is provided.

1472   Thomas, Henry. *Early Spanish Bookbindings, XI-XV Centuries.*
        London: Bibliographical Society, 1939.

        A series of 100 plates with descriptive comment and bibliog-
        raphy, preceded by a general introduction. Indexes are provided
        for authors/works and chronology. A select bibliography only.

1473   Weale, William Henry James. *Early Stamped Bookbindings in the
        British Museum*, comp. Lawrence Taylor. London: Trustees of
        the British Library, 1972.

        An illustrated survey of representative bindings; cf. also
        Weale's publications on the bindings of the Victoria and Albert
        Museum (London: Holland Publishing Co., 1962), which are mainly
        post-Renaissance.

                    E. PUBLICATION AND CIRCULATION

1474   Adamson, J.W. "The Extent of Literacy in England in the Fifteenth
        and Sixteenth Centuries." *The Library*, 4th ser., 10 (1929-30),
        163-93.

With reference to the Paston letters, Plumpton letters, Stoner papers, and other documents, the author proposes that literacy among the lower classes during this period was higher than historians have supposed.

1475 Bell, H.E. "The Price of Books in Medieval England." *The Library*, n.s., 17 (1936-37), 312-32.

Focusing upon the fourteenth and fifteenth centuries, for which more documentation is available, Bell cites specific examples of book purchases within the context of professional scribes, university stationers, and other outlets. He considers writing prices for various genres, e.g., £4 paid for a Missal in 1384, illuminating prices, and prices for materials and binding. His main conclusion is that for this period manuscript books were "essentially a luxury commodity."

1476 Davis, N. "A Scribal Problem in the Paston Letters." *English and Germanic Studies*, 4 (1951-52), 31-64.

Davis studies a group of 20 letters from Margaret Paston, 1440-78, which, although by different scribes, have certain stylistic features in common, most notably the small, compact writing and the letters *w*, *h*, *M*, and *P*. Davis suggests that these indicate publication limited to certain areas and certain traditions in transmission.

1477 Deanesly, Margaret. "Vernacular Books in England in the Fourteenth and Fifteenth Centuries." *Modern Language Review*, 15 (1920), 349-58.

This article considers the general "booklessness" of individuals from examples provided in 7,568 wills. Of these only 338 individuals bequeathed books, and these are examined by the author in terms of genre. Among the most popular are works by Richard Rolle and Nicholas Love.

1478 Delalain, P. *Etude sur le librairie parisien du XIIIe au XVe siècle*. Paris: Delalain Frères, 1891.

An account of the different methods of book distribution by the *librarius* and *stationarius*. The former sold through commissions, but these had to be approved by University authorities. The *stationarius* was less restricted. A good bibliography is included.

1479 Hunt, R.W. "Manuscripts Containing the Indexing Symbols of Robert Grosseteste." *Bodleian Library Record*, 4 (1953), 241-55.

In this article Hunt lists the manuscripts and describes the symbols briefly. For fuller explanation of these "subject" symbols see Robert Grosseteste's *Works*, ed. C.A. Callus (Oxford: Clarendon Press, 1955), pp. 121-45.

1480 Kenyon, Sir Frederick. *Books and Readers in Ancient Greece and Rome*. 2nd ed. (from 1932). Oxford: Clarendon Press, 1951.

Originally three lectures, delivered at King's College, London, March, 1932, on the use of books in Classical times. They include a discussion of the papyrus roll and the development of the codex.

1481   Kirchoff, H. *Die Handschriftenhandler des Mittelalters.* 2nd ed. (from 1853). Ösnabrück: Zeller, 1880/1966.

An account of the distribution and sale of manuscripts among European countries and England. Although somewhat general, there are some useful earlier bibliographical references.

1482   Lehmann, P. "Konstanz und Basel als Büchermärkte während der grossen Kirchenversammlungen," in *Erforschung des Mittelalters, ausgewählte Abhandlungen und Aufsätze,* I. Leipzig: Hiersemann, 1941; pp. 253–80.

A fully descriptive list of the fifteenth-century manuscripts known to have been sold in Constance or Basel, arranged by place of origin and grouped according to present collection and location. Other essays in this volume also relate to library history and book production or circulation.

1483   Loomis, Laura Hibbard. "The Auchinleck Manuscript and a Possible London Bookshop of 1330–1340." *PMLA,* 57 (1942), 595–627.

Loomis proposes that the Auchinleck manuscript of the first half of the fourteenth century was produced by scribes, five in all, working at a secular London bookshop rather than a *scriptorium.* Their purpose was to produce a popular collection for the "new English reading public."

1484   Mumby, F.A. *Publishing and Bookselling from the Earliest Times to the Present.* Rev. ed. (from 1910). London: Cape, 1954.

Originally entitled *The Romance of Book Selling,* this work surveys the history of bookselling from Classical Antiquity to modern times. The focus is upon Great Britain. A bibliography was added to the revised edition by W.H. Peet.

1484.1 Pollard, G. "Notes on the Size of the Sheet." *The Library,* 4th ser., 22 (1941), 105–37.

The author describes the two main medieval methods of writing, either from a pile of double leaves or undivided skins of parchment; either method determined the order in which the sheets were written; the latter became the method for the printed book. Pollard describes national differences in techniques and sizes, and establishes relationships between sizes of the sheet and genre, e.g., Bibles and eventually newspapers.

1485   Root, R.K. "Publication before Printing." *PMLA,* 28 (1913), 417–31.

A description of general publishing conditions during the fourteenth and fifteenth centuries, based upon evidence from Latin letters by Petrarch and Boccaccio.

1486   Scattergood, V.J. "Two Medieval Book Lists." *The Library,* 5th ser., 23 (1969), 236–9.

Lists of books from inventorial rolls in the PRO of ca. 1358 and 1388. The books belonged to William de Walcote and Sir Simon Burley. Walcote's appear to have been mostly in Latin and of an ecclesiastical nature, while Burley's reflect a courtier's taste for mainly French romances and chronicles.

1487 Schubart, W. *Das Buch bei den Griechen und Romern*. 2nd ed. (from 1907). Berlin: De Gruyter, 1921/1963.

An important work on early manuscript production. In his discussion of the form of the early codex, Schubart proposes that no significance is to be found in the absolute dimensions of breadth and height, but rather in their proportional relationship. See Turner's continued discussion of this point, item 1488.1.

1488 *Studies in the Book Trade in Honour of Graham Pollard*. Oxford: Oxford Bibliographical Society, 1975.

A collection of essays by different hands; of special interest in relation to medieval manuscripts and early books are Nicolas Barker, "Quiring and the Binder: Quire Marks in Some Manuscripts in Fifteenth-century Blind Stamp Bindings," pp. 11-32; Anthony Hobson, "The *Iter Italicum* of Jean Matal," pp. 33-62; Richard Hunt, "Donors of Manuscripts to St. John's College, Oxford, During the Presidency of William Laud, 1611-1621," pp. 63-70; Paul Morgan, "Letters Relating to the Oxford Book Trade Found in Bindings in Oxford College Libraries, c. 1611-1647," pp. 71-90; and D.G. Varsey, "Anthony Stephens: The Rise and Fall of an Oxford Bookseller," pp. 91-118. Throughout valuable bibliography is provided on a large number of related subjects.

1488.1 Turner, E. *Typology of the Early Codex*. Haney Foundation Series, 18. Philadelphia, Pa.: Philadelphia University Press, 1977.

A study of how early codices were made from the various types of gatherings, and the relationship between gathering techniques and type of material, whether papyrus or parchment. Includes a bibliography and index. For a more detailed study of the papyrus codex, with illustrations, see the author's "Towards a Typology of the Early Codex, Third to Sixth Centuries after Christ," *Codicologica*, 2 (1978), 9-14.

1489 Widmann, Hans. *Geschichte des Buchhandels vom Altertum bis zur Gegenwart*. Wiesbaden: Harrassowitz, 1952.

Based initially upon Ernst Kuhnerts's *Handbuch der Bibliothekswissenschaft*, 1931, this work presents a general history of the book trade from Classical Antiquity to modern times. Bibliographies are provided for each historical section; indexed.

1490 Wilson, N.G. "Books and Readers in Byzantium," in *Byzantine Books and Bookmen. A Dumbarton Oaks Colloquium*. Dumbarton Oaks Center for Byzantine Studies, Washington, D.C.: 1975; pp. 1-15.

One of five papers published from this colloquium (1971) on
Greek and Byzantine codicology.

F. MODERN PRESERVATION

1491   Almela Melia, Juan. *Manual de reparación y conservación de
        libros, estampas y manuscritos.* Mexico: Instituto Panamericano
        de Geografia e Historia, 1949.

        While primarily concerned with the preservation of modern
        archival material, this manual contains some references to
        methodology and technology applicable to earlier documents.

1492   Barrow, William J. *Manuscripts and Documents, Their Deteriora-
        tion and Restoration.* 2nd ed. (from 1955). Charlottesville,
        Va.: University Press of Virginia. 1972.

        With reference to documents composed of papers and inks 1400-
        1850, Barrow discusses storage conditions, de-acidification,
        and lamination. He stresses the need for collaboration with the
        scientist in all such procedures. A bibliography is included.

1493   ———. *Procedures and Equipment Used in the Barrow Method
        of Restoring Manuscripts and Documents.* Richmond, Va.:
        Virginia State Library, 1952.

        An account of research into the preservation of paper, the
        use of the roller-type laminating machine (developed by Barrow
        in 1938), and the treatment of book papers through de-acidifi-
        cation.

1494   Bordin, Ruth B., and Warner, Robert M. *The Modern Manuscript
        Library.* New York, N.Y.: Scarecrow Press, 1966.

        On the principles of collection for university and general
        libraries, methods of collecting, cataloguing, administration,
        and preservation. The author provides sample descriptive in-
        ventories, contracts, and other documents. Bibliographies are
        provided for each section.

1495   *Etudes concernant la restauration d'archives, de livres et de
        manuscrits.* Archives et Bibliothèques de Belgique, Numéro
        Spécial, 12. Brussels, Bibliothèque Royale, 1974.

        A collection of 21 papers on the technical aspects of preser-
        vation and restoration, with illustrations and bibliography.
        These are in French, Dutch, German, and English.

1496   Flieder, Françoise. *La Conservation des documents graphiques:
        Recherches experimentales,* pref. by Roger Heim. Paris: Eyrolles,
        1969.

An introduction to the conservation and restoration of books and manuscripts, and the preservation of paper documents. Illustrations, bibliography, and index are provided.

1497   Johnson, Charles. *The Care of Documents and Management of Archives*. Society for Promoting Christian Knowledge. London: The Society, 1919.

A general, introductory guide, with select bibliography.

1498   Jones, Melvyn. "Seal Repair, Moulds and Casts." *The Paper Conservator*, 1 (1976), 12-18.

A technical article on the various stages required in repairing early wax seals. Illustrated by photographs of representative seals and drawings of the techniques involved.

1499   Kathpalia, Yash Pal. *Conservation and Restoration of Archive Materials*. Documentation, Libraries and Archives, Studies and Research, 3. Paris: UNESCO, 1973.

A survey, from a chemist's point of view, of the methods, techniques, and materials employed in the conservation and restoration of archival materials. The author discusses causes of deterioration, de-acidification, restoration, and preservation, including the preservation of microfilms. Appendices include physical and chemical texts on the subject, as well as the names of international suppliers.

1500   Plenderleith, Harold James. *The Preservation of Leather Book Bindings*. London: Trustees of the British Library, 1946/1957.

A brief discussion of the causes and prevention of leather decay and some techniques for cleaning old bindings. A final paragraph discusses the care of early medieval vellum bindings. A select bibliography is provided. See also item 1431.

1501   Pollard, G. "On the Repair of Medieval Bindings." *The Paper Conservator*, 1 (1976), 35-36.

In a discussion of the repair and restoration of early bindings, the author observes that, of the bindings done in England before 1225, fewer than 500 survive.

1502   United States National Archives. *Staff Information Papers*. Washington, D.C., 1950-.

A series of papers on the practical aspects of preservation and display. Good current bibliographies are included.

1503   Vatican Library. *Conservation et reproduction des Manuscrits et imprimés anciens: Colloque international organisé par la Bibliothèque Vaticane, 21-24 octobre 1975*. Studi e Testi. Rome: Vatican: 1976.

The conference papers, on all aspects of preservation and microform reproduction. Select documentation is provided.

1504   Wächter, Otto. *Restaurierung und Erhaltung von Büchern, Ar-*
        chivalien und Graphiken: mit Berücksichtigung des Kulturgüter-
        schutzes laut Haager Kovention von 1954. Vienna: Böhlaus,
        1977.

        A comprehensive and detailed study of all aspects of restora-
        tion and preservation of manuscripts and books. Part A discusses
        types of materials--parchment, paper, leather, etc.--and part
        B types of damage, e.g., light or moisture; part C presents
        methods for restoration. Many illustrations are provided and
        there is a glossary of technical terms in German, French,
        English, and Italian.

XII. REFERENCE WORKS

The reference works selected for citation in this
section provide technical aids to the reading and
transcription of manuscripts which have been located,
identified, and related if only in a preliminary way
to other extant manuscripts bearing a textual or other
relationship. These works fall into three groups:
dictionaries for abbreviations and other technical
data; dictionaries for language; and dictionaries or
encyclopedias for other matter.

The use of abbreviations, or tachygraphy, is of some
significance for paleographers, because although it
may create difficulties in the reading of a text, it
may nevertheless provide clues to the date and provenance of a particular script. Also within this section
are cited works which might facilitate the establishment of date and provenance through chronological,
biographical, or topographical references, for these,
too, possess geographical and chronological features.
Thus, for example, the spelling of a French place-name
in a manuscript datable to the late thirteenth century
might indicate that the scribe was Anglo-Norman and
that he was, moreover, copying from an earlier exemplar
(see item 1568).

The dictionaries and specialized glossaries represent
a highly select body of reference material. Many of the
specialized bibliographies in Section I already list
the most relevant linguistic aids to individual disciplines, or else cite further bibliographies which do so.

Finally, the varied encyclopedias which conclude this
section are intended rather as a selective guide to further, more specialized works than as an exhaustive bibliography. Among these Briquet's illustrated manual on watermarks (item 1615) should perhaps be singled out as one
of the most valuable aids in establishing the date and
provenance of paper manuscripts.

CONTENTS

A. BIBLIOGRAPHICAL MATERIALS

1505   *Guide to Reference Books*, comp. Eugene P. Sheehy. 9th ed.
        Chicago: American Library Association, 1976.

        A guide to reference works in all areas of inquiry, periodi-
        cally brought up to date. The references are well-organized
        and fully annotated, often in considerable detail. An author/
        title/subject index provides a means of ready reference, other-
        wise the arrangement by language, history, then country and
        chronology tends toward some complexity. Under "Ancient,
        Medieval, and Renaissance Manuscripts." AA177-194, are listed
        bibliographies, catalogues for libraries, and studies, although
        these titles are highly selective.

1506   *Reference Sources: 1978*, ed. Linda Mark. Ann Arbor, Mich.:
        Pierian Press, 1978.

        An annual bibliography of reference works, succeeding *Refer-
        ence Book Review Index, 1970-72-*. The descriptive entries are
        arranged alphabetically, with a subject index.

See also individual Besterman bibliographies, item 9, under specific
    subjects.

B. ABBREVIATIONS OR TACHYGRAPHY

1507   Allen, T.W. *Abbreviations in Greek Manuscripts*. Oxford: Claren-
        don Press, 1889/Amsterdam: Hakkert, 1967.

        This work is difficult to use because Allen reproduces the
        abbreviations along with the entire facsimile page. They are
        indicated by brackets and arranged more or less in alphabetical
        order.

1508   Blanchard, Alain. *Sigles et abbréviations dans les papyrus
        documentaires grecs: Recherches de paléographie*. Institute
        of Classical Studies. London: The Institute, 1974.

        A short guide to Greek abbreviations in papyrus diplomatic
        texts. He discusses two systems of abbreviations and historical
        signs.

1509   Cappelli, A. *Dizionario di abbreviature latine ed italine.*
        6th ed. from the 3rd ed. of 1929. Milan: Hoepli, 1961; *Ab-
        breviationes Latines Medievales*, by Auguste Pelzer. Louvain:
        Publications Universitaires, 1964.

        Cappelli's convenient dictionary of abbreviations for Latin
        and Italian manuscripts, along with Pelzer's supplement, still
        remains the standard work on tachygraphy. It has undergone
        numerous editions and revisions since the original of 1899,
        with a German translation published in 1901. Its alphabetically
        arranged scribal abbreviations and *notae* are reproduced in
        facsimile from a variety of manuscripts, including many ponti-
        fical archives, to the fifteenth century.

1510   Chassant, Alphonse Antoine Louis. *Dictionnaire des abréviationes
        latines et françaises usitées dans les inscriptions lapidaires
        et metalliques, les manuscrits et les chartes du moyen âge.*
        5th ed. (from 1846). Paris: J. Martin, 1884.

        This dictionary is divided into two parts according to whether
        the abbreviations are Latin or French; the abbreviations are
        given in facsimile and include epigraphical inscriptions (pre-
        seventh century) and those from later Latin and French manuscripts.

1511   Christopher, Henry G.T. *Palaeography and Archives. A Manual
        for the Librarian, Archivist and Student*, with an introduc-
        tion by J.D. Stewart. London: Grafton, 1938.

        A guide to the major reference works for paleography and
        archivicology. Included is a table of Latin abbreviations with
        reference to mainly British manuscripts.

1512   Kopp, Ulrich Friedrich. *Lexicon Tironianum. Nachdruck aus
        Kopps 'Palaeographia Critica' von 1817 mit Nachwort und
        einem Alphabetum Tironianum*, ed. Bernard Bischoff. Osnabrück:
        Otto Zeller, 1965.

        Part 1 of this reissue of Kopp's early handbook is based upon
        a format similar to Cappelli's although more expanded; part 2
        provides a *Lexici Tironiani*, with Latin word and *nota* reference.
        As a dictionary of abbreviations it is more awkward to use
        than Cappelli's, but it provides more complete references
        and examples.

1513   Laurent, Marie-Hyacinthe, O.P. *De Abbreviationibus et Signis
        Scripturae Gothicae*. Rome: Institutum Angelicum, 1939.

        A specialized manual for Gothic script and punctuation,
        thirteenth to fifteenth centuries.

1514   Lehmann, Oskar. *Die tachygraphischen Urkurzungen der griechi-
        schen Handschriften.* Leipzig: 1880/Hildesheim: G. Olm, 1965.

        A discussion and dictionary of abbreviations used in Greek
        manuscripts from the earliest period.

1515   Lindsay, W.M. *Notae Latinae, An Account of Abbreviation in
        Latin Manuscripts of the Early Minuscule Period (ca. 700-*

850): *Supplement*, by D. Bains. 2nd ed. (from 1936). Hildesheim: G. Olm, 1963.

While this book deals only with earlier abbreviations, the *Supplement* includes Latin manuscripts from 850 to 1050. More detailed is Lindsay's *The Abbreviation Symbols of "ergo," "igitur"* (Leipzig: Harrasowitz, 1912).

1516   Martin, Charles Trice. *The Record Interpreter: A Collection of Abbreviations, Latin Words and Names Used in English Historical Manuscripts and Records.* 2nd ed. (from 1892). London: Stevens, 1910.

Because the Latin abbreviations are not reproduced in facsimile as in Cappelli's *Dizionario*, this dictionary is easier to use. It is, however, more limited in reference than both Cappelli and Kopp, and the Latin place-name dictionary applies only to the British Isles. Useful French abbreviations are provided in a separate list.

1517   Santifaller, Leo. *Die Abkurzungen in den altesten Papsturkunden.* Weimar: Böhlaus, 1939.

A short dictionary for abbreviations used in archival documents, mainly pontifical, for the period 788-1002.

1518   Schiaparelli, L. *Avviamento allo studio delle abbreviature latine nel medioevo.* Florence: L.S. Olschki, 1926.

A brief pamphlet on standard abbreviations for Latin manuscripts from the eighth century to the fifteenth.

1519   Wright, Andrew. *Court-Hand Restored, or the Student's Assistant in Reading Old Deeds, Charters, Records, etc.* 3rd ed. (from 1886). London: W. Brown, 1912.

Largely superseded by items 1511 and 1516.

C. CHRONOLOGY

1520   Cappelli, A. *Cronologia e calendari perpetuo.* Milan: Hoepli, 1906.

A work difficult to find, but Cappelli's practical arrangement of dates is easier to use than that found in other works on chronology.

1521   Cheney, Christopher, ed. *Handbook of Dates for Students of English History.* London: Office of the Royal Historical Society, 1945/1955.

A handy résumé of Powicke, Johnson, and Harte, item 1534. It provides a select bibliography, pp. xi-xvii.

1522   Chevalier, Ulysse, ed. *Gallio Christiana Novissima*. 6 vols.
        Valencia: J. Ceas, 1899-1916.

        A chronological list of bishops and other officials; an
        attempt (although credited with many inaccuracies and omissions)
        to reissue the original *Gallia Christiana* in *Provincias Ecclesi-
        asticae Distributa*, published in 16 vols. (Paris: 1715-1865).

1523   Delorme, Jean. *Chronologie des civilisations*. Paris: Presses
        Universitaires de France, 1949.

        Provides parallel columns of factual data (political, mili-
        tary, religious, and cultural). The Middle Ages occupies pp.
        94-203.

1524   Delisle, L. *Chronologie des bailles et des sénéchaux royaux
        depuis les originies jusqu'à l'avènement de Philippe de Valois*.
        Recueill des Historiens des Gaulles et de la France, 24.
        Paris: Imprimérie Nationale, 1904.

        Lists of royal officials with dates and other details of
        office. Continued by Dupont-Ferrier, item 1526.

1525   Duchesne, Louis. *Fastes episcopaux de l'ancienne Gaule*. 3 vols.
        Paris: A. Fontemoing, 1894-1915; 2nd ed., 2 vols. 1900-15.

        Sources and dates for the history of the early church in
        France. Each volume is devoted to a different region.

1526   Dupont-Ferrier, G. *Gallia Regia ou état des officiers royaux
        des bailliages et des sénéchaussée de 1328 à 1515*. 3 vols.
        Paris: Imprimérie Nationale, 1942-61.

        Modelled on item 1524, which this work continues.

1527   Florez, Enrique, *et al*. *España Sagrada*. 58 vols. Madrid: M.F.
        Rodriguez, 1747-1879; *Indice*, by A. Gonzalez Palencia. 2nd
        ed. Madrid: M.F. Rodriguez, 1946.

        Chronological lists, with a selection of texts relevant to
        Spanish and Portuguese history. It covers the early medieval
        period to the mid-nineteenth century.

1528   Fruin, R. *Handboek der chronologie*. Aalphen aan den Rijn:
        N. Samson, 1934.

        An abbreviated guide for Dutch chronology and church calendars.
        See also item 1536.

1529   Grotefend, H. *Taschenbuch der Zeitrechnung des deutschen
        Mittelalters und der Neuzeit*. 8th ed. (from 1898). Hannover:
        Hahn, 1941.

        The standard work on medieval computational methods, with
        emphasis upon the German tradition.

1530   LaMonte, J.L. "Chronology of the Orient Latin." *Bulletin of
        the International Committee of Historical Sciences* 47, vol.
        12.2 (1943), 141-202.

1531   Mas-Latrie, Louis comte de. *Trésor de chronologie d'histoire et de geographie pour l'étude et l'emploi des documents du moyen âge.* Paris: V. Palme, 1889.

A work largely derivative from earlier works, e.g., the Benedictine *L'Art de verifier les dates* (Paris: 1750). It is often inaccurate, but does contain useful lists of names, dates, saints, monasteries, etc. There is a valuable analysis of the contents of J.-P. Migne's *Patrologia Latina.*

1532   Maurice-Denis, Noële. *Das Kirchenjahr.* Der Christ in dem Welt, 9.6. Aschaffenburg: Pattloch, 1960.

A good description of the Christian liturgical year and a lucid account of the computation of moveable feasts, e.g., Easter.

1533   Poole, R.L. *Medieval Reckonings of Time.* Helps for Students of History, 3. London: Society for the Promotion of Christian Knowledge, 1921.

A concise student's guide to medieval reckonings and terminology for days (holy days and days of the week), months (days of the month and seasons), and years (cycles, Easter tables, and eras).

1534   Powicke, Sir F. Maurice, with C. Johnson and W.J. Harte. *Handbook of British Chronology.* London: Royal Historical Society, 1939.

This work provides chronological lists of the kings of England, Scotland, Wales, and the Isle of Man. It also includes lists of government officials, deputies of Ireland, the governors of the Channel Islands, bishops, archbishops, nobles, parliaments from 1258 to 1547, church councils from 602 to 1566, notes on calendars, and some bibliography. There is no index. Powicke and E.B. Fryde produced an updated version (2nd ed. 1961), with the "Reckonings" omitted; this was issued separately by Cheney, item 1521.

1535   Storey, R.L., gen. ed. *Chronology of the Medieval World 800 to 1491.* London: Barrie and Jenkins, 1973.

This useful work arranges approximately three years per page and enters important events for each year under a general heading, e.g., "Religion," "Literature," or "Science." A general index is provided.

1536   Strubbe, E., and Voer, L. *De Chronologie van de Middeleeuwen ende moderne tijden in de Nederlanden.* Antwerp: Standaard-Boekhandel, 1960.

A massive reference work on Netherlandic chronology, with an excellent bibliography on the subject. See also item 1528.

1537   Ughelli, Ferdinando, F. *Italia Sacra.* 2nd ed. 10 vols. Venice: Sebastiano Coleti, 1717-22.

Completed by R. Pirro, *Sicilia Sacra*, 2 vols. Palermo: 1733,
F. Matthaejo, *Sardinia Sacra* (Rome: 1768). Difficult to find
outside Italy or the major libraries, but thus far the only
comprehensive work on Italian chronology. It lists members of
the ecclesiastical hierarchy by district plus other officials
and foundations. Indexes are provided. See also item 1583.

D. BIOGRAPHY

The following list offers only specialized dictionaries; no attempt has been made to cite the many variants of the *Dictionary of National Biography* or *Who Was
Who* for individual countries. For full bibliographies of
these consult items 1505-6.

1538   Ancona, Paolo d', and Aeschlimann, Erhard. *Dictionnaire des
        miniaturistes du moyen âge et de la renaissance dans les
        différentes contrées de l'Europe*. 2nd ed. (from 1940). Milan:
        Hoepli, 1949/Nendeln/Liechtenstein: Kraus, 1969.

        An alphabetical biographical dictionary with some bibliography.
        A chronological and geographical index was added to the 2nd
        ed. See also item 1541.

1539   Baxter, J.H.; Johnson, Charles; and Willard, J.F. "An Index
        of British and Irish Latin Writers 400-1520." *Archivum
        Latinitatis Medii Aevi*, 7 (1932), 1-115.

        A descriptive list of Latin writers in Britain, with bio-
        graphical and bibliographical notes.

1540   Benedictine Monks of St. Augustine's Abbey, Ramsgate. *A Book
        of Saints: A Dictionary of Servants of God Canonized by the
        Catholic Church*. 5th ed. (from 1921). London: A. and C.
        Black/Ithaca, N.Y.: Cornell University Press, 1966.

        A handbook to all the saints in the Roman martyrology.

1541   Bradley, J.W. *A Dictionary of Miniaturists, Illuminators,
        Calligraphers and Copyists*. 3 vols. London: Quaritch, 1887-
        89/New York, N.Y.: Burt Franklin, 1958.

        Broader in scope than item 1538 above, this work also in-
        cludes brief descriptions of works and sources. Supplementary
        names have been added in an appendix.

1542   Cosenza, Mario Emilio, comp. *Biographical and Bibliographical
        Dictionary of the Italian Humanists and of Classical Scholar-
        ship in Italy, 1300-1800*. 2nd ed. 6 vols. Boston, Mass.:
        G.K. Hall, 1962-67.

        An indispensable reference work for Humanist scholars and
        one which lists the Italian Humanists with brief biographies,

principal works, and editions. The supplementary volume provides
a *Dictionary of Italian Printers*.

1543   Dauzet, Albert. *Les Noms de famille de France*. Paris: Payot,
        1949.

        A "traité d'anthroponymie française," with etymological notes
        on French family names. An index and bibliography are provided.

1544   *Dictionnaire historique et biographique de la Suisse*. 8 vols.
        Neuchatel: Administration du Dictionnaire, 1921-34.

        A useful guide to Swiss names found in medieval manuscripts.
        Not many details are provided, however, because the dictionary
        covers both medieval and modern history.

1545   *Dictionary of Scientific Biography*, ed. Charles Coulston
        Gillispie. 16 vols. New York, N.Y.: Scribner, 1970-80.

        An excellent international biographical dictionary, covering
        all periods and all fields of science and medicine. Full accounts
        are given of each individual, with bibliographical notes. Vol.
        15 is a supplement providing additional names and bibliography,
        while vol. 16 is a general index.

1546   Ekwall, Eilert. *Early London Personal Names*. Lund: Gleerup,
        1947.

        This work lists personal names found in medieval London and
        the surrounding area. Etymological notes are given, along with
        bibliography.

1547   Emden, A.B. *A Biographical Register of the University of Cam-
        bridge to 1500*. Cambridge: University Press, 1963.

        Brief biographical notes are provided, when possible, in this
        alphabetical dictionary of Cambridge students and teachers.
        Bibliographical references are made to their works when appli-
        cable. See also next item.

1548   ————. *A Biographical Register of the University of Oxford
        to A.D. 1500*. 2 vols. Oxford: Clarendon Press, 1957-59.

        Similar in format to preceding item.

1549   Eubel, Conrad, ed. *Hierarchia Catholica Medii et Recentioris
        Aevi*. 7 vols. Padua: Il Messagero di S. Antonio, 1913-68.

        Vols. 1-3 list members, with biographical notes, of the Roman
        Catholic hierarchy for the Middle Ages from 1198. These include
        popes, cardinals, and bishops, arranged chronologically within
        each country. Listing is by Latin name, but modern equivalents
        are provided in the index.

1550   Farmer, D.H. *The Oxford Dictionary of Saints*. Oxford: University
        Press, 1978.

        This work lists over 1,000 saints with cults in Britain and
        provides concise bibliographies and topographical notes on
        cult sites.

1551   Förstemann, Ernst. W. *Altdeutsches Namenbuch*. 3rd ed. 3 vols.
        in 2. Bonn: P. Hanstein, 1900-16.

        Contains both personal (to A.D. 1200) and geographical names,
        with etymological notes.

1552   Fransson, Gustav. *Middle English Surnames of Occupation 1100-
        1350, with an Excursus on Toponymical Surnames*. Lund Studies
        in English, 3. Lund: Gleerup, 1935.

        An etymological account of English surnames derived from
        professions and places. A full bibliography for other onomastic
        works is included, pp. 8-14.

1553   Frati, Carlo. *Dizionario bio-bibliografico dei bibliotecari e
        bibliofili italiani dal sec. XIV al XIX*, ed. Albano Sorbelli.
        Biblioteca di Bibliografia Italiana, 13. Florence: Leo S.
        Olschki, 1933.

        This dictionary cites Italian librarians, scholars, and col-
        lectors of manuscripts. Some entries include bibliography. An
        author/title index is provided.

1554   Glorieux, Palémon. *La Faculté des arts et ses maîtres au XIIIe
        siècle*. Paris: J. Vrin, 1971.

        A history of the faculty of the University of Paris in the
        thirteenth century, with a biographical account of its known
        scholars. For the manuscript traditions of their works, see
        item 678.

1555   Harvey, John. *English Mediaeval Architects. A Biographical
        Dictionary Down to 1550 Including Master Masons, Carpenters,
        Carvers, Building Contractors, and Others Responsible for
        Design*, with contributions by Arthur Oswald. Boston, Mass.:
        Boston Book and Art Shop, 1954.

        A useful reference book for more than architectural biography,
        since it also contains extensive bibliographical references
        for topography, genealogy, and history. Indexes are provided.

1556   Hogan, Edmund. *Onomasticon Goedelicum Locorum et Tribunum
        Hiberniae et Scotiae*. Dublin: Hodges, 1910.

        An index of Gaelic place and tribal names in Scotland and
        Ireland for the early medieval period.

1557   Mansion, Joseph. *Oud-Gentsche naamkunde*. The Hague: M. Nijhoff,
        1924.

        A well-organized reference work for early Dutch family and
        place-names. Extensive indexes are provided. See also item
        1580.

1558   Reel, Jerome V., Jr. *Index to Biographies of Englishmen 1000-
        1485 Found in Dissertations and Theses*. Westport, Conn.:
        Greenwood Press, 1975.

        An alphabetical index of "little men," as the author terms
        them, with names and information gleaned by Reel from disserta-

tions written in English 1930-70. Also included are lists of dates, counties, and professions.

1559 Russell, Josiah Cox. *A Dictionary of Writers of Thirteenth-Century England.* London: 1936/New York, N.Y.: Burt Franklin, 1971.

This useful dictionary provides biographical notes when such information is available; it also identifies writers known under more than one name, e.g., John Aschenden or Estwood or Eschvid. A briefer but more recent list appears in item 112, pp. 32-35.

1560 Searle, William George. *Onomasticon Anglo-Saxonicum, A List of Anglo-Saxon Proper Names from the Time of Beda to That of King John.* Cambridge: University Press, 1897.

A dictionary of Anglo-Saxon family names, with some brief biographies when known and references to bibliographical sources.

1561 Talbot, C.H., and Hammond, E.A. *The Medical Practitioners in Medieval England: A Biographical Register.* Wellcome Historical Publications, n.s., 8. London: Wellcome Historical Medical Library, 1965.

Names, with known biographical details, of practicing physicians such as John Crophill. Bibliographical references to sources are provided.

1562 Wace, Henry, and Percy, William C., eds. *The Dictionary of Christian Biography and Literature to the End of the Sixth Century, A.D., with an Account of the Principal Sects and Heresies.* London: J. Murray, 1911.

Revised from the earlier, four-volume edition of 1877-87 by Wace and Sir William Smith. Bibliographically out of date, but the work still supplies valuable summary biographies of early Christian writers.

E. TOPOGRAPHY

1563 Bahlow, Hans. *Deutschlands geographische Namenwelt: Etymologisches Lexikon der Flus- und Ortsnamen alteuropäischen Herkunft.* Frankfurt am Main: Klostermann, 1965.

Focuses on the philological elements in early German river and place names. Indexes and bibliography are provided.

1564 Besnier, Maurice. *Lexique de géographie ancienne.* Paris: Klincksieck, 1914.

A comprehensive and therefore succinct dictionary/handbook on place-names in all known Classical and medieval literature.

1565   Darby, Harry Clifford, ed. *Historical Geography of England before A.D. 1800*. Cambridge: University Press, 1936.

A collection of fourteen studies by different hands on British geography, pre-historic to the eighteenth century. A bibliography is provided.

1566   ———. *A New Historical Geography of England before 1600*. Cambridge: University Press, 1976.

More focused than item 1565. Extensive bibliographies and an index are included.

1567   Dauzet, Albert. *Les Noms de lieux: origine et évolution*. Paris: Delagare, 1947.

Names of French villages, towns, rivers, etc. A bibliography is provided.

1568   ———, and Rostaing, Charles. *Dictionnaire etymologique des nom de lieux en France*. Paris: Larousse, 1963.

Contains fuller etymological notes and bibliography than item 1567.

1569   *Dictionnaire d'histoire et de géographie écclésiastiques*, ed. Alfred Baudrillart, *et al*. 17 vols. in 102 fascicles. Paris: Letouzey et Ané, 1912-71.

The most complete French dictionary of this type; includes brief accounts of all matters concerning ecclesiastical history and geography: names of churches, accounts of councils, etc. Maps are included.

1570   Ekwall, Eilert. *The Concise Oxford Dictionary of English Place Names*. 4th ed. Oxford: Clarendon Press, 1960.

1571   ———. *English River Names*. Oxford: Clarendon Press, 1928/ 1968.

1572   ———. *Etymological Notes on English Place-Names*. Lund Studies in English, 27. Lund: Gleerup, 1959.

All three works provide etymological background to English place names. Useful for the paleographer are the listed historical forms.

1573   English Place-Name Society. *The Place-Names [of England]*. Cambridge: University Press, 1924-.

The Society issues fascicles devoted to place-names and place-name elements in specific counties. Included are studies in historical evidence and maps.

1574   General Register Office. *Census: England and Wales: Index of Place Names*. 2 vols. London: HMSO, 1965.

An alphabetical index of all place names in England and Wales.

1575   Grasse, Johann Georg Theodor. *Orbis Latinus*. 4th ed. (from
        1866) by Helmut and Sophie-Charlotte Plechl. Braunschweig:
        Klinckhardt and Biermann, 1972.

        A dictionary of Latin place-names, with modern German equiv-
        alents. The two parts are arranged Latin-German/German-Latin.
        The earlier editions indicate some variants later omitted.

1576   Gröhler, Hermann. *Über Ursprung und Bedeutung der französischen
        Ortsnamen*. 2 vols. Heidelberg: Carl Winter, 1913, 1933.

        An etymological dictionary of French place-names, with modern
        German equivalents.

1577   Grollenberg, L.H. *Atlas of the Bible*, trans. and ed. J.H.M.
        Reid and H.H. Rowley. London: Nelson, 1956.

        A companion to item 1591 below.

1578   Longnon, Auguste. *Les Noms de lieu de la France, leurs origines,
        leurs signification, leurs transformations*. 5 fascicles.
        Paris: 1920-29/H. Champion, 1968.

        This dictionary considers place-names of different linguistic
        (Greek, Gallic, Saxon, etc.) or other origin (ecclesiastic,
        feudal, etc.).

1579   Magoun, Francis P., Jr. *A Chaucer Gazetteer*. Stockholm: Almqvist
        and Wiksell, 1961.

        A listing and discussion of all names of geographical origin
        or connection used by Geoffrey Chaucer (conflated from papers
        published separately, 1953-55). The fullness of detail and
        etymology renders it useful for other than Chaucerian studies.

1580   Mansion, Joseph. *De voornaamste bestanddeelen der vlaamsche
        plaatsnamen*. The Hague: M. Nijhoff, 1935.

        A study of Flemish place-names, with etymological notes. See
        also item 1557.

1581   Markl, Otto. *Ortsnamen Griechenlands in fränkischer Zeit*.
        Byzantina Vindobodensia, 1. Graz: Böhlaus, 1966.

        A dictionary of medieval Greek place-names as they appear in
        early manuscripts; provided are some etymological and biblio-
        graphical references.

1582   Matthias, Walter. *Die geographische Nomenklatur Italiens im
        altdeutschen Schriftum*. Leipzig: F. Brandstetter, 1912.

        This work provides a dictionary to Italian place-names as
        they appear in Middle High German texts; some etymological notes
        are given.

1583   Muñoz y Romero, Tomás. *Diccionario bibliográfico-histórico de
        los antiguos reinos, provencias, ciudades, villas, iglesias
        y santuarios de España*. Madrid: Rivadeneyra, 1858.

Still useful, when obtainable, as a dictionary of persons, places, and churches in medieval Spain. See also item 1537.

1584   Nissen, Heinrich. *Italienische Landeskunde*. 2 vols. in 3 pts. Berlin: Weidmannsche, 1883-1909.

A descriptive geography of Italy. Arrangement is by region. A bibliography is provided.

1585   Oesterley, Herman. *Historisch-geographisches Wörterbuch des deutschen Mittelalters*. Gotha: Perthes, 1883.

An etymological dictionary of medieval German place-names. The bibliographical references to earlier nineteenth-century works are still useful.

1586   Olivieri, Dante. *Dizionario di toponomastica Lombarda*. Milan: La Famiglia Meneghina, 1931.

An etymological dictionary of Lombardy. There is a useful bibliography of Italian topography, pp. 57-64.

1587   Poole, Reginald Lane. *Historical Atlas of Modern Europe from the Decline of the Roman Empire*. Oxford: Clarendon Press, 1902.

Contains, among others, regional maps of medieval monasteries. For these see also the *Ordinance Survey Maps*.

1588   Rostaing, C. *Les Noms de lieux*. "Que sais-je?" Paris: Presses Universitaires de France, 1945.

General, with little real information. A useful guide, how-ever, for rapid identification of French place-names in their various forms and locations. For a more scholarly version see item 1568.

1589   Repetti, Emanuele. *Dizionario geographico-fisico-storico della Toscana*. 6 vols. Florence: G. Piatti, 1833-46.

Geographical dictionary of Tuscany. Vol. 6 includes intro-duction, maps, and genealogical tables.

1590   Smith, Sir William. *Dictionary of Greek and Roman Geography*. 2 vols. London: J. Murray/Boston: Little, 1873-78/New York, N.Y.: AMS Press, 1966.

A detailed reference dictionary for Classical place-names. It contains maps.

1591   Van der Meer, F., and Moormann, Christine, eds. *Atlas of the Early Christian World*, trans. and ed. Mary F. Hedlund and H.H. Rowley. London: Nelson, 1958.

This atlas contains many maps from post-apostolic times to ca. 600. A system of symbols indicates types of sites and ruins. For a companion vol. relevant to the Bible, see item 1577.

F. LANGUAGE

It would be beyond the scope of this handbook to list all language reference works relevant to the study of Western manuscripts. I have therefore selected only the most basic dictionaries, and those which specifically focus upon the medieval forms of Classical languages. Specialized glossaries will, of course, be found in most editions of early texts, and the dictionaries of various medieval vernacular languages will be listed in the bibliographies noted in Section I.

1. LATIN AND GREEK DICTIONARIES

1592   Arnaldi, Francesco, *et al. Latinitatis Italicae Medii Aevi inde ab Anno CDLXXVI ad Annum MXXII Lexicon Imperfectum.* Published periodically in *Archivum Latinitatis Medii Aevi.* 1935-72.

A dictionary for medieval Latin in Italian manuscripts; the fascicles began with A-G: 10-11 (1935-36) through to Tr-Zy: 34 (1964), with *Addenda,* 35-38 (1965-72).

1593   Bauer, Walter. *Griechisch-deutsches Wörterbuch zu den Schriften des Neuen Testaments,* trans. and rev. by W.F. Arndt and F. W. Gingrich as *A Greek-English Lexicon of the New Testament and Other Early Christian Literature.* Chicago, Ill.: University of Chicago Press, 1957; 5th ed. Berlin: Töpelmann, 1958.

1594   Baxter, J.H., and Johnson, C., with Phyllis Abrahams. *Medieval Latin Word-List from British and Irish Sources.* London: Oxford University Press, 1934.

A word-list compiled according to historical principles, with variant meanings listed according to period. The list includes only those words with non-classical meanings and does not give references to texts. Revised by Latham, item 1598.

1595   Blatt, Franz, gen. ed. *Novum Glossarium Mediae Latinitatis ab Anno DCCC Usque ad Annum MCC.* Aarhus: E. Munksgaard, 1954-.

Issued in fascicles by letter of the alphabet from an international group of contributors. Especially useful in determining national differences in medieval Latin usage and vocabulary. Accompanying indexes identify authors and texts.

1596   Du Cange, Charles du Fresne, Sieur. *Glossarium ad Scriptores Mediae et Infimae Latinitatis,* ed. Didot. 7 vols. Paris: 1840-50; ed. Favre, 10 vols. Niort: 1883-87; reissued in 2 vols. Paris: Geuthner, 1943.

The great medieval Latin dictionary upon which most others depend, at least initially. More than a dictionary, the work offers a wide range of encyclopedic information (in Latin) enlarged with each successive edition. The original edition of

Du Cange, Treasurer of France, appeared in 3 vols. (Paris: 1678) and the best subsequent edition is by Didot. A shorter version was issued in 1858 by Maigne D'Arnis, item 1600, and supplemented by Schmidt, item 1603.

1597   Lampe, G.W.H., ed. *A Patristic Greek Lexicon*. 5 pts. Oxford: Clarendon Press, 1961-68.

Based upon language from Clement of Rome to Theodore of Studium but excludes the Old and New Testaments except for the pre-Christian Psalms of Solomon and the later eleventh-century *Christus Patiens*. The editor attempts to relate words listed to earlier *lexica*, e.g., that by Liddell-Scott-Jones. A list of authors/works is provided.

1598   Latham, R.E. *Revised Medieval Latin Word-List from British and Irish Sources*. London: Oxford University Press for the British Academy, 1965.

A revised and expanded version of item 1594. The select, classified bibliography offers a useful list of medieval Latin authors and works, including medieval lexicographical texts, p. xxiii. The word-list gives no specific references, however, to individual texts.

1599   ————. *Dictionary of Medieval Latin from British Sources*. London: Oxford University Press, 1975-.

An expansion of the preceding item, proposed as a series of fascicles.

1600   Maigne D'Arnis, W.H. *Lexicon Manuale ad Scriptores Mediae et Infimae Latinitatis*. Paris: Migne, 1866/1890.

An abbreviated version of Du Cange, item 1596, with defini-tions added in French.

1601   Niermeyer, J.F., ed. *Mediae Latinitatis Lexicon Minus: A Medieval Latin-French/English Dictionary*. Leiden: E.J. Brill, 1954-76.

This dictionary intends, as the editor claims in his preface, to bring Du Cange up-to-date and to supply words and meanings lacking in items 1600 and 1603. References to specific texts in the citations are a valuable aid to translation.

1602   Prinz, O. von, ed. *Mittellateinisches Wörterbuch bis zum aus-gehenden 13. Jahrhundert*. Bayerischen Akademie der Wissen-schaften und Deutschen Akademie der Wissenschaften zu Berlin. Munich: C.H. Beck, 1959-76.

A medieval Latin dictionary which attempts to extend Du Cange in depth (with works cited from over 400 authors) and length (to the fourteenth century). Fasc. 1 provides a bibliography of the major series of Latin texts, authors, individual works, dates, and editions. The remaining fascicles, issued alpha-betically by letter, cite the Latin word, then give definitions in Latin and German.

1603 Schmidt, Charles. *Petit supplément au dictionnaire du Du Cange.*
      Strasbourg: Heitz, 1906.

      A supplement to items 1596 and 1600, with added texts and
      expanded definitions.

1604 Sophocles, E.A. *Greek Lexicon of the Roman and Byzantine Periods
      from B.C. 146 to A.D. 1100.* 2 vols. New York, N.Y.: Scribner,
      1887/Ungar, 1957.

      A dictionary of later Classical Greek and guide to Patristic
      vocabulary.

1605 Souter, Alexander. *A Glossary of Later Latin to 600 A.D.* Oxford:
      Clarendon Press, 1949.

      An invaluable list, with textual references, of late Latin
      and early Christian Latin words not found in Lewis and Short's
      Latin Dictionary.

See also items 38-39, 1505-6.

2. SPECIALIZED GLOSSARIES

1606 Axters, S. *Scholastiek Lexicon. Latijn-Nederlandsch.* Antwerp:
      Geloofsverdedging, 1937.

      A glossary in Dutch for Latin terms used in scholastic
      writings.

1607 Baudry, Leon. *Lexique philosophique de Guillaume d'Ockham:
      Etudes des notions fondamentales.* Paris: P. Lethielleux,
      1958.

      A lexicon of Ockham's terminology set within the context of
      extensive quotations. Critical discussions refer to other works
      and scholars.

1608 Berger, A. *Encyclopedic Dictionary of Roman Law.* Transactions
      of the American Philosophical Society, n.s., 43.2. Philadel-
      phia, Pa.: The Society, 1953/1968.

      This work attempts to explain technical Roman legal terms
      and to translate specialized Latin words used in a juristic
      context. Bibliographical references and bibliography are pro-
      vided, as well as an English/Latin glosary. See also item 1619.

1609 Blaise, A. *Le Vocabulaire latin des principaux thèmes liturgiques.*
      Turnhout: Brépols, 1966.

      A lexicon for liturgical Latin terms. See also items 1610,
      1614, 1618, 1699.

1610 Coppens, Dom C. *Praktisch Handbock van het liturgisch Latijn.*
      2 vols. Turnhout: Brépols, 1943.

      See items 1609, 1614, 1618, 1699.

1611   Edler, F. *Glossary of Medieval Terms of Business, Italian Series,
        1200-1600*. Cambridge: Mass.: Mediaeval Academy of America,
        1934.

        A specialized glossary for mainly Italian manuscripts of this
        period. The glossary is preceded by an introduction on origins
        and resources.

1612   Fisher, John L. *A Medieval Farming Glossary of Latin and English
        Words*. London: Published for the Standard Conference for
        Local History by the National Council of Social Sciences,
        1968.

        An agricultural dictionary, derived mainly from local Essex
        records. A brief bibliography is provided, pp. 4-5.

        North, J.D. See item 1613.

1613   Pedersen, Olaf. "A Fifteenth-Century Glossary of Astronomical
        Terms." *Classica et Mediaevalia*, 9 (1973), 584-94.

        This invaluable glossary from a fifteenth-century manuscript
        provides many explanations for the technical language of
        astronomy/astrology. A useful adaptation with English defini-
        tions may be found in J.D. North's edition of the *Works of
        Richard of Wallingford* (Oxford: Clarendon Press, 1976).

1614   Sleumer, Albert. *Kirchlateinisches Wörterbuch*. 2nd ed. with
        Joseph Schmidt. Limburg: Steffan, 1926.

        A dictionary for liturgical Latin terms, which draws upon
        such liturgical books as missals, graduals, etc. The entries
        are detailed, and bibliographical references are provided.
        See also items 1609-10, 1618, 1699.

See also items 38-39, 1304-5, 1505-6.

G. *GENERAL DICTIONARIES AND ENCYCLOPEDIAS*

1615   Briquet, C.M. *Les Filigranes*, ed. Allan Stevenson. 4 vols.
        Amsterdam: Paper Publications Society, 1968.

        An impressive dictionary of over 16,000 watermark drawings,
        originally published in 1907. Brief accounts of the origins
        of and dates for most watermarks are given, with a bibliography
        on watermarks and paper production. The reader may find con-
        sultation somewhat incommodious due to the work's arrangement
        under French names for the principal subjects of watermarks,
        e.g., *croix*, 'cross,' and to the fact that the subject of
        many watermarks is not easy to recognize in the first place.
        See next item for additions and indexes.

1616   *Briquet Album, The. A Miscellany on Watermarks, Supplementing
        Dr. Briquet's Les Filigranes*, by various paper scholars.
        Hilversum: Paper Publications Society, 1952.

1630   *Meyers Handbuch über die Literatur; ein Lexikon der Dichter
        und Schriftsteller aller Literaturen*, gen. eds. Ingrid Adam
        and Gisela Preuss. 2nd ed. (from 1964). Mannheim: Allgemeiner
        Verlag, 1970.

        A comprehensive encyclopedia for international literature
        and authors from all periods. The bibliographical appendix lists
        literary histories for most of the Western literatures.

        Müller, I. von. See item 1624.

1631   *New Catholic Encyclopedia.* Catholic University of America.
        15 vols. New York, N.Y.: McGraw-Hill, 1967.

        The most comprehensive and up-to-date encyclopedia for the
        history, doctrine, and liturgy of the Roman Catholic Church.
        Of some use still for the medieval period is the earlier ver-
        sion, *Catholic Encyclopedia* (New York, N.Y.: Catholic Encyclo-
        pedia Press, 1907-22).

1632   *Oxford Classical Dictionary*, ed. N.G.L. Hammond and H.H. Scullard.
        2nd ed. (from 1949). Oxford: Clarendon Press, 1970.

        This comprehensive encyclopedia contains signed articles on
        all aspects of Classical studies, e.g., biography, mythology,
        and science. The entries include bibliographical references,
        and a general index is provided. *Oxford Dictionaries* of similar
        format exist for other literatures, e.g., English. See also
        next item.

1633   *Oxford Companion to Classical Literature, The.* ed. Sir Paul
        Harvey. Repr. with corrections (from 1937). Oxford: Clarendon
        Press, 1969.

        This dictionary/encyclopedia gives references to persons (real
        and literary), texts, historical events, philosophical schools,
        and other matters. The account of "Texts and Studies," which
        discusses such topics as "Greek Texts," "Textual Recension,"
        and "Palaeography," provides useful summaries and bibliography.
        See also item 44.

1634   *Oxford Dictionary of the Christian Church*, ed. F.L. Cross and
        Elizabeth A. Livingstone (from 1957). London: Oxford Univer-
        sity Press, 1974.

        The standard English reference work on matters of Christian,
        history, liturgy, biography, and theology, with good bibliog-
        raphies. Arrangement is alphabetical by person, topic, work,
        or location.

1635   *Paulys Real-Encyclopädie der klassischen Altertumswissenschaft*,
        rev. ed. by Georg Wissowa, Wilhelm Kroll, *et al.* 1st ser.
        A-P, 23 vols; 2nd ser. R-Z, 8 vols; *Supplement*, 8 vols.
        Stuttgart: J.B. Metzler, 1894-1973.

        A comprehensive and detailed encyclopedia for Classical
        studies. Many items pertain to paleography and the transmission
        of texts, and bibliographies are provided.

1636   Podhradsky, Gerhard. *New Dictionary of the Liturgy*, ed. Lancelot
        Sheppard. New York, N.Y.: Alba House, 1967.

        A translation and enlarged edition of Podhradsky's *Lexikon
        der Liturgie* (Innsbruck: 1962), which provides a comprehensive
        encyclopedia for all matters concerning the liturgy up to the
        present time.

1637   *Reallexikon der germanischen Altertumskunde*, ed. Johannes Hoops,
        et al. 5 vols. 2nd ed. (from 1911-19) by Herbert Jankuhn.
        Berlin: De Gruyter, 1968-73.

        A source of detailed information and bibliographical refer-
        ences for Germanic names, places, and objects, e.g., Beowulf,
        Vistula, sword.

1638   *Reallexikon für Antike und Christentum, Sachwörterbuch zur
        Auseinandersetzung des Christentums mit der antiken Welt*,
        ed. Theodor Clauser. Stuttgart: Hiersemann, 1950-.

        This encyclopedia gives comprehensive outlines for each of
        the subjects included within the general scope of relations
        between Classical Antiquity and Chritianity, e.g., *Christus-
        bild, Dialog*. Arrangement is alphabetical by topic, and some
        bibliography is provided.

1639   Ronchi, Giullia, comp. *Lexicon Theonymon Rerumque Sacrarum et
        Divinarum ad Aegyptum Pertinentium quae in Papyris Ostracis
        Titulis Graecis Latinisque in Aegypto Repertis Laudantur*.
        5 vols. Milan: Istituto Editoriale Cisalpino, 1974-77.

        A lexicon of religious references found in Greek and Latin
        papyri of Egyptian origin, arranged alphabetically under word
        or topic. Individual manuscripts are cited under each, with
        extracts and bibliographical references. Vols. 1-4 include
        Greek words, vol. 5 Latin words (*adiutor-vesta*).

1640   *Sacramentum Mundi: An Encyclopedia of Theology*, ed. Karl
        Rahner, *et al*. 6 vols. New York, N.Y.: Herder and Herder,
        1968.

        A comprehensive survey of central theological topics, each
        followed by a brief bibliography. A concise, one-volume version
        of this encyclopedia has been edited by Rahner (New York, N.Y.:
        Seabury Press, 1975).

        Stammler, W. See item 1617.

1641   Walther, Hans. *Lateinische Sprichwörter und Sentenzen des
        Mittelalters in alphabetischer Anordnung*. Carmina Medii Aevi
        Posterioris Latina, 2. 6 vols. Göttingen: Vandenhoeck and
        Ruprecht, 1963-69.

        This work constitutes a comprehensive, alphabetical index
        of proverbs and sayings. Vol. 6 provides a name/title/subject
        index. A bibliographical "Nachträge" by Jurgen Stohlmann appears
        in *Mittellateinisches Jahrbuch*, 12 (1977), 316-33.

        Wissowa, G. See item 1635.

1642   *Wycliffe Bible Encyclopedia*, ed. Charles F. Pfeiffer, *et al.*
         5 vols. Chicago, Ill.: Moody Press, 1975/1976.

         An illustrated and bibliographical encyclopedia of the Bible,
         arranged alphabetically under name or subject. Entries are
         based upon the Vulgate and King James versions, despite the
         title.

See also items 1505-6.

XIII. MANUSCRIPTS AND THEIR CONTEXTS

Works cited in this section are intended to provide referential matter which serves to establish manuscripts within certain contexts. Many will help place a manuscript against historical, political, social, religious, philosophical, scientific, or linguistic backgrounds, and others may illustrate more precisely certain textual traditions. Those works which constitute a more detailed treatment of a particular text or genre and which provide, in effect, an index or finding list have already been cited in Section V.

CONTENTS

A. HISTORICAL AND CULTURAL

1643   Fueter, Eduard. *Geschichte der neueren Historiographie*. 3rd ed.
        Munich/Berlin: R. Oldenbourg, 1936/1968.

        A survey of historical literature, from Boccaccio to modern
        times. The author discusses schools of historical interpreta-
        tion and thought and the types of historical writing and their
        documents. Bibliographies and index are provided.

1644   Hoffmann, Hartmut. *Untersuchungen zur karolingishen Analistik*.
        Bonner historische Forschungen, 10. Bonn: L. Röhrscheid, 1958.

        An introduction to methodology in research on Carolingian
        annals, using as specific illustration the *Annales Laurescha-
        menses*, *Fuldenses*, and *Sithienses*.

1645   Huizinga, Johan. *The Waning of the Middle Ages: A Study of the
        Forms of Life, Thought, and Art in France and the Netherlands
        in the XIVth and XVth Centuries*. London: E. Arnold, 1937;
        trans. from the Dutch edition of 1919. 2nd ed., by F. Hopman,
        with Preface. Haarlem: H.D. Tjeenk Willink and Zoon, 1921.

        An assessment of cultural history for the pre-Renaissance
        period, based upon Netherlandic and French literature and art.
        For the most part a work unchallenged by more recent scholar-
        ship. The bibliography is still useful for a variety of dis-
        ciplines, e.g., history, art history, and Dutch literature.

1646   Knowles, Dom David. *The Religious Orders of England*. 3 vols.
        Cambridge: University Press, 1948-59.

        A chronological account of the establishment and survival
        of the religious orders in England. Vol. 1 considers the older
        orders and the friars, 1216-1340, vol. 2 the later period, and
        vol. 3 the Tudor period. The last vol. was abridged and pub-
        lished as *Bare Ruined Choirs: The Dissolution of the Monasteries*
        (New York, N.Y.: Cambridge University Press, 1976). The indexes
        are quite useful, while the bibliography is important for an
        account of the later dispersal of manuscripts.

1647   ————, and Hadcock, R. Neville. *Medieval Religious Houses:
        England and Wales*. Rev. ed. (from 1953). New York, N.Y.: St.
        Martin's Priory Press, 1972.

        An enlarged and revised edition of Knowles' *Religious Houses
        of Medieval England* (1940), which deals with the topography of
        English monasticism. It includes lists of houses, incomes, and
        numbers of monks from the conquest to the dissolution. Six
        maps and indexes are provided.

1648   Lagarde, Georges de. *La Naissance de l'esprit laique au déclin
        du moyen âge*. 3rd ed. (from 1935–46). 5 vols. Louvain: E.
        Nauwelaerts, 1956–70.

        This work studies the changing relationships between laity
        and religious during the thirteenth and fourteenth centuries
        as reflected in the manuscript documents of the period. Vols.
        1–3 discuss the general background from the thirteenth century,
        and vols. 4–5 focus upon the writings of William of Ockham.

1649   Laistner, M.L.W. *Christianity and Pagan Culture in the Later
        Roman Empire*. Ithaca, N.Y.: Cornell University Press, 1951.

        Originally given as the James W. Richard Lectures in History,
        Cornell, 1950–51, these lectures discuss the responses of the
        early Church to its conflict with Romano-pagan culture. Included
        is a translation of John of Chrysostom's address on "Vain-
        glory" and "Bringing up Children," the latter being concerned
        with pagan texts in education.

1650   ———. *Thought and Letters in Western Europe A.D. 500 to 900*.
        2nd ed. (from 1931). Ithaca, N.Y.: Cornell University Press,
        1957/1976.

        An account of Carolingian learning and pedagogy, which paral-
        lels item 1652 on Classical education. The bibliography offers
        a valuable list of texts on the subject.

1651   Leclercq, Jean. *The Love of Learning and the Desire for God:
        A Study of Monastic Culture*, trans. Catharine Misrahi. New
        York, N.Y.: Fordham University Press, 1961.

        A general study, originally a series of lectures delivered
        at the Collegio Sant'Anselmo, Rome, on the interaction between
        the love of literature and the desire for God among monastic
        writers such as St. Bernard. This point of view is discussed
        under headings which focus upon (1) the formation of sources
        of monastic culture, (2) eschatological themes, Biblical exegesis,
        and the Fathers, (3) types of monastic works such as histories
        and sermons, and (4) spiritual and mystical writings. Leclercq
        also offers useful and often penetrating observations on
        monastic "humanism."

1652   Marrou, Henri I. *Histoire de l'education dans l'antiquité*.
        2nd ed. (from 1948). Paris: Editions du Seuil, 1950; trans.
        George Lamb (from the 1948 ed.) as *A History of Education
        in Antiquity*. London: Sheed and Ward, 1956/1964.

        An excellent, comprehensive account of Greek and Roman theories
        of education: its methods, aims, and documents. The bibliography
        is invaluable for both primary and secondary sources.

1653   Rashdall, H. *Universities of Europe in the Middle Ages*, ed.
        F.M. Powicke and A.B. Emden. 3 vols. Oxford: Clarendon Press,
        1936.

        A history of the universities of Salerno, Bologna, Paris, Ox-
        ford, Cambridge, and other major institutions of learning in
        Italy, Spain, France, and Germany. See also items 58, 75, 88,
        419.

1654   Saunders, J.J. *A History of Medieval Islam.* New York, N.Y.:
        Barnes and Noble, 1965.

        A very general guide to the major historical events in medi-
        eval Islamic history to 1260. The account of the Muslims in
        Spain is of some interest for the paleographer; select bibliog-
        raphy.

1655   Smalley, Beryl. *Historians in the Middle Ages.* London: Thames
        and Hudson, 1974.

        An historiographical study, with reference to chronicles and
        other types of historical writing. Bibliography is provided.

B. HUMANISTIC

1656   Bacon, Hans. *Humanistic and Political Literature in Florence
        and Venice at the Beginning of the Quattrocento: Studies in
        Criticism and Chronology.* Cambridge, Mass.: Harvard University
        Press, 1955/New York, N.Y.: Russell and Russell, 1968.

        The first of three studies (*The Crisis of the Early Italian
        Renaissance*, 1955; *From Petrarch to Leonardo Bruni*, 1968) on
        the composition and textual transmission of such Humanist works
        as Petrarch's *Secretum.* The bibliographical notes are extensive.

1657   Billanovich, Giuseppe. *I primi humanisti e le tradizioni dei
        classici latini.* Discorsi universitari, nuova ser., 14. Fri-
        bourg: University Press, 1953.

        This work considers the survival and transmission of Classical
        texts in fifteenth- and sixteenth-century Italy. A bibliography
        provides access to lesser known literature.

1658   Billanovich, Guido. "Veterum vestigia vatum." *Italia mediovale
        e humanistica*, 1 (1958), 155-243.

        A well-documented account of the Humanists' search for and
        classification of Classical texts among medieval manuscripts.

1659   Bolgar, R.R. *The Classical Heritage and Its Beneficiaries.*
        Cambridge: University Press, 1954.

        A study of the Classical heritage throughout the Middle Ages,
        beginning with the educational inheritance and Patristic tra-
        dition and concluding with the end of the Renaissance and the
        appearance of new patterns in Classical education and scholar-
        ship. An appendix lists Greek manuscripts in Italy during the
        fifteenth century and translations of Greek and Roman classics
        before 1600.

1660   ————, ed. *Classical Influences on European Culture, A.D. 500-
        1500.* Proceedings of an International Conference, King's
        College Cambridge, April 1969. Cambridge: University Press,
        1971.

A collection of 27 papers. Of special interest to paleographers
are the first two, R.D. Sweeney, "Vanishing and Unavailable
Evidence: Latin Manuscripts in the Middle Ages and Today," pp.
29-36, and M.-Th. D'Alverny and M.-C. Garand, "L'Institut de
Recherche et d'Histoire des Textes et l'études des manuscripts
des auteurs classiques," pp. 37-44.

1661   Geanakoplos, Deno J. *Greek Scholars in Venice: Studies in the
        Dissemination of Greek Learning from Byzantium to Western
        Europe.* Cambridge, Mass.: Harvard University Press, 1962.

        A general background is provided to the period, followed by
        individual studies of such Greek Scholars as Michael Apostolis
        and Marcus Musurus, with a final chapter on Erasmus and his
        contributions to Humanism. Bibliographical notes and extensive
        bibliography, pp. 305-337.

1662   ————. *Interaction of the 'Sibling' Byzantine and Western
        Cultures in the Middle Ages and Italian Renaissance (330-
        1600).* New Haven, Conn.: Yale University Press, 1976.

        An interdisciplinary study of the two cultures with some focus
        upon the ecclesiastical relationships between East and West.
        Some discussion of individual scholars, e.g., Marcus Musurus.
        A full bibliography is provided.

1663   Haskins, Charles H. *The Renaissance of the Twelfth Century.*
        Cambridge, Mass.: Harvard University Press, 1927.

        An assessment of pre-Humanist culture, with detailed documenta-
        tion. This work has since been questioned by scholars on its
        basic premises, see especially W.A. Nitze, *Speculum*, 23 (1948),
        464-71, and Urban T. Holmes, Jr., *Speculum*, 27 (1951), 643-51.

1664   Kristeller, Paul O. *Renaissance Thought.* 2 vols. New York, N.Y.:
        Harper, 1961-65.

        A collection of essays on the philosophy of Ficino and others.
        Additional essays on late medieval and early Renaissance thought
        have been ed. and trans. by Edward P. Mahoney in *Medieval As-
        pects of Renaissance Learning.* Duke University Monographs in
        Medieval and Renaissance Studies, 1 (Durham, N.C.: Duke Uni-
        versity Press, 1974). These include "The Scholar and His Public,"
        "Monasticism," and "The Religious Orders." Bibliographies are
        included.

1665   Lehmann, Paul. *Pseudo-antike Literatur des Mittelalters.*
        Leipzig/Berlin: Teubner, 1927/Darmstadt: Wissenschaftliche
        Buchgesellschaft, 1964.

        The author analyzes some medieval "forgeries" of Classical
        works and provides a good bibliography.

        Mahoney, Edward P. See item 1664.

1666   Pfeiffer, Rudolf. *History of Classical Scholarship from 1300
        to 1850.* Oxford: Clarendon Press, 1976.

1667   ——————. *History of Classical Scholarship from the Beginnings
        to the End of the Hellenistic Age.* Oxford: Clarendon Press,
        1968.

        Both works survey the survival and transmission of Classical
        texts with a general account of trends in textual criticism.
        Bibliographical notes are provided.

1668   Sabbadini, Remigii. *Le Scoperte dei codici latini e greci nei
        secoli XIV e XV.* Biblioteca Storica del Rinascimento, n.s.,
        4. 2 vols. Florence: G.C. Sansoni, 1905-14; 2nd ed. Florence:
        E. Garin, 1967.

        An account of the Humanists' search for Classical texts among
        medieval manuscripts. The discussion of Renaissance Greek manu-
        scripts is of some interest. Indexes are provided for authors
        and editors/owners/copyists.

1669   ——————. *Storia e critica di testi latini: Cicerone, Donato,
        Iacito, Cleso, Plauto, Plinio, Quintiliano, Livio e Sallustio.
        Commedia ignota.* Catania: 1914/Hildesheim: G. Olms, 1974.

        A history of Classical philology, manuscript traditions, and
        the activities of the Humanists.

1670   Sandys, John. *History of Classical Scholarship.* 2nd ed. (from
        1903). 3 vols. Cambridge: University Press, 1906-08.

        The standard account of Classical scholarship, from Petrarch
        and Boccacio to American eighteenth-century scholars such as
        Hadley and Packard. Included are detailed bibliographical refer-
        ences.

1671   Smalley, Beryl. *English Friars and Antiquity.* Oxford: Basil
        Blackwell, 1960.

        This work is a lucidly written and well-documented account
        of fourteenth-century English humanism and the use of Classical
        texts, chiefly among the mendicant orders; bibliography and
        index.

1672   Ullman, B.L. *Studies in the Italian Renaissance.* Rome: Edizioni
        di Storia e Letteratura, 1955.

        A series of essays on the work and influence of, chiefly,
        Petrarch and Salutati; bibliographical notes.

1673   ——————. *The Humanism of Coluccio Salutati.* Medioevo e umanesimo,
        4. Padua: Antenore, 1963.

        An application of the general context established in Ullman's
        earlier works to the life (1331-1406) and work of probably the
        most learned and active humanist of his time.

1674   Weiss, Roberto. *Humanism in England During the Fifteenth Century.*
        3rd ed. (from 1942). Oxford: Basil Blackwell, 1967.

        Originally Weiss' Oxford D. Phil. thesis, this work has since
        received minor corrections and additions throughout successive
        editions. Weiss evaluates the influence of Humanism upon the

development of English thought and literature. These theories
are further developed in the next item.

1675   ————. *The Renaissance Discovery of Classical Antiquity.*
        Oxford: Basil Blackwell, 1969.

        A chronological account of Humanism and the discovery of
        Classical texts, from the Middle Ages and Petrarch to the search
        for "antiquities" in the fifteenth and sixteenth centuries. Full
        bibliographical notes are provided.

See also items 55-57, 647.

C. PHILOSOPHICAL

1676   Baeumker, Clemens, ed. *Beiträge zur Geschichte der Philosophie
        des Mittelalters: Texte und Untersuchungen.* 27 vols. Münster:
        Aschendorffische Buchhandlung, 1891-1928.

        A detailed, comprehensive collection of writings on texts,
        many still little-known, illustrating medieval intellectual
        history, with emphasis upon philosophical writings, e.g.,
        Witelo's *Perspectiva.* Full bibliographies and indexes are pro-
        vided.

1677   Gilson, E. *A History of Christian Philosophy in the Middle Ages.*
        New York, N.Y.: Random House, 1955.

        A lucid and comprehensive account of the major philosophers
        with emphasis upon St. Thomas Aquinas, Anselm, and Abelard.
        Included among the bibliographical references are Gilson's
        many articles and monographs on specific aspects of medieval
        thought.

1678   Kristeller, Paul O., Cassirer, Ernst, *et al.*, eds. *The Renais-
        sance Philosophy of Man: Selections in Translation.* Chicago,
        Ill.: University of Chicago Press, 1948/1956.

        A selection of works in translation, which include Petrarch's
        "The Ascent of Mount Ventoux," Lorenzo Valla's "Dialogue on Free
        Will," with other writings by Ficino, Mirandola, Pomponazzi,
        and Vives. See also item 647 above.

1679   Messenger, E.C. *History of Mediaeval Philosophy.* 2 vols. London/
        New York: Macmillan, 1926.

        The final version of Maurice de Wulf's *History of Mediaeval
        Philosophy* (1909), trans. P. Coffey as the 3rd ed. of *Histoire
        de la philosophie médiévale* and, after several intermediate
        editions, appearing in the present form with updated bibliog-
        raphies. It remains one of the better manuals for medieval
        philosophy in the comprehensiveness of the texts selected for
        discussion and in the clarity of their exposition.

1680   Poole, Reginald Lane. *Illustrations of the History of Medieval
        Thought*. London: 1884; 2nd rev. ed. New York, N.Y.: Dover
        Press, 1960.

        A close, accurate account of selected topics, especially
        ecclesiastical politics. Some translations from source material
        are provided. Bibliographies and index are included.

1681   Quasten, Johannes. *Patrology*. 3 vols. Utrecht/Brussels: Spectrum,
        1950-60.

        A summary history of the Fathers, with extensive bibliographies
        on all aspects of early Christian writings, including the litur-
        gy. Full indexes conclude each volume.

        Wulf, M.D. See item 1679.

See also items 154-8, 592-5, 677-86.

                            D. ECCLESIASTICAL

1682   Fliche, A., and Martin, V., eds. *Histoire de l'église depuis
        les origines jusqu'à nos jours*. 21 vols. Paris: Bloud and
        Gay, 1934-53.

        An important work on ecclesiastical history, issued under
        different authors on particular subjects, e.g., Louis Bréhier
        on Gregory the Great, vol. 5 (1947). General bibliographies
        and comprehensive indexes are provided.

See also items 1617, 1618, 1620, 1623, 1631, 1634, 1640.

                             E. RELIGIOUS

1683   Aigrain, R. *L'Hagiographie: ses sources, ses méthods, son
        histoire*. Paris: Bloud and Gay, 1953.

        An introduction to hagiography based upon earlier studies
        by Delehaye, see next items, but brought up to date and focusing
        more upon medieval French sources. Bibliographical notes are
        provided.

1684   Delehaye, H., S.J. *A travers trois siècles, l'oeuvre des
        Bollandistes, 1615-1915*. Brussels: Académie Royale de Bel-
        gique, 1920.

        An account of the work of the Jesuit Bollandists in hagiog-
        raphy and the foundation of the *Acta Sanctorum* series. This
        work has been brought up to date by P. Peeters, *L'Oeuvre des*

Bollandistes (Brussels: Académie Royale de Belgique, 1942),
which adds an onomastic index.

1685   ————. *The Legends of the Saints: An Introduction to Hagiog-
        raphy*, trans. V.M. Crawford. London: 1907. Re-issued with
        rev. bibliography and index from the 2nd ed. by R.J. Schoeck.
        Notre Dame, Ind.: University of Notre Dame Press, 1961.

        Still the best introduction to the nature and development of
        saints' legends. The author also discusses common themes and
        their relation to secular literature.

1686   Gerould, Gordon Hall. *Saints' Legends*. Boston: Houghton Mifflin,
        1916.

        The first full-length study of hagiography written in English
        and considering, e.g., Chaucer's use of saints' legends. For
        some indication of its many generalities and *lacunae*, however,
        see George L. Hamilton's review in *Modern Language Notes*, 33
        (1921), 230-42. See also Wolpers, item 1690.

1687   Grabmann, Martin. *Mittelalterliches Geistesleben: Abhandlungen
        zur Geschichte der Scholastik und Mystik*. 2 vols. Munich:
        Max Heuber, 1926; vol. 3, ed. Ludwig Ott, 1956.

        This work provides a general survey of medieval spiritualism
        with further bibliographical references to more specific studies
        in the field. Ott includes in vol. 3 a full bibliography of
        Grabmann's writings.

1688   Harthan, John. *Books of Hours and Their Owners*. London: Thames
        and Hudson, 1977.

        A general study of the background to personal prayer books
        and their contents, accompanied by over 90 facsimile pages from
        representative manuscripts. Each is analyzed in terms of its
        historical and artistic background, and bibliographical refer-
        ences are provided to relevant works. A select reading list on
        the subject is given on p. 185.

1689   Smalley, Beryl. *The Study of the Bible in the Middle Ages*.
        2nd ed. (from 1941). Oxford: Clarendon Press, 1952.

        A valuable and well-documented history of biblical interpre-
        tation and exegesis. Extensive indexes make this a useful source
        book of information.

1690   Wolpers, Theodor. *Die englische Heiligen Legende des Mittel-
        alters: Eine Formgeschichte des Legendenerzählens von der
        spätaniken lateinischen Tradition bis zur Mitte des 16.
        Jahrhunderts*. Tübingen: Niemeyer, 1964.

        A complete and thorough study of the genre as presented in
        Middle English texts, with an attempt to relate them to Conti-
        nental sources and parallels. The 10pp. bibliography provides
        a good basis for further English hagiographic study, although
        it appears out of date even for 1964. See also items 634-7,
        1686.

F. LITERARY AND LINGUISTIC

I have selected for this section only those literary histories of special interest for paleographers. The following may be considered useful guides to various aspects of literary manuscript studies insofar as they discuss manuscript resources or specific textual problems. Further references are listed in the bibliographies of Section I.B.4.

1691   Bischoff, B. *Mittelalterliche Studien: Ausgewählte Aufsätze zur Schriftkunde und Literaturgeschichte.* Stuttgart: Hiersemann, 1966.

This work consists of miscellaneous essays on paleography and literary history, most of them general in nature. Bibliography and illustrations are provided.

1692   Chaytor, H.J. *From Script to Print: An Introduction to Medieval Vernacular Literature.* Cambridge: Heffer, 1945.

A documented series of essays on the effect of medieval manuscript book production upon the nature and transmission of medieval poetry and prose, especially Old French. Chaytor sees a basic harmony between the physical forms of architecture and script and the main literary forms.

1693   Curtius, Ernst. *Europäische Literatur und lateinisches Mittelalter.* 8th ed. (from 1948). Bern: Francke, 1973; trans. Willard R. Trask, *European Literature and the Latin Middle Ages* (from the 1953 ed.) Princeton, N.J.: University Press, 1973.

A study of relations between Classical, Medieval Latin, and vernacular literatures. The focus is upon aspects of style and concepts of realism. The bibliographical notes are far-ranging in scope.

1694   Ghellink, Joseph de. *L'Essor de la littérature latine au XIIe siècle.* 2nd ed. Brussels: Desclée, De Brouwer, 1955.

A history of twelfth-century Latin literature, with some reference to the influences of Classical Latin literature. Good bibliographical notes plus extensive bibliography, pp. 19-32, are included.

1695   Graf, Georg. *Geschichte der christlichen arabischen Literatur.* 5 vols. Rome: Vatican, 1944-53.

An invaluable introduction to a little-documented subject. Vol. 5 contains a *Register* with bibliographies listed by genre.

1696   Kennedy, George. *A History of Rhetoric. I. The Art of Persuasion in Greece. II. The Art of Rhetoric in the Roman World 300 B.C.- A.D. 300.* 2 vols. Princeton, N.J.: University Press, 1972.

An account of rhetorical traditions; especially useful for the medievalist are those textual summaries of Cicero, Quintillian,

and some early Christian rhetoricians. Bibliography and indexes
are provided.

1697   Krumbacher, Karl. *Geschichte der byzantinischen Literatur von
       Justinian bis zum Ende des östromischen Reiches (527-1453)*.
       2nd ed. with A. Ehrhard and H. Gelzer. Munich: C.H. Beck,
       1897.

       A general history of Byzantine literature with good annota-
       tions and bibliography. It was originally issued as vol. 9 of
       von Müller's *Handbuch*; see item 1624 and next item.

1698   Manitius, Max. *Geschichte der lateinischen Literatur des Mittel-
       alters*. 3 vols. Munich: C.H. Beck, 1923-59.

       A work which is still the most comprehensive history of medi-
       eval Latin literature for the period from Justinian to the
       twelfth century. Illustrative extracts are drawn from individual
       authors, many from unpublished manuscripts. Originally issued
       in von Müller's *Handbuch* series; see item 1624.

1699   Mohrmann, Christine. *Liturgical Latin: Its Origin and Character*.
       Washington, D.C.: Catholic University of America Press, 1951.

       An introduction to the nature of liturgical Latin with some
       consideration of the current work of the Nijmegen school of
       medieval and patristic Latin studies. A good bibliography is
       provided, pp. 91-95. See also items 1609-10, 1614, 1618.

1700   ———. *Etudes sur le latin des chrétiens*. 3 vols. Rome:
       Edizioni di Storia e Letteratura, 1958-61.

       An expansion of item 1699 above, consisting of a series of
       lectures on many aspects of early Christian Latin. Each includes
       a bibliography.

1701   Murphy, James J. *Rhetoric in the Middle Ages: A History of
       Rhetorical Theory from Saint Augustine to the Renaissance*.
       Berkeley, Calif.: University of California Press, 1974.

       Although not as well organized as might be expected for a
       work on rhetoric, this book nevertheless contains much informa-
       tion on rhetoricians and their art, including reference to and
       extracts from many little-known or unpublished texts. A full
       index facilitates use. There are bibliographical notes, but for
       a systematic bibliography see item 100.

1702   Raby, F.J.E. *A History of Christian-Latin Poetry from Its
       Beginnings to the Close of the Middle Ages*. 2nd ed. (from
       1927). Oxford: Clarendon Press, 1953.

1703   ———. *A History of Secular-Latin Poetry in the Middle Ages*.
       2nd ed. (from 1934). Oxford: Clarendon Press, 1957.

       Both works provide general histories of major authors and
       works, illustrated with extracts after the model of Manitius,
       see item 1698. Extensive bibliographies are included.

1704   Strecker, Karl. *Introduction to Medieval Latin*, English trans.
        and revision by Robert B. Palmer. Berlin: Weidmann, 1957.

        A primer and introduction to the major documents in medieval
        Latin, mainly literary. The translator has brought up to date
        the bibliography of the original German edition (1928).

1705   Wilamowitz-Moellendorff, U. von. *Geschichte der Philologie*.
        3rd ed. Leipzig: Teubner, 1927/1959.

        An introduction to Classical studies and texts, especially
        Greek. The bibliography includes many of the author's publica-
        tions on specific aspects of the subject.

1706   White, T.H. *The Bestiary, A Book of Beasts, Being a Translation
        from a Latin Bestiary of the Twelfth Century*. London: Cape,
        1954/1960.

        In addition to the text, from Cambridge University Library
        MS. II.4.26, the work includes an extensive bibliography on
        the bestiary as a genre with a genealogical table of illustrated
        bestiaries and 120 individual illustrations.

                        G. SCIENTIFIC AND MEDICAL

1707   Boll, Franz. *Sphaera: Neue griechische Texte und Untersuchungen
        zur Geschichte der Sternbilder*. Leipzig: Teubner, 1903.

        A descriptive account of treatises on the spheres and their
        astronomical traditions. Extracts are included, many from un-
        published manuscripts. Extensive indexes make the work a valu-
        able encyclopedia for medieval astronomical/astrological refer-
        ences and bibliography.

1708   Bonser, Wilfrid. *The Medical Background of Anglo-Saxon England:
        A Study in History, Psychology, and Folklore*. Wellcome Histor-
        ical Medical Publications, n.s., 3. London: The Wellcome
        History of Medicine Library, 1963.

        A general account of the subject, but useful as a starting
        point for further scholarship in particular areas. Some bibliog-
        raphy is provided, as well as a general index.

1709   Bouché-Leclercq, Auguste. *L'Astrologie grecque*. Paris: E. Leroux,
        1899.

        The most complete and reliable history of early astrology
        to date. It includes 10pp. of bibliography and many illustra-
        tions and diagrams.

1710   Crombie, Alistair Cameron. *Medieval and Early Modern Science*.
        2nd ed. (from 1952). 2 vols. Garden City, N.Y.: Doubleday,
        1959.

Originally entitled *From Augustine to Galileo*, this work
provides a general history of early science from A.D. 400 to
1650. Some emphasis is given to Robert Grosseteste, see the
author's separate publications on that subject. An invaluable
bibliography is given, pp. 404-23.

1711   Grant, Edward. *Physical Science in the Middle Ages*. New York,
        N.Y.: Wiley, 1971.

        A brief history, with bibliography, of science from the early
        Middle Ages to the Renaissance. Texts which provide the docu-
        mentation are collected and published in the next item.

1712   ————, ed. *A Source Book in Medieval Science*. Cambridge, Mass.:
        Harvard University Press, 1974.

        This collection of texts includes representative treatises,
        e.g., Nicolas Oresme's *De Proportionibus Proportionum*. The
        bibliographies cite manuscripts, editions, and studies. For a
        general history of medieval science, see preceding item.

1713   Gundel, Wilhelm. *Sternglaube, Sternreligion und Sternorakeln*.
        4th ed. (from 1926). Leipzig/Berlin: Teubner, 1931/1966.

        A detailed and well-documented history of astrological beliefs.
        Gundel discusses, among many other topics, relationships be-
        tween astronomy and astrology. The appendix added by Hans Georg
        Gundel contains an extensive bibliography.

1714   ————, and Gundel, Hans Georg. *Astrologumena: die astrologische
        Literatur in der Antike und ihre Geschichte*. Sudhoffs Archiv,
        Suppl. 6. Wiesbaden: Steiner, 1966.

        A history of mainly Classical astrological literature. It
        provides much encyclopedic information in the detailed notes,
        and a full bibliography as well as an index.

1715   Gunther, R.W.T. *Early Science in Oxford*. 14 vols. Oxford: The
        Author, 1925-45.

1716   ————. *Early Science in Cambridge*. Oxford: The Author, 1937.

        Both studies provide general introductions to the early history
        of science as it centred around these universities. Several of
        the summaries of major writers, e.g., Roger Bacon, provide use-
        ful indications of textual traditions. The work is illustrated
        with some facsimiles.

1717   Haskins, Charles H. *Studies in the History of Mediaeval Science*.
        Historical Studies, Harvard. 2nd ed. (from 1924). Cambridge,
        Mass.: Harvard University Press, 1927.

        Originally a collection of articles; arranged in the 2nd ed.
        into four main topics: "The Science of the Arabs," "Transla-
        tions from the Greek," "The Court of Frederick II," and "Other
        Studies."

1718   Sarton, George. *The History of Science and the New Humanism*.
        Midland Books, MB 35. Bloomington, Ind.: Indiana University
        Press, 1962.

A reprint of the revised Colver lectures delivered at Brown University and the Elihu Root lectures at the Carnegie Institution, Washington (1930 and 1935 respectively). They give some account of fifteenth- and sixteenth-century scientific texts. Bibliographies are provided.

1719 ————. *Introduction to the History of Science.* 3 vols. in 5 pts. Baltimore, Md.: Williams and Wilkins, 1927-48; rev. ed. 1947-50.

The undisputed starting point for research on all topics in the history of science, whether writer, e.g., Hippocrates, or topic, e.g., phlebotomy. This compendious work is arranged chronologically and alphabetically, but the name and subject indexes facilitate use. Bibliographies of manuscripts and books are provided.

1720 Schefer, Charles, and Cordier, Henri, eds. *Recueil de voyages et de documents pour servir à l'histoire de la géographie depuis le XIIIe siècle jusqu'à la fin du XVIe siècle.* 24 vols. Paris: Leroux, 1882-1923.

A collection of documents on geography which cites editions and bibliographies. The maps and glossaries are particularly useful for more extended studies.

1721 Shumaker, Wayne. *The Occult Sciences in the Renaissance: A Study in Intellectual Patterns.* Berkeley, Calif.: University of California Press, 1972.

A general account of fifteenth- and sixteenth-century astrological and other writings. A limited amount of bibliography is useful for paleographers, especially that which pertains to editions of early (chiefly twelfth- to fourteenth-century) manuscripts.

1722 Société Française d'Editions Professionelles et Scientifiques. *Histoire de la médecine, de la pharmacie, de l'art dentaire, et de l'art vétérinaire,* ed. Jean Theodorides. Rev. ed. 8 vols. Paris: The Society, 1977.

A fundamental and indispensible reference work on these and related subjects. Full, individual bibliographies apply to each section.

1723 Sudhoff, Karl. *Beiträge zur Geschichte der Chirurgie im Mittelalter, graphische und textliche Untersuchungen im mittelalterlichen Handschriften.* 2 vols. Leipzig: J.A. Barth, 1914-18.

An introduction to the history of surgery, illustrated from many unpublished manuscripts and some *incunabula* with plates and transcriptions. Indexes of manuscripts conclude each volume.

1724 ————. *Ein Beitrag zur Geschichte der Anatomie im Mittelalter.* 1908.

Describes manuscripts containing treatises on anatomy, ninth to late fifteenth centuries. The author has published extensively on most aspects of medieval and Renaissance medicine, e.g., a bibliography of *incunabula* (1908), on syphilis (1925), plague treatises (1926), pediatric literature (1925), etc.

1725   Talbot, C.H. *Medicine in Medieval England*. London: Oldbourne, 1967.

A general history of practicing physicians and their documents, with a select bibliography.

1726   Thorndike, Lynn. *A History of Magic and Experimental Science During the First Thirteen Centuries of Our Era*. 8 vols. New York, N.Y.: Macmillan, 1923-58.

An encyclopedia, based upon biographical principles, of nearly every aspect of the subject of medieval magic and science. The work includes bibliographies and extensive indexes. See also item 574.

1727   Ussery, Huling. *Chaucer's Physician: Medicine and Literature in Fourteenth-Century England*. Tulane Studies in English, 19. New Orleans, La.: University of Tulane Press, 1971.

This work discusses Chaucer's knowledge of medicine as deduced from, primarily, his description of the physician in *The Canterbury Tales*. There are illustrations from and references to many contemporary medical documents, with a good bibliography.

1728   Weisheipl, James A. *A Development of Physicial Theory in the Middle Ages*. Ann Arbor, Mich.: University of Michigan Press, 1971.

A short history of "physics" with reference to Classical and medieval texts. A useful background article to this work is the author's "Classification of the Sciences in Mediaeval Thought," *Mediaeval Studies*, 27 (1965), 54-90.

See also items 167-79, 574, 687-708.

XIV. JOURNALS

Journals are placed as Section XIV in the *Handbook* in order to serve as a link between the earlier sections on paleography and codicology and the final section on textual criticism. The journals listed below should provide further bibliographical and secondary matter to manuscript study already in progress and extend it beyond the initial stages of location, identification, and preliminary study. With their specialized bibliographies and detailed studies they should also serve to prepare the way for textual editing, the subject of the final section of this Handbook.

Journals which issue periodical bibliographies on special subjects have been generally so indicated under the entry. Periodical bibliographies, which do not normally publish critical articles, have been listed under Section I within specialized fields of study; those relevant to Art History are cross-listed in Section IX; and those relevant to Music are cross-listed in Section X.

CONTENTS

A. BIBLIOGRAPHICAL MATERIALS

1729   *Abstracts of English Studies.* Boulder, Colo.: 1958–.

   Published annually, with summary reviews of articles; arranged
   alphabetically by journal; indexes in the *Supplements* for
   authors, subjects, and titles.

1730   *Bowker Series Bibliography: Sources of Serials.* 1st ed. New
   York, N.Y.: R.R. Bowker, 1977; *Supplements.*

   A general bibliography to serials, which lists about 4,500
   regular and 2,700 irregular periodicals and annuals; arrangement is by subject, with a title index; gives details of place
   of publication, whether articles and reviews, and circulation.
   See also item 1737.

1731   *British Humanities Index.* London: 1962–.

   A quarterly bibliography to over 380 periodicals in the arts;
   details as for preceding item.

1732   *British Union Catalogue of Periodicals.* London: 1964–.

   A quarterly bibliography for new periodicals, post-1960.

1733   *Index to Religious Periodical Literature.* Chicago, Ill.: 1949–.

   Published every two years; cumulative index, vol. 12 (1975-
   76); list of journals, subject index, author index with abstracts, and book review index.

1734   *International Guide to Classical Studies: A Continuous Index
   to Classical Studies.* Darien, Conn.: 1960–.

   An index to articles in Classical studies, published annually
   by the American Bibliographic Service; lists authors, articles
   (non-critical), with interim subject indexes.

1735   *International Index to Periodicals, A Guide to Periodical
   Literature in the Social Sciences and Humanities.* New York,
   N.Y.: H.W. Wilson, 1916–.

   An author/subject index to an international group of periodicals; issued at intervals.

1736   *Internationale Bibliographie der Zeitschriftenliteratur aus
   allen Gebieten des Wissens.* Osnabrück: Felix Dietrich, 1965–.

   An international index to periodical literature, with focus
   upon German resources; arrangement is by subject, with author
   indexes.

1737   *Irregular Serials and Annuals: An International Directory: A*
        Classified Guide to Current Foreign and Domestic Serials,
        Excepting Periodicals Issued More Frequently Than Once a
        Year. 5th ed. New York, N.Y.: R.R. Bowker, 1978-79.

        A directory of international publications, which includes
        irregular periodicals, proceedings, transactions, handbooks,
        and others; classification is by subject with cross-indexing
        for titles; supplemented by Bowker, item 1730.

1738   *MLA Abstracts*. New York, N.Y.: 1971-.

        Issued by the Modern Language Association as a three-volume
        annual; classified by chronological periods; gives summary
        reviews of current articles on English language and literature
        in publications for the preceding year, beginning with 1971
        (for 1970).

1739   Poole, William Frederick. *Poole's Index to Periodical Litera-*
        ture, 1802-1881. New York, N.Y.: Peter Smith, 1938.

        A subject index to 90 British periodicals for this period,
        arranged by catchword; superseded in part by *The Wellesley*
        Index to Victorian Periodicals, 1824-1900, ed. Walter E. Hough-
        ton (Toronto: University Press, 1966-); both periodicals list
        many paleographical and textual items, including some early
        lists of manuscripts in British libraries.

1740   *Serials Review*. Ann Arbor, Mich.: University of Michigan Press,
        1975-.

        A valuable quarterly review of serials such as indexes, ab-
        stracts, bibliographies, and other publications; indexes refer
        to reviews of serials in other publications.

1741   *Social Sciences and Humanities Index* (formerly *International*
        Index). New York, N.Y.: H.W. Wilson: 1907-15; 1974-.

        A guide to periodical literature; annual with quarterly issues
        and a cumulative index; arrangement is by author/subject; now
        superseded by the *Humanities Index* (New York: Wilson, 1974-),
        issued quarterly with annual cumulations.

1742   *Standard Periodical Directory*. New York, N.Y.: Oxbridge Communi-
        cations, 1964-.

        A biannual directory to periodicals published in the United
        States and Canada, excluding newspapers; arrangement is by sub-
        ject, then alphabetical by title, with cross-indexing.

1743   *Ulrich's International Periodicals Directory: A Classified*
        Guide to Current Periodicals, Foreign and Domestic. 18th ed.
        New York, N.Y.: R.R. Bowker, 1979-80.

        A directory to approximately 55,000 periodicals; arrangement
        is by main periodical entries, new periodicals (1971-), periodi-
        cals no longer published, and a title-subject index; the main
        list of periodicals is arranged by subject; includes a useful
        bibliography of Indexing and Abstracting periodicals.

1744   Vesenyi, Paul E. *An Introduction to Periodical Bibliography*.
        Ann Arbor, Mich.: Pierian Press, 1974.

        An annotated guide to periodical indexes, abstracts, union
        lists, directories, and miscellaneous bibliographies. The second
        part, devoted to periodical bibliographies, focuses upon the
        humanities and social sciences; arrangement is alphabetical by
        title; indexes are in the appendices and include subject, title,
        and author.

1745   ————. *European Periodical Literature in the Social Sciences
        and Humanities*. Metuchen, N.J.: The Scarecrow Press, 1969.

        A bibliography listing indexes and abstracts, some biographies,
        directories, and union lists; occasional descriptive comments
        are provided.

See also items 1-12, 16-18.

B. JOURNALS

1746   *Acta Musicologica*. Kassel: 1928-.

        Issued twice yearly by the International Music Society, with
        a cumulative index for vols. 1-25; articles, reviews, bibliog-
        raphy.

1747   *Allegorica*. Arlington, Tex.: 1976-.

        Issued twice yearly by the English Department, University of
        Texas at Arlington; publishes mainly literal translations for
        medieval and Renaissance literature and documents, with some
        articles on interdisciplinary topics and reviews.

1748   *American Archivist*. Chicago, Ill.: 1938-.

        Published quarterly by the Society of American Archivists,
        this review gives an annual survey of writings on archives and
        manuscripts; cumulative index, 1938-67.

1749   *Analecta Bollandiana*. Brussels: 1882-.

        Published by the Bollandist Institute and devoted primarily
        to the study of hagiographical manuscripts and texts, especially
        in context with the *Acta Sanctorum*; also issues a *Bulletin des
        Publications Hagiographiques* and a *Table Generale des Articles
        Publiés*, 1962-.

1750   *Anglia: Zeitschrift für englische Philologie*. Halle/Tübingen:
        1878-1955; 1949-.

        A quarterly review for English language and literature, with
        some articles and reviews on medieval texts and manuscripts.

1751   *Anglo-Saxon England*. Cambridge: 1972-.

A review issued annually with many articles on paleographical and textual matters relevant to Old English and Medieval Latin; publishes an annual bibliography which includes a classified section on Palaeography, Diplomatics, and Illumination.

1752   *Annales Economies Sociétés Civilisations.* Paris: CNRS, 1929-.

A twice-yearly review with articles (summaries provided in English) and reviews on early economic history; a books received list.

1753   *Annales Musicologiques: Moyen Âge et Renaissance.* Paris: 1953-.

Published annually by the Société de Musiques d'Autrefois, and contains articles and reviews on early music.

1754   *Annali dell'Istituto e Museo di Storia della Scienza di Firenze.* Florence: 1975-.

A twice-yearly review with articles and book reviews on the history of science to the eighteenth-century; a books received list.

1755   *Annuale Mediaevale.* Pittsburg, Pa.: 1960-.

An annual review published by Duquesne University on all medieval topics; bibliography, articles, book reviews.

1756   *Antike Zeitschrift für Kunst und Kultur des klassische Altertums.* Berlin: 1925-.

A quarterly review for Classical art, history, and literature; articles, book reviews.

1757   *Archiv für das Studium der neueren Sprachen und Literaturen. Herrig's Archiv.* Braunschweig: 1846-; 1952-.

A quarterly review which includes many articles, reviews, and periodical bibliographies on medieval vernacular texts and studies.

1758   *Archiv für Diplomatik, Schriftgeschichte, Siegel- und Wappenkunde.* Münster/Cologne: 1955-.

A quarterly review devoted to diplomatics and archives, especially German; articles, book reviews, bibliography.

1759   *Archiv für Geschichte der Philosophie.* Berlin/New York, N.Y.: 1918-.

Although this quarterly review covers all periods, many articles, reviews, and bibliographical references are relevant to early philosophers, philosophical questions, and their manuscript traditions.

1760   *Archiv für Geschichte des Buchwesens.* Frankfurt-am-Main: 1956-.

A quarterly review with periodical bibliography for library science; many items refer to manuscript collections and their preservation.

1761 *Archiv für katholisches Kirchenrecht.* Mainz: 1857–.

A twice-yearly review with articles and book reviews on the history of the Church; each volume concludes with a classified bibliography (*Literaturverzeichnis*).

1762 *Archiv für Kulturgeschichte.* Berlin/Cologne: 1903–.

A quarterly review of general cultural history; some articles are on textual history or the background to textual traditions; bibliographies.

1763 *Archiv für Urkundenforschung.* Leipzig: 1907–44.

A quarterly review providing articles, reviews, and bibliography on historical and archival topics.

1764 *Archives.* London: 1949–.

The journal of the British Records Association; provides an annual international list of archive societies and their publications; includes a books received list; the Association also publishes *Archives and the User* Series and occasional *Exhibition Catalogues*.

1765 *Archives et Bibliothèques.* Paris: 1935–.

A quarterly review containing periodical bibliographies on archives and bibliography.

1766 *Archives et Bibliotheẑues de Belgique.* Brussels: 1925–.

A quarterly review published by the Association des Conservateurs d'Archives de Bibliothèques et de Musées; a cumulative index has appeared for vols. 1–25.

1767 *Archives Internationales d'Histoire des Sciences.* Wiesbaden: 1919–; 1972–.

Published twice yearly, this review offers articles, reviews, and indexes on the early history of science.

1768 *Archivio Paleografico Italiano.* Rome: 1882–.

Published by the Istituto di Paleografia, which also issues *Bulletins*, 1955–.

1769 *Archivio Storico Italiano.* Florence: 1841–; 1842–1966.

A review for Italian historical documents and archives; an index for volumes 1842–1941 has been edited by E. Rossi, 1945.

1770 *Archivium.* Paris: 1951–.

An international review, published annually by UNESCO and the Conseil International des Archives; it includes an international bibliography, arranged by country.

1771 *Art Bulletin.* New York, N.Y.: 1913–.

A quarterly review for art history, especially Western, with articles and book reviews; vols. 1–21 indexed, 1950; published by the College Art Association of America.

1772   *Beiträge zur Geschichte der Deutschen Sprache und Literatur.*
       Halle: 1874–1940; 1942; 1944–54; Tübingen, 1955–.

       A twice-yearly review with articles and book reviews on German
       language and literature, some early German textual criticism;
       bibliography.

1773   *Beiträge zur Geschichte der Philosophie und Theologie des
       Mittelalters.* Münster: 1891–.

       A twice-yearly review for medieval philosophy and theology;
       articles, reviews, bibliography.

1774   *Biblica.* Rome: 1920–.

       Devoted to Biblical studies, this quarterly journal has also
       issued an annual bibliography for Old and New Testament and
       Patristic studies since 1968; a cumulative index appears approxi-
       mately every 20 years.

1775   *Biblical Research.* Chicago, Ill.: 1955–.

       A review with articles and book reviews on all aspects of
       Biblical studies and work in progress; periodical bibliographies.

1776   *Bibliofilia, Rivista di Storia del Libro e delle Arti Grafiche.*
       Florence: 1899–; *Supplements.*

       Publishes quarterly articles and bibliography on general
       bibliographical matters, manuscripts, and book decoration.

1777   *Bibliographie Papyrologique.* Brussels, 1936–.

       A quarterly review devoted to articles and bibliography on
       papyrology; published by the Fondation Egyptologique Reine
       Elizabeth.

1778   *Bibliotheca dell'Archivum Romanicum.* Geneva: 1921–.

       A quarterly review, which publishes on bibliographical studies,
       library collections, and textual matters; issued by the Insti-
       tuto Nicolas Antonio.

1779   *Bibliothèque de l'Ecole des Chartes.* Paris: 1838–.

       An important review for paleographical and textual studies
       and bibliography; published twice yearly, with a critical bib-
       liography classified by history, art, archives, diplomatics,
       and manuscripts; periodical indexes.

1780   *Bibliothèque d'Humanisme et Renaissance: Travaux et Documents.*
       Geneva: 1941–.

       A quarterly review published by the Association d'Humanisme
       et Renaissance; articles, reviews, bibliography.

1781   *Bodleian Library Record.* Oxford: 1938–.

       Published by the Bodleian Library, Oxford, once or twice per
       year; articles and notes are mainly but not exclusively on the
       library's books, manuscripts, and recent acquisitions; super-
       sedes the *Bodleian Quarterly Record*, 1914–38.

1782   *Borthwick Institute Bulletin.* Peasholme Green, York: 1977-.

An annual bulletin published by the Borthwick Institute of
Historical Research, University of York; reports on the activities of the Institute, local library holdings, and publications.

1783   *British Journal for the History of Science.* Leeds: 1962-.

A quarterly review on the history of science and mathematics;
articles, reviews, and bibliography; incorporates the *Bulletin*
of the British Society for the History of Science.

Bullétin d'Ancienne Littérature Chrétienne Latine.

See item 1864.

Bullétin d'Histoire Bénédictine.

See item 1875.

Bullétin de l'Histoire Monastique en France.

See item 1875.

1784   *Bullétin de Théologie Ancienne et Médiévale.* Brussels: 1964-.

Contains summary reviews of international books and articles
on ancient and medieval theology; arrangement is by month and
year; issued annually.

1785   *Bulletin of the American Society of Papyrologists.* Urbana, Ill.:
        1963-.

A twice-yearly review with articles, reviews, and bibliography on Classical and Byzantine studies.

1786   *Bulletin of the History of Medicine.* Baltimore, Md.: 1933-.

A quarterly review published by the American Association for
the History of Medicine, which continues the *Bulletin* of the
Institute for the History of Medicine; *Index to Volumes 1-20,
21-36*, prepared by G. Miller and L. Temkin. 2 vols., 1950-1966.

1787   *Bulletin of the Institute of Historical Research.* London:
        1923-.

A twice-yearly review with articles and reviews on medieval
and modern history and early manuscripts; reports, at infre-
quent intervals, on archival collections and methodology, with
summaries of theses produced at the Institute; some references
to manuscript sales.

1788   *Bulletin of the John Rylands Library.* Manchester: 1903-.

A review published by the Library twice yearly with articles
on rare manuscripts and books.

1789   *Bulletino dell'Archivio Paleografico Italiano.* Perugia/Rome:
        1908-; 1955-.

Published by the Instituto di Paleografia dell Universita di
Roma, on all aspects of Italian archivicology.

1790   *Burlington Magazine*. London: 1903–.

       Issued monthly, with many articles on art history and manu-
       script illumination; index for vols. 1-104, 1962.

1791   *Byzantine Studies*. Tempe, Ariz.: 1974–.

       Published two to four times per year, a review with articles
       and book reviews on all aspects of Byzantine studies; cumula-
       tive indexes.

1792   *Byzantinische Zeitschrift*. Leipzig/Munich: 1892-1913; 1924-43;
       1948–.

       A twice-yearly review with articles and reviews; the classi-
       fied bibliography lists items on Byzantine chronology, geog-
       raphy, literature, history, manuscripts, and other related
       subjects; a cumulative index for vols. 1-12.

1793   *Byzantion. International Journal of Byzantine Studies*. Paris/
       Brussels: 1924–.

       A quarterly review, with book reviews and bibliography on
       all aspects of Byzantine studies.

1794   *Cahiers de Civilisation Médiévale (Xe-XIIe Siècles)*. Poitiers:
       1958–.

       A quarterly review published by the Centre d'Etudes Superieures
       de Civilisation Médiévale; articles, reviews on architecture,
       literature, and history, with a *Chronique* consisting of a
       critical review of recent scholarship in these areas.

1795   *Cambridge Bibliographical Society Transactions*. Cambridge:
       1950–.

       A review appearing approximately every three years, with
       articles, bibliographical notes, and publication lists on all
       aspects of paleography and codicology, both early and modern;
       most items have some reference to Cambridge.

       Chronique Bibliographique. See item 1875.

1796   *Chronique d'Egypte*. Brussels: 1925–.

       A review primarily for papyrologists, published by the Musée
       Royaux d'Art et d'Histoire, Fondation Egyptologique Reine Eliza-
       beth.

1797   *Classica et Mediaevalia*. Copenhagen: 1938–.

       A twice-yearly Danish review for philology and history, pub-
       lished for the Societas Danica Indagationis Antiquitatis et
       Mediiaevi; articles and reviews, with a list of books received
       in each issue.

1798   *Classical Philology*. Chicago, Ill.: 1906–.

       A quarterly review with articles and book reviews on all
       aspects of the subject, including some items on textual criti-
       cism; bibliographies, cumulative indexes.

1799 *Classical Quarterly*. London: 1907-; 1951-.

A review published twice yearly by the Classical Association and Oxford and Cambridge Philological Societies; articles and reviews on Greek and Latin literature, history, philosophy, archaeology, and paleography; combined with next item.

1800 *Classical Review*. London: 1887-.

Published in conjunction with the preceding item, approximately three times per year; shorter articles, reviews, notices, and lists of new books on all aspects of Classical studies.

1801 *Clio. An Interdisciplinary Journal of Literature, History, and Philosophical History*. Fort Wayne, Ind.: 1971-.

A quarterly review, with articles, book reviews, and cumulative indexes.

1802 *Clio Medica*. Oxford: 1965-.

Published quarterly in tabloid format by the International Academy of the History of Medicine; articles, book reviews, and indexes.

1803 *Codices Manuscripti: Zeitschrift für Handschriftkunde*. Vienna: 1974-.

A quarterly review, with articles and book reviews on paleography and codicology.

Codicologica. See item 717.

1804 *Computers and Medieval Data Processing*. Montreal: 1971-.

Published twice yearly by the University of Montreal, Institut d'Etudes Médiévales; reviews and bibliography.

1805 *Computers and the Humanities*. New York, N.Y.: 1965-.

A bi-monthly review with reviews, notes, and bibliography, published by New York City University, Queen's College, Flushing, N.Y.

1806 *Deutsches Archiv für Erforschung des Mittelalters*. Weimar: 1819-74; 1876-85; Cologne: 1937-44; 1950-.

A quarterly review published by *Monumenta Germania Historia*, with some emphasis upon medieval history, especially with reference to texts in the *MGH* series; full bibliography, classified, in each issue.

1807 *Economic History Review*. London: 1927-; Supplements, 1953-.

A quarterly review published by the Economic History Society, with reviews and bibliography.

1808 *Englische Studien*. Leipzig and Heilbronn: 1877-1939.

A review for English language and letters, with many articles on textual criticism; an *Index* was published for 1877-98 (1902) and 1899-1917 (1924).

1809   *English Historical Review.* London: 1886-.

A quarterly review for world history, especially medieval; articles, book reviews, bibliography.

1810   *English Studies. A Journal of English Letters and Philology.* Amsterdam: 1919-.

A quarterly review for English literature and language, with some articles and reviews on medieval texts and manuscripts.

1811   *Ephemerides Liturgicae.* Rome: 1887-1936; 1948-.

Published bi-monthly, this review includes articles and reviews on all aspects of the liturgy, Eastern and Western; bibliography.

1812   *Glotta: Zeitschrift für griechische und lateinische Sprache.* Göttingen: 1909-43; 1948-.

Issued in two double numbers per year; articles and reviews on Classical languages and literature, bibliography.

1813   *Gnomon: Kritische Zeitschrift für die gesamte klassische Altertumswissenschaft.* Berlin: 1925-44; 1949-.

A monthly review for Classical studies, which provides periodical lists of new publications in paleography and Classical studies; these are generally more current than the bibliography in *L'Année Philologique.*

1814   *Greek, Roman, and Byzantine Studies.* Durham, N.C.: 1957-.

A quarterly review published by Duke University on all aspects of Classical and Byzantine studies, with an annual index.

1815   *Hispania Sacra.* Madrid: 1966-.

A quarterly review published by the Consejo Superior de Investigaciones Cientificas; articles, reviews, and bibliography on the religious history of Spain.

1816   *Historische Zeitschrift.* Munich: 1859-1943; 1949-; *Sonderhefte.* 1962-.

A bi-monthly review with articles and reviews on all historical periods; bibliographies and indexes.

1817   *Historisches Jahrbuch.* Munich/Bonn: 1880-1941; 1949-.

A review which publishes articles and reviews mainly on the history of the church in Germany.

1818   *Historisk Tidskrift.* Stockholm: 1870-.

A quarterly review for mainly Scandinavian history and documents; articles, book reviews, and bibliography.

1819   *Huntington Library Quarterly.* San Marino, Calif.: 1937-.

A review with some emphasis upon the manuscripts and special collections of the Library, but also with articles and book reviews on general bibliographical, medieval, and Renaissance topics; supersedes the *Huntington Library Bulletin*.

1820 *Indian Archives*. New Delhi: 1947–.

A quarterly review with articles, book reviews, and bibliography for mainly Indian documents; some items include the care and preservation of archival materials in general.

1821 *Irish Archives Bulletin*. Dublin: 1971–.

A periodic bulletin with articles on archival matters, mainly Irish, published by the Irish Society for Archives.

1822 *Isis*. Washington, D.C.: 1913–.

A quarterly review published by the History of Science Society, with articles and reviews on all areas; annual critical bibliographies.

1823 *Journal of Ecclesiastical History*. London: 1966–.

A quarterly review for Church and liturgical history, with articles and book reviews.

1824 *Journal of Egyptian Archaeology*. London: 1914–.

An annual journal published by the Egypt Exploration Society, with reviews and bibliography; some include papyrus studies.

1825 *Journal of Hellenic Studies*. London: 1880–.

An annual review for Greek language and literature and history; some articles and reviews cover Byzantine studies; bibliography; published by the Society for the Promotion of Hellenic Studies.

1826 *Journal of Juristic Papyrology*. Warsaw: 1946–; New York, N.Y.: 1948–.

Published (in New York) by the Polish Institute of Arts and Sciences in America; includes articles, reviews, and bibliography on early legal documents.

1827 *Journal of Medieval History*. Amsterdam: 1974–.

A quarterly review with articles and announcements of published works, and lists of new books in the field of medieval European history.

1828 *Journal of the History of Medicine and Allied Sciences*. New Haven, Conn.: 1946–.

A quarterly review for all aspects of the history of the medical sciences; articles, book reviews, bibliography; an *Index* for vols. 1-30 (1946-75) has been compiled by Manfred Wasserman and Carol Clausen.

1829 *Journal of the History of Philosophy*. Claremont, Calif.: 1963–.

A quarterly review for the history of philosophy, with articles, book reviews, and indexes.

1830   *Journal of the Society of Archivists*. London: 1955–.

A quarterly review with articles and notes on archives and their care and preservation; lists recent publication and includes the *Chronicle* of the Society.

1831   *Journal of the Warburg and Courtauld Institutes*. London: 1937–.

A quarterly journal devoted to art history, iconographical studies, and textual traditions; articles, reviews, bibliography.

1832   *Library*. London: 1889–.

A quarterly journal for library and bibliographical studies, which supersedes *Library Chronicle*, 1884–88; monographic articles, book reviews on aspects of descriptive and historical bibliography; published by the *Bibliographical Society*.

1833   *Library Association Record*. London: 1899–.

Published by the Library Association monthly, this review for library science and bibliography also issues subject indexes and pamphlets, proceedings, and miscellaneous papers.

1834   *Libri et Documenti*. Milan: 1977–.

A quarterly review with articles, notes and lists of publications mainly on local documents and collections.

1835   *Manuscripta*. St. Louis, Mo.: 1957–.

A quarterly review for paleographers and codicologists, with periodic bibliographies on related publications; also publishes news of the Vatican Library microfilm collection (see item 538) and abstracts of papers presented at the St. Louis conferences on manuscript studies.

1836   *Mediaeval Studies*. Toronto: 1939–.

Published by the Pontifical Institute of Mediaeval Studies, this journal contains articles on all aspects of medieval studies, especially philosophical and historical; cumulative indexes are issued approximately every four years.

1837   *Mediaevalia: A Journal of Medieval Studies*. Binghamton, N.Y.: 1976–.

A review with an interdisciplinary policy, which publishes articles and reviews on medieval literature, music, and history.

1838   *Medical History*. London: 1957–.

A quarterly review published by the Wellcome Institute of the History of Medicine; articles, book reviews, and bibliographies.

1839   *Medievalia et Humanistica. An American Journal for the Middle Ages and Renaissance*. Boulder, Colo.: 1943–.

A quarterly review with articles, reviews, and bibliography on all aspects of medieval and Renaissance studies; issues

periodic bibliographies on "Recent Works for Palaeographers,"
see especially vols. 2 (1971) and 5 (1974).

1840   *Medium Aevum*. Oxford: 1932-.

Published three times per year by the Society for the Study
of Mediaeval Languages and Literature, with articles mainly on
textual criticism rather than paleographical matters; each
issue includes a books received list.

1841   *Medizinhistorisches Journal*. Hildesheim: 1966-.

Published irregularly by the Akademie der Wissenschaften und
der Literatur on the history of medicine; articles, reviews,
bibliography.

1842   *Microform Review*. Weston, Conn.: 1972-.

A quarterly review containing articles, reviews, and news
of microform projects, including photocopying of manuscript
collections.

1843   *Modern Language Quarterly*. Seattle, Wash.: 1940-.

A review on all aspects of medieval and modern Western
languages, with current bibliographies of Arthurian literature
and related manuscript studies.

1844   *Modern Language Review*. London/Cambridge: 1905-.

A quarterly review published by the Modern Humanities Research
Association; supersedes the *Modern Language Quarterly*, London:
1897-1904. For studies in modern and medieval languages, with
articles, book reviews, and bibliographies.

1845   *Modern Philology*. Chicago, Ill.: 1903-.

A quarterly journal devoted to medieval and modern literature,
with some articles on textual criticism; reviews, bibliographies.

1846   *Mosaic*. Winnipeg: 1967-.

A quarterly journal for comparative literature; vol. 8, 1975,
featured articles on textual criticism.

1847   *Moyen Âge*. Paris: 1888-.

A quarterly review for medieval historical and philological
studies, especially in France and Belgium; articles, reviews,
a books received list, and bibliography; indexes.

1848   *Musical Quarterly*. New York, N.Y.: 1915-.

A review with articles and book reviews on all aspects of
music, including paleography and the interpretation of medieval
music.

1849   *Neuphilologische Mitteilungen*. Helsinki: 1899-.

A quarterly review containing articles on medieval language
and literature; an annual bibliography of medieval scholarship,

arranged by field of study, is compiled by different contributors.

1850   *Neophilologus*. Amsterdam/Groningen/The Hague: 1916-.

A quarterly review devoted to linguistic and literary subjects in medieval and modern literature.

1851   *Nuovi Studi Medievali*. Rome: 1928-52; 1960-.

A quarterly review for all aspects of medieval historical, literary, and philosophical studies; supersedes *Studi Medievali*, 1904-13.

1852   *Onomastica*. Lyons/Paris: 1947-48; *Revue Internationale d'Onomastique*, 1948-.

A quarterly, international journal for onomastic studies, especially for French place and family names; articles, book reviews, bibliography.

1853   *Paleographia Latina*. Oxford: 1922-26.

This short-lived journal of only six issues was edited by W.M. Lindsay and contains a number of invaluable articles on paleography and codicology.

1854   *Past and Present: A Journal of Historical Studies*. London: 1952-.

A quarterly review with articles and book reviews on historical studies, especially Byzantine; periodical bibliography.

1855   *Patristic Studies*. Washington, D.C.: 1922-.

Published quarterly by the Catholic University of America and includes periodical bibliographies on all aspects of Patristic studies; articles and book reviews.

1856   *Philologus: Zeitschrift für das klassiche Altertum*. Stolberg: 1846-1944; 1948; 1954-.

A quarterly review for Classical philology, with some articles, book reviews, and bibliography for manuscript studies and textual criticism.

1857   *PMLA*. Baltimore, Md.: 1888-; 1889-.

A quarterly journal issued by the Modern Language Association of America; publishes an *International Bibliography*, 1921-, see item 6.

1858   *Proof*. Columbia, S.C.: 1971-.

A quarterly journal for textual criticism; bibliographies.

1859   *Rassegnà degli Archivi di Stato*. Rome: 1940-.

A quarterly review with articles and book reviews on Italian archives and legislation; lists new publications, inventories various collections.

1860   *Recherches de Science Religieuse.* Paris: 1912-.

A quarterly review for Old and New Testament studies, Patrology, and liturgy; articles, reviews, books received lists.

1861   *Recherches de Théologie Ancienne et Médiévale.* Louvain: 1929-40; 1946-.

A review for ancient and medieval theology, published with bibliographies by the Benedictine Abbey of Mont-Cesar, Belgium.

1862   *Review of English Studies.* London/Oxford: 1925-50; 1950-.

A quarterly review for literary history and criticism; articles, reviews, and a summary of periodical literature in each issue.

1863   *Revue Belge de Philologie et d'Histoire.* Brussels: 1922-.

A quarterly review published by the Société pour les Progres des Etudes Philologiques et Historiques, with some articles and reviews on paleographical matters; bibliography.

1864   *Revue Bénédictine.* Maredsous: 1884-.

A journal devoted to historical, theological, philosophical, and literary matters which concern the Benedictine order; general indexes have been published in 1905, 1945, and 1971; published as supplements are the *Bulletin D'Ancienne Littérature Chrétienne Latine*, 1921-.

1865   *Revue des Etudes Grecques.* Paris: 1888-.

Published by the Association pour l'Encouragement des Etudes Grecques en France; supersedes the earlier *Annuaire*.

1866   *Revue des Etudes Latines.* Paris: 1923-.

A quarterly review, published by the Société des Etudes Latines, and containing many articles on medieval manuscripts.

1867   *Revue des Sciences Philosophiques et Théologiques.* Paris: CNRS, 1916-.

A quarterly review on the history of philosophy and theology; articles, reviews, and valuable summaries of current journals in the field.

1868   *Revue d'Histoire de l'Eglise de France.* Paris: 1910-.

A quarterly review for the history of the Church in France, appearing twice yearly; articles, book reviews, and bibliographies which focus upon Church archives and historical documentation.

1869   *Revue d'Histoire des Textes.* Paris: 1971-.

Published by the Institute de Recherche et d'Histoire des Textes, originally their *Bulletin*, 1953-68; contains articles and bibliography on paleography and textual criticism.

1870   *Revue d'Histoire Diplomatique.* Paris: 1887–.

A journal for diplomatics and archivicology with special emphasis upon regional resources in France.

1871   *Revue d'Histoire Ecclésiastique de Louvain.* Louvain: 1900–.

A quarterly journal with articles and book reviews on ecclesiastical history in Western Europe; the annual bibliographies are of considerable scope and accuracy; cumulative indexes are issued periodically.

1872   *Revue du Moyen Âge Latin, Etudes, Textes, Chronique, Bibliographie.* Lyons/Strasbourg: 1945–.

A quarterly review of articles, book reviews, and bibliography for Medieval Latin.

1873   *Revue Historique.* Paris: 1876–.

A journal providing articles on the general subject of history and its sources, especially for France; included are reviews of other periodicals; separate *Bulletins* are issued from time to time on special subjects.

1874   *Revue Historique de Droit Français et Etranger.* Paris: 1855–.

A journal devoted to the history of law and legal archives, especially for the medieval period.

1875   *Revue Mabillon.* Paris/Ligugé: 1905–.

Focusing on monastic history, especially for France, this journal publishes the *Bulletin de l'Histoire Monastique en France* as a Supplement, 1936-66, as well as the *Bulletin d'Histoire Bénédictine*, 1907–. The *Chronique Bibliographique* formed part of the *Revue Mabillon*, 1905-26, then appeared separately 1927-30 and 1931-35; a general index to all volumes is in *Revue Mabillon*, 233-9 (1968-70).

1876   *Römanische Quartal Schrift für christliche Altertumskunde und Kirchengeschichte.* Freiburg: 1905–.

A twice-yearly review with articles and book reviews on Church history and archives; each issue includes a books received list.

1877   *Scriptorium.* Antwerp/Brussels: 1946–.

An international review devoted to manuscript studies exclusively; semi-annual, and each number contains the *Bulletin Codiocologique*, a bibliography of articles and books on the study of texts, manuscripts, illumination, etc.; arrangement within the bibliography is alphabetical by author and some annotation is provided. A subject-index appears in the last number of each annual volume. Periodical bibliographies are provided for individual countries.

1878   *Speculum.* Cambridge, Mass.: 1934–.

A journal published quarterly by the Mediaeval Academy of America; this publication also issues *Bibliographies of Period-*

ical Literature, 1934-58, with the title changed to *Bibliography of American Periodicals*, 1959-.

1879   *Studia et Documenta Historiae et Iuris*. Rome: 1935-.

A twice-yearly review with articles and documents on the history of law, especially Roman. It also includes reviews and bibliographies.

1880   *Studia Monastica*. Barcelona: 1958-.

A twice-yearly review for the history of monasticism, especially Benedictine, published by the Abbey of Montserrat. Articles and book reviews are included, with each vol. indexed.

1881   *Studia Neophilologica: A Journal of Germanic and Romance Philology*. Stockholm: 1928-.

A twice-yearly review with articles, book reviews, and a cumulative index for vols. 1-30.

1882   *Studia Papyrologica*. Rome: 1962-.

An annual review with international articles and book reviews on papyrological studies. It is published by the Pontifical Biblical Institute, with regular indexes.

1883   *Studia Patristica*. Berlin: 1955-.

Issued every four years to publish the proceedings of the International Conference on Patristic Studies.

1884   *Studi e Problemi di Critica Testuale*. Bologna: 1970-.

A twice-yearly review for textual studies, with articles and reviews.

1885   *Studies in Early English History*. Leicester: 1960-.

An irregular review with articles and reviews on the early history of Great Britain.

1886   *Studies in Philology*. Chapel Hill, N.C.: 1906-.

Originally issued quarterly in 1906-17 by the University of North Carolina Philology Club, this publication now includes articles and reviews on many philological topics, with a periodical Renaissance bibliography.

1887   *Studies in the Age of Chaucer*. Norman, Okla.: 1979-.

A quarterly review published by the New Chaucer Society. It contains articles, notes, and reviews, mainly on literary topics, but some items on textual and bibliographical matters are included occasionally. See item 118.

1888   *Studi Medievali*. Torino/Spoleto: 1903-13; *Nuovi Studi Medievali*, 1923-27; *Studi Medievali*, *N.S.*, 1928-42.

An annual review for all aspects of medieval studies. It includes articles, book reviews, texts, and, in the *Bullettino Bibliografico*, recent publications.

1889   *Studi Storici*. Rome: 1959-.

A twice-yearly review for ancient and modern history with emphasis upon economic history. It includes articles, reviews, books received, and an index; a cumulative index appears every 10 years.

1890   *Symposium: A Journal Devoted to Modern Foreign Languages and Literatures*. Syracuse, N.Y.: 1946-.

A quarterly review with international articles and reviews, some on medieval literary and textual topics; indexes.

1891   *Tijdschrift voor filosofie*. Louvain: 1938-.

A quarterly review with articles and reviews primarily on more recent philosophical studies, but the extensive classified bibliography in each issue is of wider application.

1892   *Traditio: Studies in Ancient and Mediaeval History, Thought, and Religion*. New York, N.Y.: 1942-.

Published annually by Fordham University, this review contains résumés of the year's scholarship for such disciplines as Patristic studies and canon law. It offers articles, reviews, and bibliographies.

1893   *Vigiliae Christianae: A Review of Early Christian Life and Language*. Amsterdam: 1947-.

A quarterly review with articles and reviews on all aspects of early Christian life and thought, archaeology, and epigraphy. It includes a books received list.

1894   *Vivarium: An International Journal for the Philosophical and Intellectual Life of the Middle Ages and Renaissance*. Leiden: 1962-.

A twice-yearly publication with articles and reviews; indexed.

1895   *Zeitschrift für Bibliothekswesen und Bibliographie*. Frankfurt-am-Main: 1954-.

A journal providing articles and bibliography on library science, paleography, and codicology; supersedes *Nachrichten für wissenschaftliche Bibliotheken*; *Sonderhefte* have been issued since 1963.

1896   *Zeitschrift für deutsches Altertum und deutsche Literatur*. Wiesbaden: 1841-1944; 1948-.

A monthly review for German language and literature, with some articles and book reviews on early texts and manuscripts; bibliographies.

1897   *Zeitschrift für Kirchengeschichte*. Stuttgart: 1925-.

A review published three times per year on all aspects of Church history, including music, liturgy, and archives; articles, book reviews, bibliographies.

1898   *Zeitschrift für romanische Philologie*. Tübingen: 1877-.

    Published twice yearly on Romance language and literature, with articles and book reviews; includes the *Romanische Bibliographie* as a supplement, vol. 77- (1961-), parallel in scope to the *MLA* bibliography.

1899   *Zentralblätt für Bibliothekswesen*. Leipzig: 1884-1944; 1947-.

    An annual review published by the Bibliographisches Institut; articles, book reviews, and bibliography on library science, the classification of documents, care and preservation, and library holdings; indexes.

See also Section I, under specialized areas of study, and items 944, 1903.

XV. TEXTUAL CRITICISM

The extent of textual criticism and its many ramifications in both bibliographical and literary studies
require that this final section of the Handbook be broad
and, at the same time, selective. Section A indicates
bibliographical sources, especially in periodicals
which specify textual criticism as a special area for
study. Sections B and C include general and specific
studies, selected because they are significantly con-
tributory to the history of textual criticism, to its
methodology, or to its bibliography. Finally, Section
D looks at ways in which the computer can be used in
the editing of texts, especially for collations, and
in the compilation of concordances.

CONTENTS

A. BIBLIOGRAPHICAL MATERIALS

1900   Duplacy, Jean. "Repères historiques et recherches méthodolo-
       giques." *Revue d'Histoire des Textes*, 5 (1975), 249-309.

       A résumé of the main lines of scholarship for the period
       1881-1974, followed by a non-critical bibliography of computer
       and other mechanical methods of textual studies. Periodic
       supplements.

1901   Howard-Hill, T.H. *British Bibliography and Textual Criticism.*
       2 vols. Oxford: Clarendon Press, 1979.

       A bibliography mainly for textual problems in printed books,
       post 1475, and non-critical. There are some references to
       standard works on editing, e.g., Greg, Maas, Bowers, and Dearing
       with a useful section on book binding, pp. 175ff., and libraries,
       pp. 214ff.

1902   Peeters, Felix. "La Technique de l'édition (1926-1936)."
       Antiquité Classique, 6 (1937), 319-356.

       A detailed, critical bibliography for this period. It includes
       works and articles on all aspects of editorial studies.

1903   *Studies in Bibliography: Papers.* Charlottesville, Va.: 1948/
       49-.

       An annual journal published by the Bibliographical Society
       of the University of Virginia. While not many of its articles
       are germane to early textual criticism, see, e.g., Davison,
       item 1934, a chronological bibliography/checklist is devoted
       annually to bibliographical and textual matters, including
       incunabula.

See also Section I, under the appropriate discipline, and items 21,
    29, 54, 1835, 1839, 1858.

B. FESTSCHRIFTEN AND COLLECTIONS

1904   Autenrieth, Johanne, and Brunhölzl, Franz, eds. *Festschrift
       Bernhard Bischoff zu seinem 65. Geburtstag.* Stuttgart: Hierse-
       mann, 1971.

This Festschrift contains 37 articles, of which only the first does not deal with manuscript studies. Of these, Brunhölzl's "Zu den sogenannten codices Archetypi der römischen Literatur," is the most specifically related to problems of medieval textual criticism.

1905   Fubini, M., *et al.*, eds. *Tecnica e teorica litteraria.* 2nd ed. (from 1948). Milan: Marzorati, 1951.

The article by Alberto Chiari, "L'Edizione critica," pp. 231-95, contains a useful survey of Italian textual criticism for this period.

1906   Ganz, Peter F., and Schröder, Werner, eds. *Probleme mittelalter-licher Überlieferung und Textkritik.* Oxforder Colloquium, 1966. Berlin: E. Schmidt, 1968.

Essays on specific textual problems in Middle High German literature, including Ganz, "Lachmann as an Editor of Middle High German Texts," pp. 12-30; Heinz Schanze, "Zur Frage der Brauchbarkeit seines Handschriftenstemmas bei der Herstellung des kritischen Textes von Wolframs 'Willehalm,'" pp. 31-48; and E.J. Morrall, "The Text of Michel Velser's 'Mandeville's' Translation," pp. 183-96. Bibliographical references throughout.

1907   Gottesman, Ronald, and Bennett, Scott, eds. *Art and Error: Modern Textual Editing.* Bloomington, Ind.: Indiana University Press, 1970.

A collection of essays by Housman, Greg, Bald, and others, mainly on nineteenth- and twentieth-century editorial problems, with a bibliography, pp. 301-6. See especially the last essay, item 2053, on the ordered computor collation of unprepared literary text, which experiments on two texts of Henry James' *Daisy Miller* in a project designed "to increase the accuracy and efficiency of collating." For a later expansion of these theories, see item 2070.

1908   Hunger, H., Langosch, Karl, *et al.*, eds. *Geschichte der Text-überlieferung der antiken und mittelalterlichen Literatur.* 2 vols. Zurich: Atlantis, 1961-64.

A general history of textual traditions for Classical and medieval literature, arranged by language groups. Summaries of works, lists of editions, and bibliography. An author/work index concludes. Illustrations for some stemmata are provided.

1909   Kleinhenz, Christopher, ed. *Medieval Manuscripts and Textual Criticism.* University of North Carolina, Department of Romance Languages, Symposia, 4; Studies in the Romance Languages and Literatures, 5. Chapel Hill, N.C.: University of North Carolina Press, 1976.

A collection of papers on manuscript illumination and textual criticism, some reprinted from elsewhere; included are David Diringer, "The Book of the Middle Ages," pp. 27-37; Carleton W. Carroll, "Medieval Romance Paleography: A Brief Introduction," pp. 39-82; Frank Istvan, "The Art of Editing Lyric Texts" (originally published in *Recueil Brunel*, Paris: 1955), Cesare Segre, "The Problem of Contamination in Prose Texts," pp. 117-22; George Kane, "Conjectural Emendation" (reprinted from the *Garmondsway Festschrift*, ed. D.A. Pearsall and R.A. Waldron, London: 1969), pp. 211-25; Aurelio Roncaglia, "The Value of Interpretation in Textual Criticism," pp. 227-44; Christopher Kleinhenz, "The Nature of an Edition," pp. 273-9; and T.B.W. Reid, "On the Text of the *Tristan* of Beroul," pp. 245-71; see also Whitehead, item 1332.

1910   Martens, Gunter, and Zeller, Hans, eds. *Texte und Varianten*.
        Probleme ihrer Edition und Interpretation. Munich: C.H. Beck,
        1971.

        A collection of 20 articles, with a general bibliography,
        pp. 415-26, and index. Of interest for medieval texts are
        Siegfried Scheibe, "Zu einigen Grundprinzipen einer historisch-
        kritischen Ausgabe," pp. 1-44; Hans Zeller, "Befund und Deutung.
        Interpretation und Dokumentation als Ziel und Methode der
        Edition," pp. 45-90.

1911   Monumenta Germanica Historica. *Mittelalterliche Textüberlief-
        erungen und ihre kritische Aufarbeitung: Beiträge der Monu-
        menta Germanica Historica zum 31. deutschen Historiker*.
        Munich: MGH, 1976.

        Eight papers on textual criticism and historical documents.
        The focus is upon textual transmission and source studies.

1912   *Relazione comitato internationale di scienze storiche*, 10
        Congresso. Florence: The Committee, 1955.

        A collection of papers and reports from the tenth international
        congress for historical studies. Of some importance for textual
        criticism are F. Bartolini, "Paleografia e critica testuale,"
        pp. 423-43; and G. Post, "A General Report: Suggestions for
        Future Studies in Late Medieval and Renaissance Latin Paleog-
        raphy," pp. 407-22, which provides a survey of scholarship and
        desiderata.

1913   Spongano, Raffaele, ed., *Studi e problemi di critica testuale*.
        Bologna: R. Pâtron, 1961.

        Papers from the 1960 conference on textual criticism; important
        contributions are by Marco Boni, "Richerche di 'fonti' e critica
        testuale," pp. 93-101; and Maria Corti, "Note sui rapporti fra
        localizazione dei manoscritti e *recensio*," pp. 85-91.

1914   Thorpe, James E., and Simpson, Claude E., Jr. *The Task of the
        Editor: Papers Read at a Clark Library Seminar, February 8,
        1969*. Los Angeles, Calif.: William Andrews Clark Memorial
        Library, 1969.

        While these papers discuss the editing of post-Renaissance
        works, they also provide a useful summary of the work of
        Bowers, Greg, and others.

1915   Toronto, University of. *Conference on Editorial Problems*. Toronto:
        University of Toronto Press for the Committee, 1966-72; Toronto:

A.M. Hakkert, 1972-75; New York, N.Y.: Garland Publishing, Inc., 1976-.

A series of publications containing the papers from the University of Toronto conferences on editorial problems. They include: *Editing Sixteenth-Century Texts*, ed. R.J. Schoeck (1966); *Editing Nineteenth-Century Texts*, ed. John M. Robson (1967); *Editing Eighteenth-Century Texts*, ed. D.I.B. Smith (1968); *Editor, Author, and Publisher*, ed. W.J. Howard (1968); *Editing Twentieth-Century Texts*, ed. Francess G. Halpenny (1972); *Editing Texts of the Romantic Period*, ed. John D. Baird (1972); *Editing Seventeenth-Century Prose*, ed. D.I.B. Smith (Hakkert: 1972); *Editing Canadian Texts*, ed. Francess G. Halpenny (1975); *Editing Eighteenth-Century Novels*, ed. G.E. Bentley, Jr. (1975); *Editing Renaissance Dramatic Texts: English Italian, and Spanish*, ed. Anne Lancashire (Garland: 1976); *Editing British and American Literature 1880-1920*, ed. Eric Domville (1976); *Editing Medieval Texts*, ed. A.G. Rigg (1977); *Editing Nineteenth-Century Fiction*, ed. Jane Millgate (1978); *Editing Correspondence*, ed. J.A. Dainard (1979); *Editing Illustrated Books*, ed. W.F. Blissett (1980). The collected papers on medieval texts consider aspects of editing medieval texts, especially those for which the original manuscript is presumed lost. They include: Malcolm Godden, "Old English"; Anne Hudson, "Middle English"; Ian Lancashire, "Medieval Drama"; Brian Merrilees, "Anglo-Norman"; and A.G. Rigg, "Medieval Latin."

1916   *Zeitschrift für Literaturwissenschaft und Linguistik*. 5 (1979).

An issue devoted to problems in textual criticism. Those articles referring to medieval German texts are W. Woesler, "Funktion und Planung historischkritischer Ausgaben," pp. 13-25; R. Richter, "Zur Interpretation der Formvarianten," pp. 57-62; C. Segre, "Bemerkungen zum Problem der Kontamination in Prosa texten," pp. 63-67; and R. Kohlmayer, "Textgliederung als Rezeptionssteuerung in Handschrift und Edition," pp. 43-56.

C. GENERAL STUDIES

1917   Andrieu, Jean. "Principes et recherches en critique textuelle," in *Memorial des études latines ... offert à ... J. Marouzeau*. Paris: Société d'Edition 'Les Belles Lettres,' 1943; pp. 458-74.

In this article the author advocates evaluating all the data, e.g., archaisms, syntax, lacunae, corrections, scholia, etc. He discusses the types of common contamination in medieval texts and provides a good survey of methods and scholarship. See items 1327, 1351-2. This volume constitutes *Revue des Etudes Latines*, 21 (1943).

1918   ——. "Problèmes d'histoire des textes." *Revue des Etudes Latines*, 24 (1946), 271-314.

An expanded version of the preceding item, with a general account of developments in textual criticism and bibliographical references.

1919 Bailey, David R. Shackleton. "Editing Ancient Texts," in *Language and Texts: The Nature of Linguistic Evidence*, ed. Herbert H. Paper. Ann Arbor Center for the Coordination of Ancient and Modern Studies. Ann Arbor, Mich.: University of Michigan Press, 1975; pp. 21-32.

A general discussion of the problems of recension, scribal errors, paleography, context, and language as they relate both to ancient Eastern texts and medieval manuscripts.

1920 Barbi, Michele. *La nuova filologia e l'edizione dei nostri scrittori da Dante al Manzoni*. Florence: G.C. Sansoni, 1938.

Chapters on individual Italian texts, with a preface in which the author upholds the Lachmannian method (see item 2012), and condemns Bédier and Dom Quentin (items 1992 and 1975).

1921 Bernheim, Ernst. *Lehrbuch der historischen Methode und der Geschichts-philosophie*. 6th ed. 2 vols. Leipzig: 1908/New York, N.Y.: Burt Franklin, 1960; reprinted one vol., 1970.

A handbook for the study of historical sources, with pp. 324-561 devoted to problems in textual criticism. A full bibliography, index are provided.

1922 Bidez, Joseph, and Drachmann, A.B. *Emploi des signes critiques, disposition de l'apparat dans les éditions savantes de textes grecs et latins*. Brussels: UAI, 1932; rev. ed. by A. Delatte and A. Severyns, 1938.

The use of standard critical signs and construction of the apparatus criticus. The focus is upon complex editions, especially for papyrus texts. A bibliography is included in the introduction.

1923 Bieler, Ludwig. *The Grammarian's Craft*. 3rd ed. New York, N.Y.: Catholic Classical Association of Greater New York, 1960.

Originally published in *Folia*, 10 (1958), 3-42, this introduction to editorial methods outlines the basic problems of textual criticism and early texts.

1924 Birt, Theodor. *Kritik und Hermeneutik nebst Abriss des antiken Buchwesens*. Munich: C.H. Beck, 1913.

This work represents volume I.3 in Müller's *Handbuch* series. It outlines the main aspects of codicology and the make-up of the manuscript book, styles and categories of writing, types of textual criticism, hermeneutics, historical as opposed to literary interpretation, and other problems in early literature. An index is provided for authors and works. Cf. his earlier *Das antike Buchwesen in seinem Verhältniss zur Literatur* (Berlin: W. Hertz, 1882/1959).

1925   Bowers, Fredson. *Essays in Bibliography. Text, and Editing.*
        Charlottesville, Va.: University Press of Virginia for the
        Bibliographical Society, 1975.

        Eleven essays on textual criticism, with a checklist of
        Bowers' publications, pp. 531-48.

1926   ————. *Textual and Literary Criticism.* Cambridge: University
        Press, 1959.

        The text of the Sandars Lectures in Bibliography for 1957-
        58. Bowers discusses textual problems in the works of Shakes-
        peare and Walt Whitman, and provides a rationale for modern,
        old-spelling editions.

1927   ————. "Textual Criticism," in *The Aims and Methods of
        Scholarship in Modern Languages and Literatures*, ed. James
        E. Thorpe. 2nd ed. (from 1963). New York, N.Y.: MLA, 1970.

        General definitions of types of textual criticism, with use-
        ful bibliographical references.

1928   Boyle, Leonard E. "Optimist and Recensionist: 'Common Errors'
        or 'Common Variations'?," in *Latin Script and Letters*, ed.
        O'Meara, item 723, pp. 264-74.

        A summary of Lachmannian and Bedierian theories with an
        account of the lines of scholarship established for each.

1929   Browning, R. *"Recentiones non deteriores." Bulletin of the
        Institute of Classical Studies*, 7 (1960), 11-21.

        A summary of editorial activities of several Byzantine
        scholars and their use of earlier uncial manuscripts during
        the late Byzantine period. Browning also discusses the renais-
        sance of Classical studies in late thirteenth- and early four-
        teenth-century Nicea and Constantinople.

1930   Castellani, Arrigo. *Bédier avait-il raison? La méthode de
        Lachmann dans les éditions de textes du moyen âge.* Fribourg:
        Editions Universitaires, 1957.

        A summary of editorial tenets held by Bédier and Lachmann.
        The author sets up a hypothetical stemma of 52 manuscripts by
        which he demonstrates the difficulties of Lachmann's methods.

1931   Chaytor, H.J. "The Medieval Reader and Textual Criticism."
        Bulletin of the John Rylands Library, 26 (1941), 49-56.

        A discussion of the effect of oral-aural transmission upon
        scribal habits. A scribe copying a text would have an auditory
        memory rather than visual, and so would write, e.g., *er* for
        ar, or *es* for *est*.

1932   Clark, A.C. *The Descent of Manuscripts.* Oxford: Clarendon Press,
        1918.

        An introduction to the techniques of recension, in which
        Clark works out a system for observing omissions and determining
        line-length. He makes specific application of his theories on

the Ciceronian palimpsests, the manuscripts of Plato, and the
Paris manuscripts of Demosthenes. The work is in part based
upon the next item.

1933 ————. *Recent Developments in Textual Criticism*. Oxford:
Clarendon Press, 1914.

A survey of scholarship and an assessment of the contribution
of individual scholars.

1934 Davison, Peter. "Science, Method, and the Textual Critic."
Studies in Bibliography, 25 (1972), 1-28.

A study of the controversy between bibliographers and textual
critics, especially the traditions represented by Housman and
that proposed by Thorpe and Greg. He points out the weaknesses
of the stemmatic method, but also suggests the limitations of
the "new paradigm" represented by Kane's approach to manuscript
groups. Finally, the author advocates a more "creative" and
comprehensive approach to textual criticism.

1935 Dearing, Vinton A. *A Manual of Textual Analysis*. Berkeley and
Los Angeles, Calif.: University of California Press, 1959.

An essential manual for handling variants in order to establish
recensions, and here Dearing suggests the use of overlays of
stemmata. Bibliography is included. See item 1939.

1936 ————. *Methods of Textual Editing*. Los Angeles, Calif.:
University of California Press, 1962.

A short statement, in the form of a paper read for the William
Andrews Clark Memorial Library, of what was to become the basis
for his theories of textual criticism as set out in item 1939.

1937 ————. "Some Notes on Genealogical Methods in Textual Criticism." *Novum Testamentum*, 9 (1967), 278-97.

Aspects of the recensionist method as applied to specific
texts.

1938 ————. "Some Routines for Textual Criticism." *The Library*,
5th ser., 21 (1966), 309-17.

Further discussion of problems and solutions in handling
complex stemmata.

1939 ————. *Principles and Practice of Textual Analysis*. Berkeley
and Los Angeles, Calif.: University of California Press, 1974.

In this work Dearing abandons his system of overlays in
stemmata, and reverts to simpler methods which owe much to Dom
Quentin. In an appendix he discusses computer uses and programmes.
For an assessment of this work in relation to the general traditions established by Quentin, see Froger, item 1947.

1940 Dekkers, Dom Eligius, O.S.B. "La Tradition des textes et les
problèmes de l'édition diplomatique." *Traditio*, 10 (1954),
549-55.

In many ways this article is a review of Masai's "Principes," item 1972. Dekkers discusses the direction toward editions which he calls "documentaire," i.e., a full edition with intro- duction, notes, and other relevant matter. He argues that diplo- matic texts do have an important place, especially for texts which have undergone successive changes, e.g., liturgical and canonical, or autograph manuscripts.

1941   Dondaine, A. "Abbreviations latines et signes recommandés pour l'apparat critique de textes médiévaux." *Bulletin de la Société Internationale pour l'Etude de la Philosophie Médi- évale*, 2 (1960), 142-9.

See item 1943 below.

1942   ———. "Un cas maieur d'utilisation d'un argument paléograph- ique en critique textuelle (Vat. lat. 781)." *Scriptorium*, 21 (1967), 261-76.

An analysis of evidence for *codices descripti*, with evidence from scribal misreadings.

1943   ———. "Variantes de l'apparat critique dans les editions de textes latins médiévaux." *Bulletin de la Société Internationale pour l'Étude de la Philosophie Médiévale*, 4 (1962), 82-100.

With "Abbreviations," item 1941 above, these articles provide suggestions for selection of variants and a list of common abbreviations in an apparatus criticus.

1944   Falconi, Ettore. *L'edizione diplomatica del documento e del manoscritto*. Parma: La Nazionale, 1969.

A handbook on the methodology of editing diplomatic texts, i.e., those which are largely transcriptive and provide little critical matter. A select bibliography concludes.

1945   Fourquet, Jean. "Fautes communes ou innovations communes." *Romania*, 70 (1948-49), 85-95.

A revision of his "Paradoxe de Bédier," (*Mélanges*, Paris: 1946), influenced by Whitehead's article, item 1988. Here he largely agrees with Bédier that the many "innovations" which each copyist makes through omissions, additions, transpositions, word substitutions, etc., cannot be assessed in such a way as to make stemmata a certainty. Therefore the scrupulous editor will suggest a "Stemma dichotomique" or none at all, but the final decision should be determined by the type of text itself, e.g., Latin texts are more amenable to the method of common faults than vernacular texts.

1946   Froger, Dom Jacques. "La Critique textuelle et la methode des groupes fautifs." *Cahiers de Lexicology*, 3 (1962), 207-24.

1947   ———. "La Critique de texte: une variante de la methode de Dom Quentin." *Revue des Etudes Latines*, 42 (1964), 187-92.

From its initial position as a critical review of Dearing's *Manual*, this article goes on to assess Quentin's critical principles in general. With item 1946 above, Froger considers such problems as the means of classifying forms of the text, rather than the manuscripts which transmit it, and the unfeasibility of Dearing's negative criteria based upon the principle of exclusion.

1948   Gaskell, Philip. *From Writer to Reader: Studies in Editorial Method*. Oxford: Clarendon Press, 1978.

With representative texts from twelve printed works, including Harington, Milton, and Swift, the author shows the relationships between an author's working manuscript and various editions. He offers advice on the selection of copy text and how much textual apparatus to include. Bibliograhical references and index are provided.

1949   Ghellinck, J. De. *Patristique et moyen âge: études d'histoire litteraire et doctrinale*. Museum Lessianum, Section Historique, 7. 3 vols. Gembloux: J. Duculot, 1946-48; 2nd ed. 1949.

A detailed study of Patristic textual traditions by phases: first phase, 1439-1860, beginning with Calvinists and Socinians, second phase from the work of Gaspari to (volume 3) modern methodology. Certain Fathers are studied individually, and there is a section on subjects, e.g., the doctrine of Trinity. An appendix, critical bibliography by year of publication, and author/work/subject index conclude. See item 1971.

1950   Greg, Walter W. *The Calculus of Variants: An Essay on Textual Criticism*. Oxford: Clarendon Press, 1927/London: Folcroft Library Editions, 1971.

A study of the logic of filiation, which grew out of Greg's attempt to establish the relationship of the manuscripts of the Chester plays. He discusses types of variation, recording variation, and their resolution. Greg's theories are supported by statistical analyses in Antonín Hrubý, "A Quantitative Solution of the Ambiguity of Three Texts," *Studies in Bibliography*, 18 (1965), 147-82.

1951   ———. "Recent Theories of Textual Criticism." *Modern Philology*, 29 (1931), 401-4.

A reply to Shepard's article, item 1977, in which Shepard had attempted to apply certain critical theories proposed by Greg to actual problems of filiation and found them inadequate. In this article Greg claims Shepard had failed to understand these theories, especially his notion of the dichotomous stemma, i.e., the two-branch system, which Greg considers as the normal one as a result of decimation of manuscripts. See also Fourquet, item 1945.

1952   Grigsby, John L. "A Defense and Four Illustrations of Textual Criticism." *Romance Philology*, 20 (1967), 500-20.

In a review of four recent editions of Old French texts (by van der Krabben, Lindgren, Sweetser, and Ruelle), the author considers them comparatively under the topics motivation, organization, manuscript description, filiation and choice of base manuscript, language, and versification. In the course of these comparisons he outlines what every good critical edition should have in the way of introduction, apparatus, and textual notes.

1953   Groningen, B.A. van. *Traité d'histoire et de critique des textes grecs*. Amsterdam: North Holland Publishing Co., 1963.

A clear, concise account of the editing of a Classical Greek text. The two parts consider, first, the general history of Greek manuscripts (scribes, libraries, transmission, etc.), then study of the material (codicology), classification of errors, choice of variants. Examples are provided from specific texts.

1954   Hall, F.W. *A Companion to Classical Texts*. Oxford: Clarendon Press, 1913.

This general introduction contains sections (chapters 6-9) on aspects of textual criticism; discussed are types of errors, designation of sigla, recension, and emendation. Especially useful is a dictionary of names for collectors and institutions, e.g., "Agnesiana," designating Vercelli manuscripts.

1955   Ham, E.B. "Textual Criticism and Common Sense." *Romance Philology*, 12 (1959), 198-215.

Beginning with Housman's appeal to common sense (item 1958), Ham reviews statements on the Bédier and Lachmann issues and attempts to counteract some of the "needless compilations" multiplied by textual theorists.

1956   Havet, Louis. "Sur un principe de critique des textes: La loi des fautes naissantes." *Revue des Etudes Latines*, 1 (1923), 20-26.

With reference to his major work on scribal errors, the author here stresses that to be confident a reading is right, its variants should be explicable. See item 1351.

1957   Hill, Archibald A. "Some Postulates for Distributional Study of Texts." *Studies in Bibliography*, 3 (1950-51), 63-95.

A study of texts in manuscripts makes use of distributional and geneaological evidence, which Hill calls "comparative study," but the study of printed texts makes use of "external" evidence. He proposes a type of textual criticism which would use all three, and for this suggests the name "libristics." He describes sets of variants and their tabulation and the nature of derivation.

1958   Housman, A.E. *Selected Prose*, ed. John Carter. Cambridge: University Press, 1961.

This collection includes his famous essay on editing, "The Application of Thought to Textual Criticism," pp. 131-50, in which Housman discounts the methodical recension in favour of judicious common sense, dependant largely upon a solid knowledge of the author and his language. Also included are the introductory prefaces to Propertius, Manilius, and other Classical editions. See Housman under "Specific Problems," item 2007.

1959   Irigoin, Jean. "Quelques reflexions sur le concept d'archétype." *Revue d'Histoire des Textes*, 7 (1977), 235-45.

An attempt to clarify the use of the word to designate the origin of a manuscript tradition.

1960   ————. "Stemmas bifides et états de manuscrits." *Revue de Philologie*, 28 (1954), 211-7.

An attempt to extend the scope and utility of the two-branch system of filiation. The author begins with the supposition that a given manuscript, especially for Greek texts, offers different *etats* at different periods due to recopying, *scholia*, etc., and that these should be considered separately.

1961   Jäger, Gerhard. *Einführung in die klassische Philologie*. Beck' sche Elementarbücher. Munich: C.H. Beck, 1975.

While this work is primarily an introduction to the study of Classical texts, it presents a concise account of textual criticism and the elementary principles of editing texts from a plurality of manuscripts, pp. 42-59.

1962   Johnston, Harold W. *Latin Manuscripts; An Elementary Introduction to the Use of Critical Editions for High Schools and College Classes*. Chicago, Ill.: Scott, Foresman and Co., 1897.

In the third and final part of this introductory study, the author gives a simple but lucid exposition of the Lachmannian method, with select examples from Classical texts for the major types of manuscript traditions, e.g., unique manuscripts, all manuscripts traceable to a lost archetype, etc.

1963   Kantorowicz, Hermann. *Einführung in die Textkritik. Systematische Darstellung der textkritischen Grundsätze für Philologen und Juristen*. Leipzig: Dieterich, 1921.

An exposition of stemmatics and the psychology of scribal error. The author distinguishes *echt* ("authentic") from *richtig* ("right") readings. Three stemmata are used as illustration. A good bibliography is provided.

1964   Kenney, E.J. *The Classical Text: Aspects of Editing in the Age of the Printed Book*. Sather Classical Lectures, 44. Berkeley, Calif.: University of California Press, 1974.

The author attempts through "selective illustration" to "marry Classical scholarship with printing and bibliography." He summarizes the history of textual criticism, giving an account of Lachmann and his successors. An extensive bibliography is provided, pp. 158-62, and the excellent index of authors and subjects serves, in a sense, as a dictionary of terms.

1965   Kraft, Robert. *Die Geschichtlichkeit literarischer Texte: Eine
        Theorie der Edition.* Bebenhausen: L. Rotsch, 1973.

        A general introduction to editing texts for all periods, but
        with some discussion of early methods, e.g., Chapt. 3 ("Über
        Notwendige und Falsche Kontamination, Lesarten und Varianten")
        considers Lachmannian methods and their limitations. Chapt. 11
        outlines practical matters such as the description of manuscripts
        and the use of sigla.

1966   Laufer, Roger. *Introduction à la textologie: Verification,
        établissement edition des textes.* Paris: Larousse, 1972.

        Although this book is on post-Renaissance and printed book
        textology, it provides some lucid comments on and summaries
        of methods of classification, establishment of criteria, and
        degrees of choice which could equally well apply to early
        manuscripts.

1967   Legge, M. Dominica. "Recent Methods of Textual Criticism."
        Arthuriana, 2 (1929-30), 48-55.

        A summary of the Bédier-Quentin controversy, in favour of
        the Bédier theory generally.

1968   Lutz-Hensel, Magdalene. "Lachmanns Textkritische Wahrschein-
        lichkeitsregeln." *Zeitschrift für deutschen Philologie*, 90
        (1971), 394-408.

        A summary of Lachmann's theories (see item 2012), with critical
        reference to recent Lachmannian scholarship, e.g., Timpanaro's
        La genesi del metodo dal Lachmann, item 1983.

1969   Maas, Paul. *Textual Criticism*, trans. from 2nd and 3rd ed. by
        Barbara Flower. 4th ed. Oxford: Clarendon Press, 1960.

        Originally *Textkritik* (1927), this work makes the classic
        statement on the theory of stemmatics and the common errors
        method. It recognizes the most obvious limitation of this sys-
        tem, that the manuscript tradition be "closed." The 4th ed. in-
        cludes "Leitfehler und stemmatische Typen," from *Byzantinische
        Zeitschrift*, 37 (1937), with a response to Bédier appended.
        The Italian translation by N. Martinelli (Florence: 1952) in-
        cludes an introduction by G. Pasquali, who discusses probable
        contamination and believes that recensionist methods are only
        possible when the text is uncontaminated.

1970   Marichal, Robert. "La Critique des textes," in *L'Histoire et
        ses methods*, ed. Charles Samaran. Encyclopédia de la Pléiade,
        11. Paris: Gallimand, 1961; pp. 1247-1366.

        A general survey of all aspects of textual criticism, especial-
        ly as it pertains to historical documents; includes bibliograph-
        ical references.

1971   Marrou, H.I. "La Technique de l'édition à l'époque patristique."
        Vigiliae Christianae, 3 (1949), 208-24.

With reference to Ghellink's *Patristique*, item 1949, Marrou
makes a more precise study of editions in the early fifth century and those produced commercially. Some focus is upon the
writings and textual traditions of Sulpicius Severus, Paulinus
of Nole, and St. Augustine.

1972   Masai, F. "Principes et conventions de l'édition diplomatique."
       Scriptorium, 4 (1950), 179-93.

       Masai argues that diplomatic editions are necessary to satisfy
       certain needs, principally the need for a rapid and precise
       transcription and collation as a preliminary to later critical
       editions. They also preserve the "archéologie" of the text.
       He provides a list of critical signs to use in the text and
       apparatus of diplomatic editions. See also Dekkers, item 1940.

1973   Monat, Pierre. "Le Classement des manuscrits par l'analyse
       factorielle: Recherches pour l'établissement d'un stemma."
       Revue d'Histoire des Textes, 5 (1975), 311-30.

       An application of "analyse factorielle" or "taxinomie"--a
       mathematical and geometrical analysis of letters (axis, dimen-
       sion, etc.) and line spaces in order to determine relations
       between manuscripts--to manuscripts of Lactantius' *Institutiones
       Divinae*, Bk. IV. See Griffith, item 2002.

1974   Pasquali, G. *Storia della tradizione e critica del testo*. 2nd
       ed. (from 1952). Florence: Felice Le Monnier, 1962.

       This work discusses many similar issues and from much the
       same point of view as Maas' work, but provides more documenta-
       tion, especially from textual traditions not amenable to the
       "common errors" method. Pasquali gives a history of textual
       criticism with focus upon Lachmann and the Humanists; appendices
       are provided on Dain's work and diplomatic texts. Indexes and
       bibliography are provided.

1975   Quentin, Dom Henri. *Essais de critique textuelle (ecdotique)*.
       Paris: A. Picard, 1926.

       After Lachmann and Bédier, one of the major contributors to
       methods of textual criticism, Quentin rejects common errors
       for common readings, and demonstrates a method of comparing
       manuscripts by threes to establish filiation. In this work
       Quentin replies to an earlier, unfavourable review by E.K. Rand,
       "Dom Quentin's Memoir on the Text of the Vulgate," *Harvard
       Theological Review*, 17 (1924), 197-264, in which Rand maintained
       that such stemmata would not work. Another critic of Quentin
       is J. Burke Severs, "Quentin's theories of Textual Criticism,"
       English Institute Annual (1942), 65-93, who points out in this
       article that Quentin's method is unable to account for confla-
       tion; see also Shepard, item 1977, and Quentin's earlier
       Mémoire, item 2023.

1976   Renehan, R. *Greek Textual Criticism. A Reader*. Loeb Classical
       Monographs. Cambridge, Mass.: Harvard University Press, 1969.

       An attempt to show how Byzantine scholars "edited" texts of
       Greek authors through a collection of passages from Greek texts

(Homer to Eustathius), each illustrating a particular phenomenon, e.g., punctuation and interpolation.

1977   Shepard, William P. "Recent Theories of Textual Criticism." *Modern Philology*, 28 (1930), 129–41.

A survey of recent scholarship, then a practical test of Greg's and Quentin's theories in a particular manuscript tradition. Shepard demonstrates how it would be possible to come up with a number of entirely different stemma, especially in the application of Greg's methods. For Greg's reply, see item 1951.

1978   Stählin, O. *Editionstechnik*. 2nd ed. (from 1909). Leipzig: Teubner, 1914.

A standard, early work on textual methodology, based mainly upon Lachmann and applied to Classical texts.

1979   Tanselle, G. Thomas. "Some Principles for Editorial Apparatus." *Studies in Bibliography*, 25 (1972), 41–88.

With reference to printed books, but some of the matters are relevant to early manuscripts, e.g., describing editorial principles, the arrangement of emendations and textual notes, and the use of symbols and abbreviations. See also next item.

1980   ————. "Editorial Apparatus for Radiating Texts." *The Library*, 5th ser., 29 (1974), 330–7.

An expansion of the preceding item.

1981   Thomson, S.H. "Editing Medieval Latin Texts." *Progress of Medieval and Renaissance Studies in the United States and Canada*, 16 (1941), 37–49.

A general introduction in the form of negative criticism of how not to edit texts, with reference to some recent editions of medieval Latin texts.

1982   Thorpe, James E. *Principles of Textual Criticism*. San Marino, Cal.: Huntington Library, 1972.

This work considers the abstract and theoretical aspects of textual criticism, English and American, chiefly its aesthetics. The final two chapters are on "The Treatment of Accidentals" and "The Establishment of the Text." See also Thorpe and Simpson, item 1914.

1983   Timpanaro, Sebastiano. *La genesi del metodo del Lachmann*. Florence: La Nuova Italia, 1963.

Originally published in *Studi ital. di filol. class.*, 31–32 (1959–60), this work is a documented study of Lachmannian principles, with reference to critics such as Maas, Irigoin, Castelloni, and Fourquet. The German translation, *Die Entstehung der Lachmannischen Methode* (Hamburg: 1971), provides an enlarged bibliography.

1984   ————. *Il lapsus freudiano: psicanalisi e critica testuale.* Florence: La Nuova Italia, 1974; trans. Kate Soper, *The Freudian Slip: Psychoanalysis and Textual Criticism.* London: NLB, 1976.

An account of the psychology of scribal errors, see items 1327 and 1351 above. Bibliographical references and indexes are provided.

1985   Vinaver, Eugene. "Principles of Textual Emendation," in *Studies in French Language and Mediaeval Literature Presented to Professor Mildred K. Pope.* Manchester: University Press, 1939; pp. 351-69; repr. Kleinhenz, item 1909.

The author analyzes the mental processes involved in copying manuscripts, and looks at the types of mistakes such as homoioteleuton and dittography. In his general approach to "common errors" and stemmatic recension, Vinaver supports Bédier's textual methods. See Vinaver's edition of Malory, item 2033.

1986   Wallberg, Emanuel. "Prinzipien und Methoden für die Herausgabe alter Texte nach verschiedenen Handschriften." *Zeitschrift für romanische Philologie*, 51 (1931), 665-78.

A survey of theories held by Quentin and Bédier and a proposal that medieval authors revised and rewrote less often than Bédier implies.

1987   West, Martin L. *Textual Criticism and Editorial Techniques.* Stuttgart: Teubner, 1973.

The general introduction discusses manuscript transmission, various causes for textual discrepancy, and the evaluation of variants. The practical section in Pt. 2 deals with, among other matters, the problem of open texts. A select bibliography is provided.

1988   Whitehead, Frederick, and Pickford, Cedric E. "The Two-Branch Stemma." *Bibliographical Bulletin of the International Arthurian Society*, 3 (1951), 83-90.

The authors advocate the two-branch system for stemmata on the basis of mathematical calculation for the number of descendants. They also propose that the common ancestor of a number of manuscripts is likely to be the original "X," rather than MS. "X" connected with the original through a long series of lost intermediaries.

1989   Willis, James A. *Latin Textual Criticism.* Illinois Studies in Language and Literature, 61. Urbana, Ill.: University of Illinois Press, 1972.

A general introduction to editing Latin texts, with the first 50pp. on the general principles of textual criticism, techniques for stemma and the apparatus criticus, and types of faults. The work includes an *excursus*, practical test papers in conjectural emendation, and a glossary of technical terms.

1990   Zeller, Hans. "A New Approach to the Critical Constitution of
        Literary Texts." *Studies in Bibliography*, 28 (1975), 231-64.

        With reference to modern editions, the author outlines the
        divergent paths of German and American styles of textual criti-
        cism: German editorial procedure does not distinguish in so
        marked a way between accidentals and substantives as does Anglo-
        American practice, but rather emphasizes versions. Much of his
        discussion can be applied to the editing of early texts, espe-
        cially the matters of version (*Fassung*), authorial intention,
        and textual error (*Textfehler*).

See also items 731, 744, 748, 749, 752, 754-5, 1633, 1657-8, 1661,
    1666-70, 1674-5, 1691-2, 1698, 1705.

D. SPECIFIC TEXTUAL PROBLEMS

        The following items are highly select and have been
        limited to works or articles which illustrate a particu-
        lar textual tradition or are considered outstanding
        examples in their application of certain principles to
        individual texts. Further examples may be found elsewhere
        in this *Handbook*, notably in Section V, Special Topics.

1991   Barrett, W.S. *Euripides' Hippolytos*. Oxford: Clarendon Press,
        1964.

        This edition includes an excellent preface on editorial
        methods. See especially pp. 45-84, and cf. items 2032, 2039.

1992   Bédier, Joseph, ed. *'Lai d'ombre' par Jean Renart. SATF*. Paris:
        Firmin-Didot, 1913.

        A significant formulation of Bédier's theories on the "common
        errors" method of recension. In his introduction he criticizes
        his earlier stemma of 1890.

1993   ————. *La Tradition manuscrite du 'Lai de l'ombre': Réflexions
        sur l'art d'éditer les anciens textes*. Paris: E. Champion,
        1929.

        Originally published in *Romania*, 1928, this important state-
        ment describes Bédier's "best manuscript" theory, which arose
        out of his attack on the Lachmannian method of recension by
        "common errors."

1994   Bénevot, M. *The Tradition of Manuscripts: A Study in the Trans-
        mission of St. Cyprian's Treatises*. Oxford: Clarendon Press,
        1961.

        An account of 25 years' research toward a critical edition of
        "On the Unity of the Church," first published by Cyprian, A.D.
        251; the author's comments provide a valuable guide toward the
        methodology of handling complex textual traditions.

1995   D'Ardenne, Simonne R.T.O. "The Editing of Middle English Texts,"
        English Studies Today, ed. C.L. Wrenn and G. Bullough. London:
        Oxford University Press, 1951; pp. 74-84.

        A whimsical dialogue, read at the Conference of University
        Professors of English, Oxford, August, 1950, which considers
        scribal intention and penhabits. Particular texts discussed
        are the *Ancren Wisse* and *The Owl and the Nightingale*.

1996   Ewert, A. "On Textual Criticism, with Special Reference to
        Anglo-Norman." *Arthuriana*, 2 (1929-30), 56-69.

        An examination of contaminated traditions and variant stemmata
        for Anglo-Norman texts, with the suggestion that Bédier's methods
        are the most suitable for such texts.

1997   Faral, Edmond. "A propos de l'édition des textes anciens: le
        cas du manuscrit unique," in *Recueil de travaux offert à
        M. Clovis Brunel*. I. Paris: Société de l'Ecole des Chartes,
        1955; pp. 409-21.

        Illustrated by a Rutebeuf poem in a single manuscript, the
        author's discussion suggests methodology and technical apparatus.
        See also Hofmeister, item 2004.

1998   Frank, I. "L'Art d'éditer les textes lyriques," in item 1997
        above, pp. 463-75.

        A consideration of the editing of Provençal lyrics and the
        unfeasibility of Lachmannian principles.

1999   Frankel, Hermann. *Testo critico e critica del testo*. Traduzione
        dal tedesco di Lucianio Canfora. Bibliotechina del Saggiatore,
        31. Florence: Le Monnier, 1969.

        A selection of Frankel's critical remarks, minus specific
        examples, from his *Einleitung zur kritischen Ausgabe der Argon-
        autika des Apollonios*, 1964. Questions considered are the choice
        of manuscripts, construction of the apparatus criticus, and
        choice of variants, all with reference to his Oxford edition.

2000   Görlach, Manfred, ed. *An East Midland Revision of the South
        English Legendary: A Selection from MS C.U.L. Add. 3039*.
        Early Middle English Texts, 4. Heidelberg: Carl Winter, 1976.

        This edition provides an excellent introduction to the complex
        manuscript tradition of the *South English Legendary*, with the
        text and apparatus a good example of editing from manuscripts
        of an open text.

2001   Griesbach, Johann Jakob. *Novum Testamentum Graecae*. 2 vols.
        Halle: J.J. Curtius, 1775-77.

        In his *Prolegomena* Griesbach set out for the first time some
        "rules" for textual criticism, with two general principles and
        15 special rules, including the rule of the *lectio difficilior*.
        His purpose was to attempt to determine those readings which
        would re-establish the original text of the New Testament.

2002   Griffith, John G. "A Taxonomic Study of the Manuscript of
        Juvenal." *Museum Helveticum*, 25 (1968), 101-38.

        A clear account of the method of grouping manuscripts by the
        quantity of agreement, based in part upon precise relationships
        between letters, etc. For the method as applied to Lactantius,
        see Monat, item 1973 above.

2003   ————. "Numerical Taxonomy and Some Primary Manuscripts of
        the Gospels." *Journal of Theological Studies*, n.s., 20 (1969),
        389-406.

        See preceding item.

2004   Hofmeister, R. "The Unique Manuscript in Mediaeval German
        Literature." *Seminar*, 12 (1976), 8-25.

        A discussion of the theoretical and methodological problems
        facing editors of works surviving only in single manuscripts.
        Cf. Faral, item 1997.

2005   Hofstrand, G. *'The Seege of Troye:' A study in the Intertextual
        Relations*. Lund Studies in English, 4. Lund: G.W.K. Gleerup/
        London: Williams and Norgate, 1936.

        A study of the manuscript tradition of the Middle English
        romance and its textual variations.

2006   Horrall, Sarah M. *The Southern Version of Cursor Mundi*. I.
        Ottawa: University of Ottawa Press, 1978.

        The editor's introduction justifies and illustrates her use
        of a base text (MS. London, College of Arms, Arundel 53), with
        reference to eight other manuscripts.

2007   Housman, A.E. *The Classical Papers*, ed. J. Diggle and F.R.D.
        Goodyear. 3 vols. Cambridge: University Press, 1972.

        A collection of writings—articles, prefaces, etc.—on mainly
        Classical textual criticism. Included is his account of the
        Propertius manuscripts, I. 222-304; see also item 1958.

2008   Hudson, Anne. "Tradition and Innovation in Some Middle English
        Manuscripts." *Review of English Studies*, n.s., 17.68 (1966),
        359-72.

        A close examination of scribal methods within a limited body
        of material (the metrical chronicle ascribed to Robert of
        Gloucester, in fourteen manuscripts and manuscript fragments).
        The author points out that the survival of some forms argues
        for the importance of textual transmission among manuscripts
        and also indicates scribes' perpetuation of certain archaic mor-
        phological types.

2009   Kane, George, ed. *Piers Plowman: The A Version: An Edition in
        the Form of Trinity College Cambridge MS. R. 3. 14, Corrected
        from other Manuscripts with Variant Readings*. London: Athlone
        Press, 1960.

The introduction, pp. 53-165, provides a full description of classifications of manuscripts in an "open text" tradition and general editorial practice.

2010   Kennedy, Elspeth. "The Scribe as Editor," in *Mélanges de langue et de littérature du moyen âge et de la Renaissance offerts à Jean Frappier*. Geneva: Droz, 1970; I, 523-31.

A detailed study of scribal smoothing and contamination in Old French.

2011   Kenyon, F.G. *Handbook to Textual Criticism of the New Testament*. 2nd ed. (from 1901). London: Macmillan, 1912/Grand Rapids, Mich.: W.B. Eerdmans, 1953.

On the general principles of textual criticism (collecting the documentary evidence and then establishing its value) with reference to the manuscripts of the New Testament. Discussion includes autographs, uncial manuscripts, ancient versions, Patristic quotations, and a history of Biblical textual criticism.

2012   Lachmann, Karl. *Novum Testamentum Graece et Latine*. Berlin: G. Reimer, 1842.

In his preface and in his editions of several Middle High German texts (see Lutz-Hensel, item 1968), Lachmann established himself as the "founder of modern textual criticism"; in this work he proposes as a general principle the classification of families of manuscripts by means of "common errors" and the formation of a stemma for extant and non-extant manuscripts. This method is further explained in "Rechenschaft über Lachmanns Ausgabe des Neuen Testaments," *Kleinere Schriften zur Classischen Philologie*, ed. J. Vahlen (Berlin: G. Reimer, 1876), pp. 250-72. It was applied explicitly to the edition of a Classical text in his *T. Lucretius Cari De Rerum Natura Libri Sex*. 4th ed. (from 1850) (Berlin: G. Reimer, 1871). See also item 2018.

2013   Leach, MacEdward. "Some Problems in Editing Middle English Manuscripts," in *English Institute Annual, 1940*. New York, N.Y.: Columbia University Press, 1940/New York: AMS, 1965; pp. 130-51.

The author suggests that editing should be a matter of policy rather than principle, since every text presents unique textual problems. He discusses such matters as capitalization, punctuation, and word division.

2014   Lindsay, Wallace M. *An Introduction to Latin Textual Emendation Based on the Text of Plautus*. London: Macmillan, 1896.

A detailed study of scribal errors as found among selected Plautus manuscripts: emendation, transposition, omission, insertion, substitution, etc.

2015   McIntosh, Angus. "The Analysis of Written Middle English," in *Transactions of the Philological Society*. London: The Society, 1956-58; pp. 26-55.

The author considers in some detail the relationship between written texts and linguistic analysis.

2016   Moorman, Charles. *Editing the Middle English Manuscripts*. Jackson, Miss.: University of Mississippi Press, 1975.

An introduction to medieval English textual criticism, designed for the beginning student. It offers a survey of the major scripts, a central section with sample extracts, and a final summary of the principles of introduction, apparatus, glossary, and notes. A highly select, critical bibliography concludes.

2017   Müller, K. *Petronii Arbitri Satyricon*. 2nd ed. (from 1961). Munich: E. Heimeran, 1965.

See next item.

2018   ————. *T. Lucreti Cari De Rerum Natura Libri Sex*. Zurich: Hans Rohr, 1975.

These two editions contain a lucid introduction on textual methods. Müller discusses stemmatics, the arrangement of the apparatus, textual orthography, and other matters; in the latter item he makes critical comparisons with Lachmann's earlier edition, item 2012, in which the relative values of manuscripts, especially the Codex Quadratus, was assessed for the first time.

2019   Mynors, R.A.B. *C. Plini Secundi Epistularum Libri Decem*. Oxford: Clarendon Press, 1963.

This edition provides a detailed introduction on critical methodology, see especially pp. v–xxii.

2020   Nelson, Francis W. "Graphemic Analysis of Late Middle English Manuscripts." *Speculum*, 37 (1962), 32–47.

A detailed discussion of possible relationships between linguistics and paleography along lines established by Angus McIntosh (1956). Plates and charts illustrate the techniques described; select bibliographical references are given.

2021   Ogilvie, R.M. "Monastic Corruption." *Greece and Rome*, 2nd ser., 18 (1971), 32–34.

An illustrated assessment of the presence of ecclesiastical Latin vocabulary in Classical texts and its role in determining manuscript filiation.

2022   Paris, Gaston, ed. *Vie de Saint Alexis, poème du XIe siècle*. 7th ed. (from 1885). Paris: E. Champion, 1933.

One of the first applications of Lachmann's theories to an Old French text.

2023   Quentin, Dom Henri. *Mémoire sur l'établissement du texte de la Vulgate*. Rome: Gabalda/Paris: Desclée, 1922.

The author's *Memoire* represents his first exposition of textual methodology in the course of his role as chief of the Papal

Commission on revision of the text of the Vulgate. He attempts
to reconstruct the archetype of all known manuscripts and in
so doing to use all variants, classified into three groups with
one group representing the intermediate. His theories are further expanded with wider application in *Essais*, item 1975.

2024   Reeve, M.D. "Eleven Notes." *Classical Review*, 21 (1971), 324-9.

A group of textual notes on problematical readings in Classical texts, representing different types of problems and the
use of alternate methodologies in their solution. The author
has published similar articles in this and other journals.

2025   Reilly, James P. "A Preliminary Study of a Pecia." *Revue
d'Histoire des Textes*, 2 (1972), 239-50.

The author suggests how to handle a vast manuscript tradition
like that of Saint Thomas Aquinas through a study of its *peciae*.

2026   Reynolds, L.D. *The Medieval Tradition of Seneca's Letters.*
Oxford: Clarendon Press, 1965.

A study of manuscript transmission, with an exemplary application of stemmatic theory.

2027   Seiffert, H.W. *Untersuchungen zur Methode der Herausgabe deutscher Texte.* Berlin: Akademie-Verlag, 1963.

A general guide to stemmatic theory, which discusses textual
traditions, the nature of variants, textual construction, and,
in particular, the work of such German editors as Behrend and
Martini.

2028   Seymour, M.C., gen. ed. *On the Properties of Things: John
Trevisa's Translation of Bartholomaeus Anglicus "De Propri-
etatibus Rerum."* 2 vols. Oxford: Clarendon Press, 1975.

A critical edition of the eight extant manuscripts, which
provides a noteworthy example of group scholarship and trans-
Atlantic resources. The nineteen books of Trevisa's translation,
completed ca. 1398, have here been edited by seventeen scholars
from manuscripts in both British and North American libraries.
A third vol., containing Introduction, Commentary, and Glossary,
is forthcoming.

2029   Sisam, Celia. "Notes on Middle English Texts." *Review of English
Studies*, 13 (1962), 385-90.

Brief textual notes on difficult readings in five Middle
English texts, including the *Peterborough Chronicle* and Barbour's
Bruce. Sisam employs paleographical, historical, and lexical
criteria for her conclusions.

2030   Stevick, Robert D. *Suprasegmentals, Meter, and the Manuscript
of "Beowulf."* The Hague: Mouton, 1968.

An analysis of non-segmental linear manuscript data, which
involves spacing between morphic elements, i.e., word-separation
as reflected in scribal spacing, and graphotactic patterns.

2031   Tuilier, André. *Etude comparée du texte et des scholiés d'Euripide.* Paris: C. Klincksieck, 1972.

        See next item.

2032   ———. *Recherches critiques sur la traduction du texte d'Euripide.* Paris: C. Klincksieck, 1968.

        Both works provide model examples of detailed studies of manuscript tradition in a Classical text. See also items 1991, 2039.

2033   Vinaver, Eugene, ed. *The Works of Thomas Malory.* 2nd ed. (from 1947). 3 vols. Oxford: Clarendon Press, 1967/1971.

        The editor's introduction contains a lucid explanation of editorial principles, pp. c-cxxvi, with special reference to certain textual problems created by relationships between manuscript and early printed edition. The basis of his discussion is the fact that Caxton's edition of *Le Morte Darthur* (1485) contained the only known text of the work until W.F. Oakeshott discovered the Winchester MS. in 1934 and that the manuscript appears to be roughly contemporary with, but more authentic than, Caxton's edition.

2034   Whitehead, Frederick. "The Textual Criticism of the *Chanson de Roland*: An Historical Review," in *Studies in Medieval French Presented to Alfred Ewert in Honour of His Seventieth Birthday.* Oxford: Clarendon Press, 1961; pp. 76-89.

        A judicious assessment of Bédier's theories and those of later editors, with a reaffirmation of Bédier's conservatism.

2035   ———, and Pickford, Cedric E. "The Introduction to the *Lai de l'ombre*," ed. (from *Romania*, 94) in Kleinhenz, item 1909.

        A review of the two-branch stemma controversy and a rejection of Bédier's thesis.

2036   Wilson, Nigel G. "A Puzzle in Stemmatic Theory Solved." *Revue d'Histoire des Textes*, 4 (1974), 139-42.

        The author demonstrates that paleography can solve a puzzle in the stemmatic method by proving that two manuscripts of Callimachus' *Hymns* are by Girard of Old Patras but in different scripts, the one copied accurately from the other. The fact thus provides an exception to Maas' rule that in stemmatic theory, if MS. A is found to have all the errors of B plus some of its own, then A is thus a copy of B. See also Wilson's edition of Callimachus (1953) for some earlier suggestions of this possibility.

2037   Youtie, Herbert C. *The Textual Criticism of Documentary Papyri: Prolegomena.* Institute of Classical Studies Bulletin, Supplement 6. London: University of London Press, 1958.

        Originally the Special University Lectures in Palaeography, May, 1958. On the assumption that in transcription the sounds indicated by the signs and the meanings attached to the sounds must be revived in the mind of the transcriber, Youtie stresses the need for the textual critic to be familiar both with the

language of the author and the paleography of the scribe. He
also surveys the "accidents" to which the editors of papyrus
manuscripts may be exposed.

2038   Zetzel, J.E.G. "On the History of Latin Scholia." *Harvard
       Studies in Classical Philology*, 79 (1975), 335-54.

A useful article summarizing recent scholarship on the transmission of ancient commentaries, chiefly Latin scholia but with
some reference to Byzantine manuscripts. Relations between the
Bembine scholia of Terence and Donatus represent a paradigm
of the history of scholia from the fourth to the sixth centuries.

2039   Zuntz, G. *An Inquiry into the Transmission of the Plays of
       Euripides*. Cambridge: University Press, 1965.

An outline of textual history and survey of scholarship. For
more recent work see Tuilier, items 2031-2, and cf. Barrett,
item 1991.

E. TEXTUAL CRITICISM AND THE COMPUTER

2040   Aitken, A.I.; Bailey, R.W.; and Hamilton-Smith, N., eds. *The
       Computer and Literary Studies*. Edinburgh: University Press,
       1973.

A collection of essays which includes Wilhem Ott's "Computer
Applications in Textual Criticism," pp. 199-223, and P. Tombeau's
"Research Carried Out at the Centre de Traitement Electronique
des Documents of the Catholic University of Louvain," 335-40.
Originally papers read at the second symposium, Edinburgh, 1972.

2041   Benson, Larry D. "A Review of J.B. Bessinger, Jr.'s *A Concord-
       ance to Beowulf*. (Ithaca, N.Y.: Cornell University Press,
       1969)." *Speculum*, 45 (1970), 273-5.

The review also includes a general discussion of concordance
programming, with indication of its limitations and future
desiderata.

2042   Berger, Sidney. "A Method for Compiling a Concordance for a
       Middle English Text." *Studies in Bibliography*, 26 (1973),
       219-228.

With reference to Markman's earlier "Computer Concordance,"
item 2063, the author applies similar methodology to one particular text, in this case Laʒamon's *Brut*. He outlines the
stages involved, from a machine readable format to the final
concordance.

2043   Bullough, Vern L.; Luisignan, Serge; and Ohlgren, Thomas H.
       "Computers and the Medievalist." *Speculum*, 49 (1974), 392-
       402.

A summary report of current areas of computer studies and individual research projects, with full, bibliographical notes. See especially "Literary Data Processing," pp. 393-99, and "Musical Data Processing," pp. 399-400.

2044   Cabaniss, Margaret Scanlon, "Using the Computer for Text Collation." *Computer Studies in the Humanities and Verbal Behavior*, 3 (1970), 1-33.

See items 2066, 2070.

2045   Cameron, Angus; Frank, Roberta; and Leyerle, John, eds. *Computers and Old English Concordances*. Toronto: University Press, 1970.

A collection of 22 papers and recorded discussions from the conference of March, 1969 at the Toronto Centre for Medieval Studies. They include general topics on the use of computers in literary studies, the computer concordance project, and the use of computer processing for Old English texts.

2046   Dolezalek, Gero. "Computers and Medieval Manuscripts of Roman Law." *Bulletin of Medieval Canon Law*, 4 (1974), 79-85.

A description of the analytical bibliography of medieval Roman law manuscripts developed at the Max-Planck Institute for European Roman Law, see item 638.

2047   Fischer, Bonifatius. "The Use of Computers in New Testament Studies with Special Reference to Textual Criticism." *Journal of Theological Studies*, n.s., 21 (1970), 297-318.

A general discussion of the potential value of computers for Biblical concordances, bibliography, and especially textual criticism in the classification of manuscripts.

2048   Fossier, Lucie. "Informatique et histoire médiévale à l'Institut de Recherche et d'Histoire de Textes." *Computers and the Humanities*, 12 (1978), 109-12.

An outline of the types of computer programmes available at the Institute for research in medieval historical documents: treatment of the text, classification of documents, and analysis of content. This issue of the journal is devoted to medieval topics, see also items 2062, 2073.

2049   Froger, Dom Jacques. "La Collation des manuscrits à la machine electronique." *Bulletin d'Information de l'Institut de Recherche d'Histoire de Textes*, 13 (1964-65), 135-71.

2050   ———. "La Critique des textes et l'ordinateur." *Vigiliae Christianae*, 24 (1970), 210-17.

2051   ———. *La Critique des textes et son automatisation*. Initiation aux Nouveautés de la Science, 7. Paris: Dunod, 1968.

2052   ———. "The Electronic Machine at the Service of Humanistic Studies." *Diogenes*, 52 (1965), 104-42.

In these articles and book Dom Froger surveys potential uses of the computer for documentation (e.g., scanning manuscript catalogues), collation, and reconstruction of an archetype according to principles established by Lachmann and Quentin. Some reference is made to work done by Louis Delatte at Liège.

2053 Gibson, W.M., and Petty, G.P., Jr. "Project OCCULT: The Ordered Computer Collation of Unprepared Literary Text," in item 1907, pp. 279-300.

See items 2066, 2070.

2054 Gilmour-Bryson, Anne. "Transcription and Edition of a Medieval Manuscript with the Help of a Computer." *Manuscripta*, 22 (1978), 25-39.

An exemplar of methodology, based on Vatican Archives MS. Castel Sant'Angelo, Armandio D-207, a transcription of the trial of the Templars, 1309-10.

2055 Hirschmann, Rudolf. "A Survey of Computer-Aided Research in Early German." *Computers and the Humanities*, 8 (1974), 279-84.

A descriptive survey of conferences, published research, and international scholars.

2056 Howard-Hill, T.H. "A Practical Scheme for Editing Critical Texts with the Aid of a Computer." *Proof*, 3 (1973), 335-56.

2057 ————. "Computer and Mechanical Aids to Editing." *Proof*, 5 (1977), 217-35.

These articles assess potential equipment and methodology, mainly for modern textual criticism. Useful bibliographical references are provided.

2058 Jones, Alan; and Churchhouse, R.F., eds. The Computer in Literary and Linguistic Studies. Cardiff: University Press, 1976.

A collection of papers, some of them on textual criticism, e.g., Penny Gilbert, "Using the Computer to Collate Medieval Latin Manuscripts," pp. 106-113, and Gian Piero Zarri, "A Computer Model for Textual Criticism," pp. 133-55; see also item 2066.

2059 Kochendörfer, Günter. "Teilautomatisierung der Textkritik bei mittelalterlichen handschriftlichen Überlieferungen." *Zeitschrift für deutsche Philologie*, 90 (1971), 356-76.

A proposal for computerized classification of manuscripts, with examples of format and symbols for different types of texts, e.g., single manuscripts, groups, etc. The author suggests how contamination and special problems might be indicated and stemmata constructed.

2060 ————, and Schirok, Bernd. Maschinelle Textrekonstruktion: theoretische Grundlegung, praktische Erprobung an einem

*Ausschnitt des 'Parzival' Wolframs von Eschenbach und Dis-
kussion der literaturgeschichtichen Ergebnisse.* Göppinger
Arbeiten zur Germanistik, 185. Göppingen: A. Künmerle, 1976.

A discussion of computerized editing with examples from
Parzival and proposed solutions to some problems in data processing. Bibliography, pp. 176-82, on recent publications in
the field.

2061   Laurier, Alain. "Problèmes posés par la formalisation et l'automatisation des méthodes d'analyse de textes. Commentaires de
recherches sur un corpus de manuscrits relatant à la fondation de la ville de Florence." *Revue d'Histoire des Textes*,
13 (1972), 251-79.

A study in methodological technique in two stages: (1)
a comparative analysis of the contents of the corpus, and (2)
elaboration of a mathematical method of reconstruction of the
process of textual transmission. The author concludes that the
use of the computer can create certain problems of its own.

2062   Logan, Harry M. "KLIC: A Computer Aid to Graphological Analysis."
Computers and the Humanities, 12 (1978), 93-96.

Using *e* and *ea* spellings in the Middle English Katherine group
to determine possible provenance of the manuscripts, Logan
demonstrates how the KLIC system ("Key Letter in Context") is
able to group certain manuscripts on the basis of graphology.

2063   Markman, Alan. "A Computer Concordance to a Middle English
Text." *Studies in Bibliography*, 17 (1964), 55-75.

A detailed account of making the concordance for the works of
the *Pearl*-poet. The exemplar is expanded to more general principles and methodology by Berger, item 2042 above.

2064   Mau, J. "Affiliation Programs." *Revue de l'Organisation Internationale pour l'Etude des Langue Anciennes par Ordinateur*,
3 (1972), 63-76; and, with Ahnert, H.J., "Affiliation Programs,
II: Using the Program 'affili,'" 4 (1973), 35-43.

Based ultimately on the work of Froger (see items 1946-7),
these articles describe the stages of collation, preparation
of collation material for the computer, and the interpretation
of its output.

2065   Morton, Andrew Q., Winspear, Alban D., *et al. It's Greek to
the Computer.* Montreal: Harvest House, 1971.

An introductory account which surveys the types of problems
a computer might solve in Classical Greek texts, e.g., determining authorship or compiling a concordance. Sample texts
examined are the seventh letter of Plato, the *Epinomis*, Aristotle's *Nichomechean Ethics*, and others.

2066   Oakman, Robert L. "The Present State of Computerized Collation:
A review Article." *Proof*, 2 (1972), 333-48.

A brief description of the OCCULT and Cabaniss projects, see
items 2053, 2070.

2067   ————. "Textual Editing and the Computer." *Costerus*. n.s.,
        4 (1975), 79–106.

        A useful review and critical bibliography of recent publica-
        tions and work in progress.

2068   Parrish, Stephen. "Problems in the Making of Computer Concord-
        ances." *Studies in Bibliography*, 15 (1962), 8–9.

        An assessment of the value of computers in making concord-
        ances, with reference to early experiments with the IBM 704
        computer at Cornell in 1957 and the pilot project in the poems
        of Matthew Arnold. The author describes the stages of the
        programme, problems of spelling, punctuation, homographs, and
        other matters.

2069   Peavler, James M. "Analysis of Corpora of Variations." *Computers
        and the Humanities*, 8 (1974), 153–9.

        A description of the second step in editing from computer-
        set texts: the tabular analysis of corpus variants produced
        by collation. The author uses as the basis of his discussion
        George B. Pace's edition of Chaucer's shorter poems in the
        variorum edition.

2070   Petty, George R., and Gibson, William M. *Project OCCULT: The
        Ordered Computer Collation of Unprepared Literary Text*. New
        York, N.Y.: New York University Press, 1970.

        A descriptive account of the algorithmic method of programming,
        using as examples two texts by James and two by Melville. See
        also items 2053, 2066.

2071   Poole, Eric. "The Computer in Determining Stemmatic Relation-
        ships." *Computers and the Humanities*, 8 (1974), 207–16.

        Using a sample text from *Piers Plowman*, the author analyzes
        the statistical probability of coincident variation in manu-
        script texts in order to demonstrate a method of reconstructing
        stemmata.

2072   Silva, Georgette, and Love, Harold. "The Identification of Text
        Variants by Computer." *Information Storage and Retrieval*, 5
        (1969), 89–108.

        A descriptive account of sample collation programmes.

2073   Williman, Daniel, and Dziedzic, Margarita. "*Dictio Probatoria*
        as Fingerprint: Computer Discovery of Manuscript Provenances."
        Computers and the Humanities, 12 (1978), 89–92.

        With reference to the *probatoriae*, a thirteenth-century sys-
        tem of manuscript description based on incipits from the second
        folio, the authors suggest that the computer be used to match
        the largest possible collection of medieval *probatoria* notices
        with parallel data collected from existing manuscript collec-
        tions. Specific suggestions are made for input preparation.

2074   Wisbey, R.A., ed. *The Computer in Literary and Linguistic Re-
        search*. Cambridge: University Press, 1971.

A collection of essays, including that by Harold S. Love, "The Computer and Literary Editing: Achievements and Prospects," pp. 47-56, which discusses the enumeration of sets of texts with shared variants.

See also items 731, 1322, 1764, 1779, 1804-5, 1835, 1839, 1858.

INDEX

Listed are authors or editors, titles, and publishing institutions. Many items have been listed under more than one of these categories in order to facilitate use of this *Handbook*. Names with *de*, *van*, or *von* have been listed under the main form, with the exception of names which have become anglicized. Spanish and other double names are listed under the first component.